The World
Markets
Desk Book

Also by Lawrence W. Tuller

THE MCGRAW-HILL HANDBOOK OF GLOBAL TRADE AND INVESTMENT FINANCING

GOING GLOBAL: NEW OPPORTUNITIES FOR GROWING COMPANIES TO COMPETE IN WORLD MARKETS

FINANCING THE SMALL BUSINESS

WHEN THE BANK SAYS NO! CREATIVE FINANCING FOR CLOSELY HELD BUSINESSES

BUYING IN: A COMPLETE GUIDE TO ACQUIRING A BUSINESS OR PROFESSIONAL PRACTICE

GETTING OUT: A STEP-BY-STEP GUIDE TO SELLING A BUSINESS OR PROFESSIONAL PRACTICE

The World Markets Desk Book

A Region-by-Region Survey of Global Trade Opportunities

Lawrence W. Tuller

McGraw-Hill, Inc.

New York   St. Louis   San Francisco   Auckland   Bogotá
Caracas   Lisbon   London   Madrid   Mexico   Milan
Montreal   New Delhi   Paris   San Juan   São Paulo
Singapore   Sydney   Tokyo   Toronto

*To Barbara the diplomat, Charles and Maggie
the adventurers, and Susan the explorer, who
share the wonders of global knowledge.*

Library of Congress Cataloging-in-Publication Data

Tuller, Lawrence W.
    The world markets desk book : a region-by-region survey of global
trade / Lawrence W. Tuller-
        p.   cm.
    Includes index.
    ISBN 0-07-065478-6
    1. Export marketing—Handbooks, manuals, etc.   2. International trade—
Handbooks, manuals, etc.   I. Title.
HF1009.5.T85   1993
658.8'48—dc20   92-24542
                                                                        CIP

1 2 3 4 5 6 7 8 9 0   DOH/DOH   9 8 7 6 5 4 3 2

ISBN   0-07-065478-6   N82I

*The sponsoring editor for this book was David Conti, the editing supervisor
was Ann Craig, and the production supervisor was Donald F. Schmidt. It was
set in Palatino by McGraw-Hill's Professional Book Group composition unit.*

Printed and bound by R. R. Donnelley & Sons Company.

Contents

Part 3. Asia-Pacific

Tables

Preface

The sole purpose of this book is to provide hard, cold facts and analyses about specific market opportunities in more than fifty countries and trading regions around the world, and by so doing, to point out which countries are ripe for exporting and direct investment, which countries should be avoided, and which countries should be watched for future market development.

In today's rapidly changing world, very few business people fail to see the competitive necessity of exploiting global markets and resources. A choice between competing globally or staying at home is no longer valid. That door to isolationism closed several years ago.

The only choices now are which global markets to go after, and where to locate materials and labor at the lowest cost, highest quality, and best delivery. Unfortunately, the dynamism of world market demand and constantly shifting political priorities serve up a never-ending selection of alternatives.

Furthermore, the rules of international trade keep changing:

- As companies structured long-range plans to exploit the advent of "Europe 1992," Eastern Europe flew apart. Whole new markets opened, closed, then partially opened again.

- The clamor for joint ventures with Soviet partners was jolted by the disappearance of the Soviet Union and the birth of a hodgepodge of twelve independent republics.

- Strategies to lock competitive horns with Japanese companies evaporated as these goliaths shifted investment and trade resources to Southeast Asia and China.

- Once written off as primitive and bankrupt, Latin America began to emerge as the largest single market and natural resource depository in the world.

- Strategies to exploit the perceived financial strength of the Arab Middle East unraveled as the Persian Gulf war exposed fundamental weaknesses.

- Even South Africa, long regarded as a lost cause, began reforms that suddenly opened vast markets and natural resources to global companies.

- Just when it appeared that the Uruguay Round of GATT negotiations would open new European and American markets to foreign competition, the door closed.

- Powerful new regional trading blocs in Europe, Asia-Pacific, and the Western Hemisphere began to threaten global trade with stringent external tariffs, quotas, and import licensing, making competition even more fierce.

- Miraculously, countries around the world began to respond to pressures from the World Bank, the International Monetary Fund, and the United States to clean up their ecological garbage, creating some of the hottest markets around.

- Markets in health care, agribusiness, education, infrastructure development, machine tools, electronics, alternative energy sources, communications, and transportation are exploding throughout the world.

- Many less-developed countries now offer far better opportunities and weaker competition than mature markets.

- Cheap labor, plentiful natural resources, tax incentives, and government subsidies are attracting companies of every size and industry.

- With resources restricted at home, American, European, and even Japanese companies are finding easy R & D funding and management talent offshore.

With the whole world to choose from, selecting the right market is at best confusing; at worst, frustrating, time-consuming, and fraught with costly error. Information gathered from the U.S. government or the European Commission is often biased and incomplete. Advice from trade publications is too narrow, while that derived from international trade books is too broad—useful to the casual observer, but totally worthless as a basis for developing market strategies.

Global executives need specific facts, ideas, and recommendations that actually work. For each country and/or region they hope to penetrate, decision makers need facts and insights about market growth and demand, product trends, local and foreign competition, taxes and regulatory statutes, formal and informal trade barriers, labor and management talent, political stability, operating costs, trade and investment incentives and deterrents, and financing options.

The World Markets Desk Book is designed to provide just such information for each of the world's major trading regions, pinpointing those countries within each region that offer the best (and in some cases, the worst) opportunities for market growth and resource availability. For larger countries it even identifies the best sites for establishing facilities and offers tips about specialized niche markets. It discloses which markets to attack now—and with which products. And it lays out the most likely changes in future market conditions, enabling companies to gain competitive advantage by making trade and investment moves right now.

The book focuses on current conditions and future prospects of markets in both developed and developing countries, grouped by geographical area as follows: Part 1, North and South America; Part 2, Europe, Africa, and the Middle East; Part 3, Asia-Pacific. As a special feature for non-U.S. business executives, one entire chapter analyzes market opportunities and pitfalls for doing business in the United States.

The most difficult strategic questions today's executive must answer are: (1) which markets to attack; (2) where to source materials and components; (3) where to find capable management personnel and skilled labor; and (4) how to raise appropriate financing (a subject covered in my previous book, *The McGraw-Hill Handbook of Global Trade and Investment Financing*).

This book answers the first three questions by evaluating opportunities in each trading country—both for exporting and for direct investment—against seven key criteria:

1. Political stability

2. Economic stability as measured by a country's domestic growth, external debt obligations, and inflation rate

3. Competition, market size, and market demand for specific products and services

4. Resource cost and availability, including raw materials, labor, and management talent

5. Formal and informal trade barriers to foreign direct investment, exporting from the country, and importing to the country

6. Ease of entry, including local government regulations and incentives (e.g., tax incentives), home-country assistance, cultural hurdles, infrastructure development, and transport facilities, with specific attention to environmental deterrents and opportunities

7. The strategic position of a country with regard to trading blocs

The information and analyses contained in this volume should be viewed as a starting point, a trigger to either turn on or turn off further investigation of a potential new market.

Conditions in international trade change rapidly. Quoted economic statistics and political conditions must be replaced by updated data as it becomes available. The same holds true for government policies, aid programs, competition, and market entry requirements.

Radical changes in Eastern Europe and the former Soviet Union bear witness to the need to stay on top of current events as they unfold and to develop market strategies with the flexibility to adapt to these changing conditions.

Research for this book has been extensive. Data was solicited from every pertinent public and private source, including:

- Interviews with U.S. and foreign trade officials and company executives
- Research studies from United Nations organizations
- Public files from the U.S. departments of State and Commerce, the office of the U.S. Trade Representative, and other U.S. government and government-affiliated organizations
- Documentation from the Inter-American Development Bank, the Asian Development Bank, the European Bank for Reconstruction and Development, and the European Investment Bank
- Trade promotions from European, Latin American, and Asia-Pacific government organizations
- U.S. and foreign–U.S. chambers of commerce
- Private international trade organizations
- Publications and public records from and interviews with Big Six accounting firms, trading companies, and financing institutions
- Authoritative international trade periodicals and academic research reports
- OECD reports
- Public company annual reports
- Published international reference works
- And last but certainly not least, the personal experiences of the author and his associates

Every attempt has been made to provide current, pertinent information and analyses. The opinions and conclusions expressed are those of the author alone and do not represent the positions of governments or officials from any public or private organization other than as specified.

Although no work of this magnitude can be all-inclusive, I sincerely hope that, at a minimum, it will open doors to global market opportunities that may have been closed until now. Godspeed!

Lawrence W. Tuller

Acknowledgments

Many people and organizations from around the world have graciously contributed to this book. Without their enthusiastic support it would have been impossible to compile so much data from so many countries, much less to interpret it meaningfully. Even a full chapter of acknowledgments could not do justice to everyone. I will not, therefore, attempt the impossible, but rather single out the following individuals and organizations to whom I am especially indebted for data and insight into specific areas:

Ernest Perreault (Perreault & Co., Inc.); Ernst & Young; Caribbean/Latin American Action; the Netherlands Chamber of Commerce in the United States; the World Bank; the Australian Trade Commission; the Italy-American Chamber of Commerce; the Norwegian Trade Council; the German-American Chamber of Commerce; the Import-Export Bank of Japan; the Hungarian American Fund; the Export-Import Bank of the Republic of China; Commerzbank; the Chilean-American Chamber of Commerce in Santiago, the U.S. Agency for International Development—Bureau for Latin America and the Caribbean; Peter Whitney, Senior Advisor on the Enterprise for the Americas Initiative (U.S. Department of State); *Washington International*; and the Conference Board of Canada. A special thank you is due the Honorable Robert Ruchero, senator from the State of Yap, Federated States of Micronesia.

I apologize for being unable to include a full list of every contributor.

About the Author

Lawrence W. Tuller is a leading international consultant who has done business in Europe, North Africa, the Middle East, Asia, South America, and the Caribbean. He is the founder and president of Tuller & Co., a management consulting firm, and the author of *The McGraw-Hill Handbook of Global Trade and Investment Financing*, *When the Bank Says No! Creative Financing for Closely Held Businesses*, and *Going Global: New Opportunities for Growing Companies to Compete in World Markets*. He has an MBA from the Wharton School and is a graduate of Harvard University.

PART 1

North and South America

1
Canada

Tips to Foreign Traders and Investors

1. Plan for trade with Quebec separately from the rest of Canada, even if secession is not achieved.

2. Beware of historically low manufacturing productivity, especially in the east.

3. Make high-tech direct investments in Canada; make labor-intensive investments in the United States.

4. Use a Canadian presence to tap European markets after Europe 1992.

5. Trade with the Asia-Pacific region from a Canadian location for both exports and imports.

6. Embassy office in Washington: (202) 682-1740.

In many respects Canada and the United States are as one—with or without the U.S.–Canada Free Trade Accord (FTA) that was implemented in January 1989. In the mid–1980s, long before full implementation of the FTA (scheduled for 1995), trade barriers for many goods and services had been washed away through GATT negotiations. This resulted in 70 percent of Canadian trade flowing to the United States and 20 percent of U.S. trade flowing to Canada. Eighty percent of trade from both sides was duty free.

The border between the two countries, most of which runs through wilderness, rural areas, or water, has for decades been freely traversed by citizens of both countries. Without fences or other man-made obstructions patrolled by border guards, it is in many places impossible to know when crossing from one country to the other.

With only modest differences in dialect, most English-speaking Canadians and Americans use the same language. Although the value of the Canadian and U.S. dollars fluctuates in the exchange markets, the difference between the two has never been too great. The standard of living for most Canadians and Americans is indistinguishable. The two nations have similar consumer tastes. Market economies in both countries foster entrepreneurship and, until recently, have been competitive in world markets. The similarities are endless.

Most of the differences between this nation of 27 million people (about the same number as in California) and its assertive southern neighbor of 250 million emanate from Canada's activist government structure, which seems intent on spending taxpayers' money on a grand scale. For this, Canadians receive a womb-to-tomb health care system, a national railway, a national broadcasting system (CBC), and compassionate welfare for the old, the poor, the unemployed, and other disadvantaged groups.

A government based on semi–welfare-state principles finds ever-increasing ways to spend money it doesn't have—as Sweden learned to the dismay of its socialist backers. Canada is no different. The provinces, as well as the central government, have repressive tax structures. For example, the business tax load in manufacturing-oriented Ontario is 20 to 30 percent higher than that in comparable American states such as Ohio, Michigan, New York, New Jersey, or Pennsylvania. On the other hand, it is much lower than that of several other developed countries.

In general the growth in Canadian productivity has been declining for several years. The annual productivity growth was 2.3 percent from 1946 through 1973. It declined to an average of 0.9 percent in the subsequent 17 years ending in 1990. Meanwhile wages continued to escalate. Cost competitiveness relative to the United States has declined particularly sharply, although manufacturing productivity has slowed relative to all G7 members.

In the entire world, Ottawa's budget deficit is second only to that of the United States and soaks up more than one-third of government revenues. The government also dictates "pay equity" laws whereby jobs in which women predominate (receptionists, for example) carry the same pay scale as those composed primarily of men (janitors, for example). Although certainly nondiscriminatory, such practices have cost Canadian industry dearly.

Other factors also contribute to the country's faltering competitive status. Antitrust regulations and interprovincial trade barriers prevent companies from growing large enough to compete in global markets. Relatively little money is spent on research and development—1.33 percent of GDP in 1989, the lowest of the G7 nations.

It's hard to pinpoint the real reasons for Canadian industry's lack of competitiveness. Perhaps it is what home-grown critic Kimon Valaskakis classifies as "'a passion for bronze,' the ability always to put in the middling performance apparently appropriate to a middle-sized power." Whatever the reason, Canadian industry is paying the penalty for the allure of more attractive conditions south of the border. Since the FTA went into effect, the manufacturing sector has lost more than 300,000 jobs.

Border retailers are also paying the price of noncompetitiveness as thousands of consumers swarm across the border to shop in the United States. In 1990, Canadians made more than 51 million day trips to the United States. Officials estimate that the total in 1992 will be significantly higher. Provincial governments promise to crack down. Ontario plans an 8 percent sales tax on U.S.–purchased goods. Canadians already pay a 7 percent goods and services tax on everything in excess of duty-free limits.

Probably the greatest damage to long-term Canadian economic stability is the flood of entrepreneurial businesses to sites across the border. Buffalo, New York, a border city not known for low wages in a state not known for low taxes, has experienced a business renaissance from cross-border moves. Entrepreneurs are also moving farther south, to Pennsylvania, for example, which Americans regard as a high–labor cost, high-tax state.

An Upbeat Future

One might surmise from this bleak appraisal that Canada offers few opportunities for foreign trade or direct investment, but such is not the case. Canada remains a very prosperous nation compared to other G7 members. On the whole, Canada boasts a highly skilled work force and a well-educated, talented management pool.

Its markets, stretching from the Atlantic to the Pacific, are broad-based, diverse, and growing—especially in the western provinces. Alberta possesses rich oil fields and a variety of natural resources. British Columbia offers ready access to fast-growing northeast Asian markets. The maritime provinces of New Brunswick, Newfoundland, Nova Scotia, and Prince Edward Island sustain profitable fishing and seafood industries. Toronto, Montreal, and Vancouver are vibrant, growing metropolises with most of the beneficial attributes and few of the drawbacks of Boston, Detroit, or Cleveland.

At the macroeconomic level, Canada's future looks favorable, except in its current account balance. As Table 1-1 points out, it is forecasted to have the greatest spread between imports and exports of any G7 country. Conversely, the IMF forecast of Canada's growth in GNP is the best of the lot.

One very encouraging factor is the IMF's outlook on Canada's ability to keep its inflation rate down to 2.8 percent in 1992. The Bank of Canada (the Canadian equivalent of America's Federal Reserve Bank) prefers a slightly more conservative estimate of 3 percent. Bank officials are confident, however, that inflation will decline steadily to 2 percent by 1995.

If that is achieved, it will go a long way toward righting the country's balance of payments and improving its exchange rate vis-à-vis the United States. This in turn will make Canadian trade and investment a lot more attractive to American as well as European and Japanese companies.

Foreign investors already seem to have grasped the message. Although the gap between Canadian and American interest rates narrowed during 1991, and despite jitters about the long-term ramifications of Quebec's political

Table 1-1.   Macroeconomic Forecast Comparisons of Group-of-Seven Countries

	Real GNP/GDP percentage change			Consumer prices percentage rise			Current account balance as percentage of GNP		
	1990	1991	1992	1990	1991	1992	1990	1991	1992
Canada	0.5	-0.9	3.8	4.8	5.9	2.8	-3.3	-2.8	-2.3
United States	1.0	-0.3	3.0	5.4	4.5	4.0	-1.7	-0.3	-1.5
Britain	0.8	-1.8	2.4	9.5	5.9	3.9	-2.6	-1.1	-1.2
France	2.8	1.3	2.4	3.4	3.3	3.0	-0.7	-0.8	-0.7
Italy	2.0	1.3	2.5	6.5	6.3	5.6	-1.3	-1.2	-1.4
Germany	4.5	3.1	2.0	2.7	3.5	3.5	2.9*	-0.5*	0.6*
Japan	5.6	4.5	3.4	3.1	3.4	2.7	1.2	1.9	1.7

*Includes East Germany from July 1, 1990.
SOURCE: IMF.

future, the Canadian dollar has strengthened against the U.S. dollar to its highest level in ten years.

If, in fact, Canada can approach an inflation rate of 2 percent over the next three to four years while America's hovers around 4 percent, the two dollars could easily reach parity. The only unresolved matter is the lack of international credibility regarding the government's tightening control over the Bank of Canada. The bank will have to prove itself capable of withstanding Ottawa's fiscal machinations to materially improve the country's attractiveness for foreign investment.

Caution Alert

Two scenarios could put a damper on the outlook for Canada's economic rejuvenation: (1) a drawn-out recovery from the recession in the United States; and (2) continued ethnic unrest in Quebec which effectively destabilizes the central government.

Several underlying factors could conceivably extend substantial economic recovery in the United States well into the mid-to-late 1990s. This would have a devastating effect on the market demand that accounts for 70 percent of Canada's export trade.

The long-term destabilization of Canada's central government could wreak even more havoc on prospects for growth in both trade and foreign direct investment.

A Constitutional Malaise

Quebec nationalism has been a festering sore in the Canadian body politic since 1791 and periodically threatens to tear the country asunder. The latest controversy between French-speaking Catholic Quebec, with its own set of laws founded on the French legal system, and the rest of English-speaking Protestant Canada, founded on British common law, began in 1968 with the election of Liberal leader Pierre Trudeau as federal prime minister.

On the one hand, Trudeau tried to remove Quebec's grounds for feeling excluded from the rest of Canada and thus bind it closer to the Canadian federation. Among other moves, he continued to bring Quebeckers into top federal jobs, promoted bilingualism in government and education, pushed through antipoverty measures specifically designed for Quebec, and changed the tax system so that Quebec provided and received approximately the same percentage of federal funds.

Trudeau's second contribution was accomplished after the referendum vote in 1980. He "brought home" from Britain the constitution that had served the federation since its inception in 1867 and made it a true Canadian constitution. Trudeau then proceeded to push through an addendum to this constitution—a Canadian "Charter of Rights and Freedoms," similar to the Bill of Rights in the United States.

This left Canada with a hybrid federal system: (1) a parliamentary system inherited from Britain under which the Canadian Parliament is sovereign and human rights are protected by common law; and (2) a Charter of Rights under which the power of the state is restrained by the judiciary.

The collectivist and group protection under which French-speaking Canadians had been so long sheltered was now balanced by a charter granting individual rights to Canadian citizens as a whole. This angered Quebeckers, secession talk flared once again, and the Quebec provincial assembly passed laws granting separatist language, laws, and rights.

By the mid-1980s, Canada had a constitution that was neither fish nor fowl in terms of political philosophy. Canadian rights were protected by the Charter of Rights; but that charter could be overridden by a simple declaration from a provincial parliament.

Quebec laid out its own ground rules for acceptance of a Canadian constitution. It insisted on recognition as a distinct society. It sought to play a greater provincial role over immigration. It demanded a provincial say in appointments to the Canadian Supreme Court. It insisted on limiting federal spending power. And it demanded veto rights on constitutional amendments.

Enter the new federal prime minister, Brian Mulroney, and the Meech Lake accord of June 1987—an agreement reached regarding Quebec's demands by Ottawa and all ten provinces. But the drama didn't end there. Manitoba and New Brunswick subsequently elected new provincial governments that balked at the "distinct-society" clause, and Newfoundland's premier, Clyde Wells, withdrew his predecessor's consent. The Meech Lake accord was, after all, not an accord. Quebec, miffed by this rejection, ordered another provincial referendum vote on secession for October 1992.

Caution Alert

Indecision about so important an issue as the form of a country's constitution and whether or not the country will even remain a single entity or be separated into two distinct nations has caused a serious disruption in Canada's foreign trade. Uncertainty about laws, trade barriers, exchange rules, and workers' rights frightens foreign investors and casts serious doubt on the advisability of executing long-term commitments in Canada or with Canadian firms. Obviously Quebec's secession vote in October 1992, opposed by a majority of the province's business leaders, will be watched closely by world traders.

A Bright Spot

The constitutional hassle is mitigated somewhat by enormous trade potential. Even if the province should secede, it will continue to harbor significant potential for foreign trade and direct investment. In 1990, 77 percent of Quebec's exports did not go to other provinces but to other countries, principally the United States. Under the FTA, Quebec's access to U.S. markets is guaranteed.

The province boasts a diversified economy and a thriving metropolis in Montreal. GDP exceeds that of several European nations, including Austria and Denmark. Its insurance industry and public-private sector cooperation is the envy of the rest of Canada. With a population of 6.5 million, Quebec offers foreign trade potential with or without the other provinces.

In light of the serious constitutional issues still outstanding, the U.S.–Canada Free Trade Agreement implemented on January 1, 1989, seems to have lost its relevance. Yet the FTA incorporated many special features that have made a distinct mark on trade and direct investment between the two countries in the last three years. The FTA also possesses enormous future potential as a major stimulant for accessing markets in Mexico and the European Community.

The U.S.–Canada Free Trade Agreement

Under the FTA, all tariffs between the two countries will be eliminated by January 1, 1998. Although a few minor ones were eliminated immediately, plans call for a gradual phase-out in five to ten years in equal annual installments. All quotas, embargoes, and minimum price requirements will also be eliminated.

The agreement permits five major exceptions:

1. Agricultural quotas and price-support or subsidy programs, and restrictions on log exports of both countries.

2. Canadian protective regulations on the sale and distribution of beer. (But discriminatory pricing of distilled spirits and wine will be phased out.)

3. Restrictions on energy products as permitted by GATT for shortages, conservation, and national security.

4. Canadian regulations protecting books, magazines, newspapers, video and audio recordings, and broadcasting.

5. Government procurement preferences not covered by GATT.

When traded products are made from parts or materials imported from countries other than Canada or the United States, the FTA rules of origin provide that the products must have sufficient value added (50 percent for autos) within either country to permit them to be exported under a tariff classification different from that of the imported components. Except for apparel products made of imported fabrics, on which FTA establishes quotas for tariff-free treatment, duty drawbacks and customer user fees will be eliminated by January 1, 1994.

Although it remains unclear how much real income and productivity efficiencies will be affected over the long term, it is quite obvious that short-term dislocations will occur. P. Wonnacott, in *The United States and Canada— The Quest for Free Trade: An Examination of Selected Issues* (Institute for International Economics, Washington, D.C., 1987), identifies two major types of adjustments:

1. As plants and firms specialize for the larger U.S.–Canadian market, there will be a need to shift priorities and manufacturing capabilities *within* industries, especially in Canada.

2. As U.S. firms tend to specialize in certain products, Canadian firms in others, there will be adjustments *between* industries.

In effect, greater specialization and larger-scale plants, especially in Canada, have already contributed to disruptions in distribution channels, employment, and cross-border company migration. Companies in industries such as chemicals, electrical equipment, financial services, furniture, leather products, and metal fabrication have begun to feel the bite of dislocation. In the United States, the most vulnerable industries seem to be paper and paper products, machinery, petroleum products, and transportation equipment, according to several research studies.

Conversely, U.S. firms in previously high-tariff industries such as medical supplies, furniture, sporting equipment, building materials, and computers, can expect increasing trade with Canada.

Except for U.S.–based multinationals that saw the FTA as a way to accelerate their pursuit of cohesive North American manufacturing and distribution networks, the free trade agreement has not had much effect on either trade or foreign direct investment for U.S. companies.

Aside from the nonglobal outlook of many U.S. small and midsize firms, fear of the multi-copy paperwork needed to qualify for free trade has deterred

Table 1-2. United States–Canada Trade

	United States exports to Canada in US$ billions	Canadian exports to the United States in US$ billions
1966	7.7	6.7
1970	10.7	11.8
1980	41.3	41.0
1985	53.9	68.0
1989	74.2	85.1
1990 (Jan.–Nov.)	74.2	91.0

SOURCE: *Statistics Canada, International Business.*

all but the most aggressive. Also, even before the FTA, 75 percent of bilateral trade was tariff free and other tariffs were very low. Paperwork remains the biggest hurdle.

To qualify under FTA free trade, companies from either country must prove that their products are at least 50 percent made in one or the other country. The paperwork involved in obtaining and proving a certificate of origin—when most industries' products include components and parts from around the world and from dozens of suppliers—can be a herculean task.

Nevertheless, on the plus side, companies in virtually all industries are experiencing an attitudinal change in relationships. U.S. and Canadian customers and suppliers (on both sides of the border) are increasingly anxious to explore cross-border trade. As Table 1-2 indicates, trade through 1990 has not materially changed from historical patterns; however, executives from both U.S. and Canadian companies expect substantial increases in cross-border trade as the FTA swings into full force and the initial paperwork bugs get worked out.

Exporting from the U.S. to Canada

For U.S. companies unfamiliar with international trade, exporting to Canada provides a marvelous training ground. All the previously discussed similarities between the two cultures, one hundred years of peaceful coexistence, and the easiest, least-expensive shipping accommodations in the world—with no ocean to cross—makes learning the ropes much easier and less costly than exporting to other countries.

At the same time, benefits in market growth and increased profits can prove illusory. Exporting to Canada still requires crossing borders and coping with many of the same international trade hurdles encountered when exporting to Europe, Japan, or Latin America. Exchange-rate differences (however large or small they may be) add to trade complexities, as do language differences when selling to markets in French-speaking Quebec and paperwork for complying with tariffs and quotas. Although the FTA will phase out most trade barriers, the phase-out period extends to 1998.

The ease of exporting to Canada varies from industry to industry. Those industries in which Canadian companies have cornered the market—such as telecommunications and paper—are best left to large companies with the political and financial clout to compete at a national level.

Canada imports a great many consumer and industrial products, however, and that gives U.S. companies an edge. Since imports from Europe, Japan, and other foreign countries must contend with normal trade barriers, smaller U.S. companies have the opportunity to gain considerable competitive advantage in non-Canadian industries. Medical supplies is a good example. Canada manufactures only about 20 percent of its needs in this market, leaving the door open to foreign suppliers.

Canadian markets are highly concentrated: about 50 percent of the country's output is produced within one hundred miles of the U.S. border. This eases access to Canadian markets for exporters located in the northern half of the United States.

One of the most attractive aspects of exporting to Canada is that Canadian firms have long been accustomed to dealing with both American and Canadian suppliers, as if no border existed. Canadian customers are well educated, sophisticated buyers. They expect the same competitive price and service from American as they do from Canadian sellers. Very often payment is made in U.S. dollars if the exporter requires it, thus eliminating potential exchange losses.

Because they generally treat U.S. suppliers the same as they do domestic companies, Canadian customers also prefer to be treated the same on both sides of the border. Two practices common to U.S. exporters unfamiliar with this idiosyncrasy are major irritants to Canadian customers: the use of consignment agents to distribute goods and the use of factors to collect receivables. Most Canadian firms don't appreciate either. They want to deal directly with the company from which they purchase the goods. Canadians also dislike U.S. suppliers that cut and run, ignoring after-sale service.

Hooking up with a Canadian distributor or sales organization frequently solves the few cross-cultural problems that do arise from time to time, especially in markets demanding quick-response customer service. A Canadian marketing arm also permits the sale of products in Canadian dollars, which many customers prefer. When exporting to Quebec customers, local marketing reps or distributors are helpful with bilingual translations.

Shipping to Canada

The FTA made shipping from the United States to Canada substantially less expensive and easier than from other countries. Of course, cross-border shipping is never as simple as domestic transport, and even when shipping to Canada, it's easy for new exporters to get enmeshed in red tape. Yet, shipping to Canada is a lot cleaner than shipping to Japan or Europe.

When exporting to the north, the carrier of choice may be located on either side of the border, as long as it has the expertise and authority to operate in Canada. Several trucking companies service both markets. Canada boasts an extensive rail network stretching from the Atlantic to the Pacific. With the acquisition of the Delaware & Hudson Railway Co., the CP Rail System now connects New York-to-Washington markets with all of Canada. CP's earlier acquisition of the Minneapolis-based Soo Line accomplished the same feat for midwestern exporters.

Bureaucrats on both sides of the border have been working hard to ease the burden of excess paperwork. Beginning in 1991, U.S. exporters were no longer required to file export declarations for Canadian shipments. U.S authorities now rely on Canadian statistics to compile necessary trade reports for the U.S. Census Bureau and Commerce Department.

Even without an export declaration, however, certain cross-border paperwork is still necessary. The FTA does not eliminate tariffs on all products. Wooden doors, for example, are a protected industry in Canada and imports must be designated for resale or for personal use.

Canadian customs still requires seven forms. For each shipment they want to know the product value, end use, and destination, and the name of the Canadian customs broker handling the shipment.

Caution Alert

Cross-border shipment isn't as difficult as moving goods once they are in Canada. Each province has its own carrier regulations, as do most states in America. Many are very onerous. Only a few truck lines have operating authority in all provinces. Long-haul trucking is partially subsidized by the Canadian government, theoretically to ensure adequate cross-nation service. In practical terms, this merely opens another layer to bureaucratic mischief. Furthermore, the Canadian mail service leaves a lot to be desired.

Tax Questions

The question of how to avoid or at least minimize foreign tax liability plagues exporters the world over. It is especially bothersome to U.S. firms because of the complexity and inclusivity of U.S. tax laws. Exporting to Canada creates less confusion and incurs less tax liability for U.S. companies than exporting to any other industrialized country.

The U.S.–Canada Income Tax Treaty, executed in 1980, contains provisions designed to eliminate the potential for double taxation. The treaty provides that a U.S. exporter is subject to U.S. taxes only, unless the company maintains a "permanent establishment" in Canada. If business is conducted from that permanent establishment Canada taxes the profits generated from it.

The treaty defines *permanent establishment* as a fixed place of business through which the business of a resident of the province is wholly or partially conducted. This can include places of management, branches, offices, factories, and workshops. A person in Canada acting on behalf of a U.S. resident is tantamount to a permanent establishment "if such person possesses and exercises the authority to conclude contracts in the name of the foreign resident."

Ordinarily, this would apply to U.S. sales agents in Canada. Tax liability can be avoided, however, if a sales agent's premises are used only for advertising or "for the storage, display, or delivery" of goods. Agents and reps may solicit orders as long as the orders are accepted by a U.S.–located office of the company, and all contracts are concluded within the United States. Therefore, it's important that agents forward all orders to a U.S. office for processing and billing. It also helps to treat the Canadian sales rep as an independent contractor operating from his or her own office or home rather than as an employee.

Caution Alert

Even though the treaty shields U.S. exporters from Canadian federal taxes, all other provincial taxes and licenses remain in force. In many cases, these taxes amount to a hefty sum.

Foreign Direct Investment

In the east, reports of Canadian firms flocking across the border from Ontario and Quebec to Buffalo and towns in New England, Michigan, Ohio, and Pennsylvania dot the pages of the *New York Times* and *The Wall Street Journal.* However, a quiet revolution in reverse is occurring in the west. As the FTA encourages companies from the north to seek larger markets and lower operating costs in the United States, it also opens the door for American firms to tap burgeoning high-tech markets and technically skilled workers in Canada.

Since exporting and foreign direct investment complement each other, exporting companies cannot fully optimize foreign trade opportunities without foreign facilities. In the case of the United States and Canada, the FTA permits companies from both sides of the border to exploit direct investment opportunities in each other's backyards.

Canadian firms engaged in labor-intensive, low-margin businesses (e.g. smokestack industries, low-tech consumer goods, and so on) find wages, taxes, and other manufacturing costs more competitive in the United States.

The same holds true for companies needing direct access to very large markets and convenient distribution channels.

On the flip side, U.S. firms engaged in technology or knowledge-intensive, high-unit-margin businesses (e.g. software, telecommunications, electronics, and so on) find a large, technically skilled labor base and very concentrated, hungry markets in the western provinces. Hughes Aircraft is one such company.

Hughes found entirely new sources of skilled personnel and ready financing, along with high-demand public and private markets, north of the border. While the defense industry languishes in the United States, just the opposite holds true in Canada. Hughes found the reception so warm there that it formed a subsidiary, Hughes Aircraft of Canada, Ltd.

Hughes (Canada) established its corporate headquarters in Calgary, Alberta; opened a systems division in Vancouver, British Columbia, to develop and export air traffic control systems worldwide; set up an acoustics technology division in Winnipeg, Manitoba; and opened a precision optics plant in Midland, Ontario. The expansion was triggered by a significant order from the Canadian government to modernize its aging air traffic control system.

Ottawa is very receptive to granting government contract work to U.S. firms willing to invest in a Canadian facility. The rules are simple. In exchange for opening a Canadian headquarters, employing Canadian workers, and exchanging technical knowledge with Canadian engineers and managers, the Canadian government offers U.S. companies a wide variety of assistance programs, including tax breaks, long-term financing, and R&D incentives.

Smaller U.S. companies find that doing business with Canadian government agencies is quite different from dealing with similar agencies in the United States, because Canadian bureaucrats tend to help, rather than hinder, companies in cutting through mountains of red tape.

Welcoming U.S. direct investment obviously serves Canadian interests. The country relies primarily on its huge reserves of natural resources to sustain the economy. Diversification plans call for the development of nonpolluting industries, and the United States is the closest and largest source of such companies. U.S.–Canada business and cultural synergism makes cross-border investment the fastest mechanism to populate the country with clean industry.

The FTA apparently plays a modest role in encouraging direct investment from the United States. Its greatest contribution has been to provide U.S. companies in Canada ready access to a cheaper and more diversified base of American suppliers.

In the western provinces (and sometimes in the eastern ones as well), U.S. companies have found it both more expensive to do business in Canada and more cost-effective. In many instances, the cost differential isn't even that great. According to a survey conducted by the Ministry of Regional and Economic Development of British Columbia, leasing and building costs are comparable to those in neighboring Seattle, Washington, two hours south.

Although hourly wages are slightly higher in Vancouver, payroll taxes are about 6 percent lower than they are in the United States. Employee health costs are substantially lower. Salaries for professionals, engineers, and technical support personnel are typically lower than they are in border states. Also, with fewer openings for university graduates, the supply of professional employees, especially engineers, is much greater in Canada.

Franchising

International franchising has been growing as rapidly (or even more rapidly) in Europe as it has in the United States. Franchise fever has also hit Canada, with most franchises coming from the United States. Industry officials estimate that the Canadian franchise market topped US$90 billion in 1991, making it the world's second largest in franchise volume. According to a study from the International Franchise Association, 81 percent of U.S. franchisers with international units are in Canada. Of these, more than 50 percent chose Canada as their first venture into the international arena.

While Canada offers the same synergies for U.S companies in franchising as in other industries, it also presents the same risks as exist when opening franchises in any international market. Trade officials warn first-time franchisers to thoroughly research Canadian company law, including bankruptcy law, before venturing north. They also suggest the use of legal counsel intimately familiar with the peculiarities of both English common law and the French legal system.

MAACO Enterprises, Inc., headquartered in a Philadelphia suburb, is a good example of a midsize franchiser (1990 sales of US$270 million) that likes the northern markets so much it has restricted its international expansion to Canada. Out of 404 operating units, the auto painting and bodyworks company claims 21 in Canada. MAACO has operated a separate subsidiary in Canada since 1977. However, company officials advise that direct contact between franchisees and the home office provides better service and tighter control over operations.

MAACO anticipates that its Canadian market is ready to enter a major growth spurt and plans to more than double its number of franchisees by 1995. It views the recession-caused pool of laid-off corporate executives and plentiful, inexpensive real estate as the primary reasons for growth optimism.

Taxes

In addition to corporate income taxes, Canadian-domiciled companies must cope with provincial income taxes and a new federal tax called the Goods and Services Tax (GST). The GST rate is 7 percent and has replaced the old federal sales tax of 13 percent. The GST is very similar to the VAT or value-added tax popular with European taxing authorities. It applies to nearly all imports and all goods and services purchased in Canada.

All manufacturers and other businesses are liable for the GST, which is applied to the value added to a product or service. The tax is assessed at each stage of production and distribution; however, companies may claim full input credits for taxes paid on business purchases. End users pay the tax, which is collected at the time of purchase.

The government found that imported services are difficult to value; the 7 percent tax, therefore, applies to any service purchased within the country.

Choosing the Right Location

Each of Canada's six distinct regions offers unique advantages to foreign investors. These regions can be roughly defined along provincial lines:

1. The eastern maritime provinces of Nova Scotia, New Brunswick, and Newfoundland

2. Quebec, with the bustling, bilingual metropolis of Montreal

3. Ontario, rich in agriculture and industry, and home of the financial and educational center of Toronto

4. The two agricultural/timber provinces of Manitoba and Saskatchewan

5. Oil and natural resource rich Alberta

6. High-tech oriented British Columbia

The St. Lawrence Seaway, and thence the Great Lakes, gives ocean-going cargo ships navigable waters from the Atlantic to Duluth, Minnesota, with direct access to ports at Montreal, Quebec, and Toronto. Winnipeg has easy rail and trucking connections to Duluth.

But one of the most interesting aspects of locating in Canada is the nation's access to world markets other than the United States. With its close trading ties to Britain and its continued association with the British Commonwealth, for instance, Canada offers an entrée to the European Community that will soon be denied American-based companies.

In addition, Canada's active participation in trade and financial services with English-speaking Caribbean island states (through the Caribbean-Canada [CARIBCAN] trade accord), permits duty-free, or nearly duty-free, imports from and exports to the Caribbean similar to those covered under America's Caribbean Basin Initiative program.

On the Pacific coast, the port of Vancouver has become a bustling terminal serving Asia-Pacific shipping lanes and transpacific air routes. In fact, the opportunity to participate in cross-ocean trade with the booming Asia-Pacific region is probably the greatest advantage enjoyed by Canadian-based companies.

Asia is a major source of critical high-tech components for Canada. Nearly all semiconductors arrive from Thailand, Malaysia, or Singapore. On the flip side, British Columbia already sends 40 percent of its total exports to Asia, against 41 percent to the United States and 15 percent to Europe.

East Asia also has been a major source of capital. For instance, in 1990, Japan was the largest holder of Canadian public debt, at approximately US$40 billion.

Hong Kong capital also plays a major role. Mutual participation in the British Commonwealth gives Canada and Hong Kong especially strong people-to-people ties. Over 30,000 Canadians now call Hong Kong home. To escape from the takeover by China in 1997, many Hong Kong residents are moving their capital to Canadian banks. For a deposit of US$500,000, Hong Kong citizens can receive residence papers from Canada—one-half the US$1 million investment demanded by the United States.

The Canadian government and the financial community are working hard to encourage the relocation of entrepreneurial businesses—and capital—to Canada. In 1989, 20,000 emigrants arrived from Hong Kong; in 1990 the figure was 30,000; officials expect the 1991 figure to increase by another 25 percent, with an even bigger jump in 1992.

Such close ties to the Asia-Pacific markets give Canadian firms a unique advantage over both U.S.–based and European-based companies. Proximity, cultural assimilation, and a practically open emigration policy permit a flow of trade and capital not found elsewhere.

Canada as a whole, and British Columbia in particular, encourage foreign investments as well as joint ventures and strategic partnerships with foreign firms from all around the world.

2
Mexico

Tips to Foreign Traders and Investors

1. Get on the Mexican bandwagon with a direct investment before NAFTA is signed. Japanese and European companies will then be looking for good buys.
2. Be on the lookout for new and more stringent environmental and industrial safety regulations.
3. Make direct investments only for labor-intensive production.
4. Export capital-intensive products.
5. Use Mexico as a stepping stone to the rest of Latin America.
6. Hire a competent subcontractor to handle labor matters and relations with local bureaucrats.
7. Try maquiladoras as an entree before NAFTA.
8. Embassy office in Washington: (202) 728-1600.

The restructuring of the Mexican economy has had profound implications for the country's social structure, political institutions, and trade relationships with the rest of the world. Prior to 1985, the government pursued an economic policy of import substitution. Mexican manufacturers imported equipment and machinery as well as raw materials to produce goods essentially for domestic consumption. No one had much interest in exporting anything but agricultural products and oil.

The government tightly controlled and restricted imports, fostered the growth of local firms, strictly regulated the entrance of foreign direct investment, and induced domestic investment in priority sectors through a maze of indirect and direct subsidies. This fostered an unmanageable bureaucracy entrusted with powers over foreign trade, domestic investment, and in fact, all economic activity in the country. Such concentrated economic muscle created enormous political power in the hands of corrupt and often abusive government officials.

This self-imposed, and self-defeating, policy of industrialization by substitution didn't work in Mexico any better than it did in Eastern Europe or the Soviet Union. Although the government attempted to shape the economy with even more socially restrictive actions, the decline in agricultural exports and the depressed world oil prices tilted Mexico's trade equilibrium for financing further factory expansion. To compensate, the government borrowed heavily from international banks and governments.

In 1982, as the trade balance rapidly declined and hard-currency flows dried up, the government defaulted en masse on its external debt obligations, triggering the snowballing rounds of the now famous debt crises throughout Latin America. Eventually, in the mid-1980s, harsh decisions had to be made, and Mexico was set on its market economy course.

In 1988, newly elected President Carlos Salinas de Gortari promised economic reforms to liberalize Mexico's statist, inefficient economy and move it toward closer integration with the United States. He also instituted Mexico's version of perestroika with a series of harsh political reforms.

Hindered by the fear of losing political control, Salinas's Institutional Revolutionary Party (PRI), which has provided relatively stable civilian rule for 62 years, is moving more slowly toward reform than the U.S. government or international traders would like.

Corporatism, authoritarianism, corruption, and rigged elections remain embedded in the PRI political system. Human rights abuses are widespread. Environmental degradation causes serious concern on the part of Mexican and world leaders. Mexico City has become so polluted that many people have to wear gas masks and breathing filters when moving about.

Pressure from the United States and, to a lesser extent, from Europe caused delegates to the PRI's fourteenth national assembly in 1990 to adopt a series of new reforms which, according to party president Senator Luis Donaldo Colosio, were designed to "put an end to the political perversion of centralized decisions."

In addition to lesser points, these reforms introduced secret ballots in all internal elections (except in the selection of a presidential candidate), made party membership voluntary, granted authority to expel public officials who commit fraud, implemented steps to protect human rights, and promoted greater participation by women and young people in party affairs. To date, most of these reforms have been less than totally effective.

Notwithstanding political and social anomalies, foreign companies view Mexico's population of 86 million as a substantial untapped market and Mexico's natural-resource base, especially its oil, as a virtual gold mine of opportunity. Because of long-standing trading practices and neighborhood proximity, American companies represent far and away the largest source of foreign trade and direct investment. The eventual implementation of a U.S.–Mexico–Canada Free Trade Agreement (NAFTA) will further enhance economic growth on both sides of the border.

Even now, pre-NAFTA, Mexico represents the third-largest trading partner for the United States. Department of Commerce statistics show the combined total of exports and imports among the top five U.S. trading partners in 1990 as:

Canada	US$175 billion
Japan	US$138 billion
Mexico	US$ 59 billion
Germany	US$ 47 billion
United Kingdom	US$ 44 billion

Imports and exports shared equally in the US$59-billion worth of trade with Mexico.

Mexican Reforms

In 1985, Mexico's economic prospects looked as bleak as those of any country in Latin America. Mexico City had just been hit with a devastating earthquake, oil prices were tumbling, and foreign debt was unmanageable. Since then, although little noticed in the world community, a truly remarkable recovery has occurred. One of the world's most protected economies has become one of the most open, and one of the most spendthrift bureaucracies has become one of the most frugal.

The economy is being rapidly modernized through deregulation, privatization of state-owned industries, and massive tax reform. The Salinas government is betting the country on what historically have been its two worst enemies: private enterprise and the United States.

As in other statist countries, conversion to a market economy doesn't come easy. Much of the population has less income and more headaches than in the past. Real wages have fallen for nine consecutive years. Many goods are in short supply. Corruption and human rights abuses have not ended. More than 30 percent of the population lives in abject poverty—roughly the same percent as did back in 1980.

In 1990 the economy grew slightly less than 3 percent; about the same is predicted for 1992. That's half of what was achieved in the 1960s and 1970s. Inflation hovered around 30 percent. The nation's trade balance declined from a surplus of US$8 billion in 1985 to a deficit in 1990.

But now the worst seems over. Wages are edging upward. Inflation has stopped accelerating. Mexico has joined the GATT. And reforms to convert to a market economy are taking hold. The Mexican government took five important steps to achieve these improvements:

1. It cut spending, reducing the deficit from 16 percent of GDP in 1987 to 3 percent in 1990. As Finance Minister Pedro Aspe points out, that's equivalent to the amount of cuts from the U.S. deficit envisioned in the Gramm-Rudman Act that never happened!

2. It devalued the peso 230 percent in 1988 and then fixed it against the U.S. dollar. To keep it strong, the government further devalued the peso gradually, approximately 14 percent each year. This stabilized domestic prices and reduced fears of rampant inflation.

3. It called on business and unions to help stabilize prices and wages, contrary to the go-it-alone approach taken by governments in other Latin American countries.

4. It replaced import quotas with tariffs, and then steadily reduced tariffs. The result has been far fewer shortages of imported goods than there have been under the Brazilian or Argentine plans.

5. It negotiated a deal with foreign creditors under the Brady Plan to restructure external debt. To date, the program has been eminently successful.

Until Mexican industrial production becomes stabilized and companies begin producing for export rather than for local consumption, oil will remain the country's main export commodity. With oil at US$30 per barrel in 1990, Mexico could have picked up incremental revenues of US$2.5 billion, which effectively could have righted the country's balance of payments. With oil at US$22.50 a barrel in 1991, the country could have picked up an extra US$5 billion. Unfortunately, world prices didn't stabilize at these levels in either year.

In the face of a prolonged American recession and slow recovery, Mexico cannot count on increased tourism or nonpetroleum exports to help. In fact, the only reasonable expectation for additional foreign currency is through increased foreign direct investment—which so far has not significantly materialized. The Mexican government's intensive negotiations to arrive at a free trade agreement with the United States have very little to do with trade but a great deal to do with attracting foreign investment.

Mr. Salinas was quoted as saying that he hopes that the NAFTA will do for Mexico what joining the European Community did for Spain, whose foreign direct investment increased by US$10 billion a year after it became a member of the EC.

The North American Free Trade Agreement

Amid much hoopla, the U.S. Congress gave President Bush his requested "fast-track" authority to negotiate a free trade agreement with Mexico. Canada also expects to join, thus forming a North American Free Trade Agreement, commonly referred to as NAFTA. Some fear that bitter disputes with American trade union leaders who decry massive job losses as whole companies relocate to Mexico might derail negotiations, but that seems unlikely.

While certain firms will obviously take advantage of a Mexican labor rate ten times lower than the U.S. average, the likelihood of wholesale job losses seems remote. The cost of picking up and moving entire companies or plants is simply too high. Political and social uncertainties will discourage many small and midsize companies from making massive commitments to Mexican production lines. Furthermore, a population of only 86 million is hardly enough to justify opening local markets to the detriment of American consumers.

American environmentalists are also up in arms, citing contaminated air and polluted water already flowing across the Mexican border from maquiladora plants. Over the long haul, these destructive situations must be attended to. Indications are already surfacing that U.S. companies choosing to establish plants in Mexico will have to abide by strict U.S. environmental regulations. This of course will add to the cost of moving and help to deter companies from relocating to Mexico en masse—further damping the flames of trade union arguments.

As far as cross-border trade is concerned, a free trade agreement will do little, either to increase Mexican exports to the U.S. or to increase U.S. exports to Mexico. Tariffs have already been cut substantially, averaging a mere 9.5 percent on Mexican imports from America (with a maximum rate of 20 percent), and a measly 4 percent on U.S. imports from Mexico.

To be sure, certain industries exceed these averages. For example, the United States imposes a 13 percent tariff on imports of Mexican fruits and vegetables; a 20.5 percent tariff on imports of footwear; a 17 percent tariff on clothing; and a 9.3 percent tariff on yarn. The United States also imposes "voluntary export restraints" (VERs) on imports of textiles, cement, and a few steel products.

A free trade agreement will undoubtedly help Mexican exporters of these products. The more important result, however, will be a restructuring of the entire Mexican economy—which in turn will attract foreign direct investment, not only from the United States but from Japan and Europe.

The legacy of fifty years of import-substitution protectionism is that the government has been financing and otherwise protecting capital-intensive heavy industry; exactly the opposite of the labor-intensive industry needed in Mexico. Presumably, a free trade agreement will make capital-intensive companies noncompetitive and drive many out of business, shifting national resources to low-tech, labor-intensive companies better attuned to Mexico's economic capabilities.

Quite obviously, this should steer potential foreign investors away from acquiring heavy industry companies through Mexico's privatization program or otherwise. It should also encourage either the acquisition or the start-up of low-tech companies, similar to the assembly plants currently operating in maquiladora zones.

Foreign Direct Investment

A major segment of the Salinas economic reform program is the privatization of thousands of state-owned industries. Through 1990, the government had sold off 230 companies, raising more than US$3 billion. It has closed down many more.

These numbers include very few large privatizations, however. The government argues that they must be saved until the economy improves, so that higher prices can be obtained. Attempts to privatize some of the big ones have been less than satisfactory. For example, when the large copper mine, Cananea, was put on the block, four separate bids and negotiations evolved before the sale finally culminated, and then at a substantially reduced price.

A high proportion of privatization revenues have been used to pay down government debt, resulting in a savings of US$1 billion in annual interest payments, according to official estimates. So far, some US$6.6 billion, or 94 percent of Mexico's contingency fund reserves from the sale of the state-owned telephone company and banks, have been used to pay off about 12 percent of the country's internal debt, largely in the form of treasury securities issued by the central bank in debt/equity swaps. This has reduced the nation's debt balance to about US$48 billion.

Caution Alert

Some progress has been reached in reducing Mexico's tax rates, traditionally among the highest in North America. The top rate applied to personal income dropped to 35 percent in 1991. The corporate rate was sliced to 35 percent from an exorbitant 56 percent.

This was a good start, but then the government reversed itself. Value-added taxes have increased. A corporate tax of 2 percent of assets was enacted. Farmers, journalists, retailers, book publishers, small companies, and countless other small businesses that survived because of special tax provisions have now lost them through the closing of so-called tax loopholes.

Mexico has a long way to go to bring its tax structure into line with a competitive market economy. To date, the effect of high taxes on smaller businesses has been detrimental. Foreign traders will keep a close eye on promised future improvements.

Meanwhile the nation's currency reserves increased to a record US$16.27 billion, up US$8 billion in one year. Foreign investors from North America, Europe, and now Japan, regard this as a positive move.

Bank of Tokyo's Masami Tsutsumimoto was quoted in *Global Finance* as stating that Japanese companies are "extremely interested in the progress of the free trade agreement." Although Japanese companies will be affected by the "local content" provision of any agreement, Mr. Tsutsumimoto says that in the long run they see "significant business opportunities in the Mexican market."

Caution Alert (to U.S. Companies)

Obviously, Japanese strategies call for using Mexico under NAFTA as a foothold for additional entries to the United States and Canada. Some company officials also freely announce that they intend to penetrate Latin American markets through free trade pacts executed between Mexico and its Latin American neighbors. U.S. companies must take an active role in Latin American trade to counteract Japanese and other East Asian competition. Hemispheric free trade accords alone won't solve competitive deficiencies.

The enactment of provisions to attract foreign investments from around the world solidifies the primary goal of Mr. Salinas's economic reform package. Foreign investors may now own 100 percent of Mexican companies in most industries, although a few, such as companies in the telecommunications, utilities, and banking industries, require majority or minority ownership by Mexican interests. Recently, foreign investment opportunities have opened in the mining industry. Domestic financial markets have also been liberalized. The government hopes that these new rules will increase the flow of foreign capital, modern management techniques, and state-of-the-art technology.

According to officials from Bancomext (Banco Nacional de Comercio Exterior), the government-owned national foreign trade bank, "Mexico has made a definitive, permanent invitation to foreign investors interested in ownership and control of Mexican-based operations." Bancomext is the government's official organization for the promotion of foreign trade. It operates a network of Trade Commission offices throughout Mexico and in 36 foreign countries.

Even with the relaxation of regulations, however, foreign investment in 1989 was a mere US\$2.4 billion, increasing to just over US\$4 billion in 1991. Officials optimistically predict that 1992 will bring in close to US\$5 billion. Even that, however, falls far short of the amount needed to offset currency drains from debt payments and imports.

Investment Opportunities

The result of Mexico's economic restructuring efforts has returned the country to real growth—over 3 percent in 1990. Nonpetroleum exports quadrupled between 1982 and 1989 and now approach US\$20 billion a year. Low-cost labor (about one-half the cost in Taiwan, South Korea, Singapore, and Hong Kong) and a 2000-mile border with the United States remain the country's biggest drawing cards.

Other factors also play prominent roles in developing direct investment and trade strategies. The country has accumulated more than US$26 billion in foreign direct investments, mostly from large U.S. companies. These investments have contributed to a substantial increase in the import of capital equipment, which jumped by 36 percent in 1989—a clear indication of the country's move toward international productivity standards and competitiveness.

Unlike its East Asian competitors, Mexico has no shortage of skilled labor. The quality and training of the work force improves each year. In 1990, nearly one-third of Mexico's 86 million people were enrolled in some form of educational program. Worker training programs have doubled over the last ten years. Multinational companies such as Ford and Sony have consistently acknowledged their Mexican plants with "quality of workmanship" awards.

While U.S. annual gains in real productivity have leveled out at about 1 percent since the mid-1970s, Mexican productivity has increased at 2.5 times this rate. During the 1980s, accumulated productivity increases totaled 26 percent—a significant achievement in anyone's book.

Mexico's main nonpetroleum exports now include automotive assemblies and components, electronics, computers, appliances, plastics and plastic products, building materials (including PVC products), and textiles.

From a manufacturing perspective, the maquiladora assembly plants that proliferate in free trade zones along the nearly 2000-mile stretch of the Mexican–U.S. border already offer significant advantages for foreign investment—with or without NAFTA.

The Maquila Program

Maquiladoras are the Mexican version of shared-production manufacturing facilities, usually assembly plants. Most, although certainly not all, maquiladora facilities are owned by U.S.–based companies. They employ approximately 500,000 Mexican workers at wages that average US$1.15 per hour, according to the Department of Labor.

Maquiladora facilities now bring Mexico more than US$3 billion per year in foreign exchange. Over the last three years, growth in the maquiladora industry has averaged 20 percent per year.

The basic rules governing maquiladoras are quite simple: foreign companies operating in a maquiladora zone may bring capital equipment and production materials into the zone duty free. When the finished product, or assembly, is shipped back to the United States, duty is paid only on the labor added while in the zone. Similar provisions apply when shipping to other countries.

The Maquila program is about as close as possible to free trade without a formal government-to-government agreement. The success of maquiladoras is one reason for the lack of universal enthusiasm by U.S. companies for a free trade accord.

American FTZs

One interesting by-product of the Maquila program is the use of U.S. foreign trade zones (FTZs). Nearly every Fortune 500 company participates in the program. A company first selects an appropriate maquiladora site that meets its requirements for labor, building facilities, and proximity to markets and materials used in the production process.

Once a Mexican site has been chosen, the company chooses another site in one of the border states—California, Arizona, New Mexico, or Texas—for a complementary facility to perform testing and/or final assembly. Finished goods are then shipped either to international markets or repackaged and sold domestically. By locating in an American FTZ, these finishing steps can also be accomplished duty free.

It is not surprising that one of the highest-volume general-purpose FTZs in the country is located in the lower Rio Grande Valley town of McAllen, Texas. Practically every U.S. city along the Mexican border has at least one FTZ. Laredo, San Diego, and El Paso each have several.

Maquiladora Sales within Mexico

Maquiladoras are not used solely to produce semi-finished or finished products for sale in the United States or overseas. They also produce goods for Mexican consumption. According to the World Trade Association in San Antonio, Texas, 1989 exports totaling US$8.5 billion moved through Laredo, Texas, to Mexico, while another US$22 million in exports passed through tiny Columbus, New Mexico, on their way south. These exports to maquiladora plants presumably were to be finished and reshipped back to the United States. In fact, however, many were purchased by Mexican consumers.

An increasing number of companies are taking advantage of a little-publicized Mexican program—the Program for Temporary Import for Export (PITEX). Under this program companies operating in a maquiladora zone may spin off a new company to produce exclusively for the Mexican market. They have the choice of expanding production in an existing maquiladora company and selling the additional products within Mexico, or of switching an entire plant over to the PITEX program. Either way, companies enjoy the same Maquila program benefits.

The Mexican manufacturing sector continues to voraciously seek capital goods, especially from the United States. Companies in these industries find the average tariff of 9.5 percent easy to crank into selling prices. Exports moving through the Maquila program, or through PITEX, of course, enter the country duty free.

Maquiladoras also benefit from a reverse condition. Original supporters of the Maquila program argued that maquiladoras would not only provide jobs for Mexican laborers but also create an additional market for Mexican manufactured goods and materials. Thirty years later this prediction is coming true.

Toilet paper, soap, cardboard boxes, and other nonproduction materials have always been purchased locally. Now an American Chamber of Commerce survey shows a significant rise in the local supply of materials and components used in the production process, up to nearly 10 percent of all maquiladora purchases. Responding to cost and delivery pressures, maquiladora plant managers are increasingly developing networks of local vendors. Companies going this route report that it adds significant delivery efficiency and gives them an extra competitive edge in finished goods prices and delivery schedules.

Maquiladora Problems

Telephone service in Mexico, especially outside Mexico City and a few coastal resort areas, remains an abysmal reminder of the underdevelopment of the country's infrastructure. Placing local calls from a rural area is nearly impossible. International calls get through more frequently but are still less than satisfactory. With frequent telephone contact a way of life in American business, poor telephone service creates a major obstacle to efficient operations.

Maquiladora managers cheered the acquisition of the Mexican telephone company Telefonos de Mexico (Telmex) by an international consortium that included Southwestern Bell, Cable and Radio from France, British Telecom, and Mexico's own Grupo Carson. Their euphoria was short-lived. Powerful Telmex union workers were not satisfied with the deal and the usual horrendous service continued. Furthermore, while service is unchanged, rates have escalated. A maquila manager pays new, much higher rates for services ranging from a busy signal that overlays a conversation, to the inability of either party to hear the other.

Border Customs Officials

One of the major complaints from maquiladora operators relates to corruption and delays at Mexican customs border stations. Customs officials have acknowledged the problem but offered no solution. Finally, the Mexican government has come to the rescue. It has transferred import warehouses to entrepreneurs who, by holding merchandise in private warehouses, will presumably deny customs officials access to the goods and thus keep customs' sticky fingers out of the pie.

Environmental and Industrial Safety

Potential foreign investors should be aware of increasing pressure from U.S. activist groups against continued environmental degradation and safety hazards in foreign-owned manufacturing facilities—primarily those located in maquiladora zones.

Residents of U.S. border towns continue to raise loud objections to the air and water pollution in their communities coming from cross-border industrial plants. When President Bush requested "fast-track" authority to negotiate a Mexican free trade agreement, Congress insisted that U.S.–owned facilities in Mexico be subject to the same environmental standards as in the United States.

Until now, one of the cost-saving features of locating in a maquiladora area has been avoidance of the nonproductive pollution control or safety costs necessitated by U.S. regulations.

But time has run out. Activist groups have broken through to congressional representatives, who in turn have demanded compliance assistance from Mexican authorities. Although Mexico has environmental regulations on its books similar to those imposed in the United States, activists claim that Mexican enforcement has been all but nonexistent.

Both the U.S. Congress and the Mexican government have put maquiladora companies on notice to clean up their act or get out. This means substantial additional costs and could forestall strategic plans for new maquiladora facilities.

Red Flag

Environmental and safety regulations for new foreign investments are much stricter than in the past. Even with current lax enforcement by Mexican authorities, the government's intense desire for a free trade agreement with the United States is creating regulations and enforcement measures more stringent than current American standards. Although difficult to estimate, the added costs of compliance must be weighed against market and resource advantages.

Starting a Mexican Operation

Maquiladoras are clearly not for every manufacturing company. Aside from relaxed export and import duties, a primary advantage of manufacturing in Mexico has been and will continue to be cheap labor.

Many advocates of a free trade agreement from both sides of the border argue convincingly that even though maquiladoras offer many economic and social benefits now, more will accrue after the implementation of a free trade agreement. The fact remains, however, that most companies view the primary advantage of locating facilities in Mexico to be its abundant, low-cost labor. They are willing to put up with all the hassles discussed here, provided that a real savings can be effected through lower labor costs.

Several consultants, trade officials, and industry gurus have tried to develop cost models to help companies plan their strategies for entering

Mexican markets. None is universally applicable and none offers an easy answer.

In the end, company executives must weigh labor savings against such hidden costs as travel, communications, shipping, customs duties, financing, insurance, and internal coordination. To the extent that the end result yields higher profits, a Mexican investment can make sense.

The Best Choices

The greatest benefits of a Mexican facility tend to occur in labor-intensive industries, such as commercial electronics, auto parts and components (air conditioners, engines, transmissions), apparel, and furniture. Within the consumer electronics category, current Mexican facilities efficiently produce a wide range of products: can openers, hair dryers, toasters, coffee makers, toys, sporting goods, outboard motors, and pleasure boats, to mention only a few. Companies have also discovered that production of TVs, lamps, ceramics, large appliances, and cut flowers fit the Mexican mold.

Many products made by foreign companies in East Asia can be more efficiently produced in Mexico. Labor is cheaper, cultural differences less, shipping easier and less costly, and local markets much larger.

One way for smaller companies, perhaps inexperienced in international trade, to begin a Mexican operation at the least cost and risk is by subcontracting personnel and administrative duties to a Mexican firm. This version of shared production enables the foreign investor to concentrate on managing purchasing, production, and marketing activities while the Mexican subcontractor takes responsibility for locating and hiring workers, preparing and distributing payrolls, leasing facilities, keeping the company's books, and processing customs paperwork. Most important, a competent subcontractor can keep local government bureaucrats off the backs of foreign managers.

The subcontractor functions as a combination labor broker and administrative partner, in an arrangement commonly used for managing smaller foreign investments in the Middle East, Asia, and certain Caribbean and South American locations. The subcontractor usually bills the foreign investor a flat rate based on the number of direct labor hours worked. Current Mexican rates range from US\$2.50 to US\$4.50 an hour.

Starting in Mexico City

Although the country boasts a populace of 86 million, more than three times the size of Canada, nearly one-fourth of the population lives and works in the Mexico City metropolitan area. Table 2-1 shows a breakdown of the area's growth projections.

Administratively, Mexico City is split in two: the Federal District, which

Table 2-1.   Growth of Mexico City

	Central City	Total Metro Area
Surface area (in square kilometers)	1479	7860
Population (in millions)	10.8	19.8
Projected population (in millions)		
By the year 2000	12.0	23.5
By the year 2010	13.0	26.7
Population density (per square kilometer)	7317	2341
Growth rate (percentage)	0.3	4.4
Minimum wage (per day)	US$4	N/A

SOURCE: *Atlas de la Ciudad de Mexico.*

comprises the central city, and the surrounding metropolitan area, which is classified as the State of Mexico.

Although Mexico City does not have the tourist charm of Cancun or San Miguel de Allende, it remains a "must-stop" for many international visitors. Its museums of archaeology, modern art, manuscripts, ethnology, and natural history, along with its pyramids, galleries, and national ballet, attract millions of visitors every year. Companies interested in direct investment in the tourist industry would do well to consider Mexico City in addition to the more developed coastal regions.

Looked at from a negative standpoint, Mexico City has some major problems. Its air pollution, caused by industrial waste and a veritable army of cars, is one of the worst in the world. Traffic congestion, especially during the rush hours, is nearly impossible to negotiate. The city rests on the unstable foundation of a shallow lake bed into which the city's buildings are steadily sinking. Severe earthquakes are a constant worry. Crumbling municipal plumbing and drained reservoirs leave the city continually short of water.

Despite these obvious drawbacks, Mexico City's substantial cheap labor base and its educated, technically proficient management pool, continue to attract foreign investment of all types.

Economic Revitalization: Fact or Fiction?

While the halls of Congress and American business schools reverberate with debates about the pros and cons of free trade and the desirability of protecting local industry, employment, and social benefits, discussions in corporate boardrooms are far more pragmatic. The strategic importance of free trade cannot be overlooked; nor can related social and political concerns.

When all is said and done, the purpose of international trade is to increase long-term company profitability and return on invested capital. Most business leaders from around the world seem to understand this truism. They also understand that challenges from the international marketplace must be met with swift, decisive actions.

The implications of a North American Free Trade Agreement are staggering. Together, the three countries constitute the world's largest, and potentially its richest, consumer market.

The most relevant issues seem to center on the economic and social disparities between Mexico and its northern neighbors. Mexico's GNP is less than 4 percent that of the United States; its per capita income is US$2625, compared to the American US$21,600; its labor pool is one-fifth the size of the U.S. labor pool; and its average wage rates are one-tenth those of U.S. wage rates.

On the plus side, Mexico stands fair to be the backyard market of the future for northern companies. In 1990, its GDP grew 3.9 percent, while its industrial production grew by 5.4 percent. Investment as a percentage of GDP reached its highest point in five years: 18.9 percent. Current forecasts for growth in 1992 are in excess of 5 percent. Mexico's credit rating has been raised 5.4 points. Foreign investment reached US$4.6 billion in 1990.

Detroit's automakers, DuPont, Phelps Dodge, IMB, and General Electric, have been in Mexico for decades and are now expanding their investments. Small and midsize companies are venturing into Mexico as never before—both in and out of the Maquila zones. Japanese and German multinationals are investing billions in everything from infrastructure projects to maquiladora assembly shops. For these companies at least, Mexico's cheap labor, rising productivity levels, burgeoning market demand, abundant natural resources, and proximity to U.S. markets are more than worth the extra effort and cost.

Still, several deficiencies will take many years to rectify. Without question, foreign investment is desperately needed to correct basic shortcomings in Mexican infrastructure, telecommunications, internal transport, and environmental control.

The Mexican government is certainly taking major steps to encourage foreign companies. Deregulation and procedural simplification have opened a broad range of direct investment forms: joint ventures, full business acquisitions, trusts, "pyramided" share ownership, neutral stock options, and venture capital funds, to mention a few. The Mexican financial system is capable of handling trade finance and investment funding in the Maquila zones or in other areas of the country.

The banking industry has been strengthened through privatizations and closures: total financial institutions declined from 60 to 18. Brokerage houses, fund management, and leasing operations have all grown significantly. Many larger houses now offer full-service capabilities. Several Mexican banks are better capitalized than their U.S. counterparts.

Professionals are also beefing up their expertise and knowledge of international trade. Law firms are learning U.S. customs and tax laws. Local public accounting firms are expanding services to foreign firms. Even international consulting firms have begun to take on a professional air.

These developments are all occurring in tandem with, but prior to, the implementation of a free trade agreement. Cross-border business has developed its own dynamism. It won't wait for the politicians. Mexican, American, and Canadian business leaders are already formulating appropriate strategies for flexible participation in NAFTA. Meanwhile, European and East Asian companies have slowly but surely begun to recognize the strategic importance of close trading ties with Mexico.

3
The United States

Tips to Foreign Traders and Investors

1. Review idiosyncrasies of American tastes and product standards thoroughly before entering this intensely competitive market.

2. Don't be turned off by "Buy American" slogans.

3. Don't be fooled by the American propensity for self-deprecation.

4. Take a look at the new "investor visa" for foreigners willing to invest US$1 million in a U.S. venture that creates at least ten jobs.

5. Recognize that each state has different laws and each region different market characteristics.

6. Tap red-hot markets for electronic gadgetry, environmental protection devices, and products that make life easier for the American consumer.

7. Exploit markets and promotions for the kind of socially responsible products and management demanded by an increasing number of American consumers.

"Buy American" may be a cliché with a hollow ring, but for many Americans it stimulates a patriotic fervor that stirs hearts and opens checkbooks. Companies that choose to make a direct investment in the United States, either through a joint venture or through a business acquisition, find a market of 250 million people with the largest gross national product in the world. They also find American consumers, government agencies, and even industrial customers more enthusiastic about buying products made within U.S. borders than offshore.

At the same time, the fact that the United States imports more than it exports bodes well for companies unable to establish a U.S. presence but still eager to tap this immense market.

The U.S. market has a lot going for it. It is large, dynamic, and attracts a plethora of products and services. Corporate income tax rates are relatively low compared to European countries. Profits can be easily repatriated. A commonalty of language and fairly uniform industrial standards throughout the country makes expansion within its borders relatively simple once U.S. rules for doing business are learned.

The U.S. dollar remains the "super" currency of the world, freely convertible in any country. Best of all, the U.S. market is not very difficult to penetrate, provided certain classic pitfalls are avoided and sufficient time is allotted.

On the other hand, foreign traders and investors should not be misled by the comparative openness of U.S. business. Major obstacles have shackled more than one company trying to exploit this market. Consumer preferences, customer services, market dispersion, distribution methods, and sales techniques are substantially different from those found in other industrialized nations. The United States is a big market and products that sell in one section of the country may not sell in another.

A labyrinth of company and trade laws cause misunderstandings and confusion. So many laws from different jurisdictions are overlaid, one on the other, that it's difficult to determine which apply in specific cases. Federal, state, county, township, and city laws frequently conflict.

Tax laws also offer challenges. To a large extent the structure of a business determines the amount of taxes paid. Federal, state, county, township, and city tax laws overlap. A wide variety of special taxes must be dealt with: sales and use taxes, real estate and personal property taxes, capital taxes, franchise taxes, and a variety of other taxes that differ for each governmental unit. Fifty states and thousands of lesser government bodies make the U.S. tax structure one of the most complex in the world.

Nevertheless, companies willing and able to grapple with this maze of regulations, tax structures, market peculiarities, and distribution vagaries find the United States an extremely lucrative opportunity for gaining new markets and resources. Granted that only about 7 percent of total business receipts come from foreign-controlled companies, the fact that sales from these companies have been accelerating faster than sales from American-controlled firms gives credence to the vast opportunities for foreign investment.

In 1979, foreign-controlled companies located in the United States generated US$242 billion in sales. In 1987 (the latest year for which statistics are available), sales totaled US$685 billion—an increase of 183 percent. In comparison, the revenue of U.S.–owned companies increased just 52 percent. While these statistics are certainly outdated, U.S. trade officials believe that, based on the flood of foreign acquisitions during the late 1980s and early 1990s, total sales from foreign-controlled businesses during 1992 will exceed US$1 trillion.

The growing presence of foreign-owned properties and foreign goods continues to be encouraged—sometimes deliberately, at other times inadvertently—by generous tax breaks from Washington.

Data from the Internal Revenue Service shows that U.S. businesses owned by parent companies from Germany, Japan, Britain, France, the Netherlands, and other foreign countries claim far larger tax deductions than do U.S.–owned companies. Oversized write-offs allow these companies to file tax returns showing little or no profit and therefore requiring little or no income tax. While revenues from these companies increased 50 percent from 1984 to 1987, their tax bill went up a mere 2 percent.

The Internal Revenue Service has been especially generous to Japanese-owned American companies. Sales from these firms rose 64 percent from 1984 to 1987 to reach a total of US$184 billion. But federal income taxes from the same firms actually decreased 14 percent—from US$1.1 billion in 1984 to US$951 million in 1987. In 1988, Japanese-controlled American companies paid federal income taxes of US$510.5 million, or 6.1 percent of sales. Contrast this with an actual tax rate of 11.6 percent paid by individuals earning between US$40,000 and US$50,000.

Market Characteristics

Beyond the issue of federal income taxes, competitive strategies call for a thorough understanding of the market characteristics of U.S. trade. These characteristics can logically be categorized in eight groupings:

1. The uniquely American "will"
2. Acceptance of things foreign
3. Diversity of cultural markets
4. Product demand
5. American standards
6. Economic cycles
7. Staying power
8. Emphasis on service

The American "Will"

American customers, either industrial or consumer, show a remarkable resilience. Quick to accept new ideas; secure in the belief that, despite obvious inequities and mismanagement, the federalist system of government works to protect the rights of the individual and will not be radically altered; and convinced that a market economy will continue to expand opportunities for individuals and businesses, Americans are not afraid to criticize or to accept criticism.

Recessions and wars come and go, the rich get richer and the poor get poorer, but the work ethic still prevails. With creativity and business acumen, Americans firmly believe that they have it within their power to achieve individual success. The American "will" has often bent, but never broken in more than 200 years; nothing on the horizon indicates a change.

Americans love to criticize themselves. The Constitution and the Bill of Rights permit a degree of freedom of expression found in few other places in the world, and Americans take full advantage of it. Foreigners frequently misinterpret these criticisms as an indication that the United States is headed for disaster. Self-deprecation is an American way of life. The biggest mistake foreign traders and investors make is to believe that Americans take their self-criticism seriously.

Acceptance of Things Foreign

In line with their general openness, many Americans are more than willing to try foreign products. High-priced imported cars, designer clothing, consumer durables, films, and a variety of other foreign products have become status symbols for certain groups of Americans. Eager to try something new, consumers flock to buy Australian meat, Japanese electronic gadgets, Hong Kong clothing, Chinese shoes, and Dutch filtration systems, even though American products are priced lower and are frequently of a higher quality.

Diversity of Cultural Markets

The United States' borders have always been open to foreign immigration and foreign trade. No other country can boast such a diversity of ethnic markets. Hispanics and African Americans, East and Southeast Asians, Indians and Arabs, northern and southern Europeans, and various cultural mixes and subdivisions create an enormous market opportunity to specialize in ethnically oriented products.

Foreign traders should be warned, however, that even though these groups exhibit ethnic origins and tastes, the longer they reside in the United States the more assimilated they become in broad American markets. It is also important to recognize that most immigrants obtain U.S. citizenship eventually and adopt American characteristics and tastes rather than retaining those of their heritage.

Product Demand

It only makes sense to develop strategies that target market segments with the least competition and the greatest projected customer demand.

High-tech products are in universal demand and companies engaged in extensive R & D efforts stand a good chance of cornering a share of one or more market niches. Not only is domestic demand high; a U.S. presence opens doors to Canadian and Mexican markets as well.

American consumers love gadgets, especially those involving electronics. Japanese companies, for example, have been eminently successful in marketing an array of electronic gadgetry.

Virtually any industrial or consumer product that improves or protects the environment sells like hotcakes. Drainage and flood control pumps, biofiltration systems, solid-waste conversion equipment, drinking water filtration products, and oil refinery and chemical plant air cleaners, are examples of booming markets.

American consumers spend millions every year on imported ethnic foods, specialty fruits and vegetables, and nutritional diet foods. Physical fitness products are also hot items.

It's important to bear in mind that in the 1990s American culture is placing a high value on physical fitness, environmental clean-up and protection, and products that make everyday living easier. These are some of the hottest markets to go after.

American Standards

Foreign companies frequently underestimate the American preoccupation with homegrown standards. Regardless of the rest of the world, Americans are not prone to change the standards they have been accustomed to for generations. Here are some examples of product standards that Americans insist on:

Product Literature and Advertising.   If product literature and advertising do not employ American English, which differs materially from English English, Americans won't get the message. Foreign traders would be wise to brush up on their "Americanese" before entering U.S. markets.

Paper and Packaging Sizes.   A quart is a quart; a pint is a pint; a gallon is a gallon. The alcoholic beverage industry converted to liters some years ago, committed huge sums to modify bottle size and labeling, and then learned that Americans do not think in terms of liters. Some claim that this marketing error contributes to the continuing downward trend in the sales of imported liquors.

Measurements.   The metric system is not widely accepted in American markets. Some products get by using these measures; most do not.

Safety.   Product safety standards are set by federal government agencies. In spite of their abhorrence of big government, American consumers listen carefully to product safety pronouncements. More than one automobile model, toy, prescription or over-the-counter drug, cereal, and snack food has failed to meet safety standards and been recalled from the market.

Economic Cycles

The ideal time to enter U.S. markets is immediately prior to the introduction of competing products. With the exception of high-tech gadgetry, however, this seldom occurs.

That being the case, entry should be timed to coincide with the beginning of the upward trend in an industry's economic curve. The U.S. government has an abundance of historical and forecasted data relating to economic curves in virtually every industry. Research in this area can prevent serious misjudgments regarding competition and market demand.

A second point relates to the length of time it takes to penetrate U.S. markets. A good rule of thumb is that market penetration takes approximately the same amount of time as it would to start a business from scratch in the foreign company's home country. If that is five to eight years, the same time frame should apply to penetrating U.S. markets. Obviously many companies have shortened the period through effective advertising and sales promotions. And of course some market niches accept new competitors faster than others. Still, the above rule of thumb is not a bad measure for strategic planning.

Staying Power

Staying power is extremely important to American customers. Too many times in the 1960s and 1970s foreign imports and foreign-controlled companies seemed to come and go overnight. A good example is the Yugoslavian automobile, the Yugo. Another is the Volkswagen production facility in New Stanton, Pennsylvania.

Americans want to be certain that a company will be around in the future to repair the product or provide other after-sale service. Americans may be keen on foreign products, but not so much that they will buy from anything less than what they perceive to be a permanent member of the marketplace.

Emphasis on Service

Intense competition in virtually every industry gives customers the edge in choosing which products to buy. With this edge comes a strong demand for service.

Regardless of a product's utility, or in many cases its price, the customers' loyalty (to the extent that it exists at all) goes to companies that pamper them with iron-clad guarantees and out-of-the-ordinary after-sale service. Although certainly important in many other countries, service is the name of the game in the United States. Outstanding customer service remains the fastest and least-expensive way to penetrate American markets.

The banking industry is a major exception to this commandment. Based on cost and availability, cross-border money attracts customers far more than services offered by the bank.

Economic Future

Part of any strategy that includes U.S. trade or investment must take into account the state of the economy and its relationship to global trade. Shortsighted plans that ignore the underlying economic strengths and weaknesses of the customer's country will assuredly lead to erroneous and potentially dangerous conclusions.

Several conflicting scenarios have been advanced by noted authorities about how strong the recovery will be from the 1989–1992 recession and the effect of an American downturn on world trade. But most economic predictions are meaningless to company strategies without an explanation of the factors underlying economic swings. With such factors in mind, executives should be in a better position to judge the efficacy of alternative market strategies on their own.

Five major factors dampen enthusiasm for a robust recovery of the American economy.

1. Lack of consumer confidence

2. Unwieldy debt burdens

3. Restructuring of the banking system

4. Precarious government fiscal policies

5. Slackening exports

Consumer Confidence

Recovery stimulants to every recession since 1945 have come from one or both of two sources: (1) an increase in consumer spending; and (2) pump-priming by the U.S. government. Except for a modest spurt in durables, consumer spending remains far less than that needed to jolt the economy.

During 1992, conflicting interpretations from a variety of pollsters have indicated two conditions not present during prior recoveries: (1) more than US$3 trillion in consumer debt; and (2) a predominantly white-collar unemployment rate approaching 7 percent. The Fed's attempts to jump-start the economy by tinkering with discount rates have done little to boost consumer confidence.

The second traditional stimulant, federal pump-priming, was hampered by similar conditions. Despite substantial cutbacks in defense spending, the federal budget deficit continued to grow under the prodding of outmoded supply-side federal policies. Without major sources of new revenue, the federal government remains prevented from pouring additional funds into the economy.

On the contrary, politicians view fiscally prudent tax increases and the reallocation of federal spending programs as politically unacceptable. Boxed in by debt and fiscal paralysis, consumers viewed government economic policies as inept and useless for stimulating economic recovery. Consumer confidence dropped to the lowest level since the Great Depression, slowing recovery even further.

Debt Burdens

Both consumer debt and business debt are at an all-time high, each exceeding US$3 trillion. Echoing the debt-crazy theories popular during the 1980s, economists such as MIT professor Rudiger Dornbusch firmly believe that the level of debt isn't important as long as interest rates remain low. They point to a decrease in commercial paper rates from 16 percent in 1983 to less than 6 percent in 1991 as evidence that "even with high debt ratios, interest burdens are not oppressive." From this they draw the conclusion that consumers should have been on a spending spree in 1991—which of course they were not.

Not only did consumers stop spending, the number of personal and business bankruptcies continued to skyrocket. Dun & Bradstreet reported that business failures increased 54 percent in the first quarter of 1991—the biggest jump in seven years.

The net liabilities of these 20,811 failures totaled US$29.6 billion, causing a devastating bad-debt effect on other companies and creating another major reason for a slow recovery. Although business failures are predicted to decrease in 1992–1993, much of the damage has already been done, especially to the many smaller businesses that employ a large percentage of the U.S. work force.

Banking Bust

The U.S. banking industry began deteriorating in the late 1980s when it became clear that loans made to developing country governments, primarily in Latin America, would never be repaid. The 1989–1992 recession resulted in unfilled offices, factories, apartment buildings, and hotels. Owners defaulted and banks were left with equally sizable unpaid real estate loans.

The collapse of the junk bond market and the previously mentioned rash of business failures, many of which were victims of high leverage buyouts during the raging 1980s, further crippled the banking industry. The collapse of the savings and loan industry drove the final nail into the coffin.

The domino effect of bank failures ricocheted through the insurance industry, investment banking, and other financial services, further dampening enthusiasm for the increased lending that might stimulate consumer and business spending.

As long as the stock market held and major corporations sported better credit ratings than banks (allowing them to tap public bond markets), the withdrawal of banks from credit markets wasn't as severe as it could have been. Nevertheless, the credit crunch did stop smaller businesses and consumers from borrowing more to spend more.

Although foreign banks are also encroaching on the American scene, their impact to date has been minimal.

Fiscal Austerity

As previously mentioned, prudent federal fiscal policy has been notably absent for more than 15 years. Normally, a recovery would be stimulated by fiscal policies aimed at increasing government spending levels on domestic programs. But the composition of the federal deficit is different this time around than in the previous recoveries of the mid-1970s and early 1980s.

Nearly one-third of the federal deficit results from government bailouts of the savings and loan industry. Interest payments are running at an all-time high. A deficit consisting primarily of bailouts and interest payments is far less a stimulator than one consisting of big jumps in defense spending or income tax cuts.

State and city treasuries across the country face equally hard times and cannot assist in a recovery. New York, New Jersey, Massachusetts, and Rhode Island remain in a precarious position. Bridgeport, Connecticut, pleaded bankruptcy. Philadelphia avoided massive default by a hair's breadth. Federal cutbacks in allocated funds to states and cities during the 1980s caused local governments to raise taxes and cut spending—certainly not economic stimulants.

Foreign Trade

Except for brief periods of small surpluses, the United States continues to run a trade deficit, importing more than it exports. The dollar is no longer as competitive as it was during the 1980s and early 1990s. Foreign investment in the United States has slowed. The rapid export growth that buoyed the economy during 1988–1990 has tapered off and the OECD forecasts approximately equal increases in exports and imports for 1992.

This makes foreign trade or massive injections of foreign investment unlikely stimulants. Japan, Germany, and the rest of Europe have their own economic and fiscal problems. If substantial recovery is to come to America, it must start at home with internal economic growth.

Although the country's trade balance continues in the red, the deficit is shrinking, giving rise to modest optimism. Table 3-1 shows historical and projected trade balances. More optimistic for 1992 than national forecasters, the OECD projects substantial gains in consumer spending and private investment, as shown in Table 3-2.

Table 3-1.   United States Trade Balances
(Seasonally adjusted, in US$ billions)

	1989	1990	Projected 1991	1992
Exports	360.5	389.3	405	443
Imports	475.3	498.0	484	524
Trade balance	-114.9	-108.7	-79	-82
Current account balance	-110.0	-99.3	-9	-58

SOURCE: OECD.

Table 3-2.   Demand, Output, and Prices in the United States
(Percentage change from previous period)

	1988	1989	1990	1991	1992
Private consumption	3.6	1.9	1.0	0.1	2.6
Government consumption	0.2	2.3	2.8	1.1	-0.6
Private fixed investment					
Residential	-0.8	-4.0	-5.3	-13.8	9.0
Nonresidential	8.3	3.9	1.8	-4.7	6.4
Total domestic demand	3.3	1.9	0.5	-0.9	3.3
GNP at market prices	4.5	2.5	0.9	-0.2	3.1
Consumer prices	3.9	4.5	5.0	4.3	3.9

SOURCE: OECD.

Although these projections are certainly encouraging, the OECD, not noted for its conservatism, traditionally overforecasts the timing and magnitude of upturns and underestimates the severity of downturns. Furthermore, statistics compiled from gross, consolidated data do not necessarily reflect conditions in specific markets, industries, or regions of the country, which in the United States experience extremely diverse economic fluctuations.

The impact of the United States' economic slowdown on the rest of the world has been substantially less than in previous recessions. One reason for this is the strength of the Japanese and German economies. Another reason is the stability brought to Europe by the progress of the European Monetary System. A third reason is the relative strength of major multinational corporations with firmly established operations throughout the world.

Foreign Direct Investment

Throughout the halls of Congress lobbying groups echo cries of "protect America." Editorials and special reports in major newspapers decry the "sellout" of American property and businesses to foreigners. Media analysts denounced the Japanese purchase of a share of Rockefeller Center as a "traitorous sell-off of America's heritage."

Such antagonism might frighten off unwary foreign investors, but it shouldn't. This is merely another example of Americans exercising their right to free speech and free press. Radical activist groups might parade with placards and the media may wave scare-tactic banners, but the majority of American businesses and consumers continue to demand innovative products (and of course money) from abroad.

The latest statistics show that in 1989, foreign direct investment accounted for a mere 3 percent of domestic net worth, or US$550 billion. That compares to US$800 billion in direct American investment abroad. Clearly, worries about a "sellout" have been grossly exaggerated.

Special interest groups exert powerful influences over federal legislation. The spurt of Japanese acquisitions of American companies caused a bill to be introduced in the House of Representatives labeled the Technology Preservation Act (TPA) to ensure that foreign direct investments will be done only on American terms. The bill was designed to amend the so-called Exon-Florio provision of the trade bill of 1988. Exon-Florio (which lapsed in mid-1990) gave the President authority to review foreign takeovers of U.S. companies that might impair the nation's "national security." Under both presidents Reagan and Bush "national security" has been narrowly defined as relating almost entirely to military secrets.

Congressional protectionists claim that the vetting process under Exon-Florio worked too well, subjecting a mere 12 cases—out of a total of 575 cases reviewed—to 45-day investigations. Only one case, that involving the China National Aero-Technology Import and Export Company's proposed acquisition of Mamco Manufacturing, was blocked.

Caution Alert

In late 1991, special-interest protectionist groups pushed Congress to enact the TPA. The bill introduced explicit criteria for vetoing a foreign-acquisition: namely, that the foreign takeover impairs "the industrial and technology base of the United States"— whatever that means. The TPA also empowers the President to demand written assurances from a potential foreign buyer of its "plans and intentions"—in other words, its business secrets. It will pay to watch this legislation and others like it very closely. Protectionist legislation could kill otherwise valuable investment opportunities.

Fortunately, this type of protectionist thinking is isolated in a minority of lobbying groups and congressional leaders. And rightly so, as statistics from the Department of Commerce clearly show.

According to the Commerce Department, the share of foreign investment flowing into high-technology businesses remained practically constant from 1980 through 1989 at 11 to 11.5 percent. The Commerce Department reports that, as measured by royalties and license fees, technology transfers from foreign companies to American affiliates were five times as great as transfers out of those affiliates. Furthermore, 75 percent of all technology transfers out of the United States are to American-owned foreign affiliates: a trifling 2 percent transferred to foreign-owned companies.

Americans love charts, graphs, tables, and statistics compiled from pollsters in every walk of life, as witnessed by the rise in popularity of the newspaper *USA Today*. Not infrequently, such unscientific surveys of American consumers and businesses give a more reliable reading than professional economists' mathematical forecasting models.

One such poll was conducted by American Business Information of Omaha, Nebraska. This company specializes in counting telephone directory Yellow Pages listings from across the country to determine which business categories have grown or shrunk from the previous year. The results are shown in Table 3-3.

Table 3-3. Growing and Declining Businesses in the United States

	Number of businesses by end of 1990	Percentage change
Ten Biggest Gainers		
Facsimile transmission equipment	10,830	47.7
Moving supplies/equipment renting	11,774	41.3
Convenience stores	17,235	41.1
Environmental services	6,238	40.5
Yogurt producers	5,598	27.9
Collectibles retailers/producers	6,476	27.1
Asbestos removal services	3,028	26.5
Recycling centers	5,883	26.3
Disc jockey radio stations	3,321	24.4
Bed and breakfast establishments	5,526	24.0
Ten Biggest Losers		
Home-planning services	1,620	-20.6
Commercial refrigeration	2,776	-20.4
Video recorders	10,591	-19.0
Air conditioning (room units)	3,639	-15.8
Microwave ovens	3,756	-15.3
Kitchen ranges and stoves	5,085	-14.5
Metal windows	2,290	-14.5
Dishwashers	3,671	-14.4
Auto rustproofing	1,896	-14.2
Scalp treatment services/supplies	2,341	-12.7

SOURCE: *American Business Information.*

Foreign investors and traders shouldn't put undue reliance on surveys of this type. Most are skewed toward the pollster's prejudices. They do indicate general trends, however, and therefore might be of value in judging market opportunities.

A Bright Spot

Traditionally, recessionary pressures cause certain industries to suffer more than others. Machine tools and segments of the electronics industry in 1981–82 and commercial real estate and banking in 1989–1992 are prime examples. Foreign companies seeking direct investment opportunities, and having access to offshore capital, can usually find significant bargains in these depressed industries. The American hospitality industry presents just such an opportunity.

At last count the Resolution Trust Corp. (RTC), a federal government organization formed to take over defaulted properties from the savings and loan industry, owned nearly 200 operating hotels. The cost of these properties to the RTC is of course the amount of the defaulted, and guaranteed, mortgage.

To get out from under and at the same time save taxpayers the continuing funding of operating businesses, the RTC is generally willing to part with these properties at a fraction of the mortgage balance. Whereas a typical first-class hotel (outside New York) costs approximately US$80,000 to US$100,000 per room to build, many can be purchased from the RTC at US$10,000 to US$20,000 per room. The 1991–1992 trend is for foreign companies to purchase hotels and permit American exowners to continue running them.

RTC properties are not the only hotels being gobbled up by foreign investors. East Asian companies have led the charge. During the last couple of years, Korean firms have been highly visible in southern California, investing in excess of US$500 million in hotel acquisitions. In Hawaii, Japanese investors already own 60 percent of available hotel rooms.

Two internationally known U.S. chains divested: Holiday Corp. sold out to London-based Bass PLC for US$2.2 billion, and Ramada, Inc. turned over properties to a Hong Kong firm for US$540 million.

The giant Canadian hotel chain, Toronto-based Canadian Pacific Hotels & Resorts, penetrated the U.S. market by acquiring an 80 percent interest in MetHotels of Phoenix, Arizona. MetHotels operates the Doubletree and Compri hotel chains in the Southwest. MetHotels is also building a hotel in Japan that gives Canadian Pacific a toehold in that lucrative market.

Although these chains had not defaulted on mortgages, and therefore were not part of the RTC sell-off, prices paid by foreign investors were substantially discounted, according to Richard Kateley of Real Estate Research Corp. of Chicago.

Hotels are not the only recession-generated opportunity for foreign investors. On a lesser scale, hundreds of thousands of entrepreneurial and midsize companies face enormous debt problems. Temporarily declining markets drain cashflow and make debt service obligations unmanageable.

These companies can be found in virtually any industry. Most are manufacturing or distribution firms. In nearly every case a foreign investor can purchase 100 percent or controlling interest in these troubled companies at a fraction of market value. The fastest way for interested parties to explore such possibilities is to work through a U.S. consulting or legal firm. In addition, many regional banks have special nonperforming-loan work-out departments that can be contacted directly for potential acquisitions.

Choosing the Right Location

Not infrequently, the sheer vastness of the United States inhibits foreign investors. Each section of the country has its own commercial and cultural characteristics. Each state has its own set of corporation and tax laws. Each region has unique cost structures for labor, facilities, and insurance. Many locations offer opportunistic access to overseas markets: others do not. And several states and cities actively seek foreign investors with tax incentives and labor subsidies.

State recruiters are putting out the welcome mat, not only for the Sonys and Basses and Siemenses of the world, but also for lesser-known foreign firms employing dozens, not hundreds or thousands. McKinley Conway, publisher of *Site Selection and Industrial Development* magazine was quoted as stating, "For every company that has already spread its wings globally, there are many that have not, and those are the companies that are now starting to move into the United States."

Foreign companies have built or expanded only 865 U.S. industrial sites since 1988. That's a mere 6 percent of the total number of projects, according to *Site Selection*. But the flow of overseas investment has been constant. The American open-door policy will bring thousands more in the future and states are vying hard to attract them. According to *Site Selection*, the most active states are shown in Table 3-4.

Table 3-4.   States Attracting the Most Foreign Direct Investment*

	New foreign manufacturing sites	Manufacturing jobs
Ohio	76	82,800
Florida	72	N/A
North Carolina	69	87,200
South Carolina	64	N/A
Texas	54	78,000
California	51	145,400
Georgia	47	59,900
Virginia	46	N/A
New York	45	82,000
Tennessee	40	61,700

* As of 1988–1990.

NOTE: In addition, new sites in Pennsylvania created 89,500 jobs, in New Jersey 72,000 jobs, and in Illinois 86,000 jobs.

SOURCE: *Site Selection and Industrial Development*; U.S. Department of Commerce, Bureau of Economic Analysis.

Various factors enter into the decision to choose one state or region over another: among them are labor availability and cost, local management talent, operating costs, strength of labor unions, tax incentives/penalties, company laws, political concessions, site availability, cultural receptivity, and access to domestic and international transport.

No single state excels in all categories. In many respects, choosing the right state is similar to choosing a country in Europe to tap European markets.

Two peculiarities in the state-federal system of government should be clarified. First, each state has the authority and responsibility to raise state revenues through a series of income, sales, use, property, and other taxes. These taxes overlay the federal structure and are in addition to, not in lieu of, federal taxes.

Second, each state has its own governmental bodies patterned after the federal government: the executive branch headed by a governor; a two-segment legislative branch which includes a senate and a house of representatives; and a judicial branch headed by the state supreme court.

State laws, like state taxes, are in addition to, not in lieu of, federal ones. State courts adjudicate state laws: federal courts handle federal laws. This system of complementary laws is unique to the United States and can be confusing for first-time foreign investors. Attorneys licensed to practice in the state of choice are a necessary adjunct to a firm's investment strategies.

Although the task of describing the investment pluses and minuses in all 50 states exceeds allotted space, a few major foreign trade regions can be highlighted.

The Mid-Atlantic Region

The Mid-Atlantic region consists of the states of New York, New Jersey, Pennsylvania, Delaware, Maryland, Washington, DC, and the northern part of Virginia. Characterized by a labor-intensive manufacturing base, New York, New Jersey, and Pennsylvania, along with several midwestern states, have historically provided the industrial muscle for American heavy industry.

- One of the most influential financial centers in the world, New York City is also home to a melting pot of cultures and therefore to significant ethnic markets.

- Cities in upstate New York actively pursue high-tech firms that can utilize its large, highly skilled technical labor base and low-cost facilities and/or need immediate access to Canadian markets.

- Massive marine and bulk cargo ports at Newark and Elizabeth, New Jersey, give the whole area a valuable leg-up on foreign shipping.

- Northern New Jersey also offers ready access to highly educated management talent and a more-than-sufficient labor pool.

- The beltway around Philadelphia has become a locus of computer and other high-tech companies as well as of the pharmaceutical industry.

- On the down side, labor and facilities costs in the New York City/northern New Jersey area approach the highest in the country. City and state taxes are outrageous. Tightly controlled trade unions represent virtually all labor in the area, making attendant costs very high. (In southern New Jersey, labor is less expensive and local taxes are lower.) The region also has some of the strictest environmental laws in the nation. In many cases this means incorporating an expensive clean-up job.

- Farther south, along the Atlantic seaboard, Delaware, Maryland, and northern Virginia offer specific attractions to foreign trade and investment.

- Maryland's seaport facilities and proximity to Washington have brought it a reputation as a convenient location for ocean shipping and access to the federal government.

- With some of the best port facilities in the nation, significantly lower labor costs, far less influence from trade unions than the north, and a large, highly educated white collar pool, Baltimore in particular has become a center for high-tech and biotechnology firms.

- Northern Virginia has become a busy and important satellite of Washington, DC.

- Delaware is noted for the most favorable political and business tax climate in the country.

Florida

Florida is the acknowledged headquarters for trade with Latin America (other than Mexico, which trades heavily with Texas and the other southwestern states) and the Caribbean. According to the Florida Department of Commerce, two-way international trade exceeded US$30 billion in 1989. Local estimates put the growth in excess of 10 percent per year, despite recessionary pressures in the rest of the country.

In addition to access to Latin American and Caribbean markets, products ranging from agricultural goods to machine tools pass through the FTZ ports at Tallahassee, Jacksonville, Tampa, Orlando, and Miami. More than one hundred U.S. and foreign banks supply some of the easiest and least-expensive financing in the country. An educated, bilingual work force with ties to Latin America enhances communications and cultural cohesion with customers in those countries. Labor costs are very low compared to the north. (There are virtually no trade unions in Florida.) And Florida boasts one of the lowest and fairest personal and corporate tax structures in the country.

On the down side, Florida's remote location from many American consumer markets makes inland freight costly and slow. Heavy industry is not encouraged. Access to Pacific markets is difficult except through the Panama Canal.

New England

Logistically, New England is hard to beat. The region has ready access to mid-Atlantic markets and New York City. It boasts the air terminal closest to Europe, deep-water ports, and immediate proximity to Canada. High-tech and development firms dot Boston's periphery. The entrepreneurial spirit has spread to Connecticut and Rhode Island. New Hampshire's disdain for taxes of any kind provides a unique incubator for start-up companies and related service industries. Affordable real estate and labor are plentiful in Vermont.

The region is blessed with a surplus of highly skilled labor and educated management talent. Boston's brain bank is well known throughout the world.

On the down side, the New England banking industry is in dismal shape, making financing difficult. Trade unions continue to play a major role in keeping wages high in Massachusetts and Connecticut. State tax structures in these two states also rank with the highest in the nation. The fiscal condition of both states is in disarray, necessitating additional taxes in the future.

Washington State

A mere two days' sailing time to Japan, Seattle has become the gateway to northern Pacific Basin trade. The Port of Seattle is the number-four container port in the nation. The region boasts a skilled labor force: many workers have been trained at the huge Boeing facility.

Wage rates are relatively high. State tax structures are moderate compared to California, New York, Massachusetts, and Minnesota.

Washington state's remote location is the region's major disadvantage. Because of its position in the far northwest corner of the country, moving goods and people to East Coast and southeastern markets is more difficult and time-consuming than it is to Japan. Foreign investors looking for proximity to the Asia-Pacific and Canadian markets will find Washington attractive. Those more interested in domestic markets might do better elsewhere.

Southern California

Blessed with a high-tech labor pool, excellent port facilities, an enormous local market, and a broad manufacturing, retail, distribution, and service base, southern California has become the location of choice for thousands of foreign investors.

Southern California's immediate access to Mexican markets, its excellent shipping and transport facilities to Hawaii, and its position as a natural jumping-off point to Australia and the South Pacific, all open significant international trade possibilities. Large Hispanic and Asian populations boost local ethnic markets.

Conversely, southern California is closely tied to the aerospace and defense industries, which probably will be in a down cycle for several years to come. Like other West Coast locations, it is geographically separated from midwestern and eastern markets by large distances and the Rocky Mountains. The California tax structure is one of the most burdensome in the country. Labor unions from the aerospace industry remain strong, keeping wage rates at a high level compared to surrounding states.

Foreign Trade Zones

Although nearly every trading country in the world utilizes foreign trade zones (FTZs, or "free zones" as some are called), they are most prominent in the United States. At last count the United States had more than 150 fully licensed, operational FTZs. Only West Virginia and Idaho are without. Texas has 16 FTZs.

As foreign traders are well aware, FTZs provide a means to transship goods between countries without paying customs duties. In the United States, FTZs may be used for storage, distribution, assembly, light manufacturing, modifications of products, or transshipment. Goods held in FTZs may be sold, exhibited, broken up, repacked, repackaged, graded, cleaned, and mixed with other foreign or domestic merchandise. Value may be added to goods after they have been brought in. The goods can then be shipped to a foreign destination without customs duties in either direction. Of course, customs duties do apply when goods are shipped to U.S. markets.

American FTZs have many uses. One very popular scheme is to time the shipment of semi-finished goods to an FTZ to maximize home country financing channels and shipping availability prior to the opening of American markets or import quotas. Goods are held in the FTZ until market conditions change; then they are assembled and shipped.

Domestic materials, subassemblies, or other components may enter FTZs free of duty, quotas, or taxes, providing customs officials are notified. These American-made goods can then be combined with foreign goods for ultimate shipment. Certain domestic items are prohibited from being processed while in the zone. Among these are domestic distilled spirits, wine, beer, and a limited number of other kinds of merchandise.

Uniquely American Opportunities

From time to time there arise certain sociopolitical trends of special significance to foreign investors and traders. Socially responsible investment and environmental protection are two trends gaining increased support from American consumers.

Federal and state political pundits have been quick to jump on the environmental bandwagon, passing legislation that requires companies to clean up their past errors. Few have yet to see the wisdom of urging the business community to promote environmentally safe or socially responsible policies. Slowly but surely, however, an increasing number of U.S. companies are taking advantage of these phenomena, recognizing the substantial competitive edge that can be achieved thereby.

Granted, much of the consumer attention to date has centered on what critics call "New Age nuttiness." This activity has included the refusal to buy stocks in companies that produce cigarettes, liquor, or birth-control pills, the boycotting of companies that trade with or have investments in South Africa, and the chastising of companies that operate gambling casinos.

According to one liberal trade group for socially conscious investors, the Social Investment Forum of St. Paul, Minnesota, social investment assets currently total US$625 billion.

A far more important aspect of the explosive growth in social investing was defined by ethics expert Kenneth Goodpaster. He claims that this explosive growth is part of a much larger phenomenon: the increasingly militant demand by corporate "stakeholders"—consumers, employees, local communities, and shareholders—"to have their voice heard in the corporate decision-making process."

Hardly anyone who has followed the abortive actions of Wall Street tycoons Michael Milken or Ivan Boesky or the unconscionable actions of many public servants in Washington and state capitols can be ignorant of the vast increase in unethical practices in both the private and public sectors.

The situation is similar with regard to environmental protection. It is difficult not to be aware of the ecological damage done by dolphin-snaring fishing nets, offshore dumping of medical refuse, and indiscriminate deposit of toxic industrial waste in wilderness areas.

Without belaboring the point, many legitimate, socially conscious consumer groups have begun not only to avoid investing in equity and debt issues of companies with unethical management or environmentally destructive practices, but also to avoid buying products from them.

Two widely advertised results are the financial damage done to the Exxon Corporation by consumers who boycotted their products at the gas pump after the Valdez oil spill, and the rapid agreement by American tuna processors not to buy tuna caught with dolphin-snaring nets.

Consumer groups are beginning to have a profound effect on American business, although to date, few large corporations have given more than lip service to the trend. Many small and midsize companies, however, are steadily gaining market share by following socially conscious policies and then advertising this to consumers.

The impact of these trends on foreign traders and investors is twofold. First, the acquisition of or joint venture with a U.S. company might carry the foreign company's name or product identification. By overtly marketing these products as environmentally safe and by building a public image as a socially conscious, ethical company, significant competitive advantage can be achieved over less responsible U.S. competitors.

Second, products and packaging that meet environmentally safe standards, technology that processes goods in an environmentally safe manner, and equipment that operates without damage to the earth, air, or water, are new markets that are just now beginning to be sought after by a few U.S. producers. Bringing such products, technology, and equipment to U.S. shores will offer significantly greater market opportunities than playing follow-the-leader.

The environmental movement is much further advanced in the United States than in either Europe or Japan; it is decades ahead of Latin America and East Asia. Companies that carve a niche in this lucrative American market should be in an excellent strategic position to use it as a product and a market testing ground for future sales throughout the world.

America's Offshore Markets

One of the by-products of entering the American market is the opportunity to exploit special financing and tax breaks open to American-based companies with branches in American-owned offshore locations, such as Puerto Rico, the Virgin Islands, Guam, and the Northern Marianas. Not only are tax laws more lenient and financing more available; these offshore possessions also offer the opportunity to tap potentially explosive regional markets and low-cost labor.

Strategically located in the Caribbean and the Pacific, these possessions provide interesting bases for exporting to Latin America and East Asia respectively. Furthermore, since these islands are not fully developed, local market demand is burgeoning for a variety of products. (Chapter 5 looks at the especially beneficial markets in the Caribbean; Chapter 32 covers the Pacific.)

4
Latin America

Tips to Foreign Traders and Investors

1. Don't be dissuaded by dire economic predictions. Many Latin countries thrive on foreign goods and services not recorded in official statistics.
2. Check out direct investment opportunities in the English-speaking Caribbean states, Venezuela, and Chile as the best locations.
3. Get trade and investment financing from U.S. and multilateral aid agencies.
4. Use the "underground" system wherever possible. It's cheaper—and it works with hard currency.
5. Be prepared to work with a cash economy. Distrust of banks persists.
6. Stay away from the poorer countries, such as Peru, Bolivia, El Salvador, and Nicaragua, for the time being. The risks are too great and the returns too small. Check back in five to seven years.
7. Embassy offices in Washington

   Peru: (202) 833-9860
   Bolivia: (202) 483-4410
   El Salvador: (202) 265-3480
   Nicaragua: (202) 687-4371

Although Spain, Portugal, Germany, and a few other European nations continue to be modestly attracted to Latin America, their main interest lies in getting the European Community programs off the ground. Exploitation of developing markets by French, British, Italian, and Belgian companies focuses primarily on excolonial African countries. Although companies from Japan and the "four Tigers" sense market opportunities in South America and have made modest investments, they remain committed to further East Asian and Pacific development.

European and Asian companies may have moderate long-term interest in the region, but for U.S. companies, Latin America offers lucrative market and resource opportunities right now. To delay is to miss getting in on the ground floor. To ignore the region is to lose substantial competitive advantage, not only in U.S. and North American markets, but throughout the world. What Southeast Asia and the Pacific are to Japanese companies, Latin America is to U.S. firms.

President Bush's "New World Order" may have a hollow ring to Europeans and Asians, but to Americans it signals the start of a new era of global competitiveness, beginning with easily accessible markets and resources close to home. When the president boarded the plane for his 1990 Latin American junket, his "Enterprise for the Americas Initiative" called for a hemispheric free-trade zone and an "economic partnership" with Latin America based on "trade, not aid."

This proposal represents an ambitious plan for economic recovery and regional integration. It gives hope once again to Latin America's poverty-ridden, debt-burdened nations. And it opens the economic door to American-based firms with the foresight to develop trading ties and investment opportunities throughout the Americas.

Fortunately for American and Canadian companies, the rest of the world doesn't take the president's platitudes seriously. All the better, if it delays the entrance of Asian and European competitors.

On the flip side, many American executives don't take Latin America seriously, either. Why struggle with developing countries that have a history of political upheaval, protectionism, and environmental and human abuses, when developed markets beckon in Europe and Asia? Why risk the fate that has befallen Anaconda, Ford, Mobil, General Electric, and United Fruit in years past, when greater returns can be realized across the oceans? Why enter a region that American banks have already written off as unreliable?

The answers seem too obvious to list. North American firms find Latin America attractive because:

- Consumer markets are as great or greater than those in Europe and Japan.
- Coming industrialization and infrastructure buildup will require enormous imports of capital goods and services.
- The region boasts immeasurable natural resources.
- Labor and other operating costs are very low.
- A management cadre is being formed.
- Rejuvenated financial systems and external aid agencies provide many financing options.
- Major competition from European and Asian firms has not yet materialized.

- Regional proximity, low operating costs, and easy market penetration offer far better returns than transoceanic trade or investment.

Obviously, all is not rosy. Many obstacles must be overcome. One of the most serious is Latin America's continuing socioeconomic illness. No one questions the region's massive headaches, and market strategies must recognize both the seriousness of these maladies and the potential for rectifying them through foreign trade and investment.

Economic Reforms

The 1989–1992 U.S. recession and skyrocketing oil prices from the Gulf war hit most Latin countries hard. Argentina and Brazil, the region's two largest economies, pushed the region into a slight decline in output of 0.7 percent during 1990.

Inflation remains high in many countries. Government austerity measures to control inflation have had a negative impact on output growth. With a few exceptions, investment has stagnated or declined. Even with restructuring, high debt service payments have continued to sap the economic strength of several nations.

Output in Argentina and Peru contracted for the third consecutive year. Brazil experienced a severe recession. Macroeconomic imbalances caused Nicaragua's economy to contract a whopping 5.5 percent. Governmental austerity programs restricted domestic demand in Honduras.

Other countries weathered the recession much better. Energy-exporters Venezuela and Ecuador actually improved their growth performance. Chile's intentionally tightened monetary policy constrained GDP growth to 2 percent after a smashing 10 percent growth in 1989. Costa Rica and Paraguay also intentionally restricted rampant growth. Venezuela's growth rate topped 4.4 percent; Colombia hit 3.5 percent; and Bolivia registered 2.5 percent. Ecuador broke even.

Nearly all Latin governments have embarked on the road to market economies. Bolivia, Peru, and Venezuela have simplified their tariff structures and are gradually reducing tariff levels. Argentina and Brazil have done the same. The Colombian government has reduced the list of goods subject to import licenses. It has also initiated measures to encourage foreign direct investment, including rules that open new areas for foreign capital participation. Most countries now treat foreign investors the same as nationals.

Deregulation has also occurred in certain sectors. Argentina has deregulated its oil industry. Brazil has deregulated its airlines and the distribution of fuel and petroleum by-products. Many countries have reduced or abolished price controls and reduced subsidies. The relationship between public and private sectors is being revised in Argentina and Mexico, resulting in huge privatization programs.

All Latin nations have begun to give intraregional trade increased emphasis—driven no doubt by the formation of trading blocs in Europe and Asia. The Southern Cone Common Market, the Andean Group Trade Pact, the Central American Common Market, and a variety of other bilateral and multilateral trade agreements have been executed and revitalized. Most governments now regard exports as the primary stimulant driving economic growth. President Bush's "Enterprise for the Americas Initiative" merely added fuel to the already-blazing intraregional trade fire.

The combination of intraregional trading blocs, major economic reforms, and the fact that all Latin countries (except Cuba and Haiti) now have democratically elected governments, should force recalcitrant American and Canadian companies to reassess their participation in the region. Many are now developing long-term trade and investment strategies to strengthen their competitive positions as the region develops.

The year 1991 was the turning point in many Latin countries, according to a report from the United Nations Economic Commission for Latin America and the Caribbean (ECLAC). Focusing on Argentina, Brazil, Colombia, Chile, Ecuador, Mexico, Peru, Uruguay, and Venezuela (which together account for 90 percent of the region's population and gross domestic product), the report disclosed that the region experienced a rise in per capita output for the first time in four years. Hyperinflation came under control. Foreign direct investment began returning. As Isaac Cohen, director of the commission's Washington office, stated, "The years of stagnation seem to be over."

ECLAC predicts that in 1992, the nine countries in its survey will have a combined growth rate, in real terms, of 2 percent. It goes on to say that, without the protracted recessions in Peru and Brazil, the regional growth rate would actually be about 4 percent—higher than the United States. Inflation, which stood at 1200 percent in 1989 and 1990, has been reduced to 300 percent. Inflation for most of the region is under control. Outrageous rates in Brazil and Argentina persist, however, buoying the average.

To analyze economic progress, the commission's report divides the region into three categories. The first consists of Mexico, Colombia, Chile, and Venezuela, which ECLAC claims "have assimilated the cost of adjustment and are now on the threshold where they can start fast growth." The second strata includes Argentina, Brazil, and some medium-size countries which are "also on their way, but with a lot more fragility." The third group includes countries such as Peru, Nicaragua, and Haiti that "have not advanced very much in undertaking major changes" and "will probably have a rough time of it and will need greater international cooperation."

According to Otto Reich, former U.S. ambassador to Venezuela, "The turnaround in Mexico, Venezuela, and Argentina is almost as dramatic as the change in the Soviet Union."

Table 4-1 shows the clear progress in the region's six major trading nations.

External debt continues to hamper the region's free-market growth. As Horst Schulman of the Washington-based Institute of International Finance

Table 4-1. Key Growth Comparisons

	Real GDP percent change			Consumer price percentage			
	1988	1989	1990	1988	1989	1990	1991
Argentina	-2.7	-4.4	-1.5	343	3195	2315	115
Brazil	-0.2	3.2	-4.6	683	1287	2928	387
Chile	7.4	10.0	2.1	15	17	26	24
Colombia	4.1	3.6	4.2	28	26	29	31
Venezuela	5.8	-8.7	5.2	30	84	41	34
Mexico	1.3	3.1	3.9	114	20	27	22

SOURCE: EIU Country Risk Services; Datastream; press releases.

has stated, "Arrears are a country's worst foe on the road to reestablishing full creditworthiness."

Total debt for the region in 1990 was US$417 billion, placing a heavy debt-service burden on already shaky economies. Nine countries remain in arrears. Although interest rates have fallen from an average of 10.75 percent in 1989 to 5.75 percent in 1991, Argentina and Brazil are still making only 30 percent of payments due.

Even with continuing debt-service problems, Latin countries are gaining favor in financial markets, as reflected by the increase in secondary market debt prices in Table 4-2.

Under their former military dictatorships and authoritarian rulers, Latin countries sought to attain self-sufficiency mainly by building up domestic industries behind closed tariff walls. Governments discouraged foreign investment as "imperialist." Exports were disregarded. Economies were fueled by federal deficits. Whenever jobs were at risk, the state took over private companies. The more that governments could "stick it to" foreign banks, the better. They accepted skyrocketing inflation as a way of life.

Now, for the most part, these old ways have been rejected.

New, democratically elected governments have done an about-face in their economic philosophies. New paths have been set to avoid fiscal deficits and

Table 4-2. Selected Secondary Market Debt Prices

	Percentage of face value			
	1988	1989	1990	1991*
Chile	61	60	62	89
Colombia	65	56	60	76
Venezuela	55	38	35	70
Brazil	46	37	25	24
Argentina	32	20	12	38
Mexico	50	40	37	60

*Estimate
SOURCE: Salomon Brothers; VEPAL; *LDC Debt Report.*

restrain monetary growth. Economic reforms have liberalized currency controls, kept exchange rates reasonable, slashed import tariffs to 20 percent or less, encouraged exports, abolished export taxes, kept real interest rates positive, and privatized, privatized, privatized.

As Latin America learned earlier and Eastern Europe is learning now, conversion to free markets does not come without a steep social price. The slash in government spending meant severe reductions in basic services: water, hospitals, schools, sewers. Imports were cut by two-thirds. Domestic output sank, thereby reducing available consumer goods. Real wages dropped through the floor. Unemployment rose. Income inequalities spread.

Also, as government leaders discovered, the "quick fix" didn't work. The only way to improve conditions was for the people to tough it out until free markets took hold. In some countries, like Mexico, this is already occurring. In others, like Peru, Guyana, and Suriname, the road still slopes downward. In large part, however, current policies continue to push foreign trade and investment urgently as the only feasible solution.

Trade and Direct Investment

Although risks abound, the time is ripe for foreign companies to begin exploiting both market opportunities and resource acquisition—at least in Argentina, Brazil, Colombia, Chile, and Venezuela, the five most progressive South American countries. Costa Rica, Guatemala, and Panama also offer interesting strategic possibilities.

In addition to encouraging trade with U.S. and Canadian companies, several countries are pushing for trade and investment from historically related East Asian nations. The Japanese–Latin American connection that one hundred years ago furnished Japanese laborers for cheap agricultural work on Latin ranches and estate farms still lives. The children of Mexico's president Salinas attend a Japanese school; the current Peruvian president is the son of Japanese immigrants. Active solicitation of Japanese, South Korean, and Chinese investments is beginning to bear fruit, as companies from each country scour the Latin American landscape for infrastructure and commercial projects.

Several countries nurture a strong industrial base and expanding manufactured exports. The Hong Kong-based *Far East Economic Review* comments that Latin exports are well on the way to beating out Asian products in price, quality, and delivery.

Brazil is far and away the biggest regional industrial power and exporter. Even during the worst of its debt crisis, manufactured exports increased, showing a 50 percent gain between 1981 and 1988. Steel still leads the pack, with transportation equipment, chemicals, machinery, and footwear close behind. Brazil also exports automobiles and auto parts to the United States, Canada, and the Middle East. Toyota, which already assembles commercial vehicles in Brazil, is seriously considering entering the automobile market.

Japanese electronics manufacturers Sony, Matsushita, and Sanyo have extensive operations throughout the region and are now allowing these subsidiaries to compete with Asian locations for components and finished products.

Chile has become the Latin American darling of international investment bankers. Beginning its market-oriented, trade-liberalization reforms as early as 1974, the nation produced growth rates in the 8 to 10 percent range over the last few years. Textiles, clothing, plastic goods, and household electrical products are the country's major manufactured exports. Privatized steel, petrochemical, and sugar industries are approaching competitiveness. Foreign direct investment continues to pour into Chile to support industrial upgrading.

Even Argentina, hit by a sharp drop in commodity prices in the 1980s that resulted in hyperinflation and a stagnated economy, doubled its manufactured exports over a ten-year period.

Increasingly, Latin America's interests are defined in trade terms. Encouraged by the World Bank, governments have moved toward the adoption of export-led policies as the foundation for economic growth. Imports are also escalating, primarily to upgrade the productivity of the region's manufacturing sector with state-of-the-art machinery and equipment.

The United States is far and away the largest exporter of both goods and services to Latin America. American companies export approximately US$15 billion in goods per year; more than ten times the amount exported to Eastern Europe.

On the reverse side, American companies import a great deal more from South America than they export. In the past ten years, a substantial U.S. trade surplus with South America turned into a deficit.

U.S. companies experience far fewer trade headaches in Latin America that in Eastern Europe. Even under military dictatorships, Latin countries have a long history of an active private sector. Their entrepreneurs don't need to be tutored in the basics of free enterprise as is the case with their Eastern European and Soviet counterparts. Huge privatization programs proceed faster and with fewer obstacles than do similar efforts in Poland, the Czech and Slovak republics, or Hungary.

In addition, U.S. companies have a wide range of financing options at their disposal. Eximbank supports both buyer and seller credits to most Latin countries. The Caribbean Basin Initiative supports trade finance with Caribbean and Central American companies. The Overseas Private Investment Corporation (OPIC) offers a variety of direct investment funding schemes, as well as excellent political-risk insurance coverage.

The Inter-American Development Bank, through its subsidiary the Inter-American Investment Corporation, actively assists U.S. companies to finance investments. Puerto Rico's Section 936 program has over US$1 billion available for smaller direct investments, with interest rates at less than LIBOR (London Interbank Offered Rate). Lack of financing should never be a reason to avoid either trade or investment in Latin America.

Fresh Capital

With foreign banks weary of lending money that never gets repaid, most Latin countries are turning to foreign direct investment and international capital markets as primary sources of fresh capital to keep their economic engines humming.

It is usually much easier and faster to arrange for financing a direct investment in Latin America than in any other developing region. An array of bilateral aid agencies from the United States, Britain, Canada, Germany, the Netherlands, and Denmark, as well as other European countries, have funds available for private investment.

Multilateral agencies from the World Bank, the European Investment Bank, and the Inter-American Development Bank support a variety of aid programs that filter through local development banks.

Latin American government bonds and state-controlled company issues are attracting billions of dollars in foreign capital for the first time since before the 1982 debt crisis. A good example is Brazil's state-owned oil giant, Petrobras, Inc., which tapped Eurobond markets for two issues of US$250 million and US$200 million.

Other Brazilian companies followed suit. Companhia Vale do Rio Doce, a giant mining company, went after a three-year Eurobond issue of approximately US$200 million. The National Development Bank went for a US$55-million issue to refinance its debt. Telebras, the state-controlled telephone company, is placing a five-year US$200-million bond issue.

Brazil alone brought in an estimated US$5 billion in foreign capital during 1991.

The Argentine government also entered international capital markets, floating its first bond issue in nearly a decade.

International markets are not only receptive to giant companies and governments. Several smaller Latin firms have also received a warm welcome. In Brazil, for instance, companies have raised over US$1 billion with commercial paper, debentures, and other instruments. The latest fad has been dubbed "securitization of export receivables." Investors pay the exporter when products ship. Upon receiving the goods, importers then repay this "securitized" advance directly to the exporter's lenders and investors. The exporter gets immediate cash, and the banks and investors mitigate country risk.

Meanwhile, emerging stock markets throughout South America, Central America, and the Caribbean are beginning to support active trading in government and private issues, as well as new debt and equity issues from local and foreign companies. New highs have been spurred largely by foreign investors, who are snapping up assets in privatization programs, often through debt/equity swaps.

The Buenos Aires stock market rose an unbelievable *fourteenfold* in the first three weeks of August 1991, as daily volume jumped from US$8 million to US$115 million. An official from Argentina's National Securities Commission believes that mutual and pension funds are coming to the country because they see Argentina as the next significant emerging market.

Brazilian capital markets are also booming. Salomon Brothers, James Chapel, and Bear Sterns have begun trading on Brazil's exchange. Other foreign investment banks are certain to follow, not only to Brazil, but to other Latin American countries, as governments relax exchange regulations.

Clearly, with debt and equity capital once again flowing, foreign investors should have little difficulty overcoming the continued reluctance of foreign banks—and foreign export credit agencies—to handle the financing side.

Regional Trading Blocs

The homogeneity of Latin America offers some interesting possibilities to companies established in the region. All Latin countries have a trading heritage dating back centuries. Spanish is the common language throughout the region (with the exception of Brazil, where the language is Portuguese). An indigenous manufacturing base has produced a century of trained labor. An educated elite offers a reservoir of management talent. Vast deposits of minerals, energy resources, timber, and agricultural commodities support the region with plentiful raw materials.

For fifty years, Latin countries have produced primarily for domestic consumption. Although the new trading emphasis encourages exports to Europe and the United States, little attention has been paid to trade with neighboring countries. Now, for the first time, rapidly forming regional trading blocs are shifting the balance and offer significant opportunities for intraregional trade.

New trading alliances pop up like spring buds. A listing one month is out of date the next. The major free trade agreements in place at the beginning of 1992 included:

- The Southern Cone Common Market—Argentina, Brazil, Uruguay, and Paraguay
- The Andean Group Pact—Bolivia, Colombia, Ecuador, Peru, and Venezuela
- The Group of Three trilateral agreement—Mexico, Venezuela, and Colombia
- A Chilean trade accord with Argentina, Venezuela, and Colombia
- A rejuvenated Central American Common Market
- The revived Eastern Caribbean Common Market
- The Caribbean Basin Initiative
- The Caribbean-Canada Free Trade Agreement
- The pending North American Free Trade Agreement
- The Lomé IV Convention

In addition, several bilateral agreements have been negotiated between nations in different trading blocs.

Free trade does not necessarily mean a complete absence of tariffs or quotas—although this does happen in some cases. Most of these agreements offer substantially reduced tariffs, licenses, and quotas, as well as preferential trade treatment between members. Companies within these countries gain competitive advantage with less costly material and equipment imports, reduced quotas for exports, and preferential trade finance.

Foreign companies wishing to avail themselves of the strategic benefits of these trading blocs should establish facilities in the appropriate country or countries as early in the game as possible. Multinational corporations, primarily from the United States, but also from Japan, Taiwan, Hong Kong, Germany, Spain, France, and even Saudi Arabia, have already begun to move in. Plenty of room remains for smaller companies, however. In fact, most local firms prefer to enter a joint venture or strategic alliance with a smaller firm rather than a giant.

The Paradox of Poverty and Other Hazards

Much has been written about Latin America's catastrophic debt condition, hyperinflation, collapsed financial systems, and extreme poverty levels. If the story ended there, the populations of Brazil, Argentina, Colombia, Venezuela, and Chile would create a poor market for foreign products, and their countries would be a poor target for foreign direct investment. In fact, if reports by the OECD, World Bank, and media were to be believed about prevailing social and economic conditions, it would seem only reasonable to expect continual armed revolt by disgruntled citizens throughout the region.

But nothing is further from the truth. Although many rural communities do suffer unconscionable poverty, vast segments in most Latin countries enjoy many of the same luxuries as consumers in Europe, the United States, or Japan. How can that be? Because of a booming black market economy.

Accounts from foreign traders describe underground economies as the fastest growing markets in Latin America. In Brazil, for instance, estimates place the underground economy at 50 percent of the total GDP. That amounts to billions of dollars flowing into and out of Brazil without being accounted for in official economic statistics—and without being taxed. The underground economy is the most likely explanation for bustling consumer markets and a high standard of living at a time when official statistics show the country flat on its back.

Through various press releases, some trade experts claim that the underground market throughout Latin America is growing at a 7 percent clip—compared with 3 percent for legitimate economies. This market includes about 30 percent of the "economically active population" in South America, especially in rural areas where the underground economy is about the only one functioning.

Most goods are sold by street vendors or via word-of-mouth contacts. Middlemen flourish as the brokers of foreign goods, bringing in cross-border products demanded by specific market segments. Government officials are usually well aware of these underground markets, but since they satisfy the needs of the populace, do nothing to stop them. Foreign exchange "gray markets," especially in U.S. dollars, also flourish. Traders frequently find street exchange rates more favorable than official ones.

It would clearly be inappropriate to recommend that foreign companies actively solicit trade in these markets—even though in many cases they are sanctioned by government bureaucrats. However, for those so inclined, contacting local middlemen is relatively simple. Any international consultant, as well as most local attorneys and bankers, know how it's done.

One of the interesting by-products of underground markets is that the sale of foreign-made VCRs, TVs, clothing, furniture, office equipment, computers, and virtually every other consumer product (as well as many industrial products) has forced local manufacturers to begin manufacturing or distributing them also. The infamous "law of similars," so pervasive for so long in Brazil, prohibited the import of any product manufactured locally. When black market products captured large consumer markets, local manufacturers began copying these products in self-defense.

Copying is as much of a threat in Latin America as it is in East Asia. Laws protecting intellectual property and their enforcement are so loose as to be practically nonexistent. About the only feasible protection for foreign companies is to join forces with a local partner with the clout to prevent such thievery, or at least with sufficient market intelligence to tell the foreign partner when to take action. Most foreign companies practice the same grandfather-generation technology in Latin America as in other developing countries, thus safeguarding current patents and processes.

Local Government Contacts

Local government influence in virtually every walk of life, including foreign trade, is pervasive throughout the region. Governments in Argentina especially, but also in Brazil, Colombia, and other countries, thoroughly scrutinize each and every foreign trade transaction. Violations of local regulations about licensing, quotas, or price setting bring heavy penalties. The solution? As in other areas, a local partner with bureaucratic clout is the only feasible way to smooth the way.

Getting Paid

Many Latin governments, especially in South America, have a way of holding up legitimate payment for imports. Even when a local partner breaks the logjam, payment might come in local currency, which in most cases is totally worthless in foreign exchange markets. U.S. dollar or other hard-currency reserves tend to be in short supply and reserved for government-designated critical imports.

South American companies experienced in foreign trade recognize this problem for foreign exporters. To compensate for low reserves, they can usually obtain special hard-currency allocations from:

1. Their home country export credit agency
2. A bilateral aid agency, such as the U.S. Agency for International Development
3. A multilateral institution like the World Bank
4. A local development bank (although this funding is usually reserved for capital investment)

Many South American exporters have developed a somewhat backhanded way of accumulating hard-currency reserves. They sell to a foreign buyer at a price lower than market, payable under standard terms. A second part of the transaction involves another payment in hard currency by the foreign buyer directly into a foreign bank account that the exporter opens in the customer's country. These hard-currency reserves are then accumulated to pay for additional imports.

Trading with a Latin American subsidiary of an East Asian, European, or North American parent presents no difficulty at all. These companies can always draw on hard currency from their parent.

Of course, as a last resort, foreign traders can work a countertrade deal, perhaps with coproduction or buy-back arrangements. However, countertrade is not recommended for smaller companies without experienced personnel to manage the transactions.

Peru, Bolivia, El Salvador, and Nicaragua: Backward Countries with Potential

Several countries in Latin America are so far in the economic hole that prudent marketers will wait a few years to begin serious trading or investing there. Eventually opportunities in one or more of these nations will open. Several already have abundant natural resources and cheap labor, but their political, social, and financial institutions are in such disarray that only the most adventurous will exploit opportunities there now.

Peru, Bolivia, El Salvador, and Nicaragua appear to be the four third-tier nations with the best chance of developing into viable trading partners.

Peru

So long misgoverned that its external debt is selling below 10 cents on the dollar, and possessed of a turbulent political environment in which conducting business resembles a crap shoot, Peru has a long way to go to catch up with the rest of newly democratized Latin America. Shortly after Alberto Fujimori was elected president, taking over a country wrought by years of corruption and fraud from ex-president Alan Garcia, he unleashed a set of more than 100 draconian reforms aimed at correcting the mismanagement of years of military dictatorship in a few months. His primary goal was to initiate structural adjustments directed toward a massive conversion from state control to free markets. The idea was to gain the support of the IMF and World Bank, which in turn would release desperately needed aid funds. This he achieved.

Foreign and local investors alike are now protected by investment guarantees from OPIC (for American investors) and MIGA, with full permission to repatriate earnings and access necessary foreign currency.

Fujimori also initiated a wide-reaching privatization program to sell state-owned companies in mining, oil, fishing, telecommunications, air, sea, and rail transport, electricity generation and distribution, water systems, and, of course, the cholera-infested sewage system. Liberalization of the Lima Stock Exchange brought in a flood of foreign capital, especially from Chile, Peru's neighbor to the south.

Such reforms look good on paper, but so far few have taken hold in practice. Why? Because of wars raging on two fronts: an uncontrolled drug war initiated by Colombia drug czars and fed by Peru's coca plant farmers, and a ferocious guerrilla war waged by the bloodthirsty Shining Path movement. Fujimori's objective of dismantling the country's protectionist and statist economic policies has been to a large extent stymied by these two increasingly violent wars. His unilateral decision in early 1992 to disband the Peruvian congress and put the constitution on hold jeopardized even the few gains that had been made.

Meanwhile the Peruvian people suffer. The minimum legal wage in Peru is US$35 a month—one-eighth what the United Nations judges necessary to sustain a family. The nation has faced three consecutive years of massive recession, with the economy shrinking by 25 percent. With luck, Fujimori's policies may now have stopped the bleeding. However, statistics are somewhat meaningless, with as much as 50 percent of the nation's output in unreported and illegal coca plant production and drug-related businesses.

Foreign traders wishing to export to Peru should find hard currency available from coffers being filled by a rash of surprising investments from East Asian companies. According to the Peruvian economic ministry, the best products to export to Peru are: oil and gas products, mining equipment, machine parts, food processing equipment, vegetable oil, insecticides, medical supplies and equipment, fertilizers, plastic consumer products, and construction equipment.

Peru participates in the Andean Pact Trade Preference Act and is eligible for preferential trade to and from the United States under provisions similar to those of the Caribbean Basin Initiative.

Bolivia

Bolivia was almost as badly off as Peru a few years ago but has made greater strides toward rejoining the world community. For the first time in over a decade, Bolivia's economy has begun to grow faster than the population. The most positive sign is a 4 percent growth in 1991, against a steady 2.6 percent for the last four years. Inflation appears to be stabilizing at 15 percent—remarkably low for Latin America—after averaging 8000 percent as recently as 1985. Interest rates are the lowest in five years.

New mining and investment laws have jump-started mining exploration after thirty years of stagnation. The fiscal deficit should reach a mere 2.5 percent of GDP in 1991. Of the sixty-plus state-owned companies in the privatization program, only six or so are going concerns, but at least their losses have been reduced. Flight capital is returning from Miami with deposits in the Bolivian banking system rising from US$400 million in 1989 to US$1 billion through mid-1991.

On the downside, private investment remains a paltry 3 percent of GDP, and expenditures on imports are substantially more than the government forecasted.

One of the biggest problems facing President Jaime Paz is the sharp class demarcation in Bolivia's social strata. About one million of Bolivia's population of seven million are members of the top economic class, living as comfortably as many Americans, and having adequate health care and educational opportunities. Below them come three million urban dwellers who also enjoy reasonable Bolivian living standards. Then the problems start.

Next in line are two million or so members of the urban poor who barely scrape together enough to eat. At the bottom of the heap are at least one million rural dwellers who live in abject poverty, with living standards and occupational tools reminiscent of the eighteenth century. Although literacy for the country at large has reached 63 percent, in the lowest two economic classes it's closer to 2 percent. Per capita income for 1990 was a startlingly meager US$760. It is the needs of the bottom two economic classes that president Paz must address if Bolivia is ever to regain status as a viable trading partner in the world community.

Of nearly equal importance is the pervasive drug trafficking industry spilling over from neighboring Peru and Colombia. It is through this underground society that Bolivia's poor farmers and rural dwellers make a subsistence living.

On the trade front, Bolivia exported approximately US$926 million in 1990 and imported US$716 million, according to official statistics. Unofficially, by including the thriving cocaine trade, export figures could probably be quadrupled, at least.

The government's ambitious economic reform programs started as far back as 1985. To date, the government has abolished foreign exchange restrictions, lowered tariff rates to 5 percent for capital goods and 10 percent for all other imports (the lowest in the Andean group of nations), eliminated most import restrictions, and effected significant fiscal reforms through massive government austerity programs. A bilateral free trade framework agreement has been signed with the United States.

The nation's infrastructure remains in serious disrepair, although in 1991 the government allocated 50 percent of its budget for rebuilding.

Mining and hydrocarbons represent approximately 70 percent of the country's official exports. Primary metals include tin, lead, zinc, silver, cadmium, and gold. Special tax incentives have been enacted to encourage foreign investment in joint ventures with the state-owned oil company YPFB. Although most petroleum exports go to neighboring Argentina, Bolivia is soliciting U.S. companies for drilling equipment, seismic drilling services and studies, duct equipment, and other products to help develop potentially large oil and natural gas reserves.

The Bolivian government considers agriculture to be its most important sector, producing soybeans, lumber, coffee, and fruits. Its major export markets are Argentina, Chile, and Brazil.

Bolivia's manufacturing sector is very small and consists mainly of artisan jewelry, wood furniture, textiles, beer and liquor, ceramics, leather goods, alpaca, llama wool products, and wood handicrafts.

The country has one free trade zone, similar to the maquiladora program in Mexico, operating in the northern border town of Cobija. No duties are assessed on goods entering or leaving the zone.

El Salvador

Despite his country's twelve-year civil war, Salvadoran president Alfredo Christiani's government has enacted free market programs that are steadily improving the economic climate. In 1991, El Salvador's respectable GNP growth rose to more than 5 percent, with the agricultural sector recording the biggest gain. Inflation dropped to 19 percent.

Several facets of the programs were specifically designed to attract foreign investors. Among the most significant were:

- Removal of price controls on 240 consumer goods
- Implementation of anti-inflationary monetary policies
- Limitations on the monopoly buying and export authority of the national coffee, sugar, and cotton industries
- Reduction of import duties to a range of 5 to 35 percent

- Gradual introduction of a floating exchange rate
- Legalization and licensing of foreign exchange trading houses

One result of these reforms has been a jump of over 60 percent in nontraditional exports to countries outside Central America.

Other actions also register the country's improved economic condition. El Salvador joined the GATT in mid-1991. It fashioned a structural adjustment program in compliance with IMF requirements and arranged a World Bank structural adjustment loan to be disbursed during 1991–1993. It rescheduled its external government debt with the Paris Club creditor countries.

The Salvadoran government realized that specific incentives were needed to bring foreign investment to this war-torn country and passed several legislative acts exclusively for the benefit of foreign companies. Among the most important were:

- Full repatriation of profits (except for service and commercial activities, which limit remittances to 50 percent)
- Complete foreign management of foreign company investments
- Unrestricted remittance of interest and capital on external loans
- Guaranteed security for foreign currency accounts
- A ten-year tax exemption for income and asset/equity taxes to firms locating in a free zone and exporting 100 percent of production outside Central America
- Duty-free imports of machinery and equipment, tools, spare parts, lubricants, and fuels for free zone facilities

The Salvadoran government encourages imports of specific goods. Among those listed as high-demand products are: telecommunications equipment, power generating equipment, fertilizers, textile and apparel machinery, woodworking equipment, and a wide range of consumer goods—especially basic goods such as apparel, processed food, appliances, and other household products.

Despite El Salvador's earnest attempt to attract foreign investment and increase global trade, many foreign companies still consider the financial risks resulting from the government's long civil war with left-wing guerrillas (which ended with a truce in early 1992) to be too great for serious direct investment consideration. Gradually, the nation is beginning to right itself, however. Its honest efforts at trade and tourist promotions, especially those aimed at the United States, will undoubtedly attract greater interest as time passes. For the moment, trade and investment in El Salvador's markets should be considered strategically as a long-term proposition. Other countries offer fewer risks and greater returns in the short term.

El Salvador's relatively small population of five million limits domestic market opportunities. Its corporate tax rate of 38 percent on branch profits is still too high, compared to other countries in the region. Nevertheless, the nation boasts a strong entrepreneurial class, skilled and willing workers, and relatively low labor and overhead costs.

Nicaragua

Although widespread civil war in Nicaragua has stopped, the legacy of exdictator Daniel Ortega's Sandanista regime hangs heavy. To remain in office, President Violeta Chamorro's government found it necessary to make concessions to the Sandanistas. Although Contra forces laid down their arms, the country faces an uphill climb out of its economic quagmire. Still, some progress has been made.

The U.S. trade embargo has been lifted. Eximbank and OPIC have added Nicaragua to their list of acceptable countries. An economic reform package started the ball rolling toward more liberalized investment and trade regulations. Among the key features are:

- Guaranteed repatriation of profits

- Guaranteed repatriation of capital after three years

- Guarantees against expropriation for ten years

- Tax rates on investment earnings that will not increase beyond those in effect at the time the investments were made

- The establishment of free trade zones to provide duty-free import of materials (if not available in Nicaragua), vehicles, and facilities for employees

- Free-zone, 100 percent tax exemption for the first five years and 60 percent exemption thereafter

- No geographic restrictions for establishing new free zones

- Up to 100 percent import duty exemption, depending on the percentage of output exported

- Up to 80 percent reduction of property tax

- Export contracts available for ten years

- Tax credit of 10 to 23 percent, depending on projected employment generation, export destination, and foreign exchange earnings

The first official U.S. investment mission sponsored by OPIC arrived in Nicaragua in June 1991. It included senior representatives from several U.S. companies, including Apple Computer, Citibank, Ralston Purina, Robinson Lumber Company, Rosario Resources Corporation, and Sprint International. The mission's purpose was to meet with local business leaders and potential joint venture partners, as well as to discuss key business issues with government officials.

Despite Nicaragua's obvious attempt to rejoin the world community, Ortega's legacy persists, evidenced by continued armed skirmishes between Sandanista loyalists and government troops. As in El Salvador, the risks for most smaller companies in such uncharted waters probably exceeds the potential gains for the immediate future. Eventually—if and when the political cauldron stops boiling—the country could become a viable trading partner. Until then, better opportunities can be found elsewhere in Latin America.

For those companies still intrigued by Nicaraguan prospects, the government trade commission lists the following products as most likely for foreign trade. For export to the country: chemicals and resins, cereals, agricultural and industrial machinery, vehicles and parts, fertilizers, and paper products. For import from the country: beef, coffee, cotton, sugar, bananas, tobacco, sesame, seafood, textiles, fruits and winter vegetables, and light-assembly electronics and plastic goods.

Nicaragua also has a large reserve of untapped fisheries resources, including lobster, shrimp, and squid. Aquaculture should become a major export industry in the future.

Exports of US$292 million against imports of US$656 million gave Nicaragua a substantial trade deficit in 1990, further dampening the country's financial capability.

Nicaragua has a relatively small population of 3.6 million, making domestic markets quite shallow. Unemployment—at a horrendous 26 percent—is attributable mostly to years of Sandanista and other military rule. Inflation in 1990 was still a serious problem, reaching nearly 2000 percent, although one year later this had been dramatically reduced to double digits.

Until Nicaragua, El Salvador, Bolivia, and Peru reach an effective end to their respective socio-political difficulties, traders and investors will find better strategic market opportunities and more readily available local resources elsewhere in Latin America.

5
Chile

Tips to Foreign Traders and Investors

1. Take a close look at periphery and complementary products needed for air pollution control: this is the next big growth area.

2. Export support products needed for growing the small businesses that are rapidly forming in Santiago's new shopping malls and office buildings.

3. Hold off direct investment plans until after the 1993 election.

4. Hire local managers and use local financing—or join forces with a local partner—to help jump political hurdles.

5. Don't be put off by peripheral money launderers. They won't bother you if you don't bother them.

6. Embassy office in Washington: (202) 785-1746.

Of the twelve independent countries in South America, Chile has progressed the fastest and the furthest toward a free market economy. President Patricio Aylwin gained a head start on the rest of South America by inheriting a finely tuned (for Latin America) economy and a relatively stable social structure from the strong-arm dictator General Augusto Pinochet. Instead of launching the kind of radical reforms characteristic of other newly elected governments, Aylwin merely needed to improve on an already functioning semimarket economy.

Granted, Chile's vibrant economy is undergoing growing pains: its GNP grew a mere 2.1 percent in 1990 after four years of averaging 7 to 10 percent. Inflation is gradually coming under control, although officials predict a 20 to 30 percent rate for the next couple of years.

An unexplained inflow of U.S. dollars led to an overvaluation of the Chilean peso. This in turn reduced the value of dollar investments and hurt exports.

Chile is certainly not reverting to out-of-date statist policies. But new incentives for economic growth and for a broadening of its entrepreneurial base are obviously needed. As in every other developing country, the best way to achieve growth is through increased foreign trade. And the most effective way to broaden the business base is with foreign direct investment.

The Chilean government has already won the battle against a protectionist business class. Consumers are well aware of the benefits of global market access. Foreign trade officials claim to be convinced that Chile must now make the final leap toward establishing a firm market base that rejects populists, money launderers, and revolutionaries. That seems to be exactly what government leaders are doing.

In 1991 Chile and the United States signed a free trade framework agreement. As President Bush's "Enterprise for the Americas Initiative" builds steam, Chile will most likely be the first to actively participate, placing the country in a strategic position from the vantage point of North American firms as well as those from Europe and Asia.

All import tariffs have now been reduced to 11 percent from an already low 15 percent. Business leaders want further reductions. Far from drying up, foreign investment continues to flow, and the North American–Chilean Chamber of Commerce, based in New York, has been a major stimulus. This organization was formed in 1977 by a group of Chilean, American, and Canadian business executives to improve trade and commerce among the three countries. Its original purpose was to expand Chile's trade beyond a monoproduct economy, based on copper exports, to one of diversified commercial products and services. Officials from the organization proudly point out that foreign investment during 1990 hit US$1.1 billion. That's a growth of 11 percent from the previous year—a significant amount when compared to a GNP of only US$26 million.

In 1990, Chile signed a restructuring agreement with commercial bank creditors totaling US$4.6 billion. The effect was to reduce debt-service payments by almost US$2 billion during the 1991–1994 period. Debt restructuring was an important step because it smooths out repayments of nearly US$1.1 billion that would have been due between 1991 and 1993. This, in turn, permits the government to spend more on domestic projects.

One of the features of the restructuring agreement was a new government issue, totaling US$320 million, placed in the Eurobond market. This marked the first return of a debt-laden Latin country to private capital markets since the debt crisis began in 1982. (It also very likely signals the beginning of the end for Latin America's fiscal mismanagement fiasco.)

With Chile's foreign debt trading at about 90 cents on the dollar, debt/equity swap bargains have vanished. While they lasted, however, many foreign companies took the bait. In 1989, for instance, debt/equity swaps accounted for investment of US$1.3 billion. In an effort to further stimulate interest from small and mid-size foreign companies, the Central Bank reduced the minimum investment level to only US$5 million.

Foreign Trade

Copper continues to be the major Chilean export, accounting for about 45 percent of the country's total exports of over US$8 billion. Fruit and nuts, fish products, and cellulose and pulp account for another 30 percent, with the balance coming from women's apparel, gold, frozen foods, industrial machinery, and even a small amount of biotechnology products. The full list of export products totals approximately 1500 items.

On the import side, products range from earth-moving equipment to cosmetics. American companies account for about 20 percent of Chile's imports and have concentrated principally on basic goods such as factory machinery, tools, transportation equipment, chemicals and lubricants, and telecommunications equipment.

In 1990, according to the U.S. Department of Commerce, U.S. capital goods exports in US$ millions were as follows. (The percentages represent change from 1986.)

Specialized industrial machinery	240 (+240%)
Nonspecialized industrial machinery	102 (+254%)
Power-generating equipment	56 (+96%)
Metal-working machinery and equipment	25 (+500%)

Additional imported products in high demand include: mining machinery, food processing and packaging equipment, leather goods, fish farming services and technology (principally salmon and turbot), woodworking equipment, dried and frozen foods, toys, furniture, computer hardware and software, medical instruments and disposable supplies, air conditioning and refrigeration equipment, textile machinery, and security and safety products.

Table 5-1 from the Chilean-American Chamber of Commerce in Santiago summarizes total exports and imports for the five years ending in 1990.

Table 5-1. Chilean Trade Summary

| Year | US$ millions | | | | |
	Copper exports	Other exports	Total exports	Total imports	Trade balance
1986	1757	2442	4199	3436	+763
1987	2235	2989	5224	4396	+828
1988	2636	3636	7052	5292	+1760
1989	4021	4059	8080	7144	+936
1990	3795	4515	8310	7710	+600

SOURCE: Chilean-American Chamber of Commerce; *Export Today.*

Foreign Direct Investment

The government is earnestly trying to expand the country's manufacturing base, both for domestic consumption and for export. A wide variety of industries are attractive to foreign investment, although many require additional imports of equipment and technology to round out production and service capabilities. Among those industries heading the list are telecommunications, food processing, agribusiness, shipbuilding, forestry and woodworking, and pulp and paper production.

Hotels, office buildings, shopping malls, and medical and dental clinics are springing up in and around Santiago. These private sector developments desperately need such diverse products as furniture and fixtures, elevators, security systems, building cleaning and maintenance supplies, restaurant and bar supplies, and so on.

A wide variety of opportunities exist for foreign participation in the service sector, which currently represents 45 percent of the nation's GDP. Management consulting, computer services, pension funds, private health services, banking, and insurance products are a few of the booming industries in this segment.

Taxes and other disincentives continue to hamper the development of a middle class of entrepreneurs. A 50 percent tax on personal income above US$30,000 makes it difficult for small business people to accumulate enough cash to start a new business. Executives of companies already established avoid this tax by reporting their income as corporate income, which is taxed at a mere 15 percent. Furthermore, recent changes in labor laws make it more difficult for small businesses to hire and fire employees while the same changes have little effect on larger firms.

Large U.S. companies have had a presence in Chile for years. Some of the biggest include Exxon, Phelps Dodge, Scott Paper, W. R. Grace, General Motors, and St. Joe Minerals. Both Citibank and Bankers Trust maintain active branches there. Although enormous opportunities exist for smaller companies, few have taken the plunge.

The Chilean government has long viewed foreign investment as a partnership venture that produces benefits for all economic sectors. It is no longer fashionable to tell the "Yankee imperialists" to go home. On the contrary, both the Chilean government and the private sector welcome foreign investors from all countries—including, and most especially, the United States.

The Chilean-American Chamber of Commerce reports that over the last 15 years, 3000 contracts have been signed with companies from 53 different countries. Total overseas investment exceeds US$5 billion, with U.S. companies accounting for approximately 25 percent. The organization also reports that over one-third of foreign companies have recapitalized their original investment or renegotiated new deals for further ventures.

Relative to other Latin countries, the Chilean bureaucracy is tolerable, its tariffs are low, and the work force capable. The government has enacted a reasonably fair corporation tax system and foreign investment laws. Profits may be repatriated three years after the initial investment occurs.

Unemployment runs about 5 to 6 percent and workers are fairly highly skilled. Minimum wages run about US$85 per month. A small but technically capable management pool exists. Literacy approaches 96 percent.

Most foreign companies are taxed at the rate of 35 percent on unremitted profits rather than at the 15 percent assessed local companies. However, profits reinvested in Chile are not subject to any tax. There is also a value-added tax of 18 percent.

Copper and lumber continue to be the favorite industries for foreign investors. Approximately 56 percent of the total 1990 investment of US$1.1 billion went into these industries. Generous government incentives tempt companies to invest in reforestation and selective tree harvesting. A lumber derivative, cellulose, is also a good choice. According to a recent study by the World Bank, other hot markets for foreign investment include textiles, packaging, explosives, and plastics.

Political Activities

Money laundering continues to plague the country. Officials from the Central Bank claim that many of the U.S. dollars flooding the market come from the northern part of the country, where drug traffickers bring in dollars from Peru to trade for Chilean pesos. The process is pathetically simple. For example, a person can buy an expensive house for dollars, sell it immediately at a much lower price for pesos, deposit the pesos in a local bank, and have the bank record the deposit as coming from the sale of a house—which of course is true, and perfectly legitimate.

Other questionable dealings have also tarnished the country's international image. The Bank of Credit and Commerce International (BCCI) made several attempts to open a branch, all turned down. Eventually, however, former BCCI stockholder Ghaith Pharaon turned a US$45 million debt swap into a US$60 million investment to build a Hyatt Hotel.

The Bin Mahfouz family of Saudi Arabia—formerly a 20 percent owner of BCCI—acquired 62 percent of the giant industrial holding company Pathfinder Chile. Although both investments were apparently legitimate, the inferences that can be drawn from these transactions cast a dark shadow on Chile's image as a location for legitimate, safe, direct investments from international companies.

Domestically, finance minister Alejandro Foxley is under the gun, with municipal elections scheduled for mid-1992—the first in twenty years. Presidential and congressional elections will be held in late 1993. The parties of the governing coalition, the Concertacion, are already jockeying for position, demanding that more money be spent for social improvements, to give voters more than just a "warm democratic feeling."

Such efforts bode well for foreign investors and traders. A country with a population of thirteen million (about one-half the size of Canada's) desperately needs massive government spending to rebuild its crumbling infrastructure and bring in the myriad of products, equipment, and services needed to operate social programs.

A few of the items on President Aylwin's US$2.35-billion public spending program include: new roads, refurbished ports, a rehabilitated and expanded rail system, water pumping and purification systems, sewage drainage and sanitizing, primary and secondary schools, health care, worker training programs, low income housing, and shopping malls.

The government also recently announced a US$1.6-billion irrigation project to double the acreage available for cultivation.

Environmental Opportunities

Another very interesting opportunity for foreign trade and investment exists in the correction of Santiago's horrendous air pollution problem. As with other major cities in developing nations (such as Mexico City), Santiago's air pollution is so bad that asthma and chronic pneumonia force schoolchildren and adults alike to wear gas masks when outside.

The greatest sources of pollution are Santiago's 14,000 smoke-belching buses, 8000 taxis, and 285,000 private cars—all operating on low-grade diesel fuel and old replacement parts imported from abroad. The country's vehicle-inspection system is "riddled with fraud," according to environmental officials. Many vehicles emit large doses of carbon monoxide and sulphur. In addition, about 3000 factories, located throughout the city in residential areas, and monitored by only five city inspectors, spew out very high levels of carbon, sulphur dioxide, nitrogen dioxide, and other gases. Last but not least, traffic kicks up large amounts of dirt and dust from unpaved roads, and the arid climate prevents plants from growing in many parts of the city, contributing to the dust storm.

For those not familiar with the city's geography, Santiago sits in a valley between high mountains. Thermal inversions, well known to residents of Los Angeles, Cincinnati, and Mexico City, trap warmer air—with all its pollutants—close to the ground. Wind currents do little to diffuse contaminants, and the result is suffocatingly dirty air.

Although not a very nice place to visit and a much worse place to live, Santiago's malaise will be a bonanza to foreign investors with the wherewithal to design and/or sell pollution-control products and supplies. As the general election in 1993 nears, it's a lead pipe cinch that government programs will be initiated to attract foreign assistance to clean up this mess. Some have already started.

The government recently initiated a spending spree to acquire environmental protection systems, filtration systems, engineering know-how, and new environmental clean-up technology. Catalytic converters are likely to be required before the 1993 election. Lead-free gasoline has already been introduced. Relatively strict automobile maintenance requirements have recently been enacted.

Aside from government programs, the private sector in and around Santiago already experiences difficulty in attracting qualified workers and managers. Inevitably, private companies will take it upon themselves to bring in appropriate pollution remedies. The greatest stimulus, however, is likely to come from voters.

6
Venezuela

Tips to Foreign Traders and Investors

1. Use Venezuela as a jumping-off point for trade with South America.
2. Enlist expatriates as supervisory personnel.
3. Concentrate on exports to get acclimated to government red tape before making a direct investment.
4. Establish a local facility to get in on currently forming Caribbean Rim trading blocs.
5. Embassy office in Washington: (202) 342-2214.

After ten years of fostering an international image as a country with a thriving oil industry and a spendthrift government, Venezuela is finally breaking the mold. The election of President Carlos Andres Perez in 1989 marked the beginning of government reform efforts to throw out contradictory policies that had kept the country locked in mismanagement and economic stagnation despite its enormous oil wealth. Foreign traders will well remember Perez's last term in office (from 1973 to 1979) when he forced the takeover of foreign-owned oil companies and extended state control over the economy in all directions.

But like many leaders in Eastern Europe and the former Soviet Union, Perez has adopted a fashionable new modus operandi amid applause from foreign multinationals, bankers, traders, and investors.

The government's reform efforts are similar to those enacted with such resounding success in Chile and Mexico, although Venezuela's timetable will undoubtedly be longer; it may be two to three years before major results can be measured.

The restructuring of Venezuela's external debt under the Brady Plan was the impetus to reform. New discount bonds, par bonds, "step-down," "step-up" bonds, and 91-day bills with buy-back provisions offered creditors a choice of options, lending credence to the government's sincerity for repayment. This restructuring occurred coincident with forecasts of rising oil prices from the Gulf war.

As prices climbed, the economy looked sounder and many bank creditors opted to retain their claims rather than go for discounted repayment, further strengthening the nation's position in world financial markets.

In addition to debt restructuring, the reform package included slashing import duties, joining GATT negotiations, floating the bolivar exchange rate, reducing the central government's deficit, slicing subsidies of public services, and eliminating price controls on most goods and services. Inflation peaked at 81 percent in 1989 and then settled in at around 25–30 percent by 1991–1992. The country continues to grow annually at a 6 percent clip.

Foreign Trade

Venezuela provides an excellent jumping-off point for foreign companies just beginning to develop a Latin American trade program. A biparty, democratically elected government has functioned reasonably effectively since 1958. Thanks to its vast oil reserves and—compared to Mexico—its small population (19.7 million), Venezuela is one of the richest countries in South America. Its per capita income reached US$2700 in 1991. Inflation remains too high, but recent government fiscal and monetary policies should keep the rate tending downward.

Although Venezuela remains an oil-based economy, it does have a developed industrial sector, primarily in mining and automobiles. The United States is still the country's largest trading partner, although capital goods imports from U.S. companies are trending downward. Imports of power generation equipment totaling US$130 million in 1990 showed a decrease of 26 percent. Imports of industrial machinery were US$603 million, a drop of approximately 13 percent. Conversely, imports of U.S. metal-working machinery increased 73 percent to US$83 million.

Petroleum remains the most important industry in Venezuela, accounting for approximately 17 percent of GDP and four-fifths of export earnings. Bauxite, aluminum, iron ore, agricultural products, and basic manufactured goods also share in export earnings. However, agricultural and manufactured exports are receiving the greatest impetus from the government's economic reforms. Of the work force, service companies draw 56 percent, the industrial sector 28 percent, and agriculture 16 percent.

The United States continues to be Venezuela's most important export market, capturing 53 percent of the total, compared to Germany with 5.3

percent and Japan with 4.1 percent. Major exports to the United States include crude oil, aluminum, steel products, ore, coffee, fish, cement, and gold. In 1990 total exports reached US$17 billion.

On the import side, the country brought in US$6.8 billion of products and services in 1990. Major imported products included foodstuffs, chemicals, consumer and industrial manufactured products, industrial machinery, transport equipment, auto parts, telecommunciations equipment, computers, medical diagnostic and treatment equipment, chemical processing machinery, and industrial instruments. Of the suppliers, 44 percent were from the United States, 8.5 percent from Germany, 6 percent from Japan, 5 percent from Italy, and 4.4 percent from Brazil.

Major imports from the United States included construction and oil drilling machinery, transport equipment, chemicals, wheat, and grains.

Foreign Direct Investment

Venezuela's foreign investment climate has improved immeasurably since 1989. Following the free market path of other South American countries, Venezuela shows little likelihood of enforcing another round of private industry nationalization. On the contrary, long-term prospects for major intraregional growth, at least over the next twenty years, appear very good. Liberalized foreign investment laws, a working banking system, strengthened capital markets, one of the better infrastructures in the region, and an avowed desire on the part of the government to broaden the country's manufacturing sector make this an ideal time to establish a Latin outpost in Venezuela.

The country is strategically located for trade with the Caribbean and Central America and easily accessible by air and sea from U.S. Gulf and East Coast ports. Venezuelan shipping and air facilities are some of the best in South America.

Many foreign nationals were drawn to the nation by high salaries in its oil industry. A fairly large percentage of these expatriates found the climate and economic opportunities to their liking and now form a significant part of the country's management talent pool. Venezuela's literacy rate tops 85 percent, making the labor force highly trainable.

Although periphery petroleum products and services offer the most visible opportunities, other markets also need foreign technology and products. Computers and software, health care services and products, processed food, automobile parts, mining services and periphery equipment, tourist facilities, pleasure boats, and seafood farming are major industries to investigate. Private aircraft, services, and parts make up a rapidly growing industry. Ground and ocean transport equipment and services also offer opportunities.

Corruption in government and in the private sector continues to keep American and some European companies from doing business in Venezuela. As in so many other Latin countries, the best way to cope with bureaucratic interference is through a national partner. Many foreign companies find that a well-connected individual serves this purpose best, although local corporate partners are also popular.

According to Venezuelan central bank reports, accumulated foreign investment totaled a meager US$2.4 billion through 1988, with the addition of only US$600 million during 1989–1990. But central bankers see the growth just now beginning, as foreign companies position themselves for major roles in the nation's new US$11.6 billion "megaprojects" program in the energy, mining, metals, tourism, and paper industries.

A privatization program to sell off more than four hundred state-owned companies was implemented in 1990. Of the two basic ways to privatize, Venezuela chose the slower path, whereby ailing companies are turned around before being sold (as was done in the United Kingdom, Chile, and Mexico). This contrasts with Argentina and Brazil, both of whom opted for the fast track: that is, selling state-owned companies without refurbishing them.

The vice president of Venezuela's privatization committee, Isilio Arriaga Cornieles, pushed for the slow approach, recognizing that, without the right framework, economic instability can cause investors to pull out, thus making it necessary to privatize all over again. Miguel Rodriques, the country's minister of planning, argues, "In order for a privatization to be successful, it has to be transparent, legally well-backed, and protected." It took Venezuela two years to get its first company ready for privatization.

Foreign investors looking at privatization as a means of establishing a Venezuelan facility will probably applaud Rodriques's approach over the long run, even though it takes longer to get up and running.

The Caracas Stock Exchange is promoted as a thriving, emerging capital market exhibiting spectacular performance. Foreign observers note, however, that trading is thin, restricted, and unfair to minority holders. The exchange's regulatory body appears to be ineffective and the 50 percent tax on capital gains is frequently not adhered to by traders.

Economic Reforms

Economic reforms under President Carlos Andres Perez have been significant. Foreign exchange restrictions have been lifted. Import licenses and permits, long the bane of many Latin countries, including Venezuela, have been removed on all but 17 agricultural and medical products. Only 192 products remain covered by import quotas. An extremely complicated tariff structure has been simplified, reducing tariff brackets from 41 in 1989 to 4 in 1991. The maximum duty rate, once 135 percent, will be slashed to 20 percent by 1993.

Venezuela is also seeking membership in the GATT, which will bring the country's international trade policies more into line with other industrialized nations. Foreign investment laws have been revamped, allowing foreign companies to invest in most sectors of the economy. Cumbersome approval procedures have been changed. Foreign companies need only register with the government to be allowed entrance.

Limits on profit repatriation have been removed. Foreign companies are permitted to borrow from local banks and participate in the Caracas stock market. The overvalued bolivar has been set afloat. The central government's deficit is being curbed and subsidies of public services reduced. Price controls on nearly all goods and services have been removed.

Caution Alert

Certain obstacles continue to plague foreign exporters and investors. Corporate tax rates remain unreasonably high at 50 percent. The economy is still overly dependent on oil exports, and Venezuela's fortunes rise and fall with world oil prices. Minor customs bureaucrats and annoying red tape persist at the country's ports and terminals. Inflation continues to erode the bolivar, and most foreign traders insist on U.S. dollar payments.

Although many reforms have been put in place, much remains to be done. The Venezuelan bureaucracy remains horrendously cumbersome. Corruption, both within and outside of government circles, continues to be a problem for foreigners doing business in the country. Although growing, the private sector is still relatively small compared to Chile and Mexico. In addition, many companies have been protected by decades of cartels and favoritism from government bureaucrats.

Future Outlook

Overall, the outlook for future trade and investment with Venezuela looks promising. The nation boasts five conditions that could conceivably make it a major force in Western Hemisphere trade:

1. Vast mineral wealth, especially oil
2. An abundance of hydroelectric power
3. A large pool of national and expatriate management talent
4. A highly literate population and a trainable labor force
5. A strategic location and favorable climate

In addition, recent trade agreements with Andean nations and Mexico, together with pending free trade arrangements with Central American and Caribbean nations, could make Venezuela an ideal location for companies wishing to exploit future trading blocs.

Whether Venezuela's government will continue to encourage conversion to a free market economy remains uncertain, although developments in 1992 look positive. The IMF and the U.S. government are both optimistic and continue to support the country's reform programs. Unscathed by the drug cartels and guerrilla warfare so prominent in other South American countries, democratic Venezuela appears to have turned the corner. To foreign companies willing and able to tough it out during the conversion period, Venezuela's future prospects as a growth market look very good.

7
Colombia

Tips to Foreign Traders and Investors

1. Proceed very cautiously with investment strategies. The government still protects many local businesses, creating unmanageable competition.
2. Insist on hard-currency payment for exports. The country has ample currency reserves.
3. Do not even consider a facility other than in Bogota or Cartagena.
4. Stay alert to the strategic advantages from new trade pacts with Mexico, Venezuela, and Panama that may evolve.
5. Get necessary financing outside of Colombia.
6. Embassy office in Washington: (202) 387-8338.

Mention Colombia, and drug cartels and guerrilla violence immediately come to mind. The international press, especially in America, has been quick to sensationalize Colombia's misfortunes—not altogether inaccurately. Over the past sixty years, 95 percent of Colombia's elections have been held under a state of siege. In Medellin, seat of the most powerful drug cartel, more people have died since 1988 than in the war in Lebanon.

The primary cause of violence is drug trafficking. The power and money derived from drugs—over US$50 billion a year—continue to be the fundamental elements destabilizing the nation. In effect, the drug czars have created a state within a state, retaining their power with bribes, death threats, and the killings of more than two hundred judges.

Guerrilla warfare is a second destabilizing force. For thirty years, guerrilla bands numbering upwards of 8000 seasoned fighting men throughout the country have battled poorly led and trained, badly demoralized, and often abusive government troops—as well as each other.

On the surface, drug lords and guerrilla wars are enough to keep any sane foreign trader away from Colombia. In fact, however, substantial market opportunities exist in this country of 33 million. The light at the end of the tunnel can be seen in the radical changes invoked by president Cesar Gaviria Trujillo. President Gaviria's major objective continues to be the restructuring of the Colombian state, with the goal of permitting it to rejoin the world community.

He is making progress. In less than a year, Gaviria defused a murderous drug war, coaxed some of his country's top cocaine dealers into jail (including Pablo Escobar, the most violent of the Medellin drug czars), and oversaw the writing of a new constitution. Talks with guerrilla leaders began in Venezuela in mid-1991, but soon broke down. Smaller guerrilla groups were persuaded to lay down their arms, form a political party, and elect representatives to the national assembly.

The rest of Colombia is changing fast. When the guerrillas began fighting in 1960, the average Colombian was a poor, uneducated farmhand whose only alternative to a tight, oppressive government was to take up arms alongside the guerrillas. Now, most Colombians live in cities, comprising a rapidly growing middle class with enough income to own cars and moderate housing. A federal court system has been redesigned. Constitutional rights are being observed. A unicameral Congress is being set up.

According to informed observers in Mexico and the United States, the events of 1990 and 1991 are signs of a transformation more important than any that has taken place in Colombia in a hundred years.

A Trading Partner

Colombia has a unique strategic location on the South American continent, adjoining Panama in Central America and with coasts on both the Pacific Ocean and the Caribbean Sea. It has a wealth of natural resources, including hydrocarbons, coal, oil, nickel, emeralds, gold, and platinum, as well as abundant forests and fertile agricultural land. Sixty-five percent of the population lives in the urban areas of Bogota, Cali, Medellin, Barranquilla, Bucaramanga, Cartagena, Cucuta, Pereira, and Manizales.

While all other Latin countries suffered to varying degrees from the "lost decade" of the 1980s, Colombia's economy enjoyed a sustained growth of 4 percent on average. It incurred a relatively modest level of external debt on which payments have been made regularly and uninterruptedly.

Colombia's main industries include coffee, bananas, cut flowers, exotic fruit, textiles, chemicals, light manufactured products, and more recently, capital goods such as automobiles and spare parts. Its principal exports consist of coffee, flowers, textiles, food, and leather goods. Exports flow mainly to the United States and Europe, with lesser amounts to Japan and Asia.

On the import front, the government dismantled administrative restrictions on imports, and tariffs are being reduced over several years. The best prospects for exports from foreign firms are: computers and software, telecommunications equipment, oil and gas field equipment, aircraft and avionics, electronic components, security and safety equipment, medical diagnostic and treatment equipment and products, food processing and packaging equipment, electrical power-generating equipment, auto parts and accessories, waste management and disposal products and equipment, and water purification systems.

Foreign Direct Investment

Foreign investment has been at unacceptably low levels for several years, and was practically nonexistent from 1985 to 1989. Excluding mining and petroleum industries, foreign direct investment has averaged a mere US$59.4 million. This condition existed in all Andean Pact nations and was a deliberate attempt to protect local companies. The "law of similars" was vigorously enforced.

New laws have now been adopted to include both direct and portfolio foreign investments. These laws are based on three principles:

1. *Equal treatment.*   Treating foreign companies the same as Colombian nationals, except for fiscal and exchange issues

2. *Universality.*   Allowing foreign investment in all sectors except those affecting national security, defense, and the disposal and elimination of toxic, dangerous, or radioactive waste not produced in the country

3. *Automaticity.*   Granting a general authorization to foreign companies except in the financial sector, in hydrocarbons and mining, in activities related to the supply of public services, and in activities covered by insurance mechanisms for noncommercial risks

The only requirements for foreign companies to begin doing business in Colombia are to register at the exchange office of the central bank and to comply with the same requirements that local companies must follow. Profits, capital, and gains on the liquidation of investments may be repatriated.

An additional incentive reduced the remittance tax from 20 to 12 percent. Taxes are completely exempt in free zones.

Colombia also subscribes to the United Nations Multilateral Investment Guarantee Agency (MIGA) and is entering into several bilateral investment and trade agreements with neighboring countries.

In the area of foreign investment, the government's economic reforms have abandoned nearly all restrictions on new investment and revamped the country's exchange control system. A major labor reform measure adds flexibility and transparency to labor markets.

Privatization is progressing slowly. Railways were the first to go private. Although monopolistic privileges granted to Colombia's state-owned shipping fleet reduced shipping costs, transportation, telecommunications, power generation and distribution, telephone systems, the financial sector, and seaports remain thirty years behind the times. Such antiquated businesses do not attract many buyers.

Major opportunities exist for foreign companies in five areas:

- The production of intermediate goods
- Capital goods (especially for agroindustrial projects)
- Forestry
- The exploitation of sea products
- The conservation and dehydration of agricultural products and fruit

Despite the government's renewed emphasis on developing an international trade presence, Colombian output, exclusive of coffee and certain minerals, remains focused inward. The total industrial sector is 30 percent smaller than that of Venezuela. U.S. exports to the country have been very meager, in part due to the relatively small size of Colombian firms and their concentration on internal markets. Fears raised by cocaine trafficking and guerrilla warfare have also clearly deterred foreign firms from active trade.

Caution Alert

Another element that makes Colombia a second-rate trading partner is the abominable shape of its financial sector. While local banks such as Banco Popular with 188 branches have the ability to handle short- and medium-term trade finance, investment banking has been dormant since the 1960s. Foreign companies have little chance of financing projects locally unless they can obtain funding through multilateral aid programs.

Future Outlook

Although Colombia has definite trade and investment potential, neither the government nor local business leaders have completely thrown off the yoke of protectionism.

While neighboring countries are actively soliciting trade with North America and Europe, Colombia seems content to feel its way slowly through the maze of international free market policies.

While Venezuela, Panama, Bolivia, and the Caribbean nations work toward bilateral and multilateral free trade agreements, Colombia remains reticent to advance beyond the slow reduction of tariffs and quotas.

No doubt, unresolved guerrilla activity and the pervasive power of drug cartels color the country's foreign trade and investment policies. However, there remains an underlying distrust of foreigners and monopolistic favoritism toward local business cartels. Until business leaders genuinely want open trade with the rest of the world, Colombia seems doomed to remain a second-class trading partner.

8
Argentina

Tips to Foreign Traders and Investors

1. Don't be misled by enthusiastic government announcements promoting trade deregulation. Competition with local cartels is still tough.

2. Use a knowledgeable local partner to break into banking circles and major markets.

3. Check out trade and investment opportunities in Argentina's hottest growth markets: tourism, health care, and pharmaceuticals.

4. Stay away from direct investments in industries dominated by large local firms. The cartels will beat you every time.

5. Form a joint venture with an influential local partner to exploit bureaucratic favoritism.

6. Be careful of new peso currency as payment against exports. Inflation could erode it as easily as it did the austral.

7. Embassy office in Washington: (202) 939-6400.

Argentina was among the last to recognize free market, export-led growth as the fastest and most beneficial way to right a staggering nation. Although President Carlos Menem initiated economic reforms as early as 1989, when average tariffs were at an oppressive 38 percent, only late in 1991 did the government take serious steps to bring the country into the foreign trade arena.

On November 1, 1991, Argentines awoke to learn that their president had reversed fifty years of state control with the stroke of a pen. In a breathtakingly daring move, President Menem completely deregulated the country's economy, effective immediately. The presidential order dubbed "the

Economic Deregulation Decree," did away with many federal regulatory agencies, cut export taxes and road duties, and encouraged the import of cheap products and services. The order also banned all restrictions on the sale of goods and services, deregulated road freight, closed down the national grain and meat boards, did away with most regulations affecting imports and exports, told ports to stay open 24 hours a day, and took on the pharmaceuticals lobby by lifting restrictions on the import and sale of medicines.

By far the most dramatic change, however, was the presidential order to end industry-wide bargaining agreements. Much of Argentina's economic malaise, as well as much of its political and social upheaval over the last fifty years, could be traced directly to the extraordinary, far-reaching power of the country's labor unions. According to international observers from the United States, Europe, and the United Nations, the control exercised by organized labor over politicians, trade policies, the business community, and social programs had been the overriding force behind the depletion of Argentina's gold reserves, industrial base, and financial institutions. In effect, labor unions had built a wall around the country, keeping foreigners out, Argentines in, and militant dictators in power.

Obviously, organized labor has objected strenuously to the presidential decree that now allows businesses to negotiate wages, benefits, and conditions directly with employees instead of via national unions. As José Pedraza, a spokesman for the two-million-member General Workers Confederation commented, "It undoubtedly is going to have an impact on a whole range of social, political, economic, and cultural activities"—a gross understatement!

Red Flag

Whether the unions will once again force a wholesale retreat from the government's free market policies remains to be seen. In any event, foreign companies looking to Argentina as a viable trading partner or as a logical site for direct investment should be forewarned that history could easily repeat itself. The Argentine economy is not yet out of the woods and the unions have not been completely defused.

Such deregulation moves sound very impressive, but foreign companies should realize that the state can only deregulate what it has itself regulated. Many of Argentina's trade restrictions are perpetrated by private agreement, not state decree.

For instance, local banks will only open accounts for people who own property. Corrupting influences between state bureaucrats and private companies still persists, permitting a wide range of favoritism. Industry cartels are as much in evidence today as before deregulation.

How many non-state controlled business practices Menem will be successful in eliminating is anyone's guess. Based on his performance so far, however, his chances appear better than even.

Foreign Direct Investment

In 1989, when the previous government of President Raul Alfonsin turned the reins over five months early to Carlos Menem, few outsiders believed that the Peronist Party, with its tradition of populist government and labor support, would implement the kinds of radical reforms the country needed. But Menem surprised his critics. He began a series of significant trade and investment reforms to end fifty years of isolation and inward-looking development, open the Argentine economy to foreign competition, and reenter global markets.

Soon after taking office, the Menem government began passing legislation that essentially provided the same treatment to foreign investors as that accorded national firms. The basic idea was not only to attract foreign capital, but to entice the return of an estimated US$40 billion of Argentine flight capital that the large upper and middle classes had moved to foreign banks.

Repatriation of capital is now permitted. The peso (formerly called the austral) is fully convertible to the dollar in a free foreign exchange market. The private sector has no limitations on maintaining dollar deposits inside or outside Argentina. Investment registration is required only for statistical purposes. Foreign firms have free access to local capital markets.

Caution Alert

Beginning January 1, 1992, the Argentine government issued a new currency called the peso to replace the austral. One peso equals 10,000 australs or one U.S. dollar. The peso is also subject to the same inflationary devaluation pressures as the austral.

U.S. companies will find OPIC open to insurance guarantees for any investment approved by the Argentine Ministry of Economy. In turn, the Argentine government has established semiautomatic ministry approval of OPIC investment-coverage applications.

Although certainly not a flood, new capital has begun to flow into the country. Those industries attracting the most foreign investment are oil and gas, food processing, hotels and restaurants, textiles, semifinished agricultural goods, banks, retail stores, and wholesale distribution centers.

Setting up a production facility in Argentina can be tricky, in that business cartels and government favoritism continue to play major competitive roles. A lingering mistrust of foreigners, held over from old regimes, makes it difficult to penetrate both the upper social strata and the upper echelons of the business community. Nevertheless, many companies have found an Argentine facility more than worthwhile, especially when teaming up with an influential Argentine partner.

This country of 33.3 million people offers a diversified industrial base and a skilled labor force (unionized, of course) totaling 12.5 million workers. It also boasts a substantial cadre of upper- and middle-class managers more than capable of competing at the international level.

In 1991, per capita GDP hit US$3108 and unemployment held at 6.2 percent, even though the nation's growth rate was a meager 1 percent. Total exports exceeded US$10.5 billion, while imports were held to US$5 billion, creating a large trade surplus and a burgeoning foreign currency reserve.

Argentina's corporate tax rates are reasonable relative to other Latin countries, but certainly not low. The income tax rate is 20 percent; the capital gains rate runs 20 to 36 percent; and the branch tax rate hit 36 percent in 1991. A value-added tax of 15.6 percent and various local taxes are also in effect. Since all foreign exchange controls have been eliminated, transactions are conducted at free market prices set by supply and demand.

In 1991, government austerity measures began to harness inflation. By 1992, it had settled in the 25 to 30 percent range: a far cry from the previous 18,000 percent! Multinational aid agencies are beginning to recognize Argentina's progress toward economic reform. The IMF approved a US$1.04-billion standby loan, unlocking a further US$325 million from the World Bank.

The booming Buenos Aires Stock Exchange offers a good opportunity to raise debt and equity funds locally. Until recently, a hyperinflation percentage rate measuring in the thousands has prevented the massive inflows of foreign capital originally envisioned. However, this situation is rapidly changing.

The nation's privatization program is gathering speed. Argentina opted for the fast-track privatization approach, believing that it would take too many years to get state-owned companies sufficiently straightened out for private investors. The national airline, railroads, state telephone companies, two TV stations, resort facilities, oil and gas concessions, 6200 miles of road-maintenance concessions, port facilities, and many other businesses have been sold through a combination of debt/equity swaps (usually 80 percent of the sell price) and fresh capital.

Through 1991, over US$8.5 billion had been raised, and the government hopes to raise another US$1.7 billion in 1992. If the plan is successful, the nation's private external debt will be liquidated. Argentina ranks third behind Chile and Mexico in its privatization sell-off. Although most large businesses have already been auctioned, plenty of small ones remain for interested foreign investors.

Foreign Trade

Foreign trade policies have been liberalized even more than foreign investment regulations. Argentina now maintains a three-tiered import tariff schedule:

- 22 percent for finished goods with domestic competition
- 11 percent for intermediary goods with domestic competition
- 0 percent for primary goods without domestic competition

In addition, the government has liberalized special protection laws for electronic equipment and computer imports. It has also done away with the last of its dreaded import licenses.

High fees charged by port authorities still rankle foreign shippers, but the presidential decree previously discussed should alleviate the situation here as well.

The United States continues to be the largest importer of Argentine products, taking 12 percent of the nation's total exports. On the flip side, U.S. companies provide 29 percent of Argentine imports.

The best prospects for exports to Argentina are: medical equipment and supplies; construction materials and equipment; electronics; clothing and textiles; optics; power tools; laboratory equipment; security systems; chemical products; pharmaceuticals; computers, peripherals, and software; aircraft and aircraft parts; office equipment and supplies; synthetic resins, rubber, and plastic materials; pesticides; civil engineering and other construction services; and monitoring instruments and instrumentation.

Also in high demand are: machinery and equipment for oil and gas field exploration, refining, and transport; telecommunications; food processing and packaging; agriculture; and textile manufacturing.

Sixty percent of Argentina's exports are agricultural products: grains, oilseeds, sugar, tobacco, fruit, and cotton. Nonagricultural exports include meat; crude oil and petroleum products; steel plates, sheets, pipe tubes, and fittings; and aluminum.

The early effect of trade liberalization policies created a trade surplus of US$8.2 billion. Subsequently, an internal recession dampened consumer buying. At the same time, Argentine consumers began showing their preference for imported goods, and the trade surplus began to shrink.

President Menem's U.S. visit to drum up additional foreign investment and support for expanded trade opened doors even further. While promising continued commitment to a market-driven, free trade economy, Menem announced that his country was about ready to participate in a debt-reduction program. At the National Press Club in Washington, D.C., President Menem announced, "I believe by the end of next year [referring to 1992] we will have access to the Brady Plan."

Menem made this prediction a day after signing a precedent-setting investment protection treaty with the United States. The Bilateral Investment Treaty is the first with a Latin or Caribbean country since President Bush announced his "Enterprise for the Americas Initiative."

The treaty guarantees the right to invest on terms no less favorable than those accorded domestic or third-country investors. It also guarantees the free transfer of capital, freedom from performance requirements of any kind, access to international arbitration, and internationally recognized standards of compensation for expropriation of private property.

In effect, economic reforms that were legislated internally by the Argentine government have now been ratified internationally in the country's first treaty with a major world power. The signing of the treaty led Deputy U.S. Trade Representative Julius Katz to remark, "It signals that Argentina is a good and suitable place for U.S. investment and will further strengthen economic links between our countries."

Argentina might indeed boast that it has "come a long way, baby"—from being an out-of-control economy ruled by an isolationist regime only a few years ago to assuming its new role as the first official U.S. trading partner in South America.

9
Brazil

Tips to Foreign Traders and Investors

1. Don't make a direct investment in Brazil without prior experience in other Latin countries. The closed business community and bureaucratic red tape are too much for beginners to master.

2. Lay the groundwork now for getting in on the inevitable boom in environmental products and services as well as computers.

3. Raise capital through local stock exchanges only with an experienced Brazilian broker

4. Beware of state and municipal laws that differ from federal regulations.

5. Get to know the underground economy quickly. This is the best place to make business contacts.

6. Seriously investigate direct investments as long-term commitments. This is the place to be to tap the new Southern Cone Common Market (MERCOSUR).

7. Embassy office in Washington: (202) 745-2700.

A nation of 155 million people (two-thirds the population of the United States), Brazil presents foreign firms enormous market and resource opportunities and at the same time immense challenges. Of all the South American countries, Brazil continues to have the largest foreign trade base; yet it has progressed the slowest toward a free market economy. Economic reforms have been meager, external debt remains unmanageable, inflation continues to eat into the nation's economic fabric, and political dysfunction plagues the federal government.

The sheer size of the country (comprising half the South American continent) and the concentration of economic power in the few metropolitan areas makes nationwide economic reforms extremely difficult. Furthermore, the unique three-tiered governmental structure, with its widely shared political, economic, and social powers, makes governing the nation cumbersome. Governmental responsibilities are shared by:

- A federation of 26 states
- A Federal District comprising the national capital of Brasilia
- A conglomeration of 4300 municipalities

Such sharing of governmental power gives Brazil the most widely decentralized form of federation of all the developing countries. Less than 50 percent of total government expenditures are controlled by the federal government. The new Brazilian constitution, enacted in 1988, gives broad, autonomous powers to states and municipalities in both tax and expenditure functions.

In other federations, municipalities are usually subservient to state governments. In Brazil, they are recognized as independent governing bodies on a coequal status with states. Among other activities, municipalities are responsible for intracity public transport, preschool and elementary education, preventive health care, land use, and historical and cultural preservation.

Federal and state governments share responsibility for the nation's health, education, culture, environment, agriculture, food distribution, housing, sanitation, social welfare, police, and hydroelectricity generation. International trade, the banking system, the nation's currency, and regulation of interstate public industries are the sole responsibility of the federal government.

Although major trade and investment policies are established at the federal level, states and municipalities have a great deal of leeway for approvals, licenses, and other regulations. For foreign investors, compliance with state and local requirements can often be as cumbersome as federal regulations. Also, bureaucratic delays and "satisfaction" payments increase under such a decentralized governmental structure.

The United States also has a decentralized form of government—not totally dissimilar to Brazil's—that has worked well for two hundred years, so clearly the fault does not lie entirely in decentralization. The blame must be laid at the feet of the elite class, whether in government office or in private business, for caring more about short-term profits (which can always be made during hyperinflation by raising prices) than about long-term national stability.

Though President Fernando Collor de Mello has tried to enforce austerity measures, he has no one behind him: not the Congress, not organized labor, and not the private business sector. Although he has praised the virtue of free markets, his insufficient backing forced the president to reinstate price controls in late 1991 on 53 basic food and drug products. He put the entire blame for this retrenchment on the elite class of private businessmen who refused to cut profit margins even in times of deep recession (depression?).

On the other hand, allegations that his wife, as president of the Brazilian

Assistance Legion, handed out hundreds of thousands of dollars in contracts to her relations makes Mr. Collor's moral high ground appear a bit shaky.

In addition, privatization plans to sell 27 state-owned companies have been blocked by trade unions and business groups that benefit from their inefficiency. In late 1991, the government broke the deadlock and made its first sale: Usiminas, the largest steel mill in Latin America.

Key Considerations for Foreign Investors

Brazil has the fifth-largest landmass in the world. It is blessed with an abundance of natural resources, including timber, energy, a wide variety of minerals, agricultural land, and fresh water. It also boasts a broad manufacturing base with plentiful, low-cost labor and a good supply of management talent. Brazil's infrastructure is fairly well developed by South American standards. It has diverse, widespread domestic markets. Most raw materials necessary for the production of goods are readily accessible within the country.

The current generation of foreign traders finds it hard to remember that prior to the 1980s Brazil had what was probably the most vibrant economy in the world. Seventy years ago, Brazil had a per capita income about one-thirtieth that of Argentina. But by the 1970s the country was far richer than Argentina. This dramatic leap forward was due mainly to a rapidly accelerating industrial base and to flamboyant foreign trade, although Argentina's catastrophic demise under Perón and later rulers also contributed to the disparity.

Until 1980, Brazil had enjoyed forty years of practically unbroken annual expansion of real output: the economy grew at an average of 7 percent per year—a remarkable feat by anyone's standards. Real GDP, according to the World Bank, grew about 4 percent per year—a rate exceeding that of the United States.

In 1980, per capita GDP stood at US$2450. The economy was well balanced, responsive, and the tenth-largest in the world. It boasted hundreds of thousands of successful entrepreneurial businesses as well as many world-class corporations. Even today, 60 percent of Brazil's exports are manufactured products. The nation also has accumulated the largest amount of foreign direct investment in the Third World: US$32 billion. Truly, Brazil cannot be considered a sleepy coffee republic, as some would have us believe.

Foreign investors would be well advised, however, to recognize that all is not as it seems from official government statistics. The failure of government—especially at the federal level—to control inflation and all its related side effects has spawned an enormous underground economy. Some estimates place it at as much as 50 percent of official GDP.

This is not an underground economy working to provide goods and services to rural peasants or nefarious street bankers. It is the principal means of livelihood and the major source of goods and services for a large, healthy, well-to-do middle class. Away from Rio, São Paulo, and Brasilia, middle-class Brazilians live as comfortably as their suburban American counterparts.

With all these assets going for it, one must ask why is Brazil floundering like a drunken giant when it could be a leader in world trade and economic growth?

The answer can be found in the completely inept management of the nation's federal government. Regardless of who has held the presidential seat, the country has been all but bankrupted by consistent policies directed toward increasing the wealth and well-being of controlling bureaucrats rather than toward the long-term well-being of everyday Brazilian citizens.

According to the World Bank's *World Development Report, 1991*, Brazil's total external debt stood at over US$111 billion in 1989, as compared with US$95 billion for Mexico and US$62 billion for India, the second- and third-highest debts in the developing world. While Mexico is well on the way to liquidating its foreign debt, Brazil only began its restructuring efforts in 1992.

Brazil's chaotic economic state can best be illustrated by the revolving-door changes effected over the last five years. During this period the country has seen ten finance ministers, ten central bank governors, five separate "shock therapy" economic reform packages, and four currencies. Today's cruzeiro has the equivalent value of 1 million cruzeiros in 1986. Inflation rates are so high that they are practically immeasurable, pushing 3000 to 8000 percent per year.

Comparison with other countries points up the severity of Brazil's inflation. From 1960 through 1989, the world price level multiplied eleven times, the worst global inflation ever recorded over a thirty-year period. In all of Latin America over the same period, prices multiplied 244,000 times. In Brazil, prices multiplied 29 million times! The drunken giant's chronic inflation problem has indeed separated Brazil from the rest of the world.

Real GDP in 1991 was 10 percent below that in 1986 and real GDP per capita was about 10 percent less. The economy continues to contract, year by year, while government officials push inept policies that do nothing more than hasten national bankruptcy.

Corruption, bribes, and kickbacks line bureaucratic, corporate, and union pockets while Brazil's citizenry makes its living in the underground market.

Despite these obvious deterrents, the country offers foreign investors some interesting possibilities. Brazil has

- A substantial export-oriented agricultural base with 90 percent of available land not yet under cultivation
- A huge reservoir of untapped mineral resources
- A well-established, functioning, and growing industrial base
- Plenty of available, low-cost energy from massive hydroelectric facilities, as well as alternative energy sources like alcohol
- A large urban population with more than adequate disposable income
- Serviceable overseas transport through ports and air terminals

Table 9-1. Foreign Direct Investment in Brazil by Country*

	US$ millions
United States	28.4
Germany	15.7
Japan	9.6
Switzerland	9.4
United Kingdom	6.2
Canada	4.6
France	4.3
Sweden	1.8
Other	20.0

*In 1989.
SOURCE: Central Bank; Bank of Brazil; Brazilian-American Chamber of Commerce.

Foreign firms are subject to the same company laws as national firms, except in oil exploration, drilling, and refining, domestic transport, all media industries, and mineral extraction. These industries remain off-limits to all foreign investment.

Although state and municipal laws affect trade, raw material acquisition, land use, and workers' rights, company organizational structure and corporate laws are set by the federal government.

Table 9-1 shows the breakdown of Brazilian foreign direct investment by country of origin.

Economic Reforms

Economic reforms from President Fernando Collor de Mello have helped stimulate a modest amount of foreign investment, but that's about all. His macroeconomic reforms to stabilize inflation by freezing prices and seizing private bank accounts have failed miserably. Microeconomic reforms have worked somewhat better.

Many obstacles to foreign trade have been removed. When Collor took office 1500 items were prohibited from import. Now all can be brought in. Most quotas and import licenses have been removed or substantially reduced. Quotas restricting imports of manufactured products have been removed.

Average tariffs still run at an exorbitant 25 percent, although the government is committed to reduce this to 14 percent by 1994, under the MERCOSUR free trade agreement executed with Argentina, Uruguay, and Paraguay. Foreign investment in mining and some other industries is still limited by the constitution, but efforts are being made to change that as well.

A significant amount of bureaucratic red tape affecting the flow of imports and exports has been done away with, although much still remains. Anticompetitive regulations that once affected most ports, transport, petroleum retailing, and telecommunications have been eliminated.

Privatization has started, but progresses at a snail's pace. By the end of 1991, only four state-owned companies had been sold or were about to be sold. The Brazilian government is trying hard to effect debt/equity swaps as part of the privatization program. With secondary market debt trading at about 25 cents on the dollar, this could be a very attractive means for foreign companies to gain a Brazilian foothold.

Debt/equity swaps could also assist the government reduce its exorbitant external debt. In fact, in the foreseeable future it may be the only feasible way. Most of the debt has already been restructured but not reduced. Even after the restructuring, the government proceeded to default on newly structured interest payments.

Economic reforms may not be Brazil's strong suit, but there can be no question that foreign firms with the staying power and fortitude to weather the country's hyperinflation, underground economy, government bungling, and horrendous bureaucratic corruption should find substantial market opportunities.

A small glow is beginning to light the horizon of Brazil's financial woes. In mid-1991, Brazil's new economics minister, Marcello Marques Moreira, took steps to further open the country to foreign companies by eliminating long-standing barriers and disincentives in the country's stock market. As a result, the leading São Paulo index soared, stimulating the country's elite corporations to reenter financial markets, this time with new, securitized asset financing.

Companies such as IBM do Brasil, Alcoa do Brasil, state-owned oil giant Petrobras, the mining company Companhia Vale do Rio Doce, and two subsidiaries of the international grain trader Bunge & Born have obtained new financing by securitizing their export orders. The only risk to investors is that the companies will not perform, but most investors believe this to be a small risk from such well-known multinationals.

Major exporters are also the favorites of foreign institutional investors in the newly liberalized Brazilian equity markets. Until Moreira's reform moves, foreigners could only invest in the stock markets through Brazilian-managed country funds. In addition, they had to pay a 20 percent capital gains tax and suffered profit remittance restrictions.

Now foreigners can deal directly with brokerage houses with no limits on the number of shares that can be purchased in a single company. They are exempted from the capital gains tax, but still must pay a tax of 15 percent when profits are remitted. Local investors continue to pay a 25 percent capital gains tax.

Both the corporate income tax rate and the branch tax rate are at an acceptable, although certainly not low, 30 percent.

Foreign Trade

As far as exporting to Brazil is concerned, foreign companies would do well to work through local attorneys and trade counsels to keep abreast of ever-changing import tariffs, quotas, and currency modifications. Under any circumstances, with hyperinflation continuing, foreign exporters would be foolish not to demand payment in hard currency through a letter of credit guaranteed by an American, European, or Japanese bank.

Currently, more than 50 percent of Brazilian imports are comprised of the following: organic chemicals, aircraft and aircraft parts, telecommunications equipment, parts, and services; coal; electronic components; machine tools; medical supplies; health care, diagnostic, and treatment equipment; and computers, computer parts, and software.

The special case of computers needs clarification, however. As far back as 1974, Brazil established a ban on all computer imports in an attempt to stimulate a homegrown computer industry. Seventeen years later, Brazilians would much rather import computers that work and can be bought for a reasonable price than continue with their own that don't work and are priced out of reach for most people and businesses. The problem evolved because along the way Brazilian firms stopped investing in computer technology. They are still producing to 1980 standards.

President Collor has now announced that he plans to end the import embargo by October 1992, permitting computer imports and the formation of joint ventures between Brazilian and foreign companies. The bill before the Brazilian congress to accomplish this, however, is full of caveats that make the bill practically worthless. For instance, one requirement states that computers exported from Brazil by a joint venture must carry the name of the Brazilian exporter. It's hard to imagine Toshiba or IBM agreeing to put the name Ferreira da Silva on their computers. But who can say?

In addition to these products, Brazil needs nearly all types of machinery and equipment. In 1990, the United States alone exported to Brazil over US$800 million in capital goods, primarily industrial machinery and power-generating equipment. Exports of specialized industrial machinery have nearly doubled since 1986.

Within the next few years, demand will accelerate for all types of environmental protection and clean-up products, services, and equipment in the areas of air quality, waste management, reforestation, and water purification.

The 1992 United Nations worldwide "Earth Summit" conference in Rio de Janeiro began stimulating interest in environmental products and services two years before it convened. Such interest will undoubtedly continue for the foreseeable future, according to U.S. trade officials and U.N. forecasts. Currently, the United States is aggressively pursuing environmental protection measures throughout Latin America, spearheaded by the Environmental Protection Agency's experimental projects in Puerto Rico.

Caution Alert

It's almost mandatory to join forces with a Brazilian partner to cut through port and inland transport red tape. It appears unlikely that this will change in the foreseeable future, regardless of new government reforms. The income to port officials is too great to assume that they will willingly give it up.

Table 9-2.   Major Brazilian Trading Partners

	US$ billions
Largest Importers	
United States	8.7
Netherlands	2.6
Japan	2.3
Germany	1.4
Italy	1.4
Largest Exporters	
United States	3.1
Germany	1.4
Iraq (primarily weaponry)	1.2
Japan	1.0
Saudi Arabia (primarily weaponry)	.9

SOURCE: Central Bank, Boletim Mensal, June 1990.

Table 9-2 lists Brazil's major trading partners.

Future Outlook

Industry leaders from Europe and the United States, along with international observers from multilateral agencies, have been especially critical of Brazil's governmental floundering over the last twelve years. It is certainly easy to lay the blame for fiscal bankruptcy and hyperstagnation at the doorstep of elected leaders. Particularly during a recession, this gambit plays out in all developed countries, including the United States.

It is also easy to blame elite corporations for subordinating social welfare to economic greed, thus identifying big business as the whipping boy for economic perturbations. Corporate America has certainly felt such a sting, as have large corporations in Britain.

To a large extent Brazil has, in fact, been mismanaged. Certainly large public and private businesses are not blameless. Nevertheless, in countries with elected governments, it's hard to argue that the people aren't getting what they deserve. After all, that's democracy.

Brazilians have been accustomed to living with outrageous inflation for generations, apparently liking the results—or at least not disliking inflation enough to sacrifice living standards to do away with it. Americans and Europeans do not occupy the moral high ground here either.

What cannot be ignored, however, is that the muddling of the 1980s did set up a democratic government structure, decentralized along the same lines as the United States. It has survived the test of time as a solid democratic forum, with well-protected civil liberties and the rule of law. In many respects the Brazilian form could be a model for the rest of Latin America.

As so eloquently stated in *The Economist*, "One reason the underdeveloped world is underdeveloped, . . . is that institutions still matter less there than the qualities of the people who happen to be at the top." Brazil has been notoriously unlucky in having leaders who placed their personal interests above those of the institution. Mexico has benefited from just the opposite situation.

Whether Brazil will find the right leaders in the future is open to question. Certainly the country has the potential to become a major force in the global arena. Perhaps the stimulation of and the controls exerted by forming trading blocs will help Brazil turn the corner. Although it's too early to tell, many international traders are banking on Brazil to right itself eventually and become a major trading partner. Of all the countries in Latin America (with the noted exception of Mexico), Brazil probably has the best opportunity for sustainable, long-term economic growth.

10
The Caribbean Basin

Tips to Foreign Traders and Investors

1. Smaller companies or those inexperienced in foreign trade will do well to look at the Caribbean Basin. It's the easiest and cheapest place to start, and an excellent classroom.

2. Be sure to understand all CBI provisions before making a direct investment.

3. Don't bother with local joint venture partners. They are not necessary for most countries in the region.

4. Check out financing from several U.S. government agencies, including Puerto Rico's 936 program.

5. Don't hesitate. Make an investment in this region before more trading blocs are formed.

6. Stay away from the Dominican Republic until 1994, except for the tourism industry.

7. Don't bother with the French islands. Their markets are too difficult for any but French companies to penetrate.

8. Definitely open a facility, or at least a trust, in the Cayman Islands or Panama. Take advantage of zero taxes while in the region.

9. Embassy offices in Washington

   Antigua and Barbuda: (202) 362-5122
   Bahamas: (202) 944-3990

Barbados: (202) 939-9200

Belize: (202) 363-4505

Dominica: (none)

Grenada: (202) 265-2561

Guyana: (202) 265-6900

Jamaica: (202) 452-0660

Montserrat: (none)

St. Kitts-Nevis: (202) 833-3550

St. Lucia: (none)

St.Vincent/Grenadines: (none)

Trinidad & Tobago: (202) 467-6490

Dominican Republic: (202) 332-6280

Cayman Islands: (none)

Nations of the Caribbean Basin have long been derogatorily referred to as "banana republics," suggesting that they are merely inconsequential satellites of the United States and European colonial powers. It is certainly true that prior generations from developed nations persistently raped the Caribbean Basin of its natural resources, agricultural products, and very cheap uneducated labor. A number of industrialized nations once also used the Caribbean Basin as a dumping ground for human and industrial waste.

The United States has long kept the region under its wing for reasons other than trade. During two world wars and the Cold War, the Caribbean Basin served as a frontline defense against European adversaries. In fact, the United States purchased the Virgin Islands from Denmark in 1917 specifically to provide a defense outpost against German attack.

The Caribbean Basin region began maturing as viable independent states during the 1960s and today represents unusual market and resource opportunities for foreign trade and investment. For American and Canadian companies, the region serves as an easy entree to global trade and a key site from which to exploit currently forming Western hemisphere trading blocs.

For European and Asian companies it holds the promise of providing access to U.S. and Canadian markets through free trade agreements, without incurring the cost and legal hassle of investing directly in either country. The tax-haven status of several states appeals to companies and individuals from a variety of developed, high-tax nations.

The region also has obvious drawbacks. Domestic markets are very small and relatively undeveloped. The region consists of more than thirty separate countries, territories, colonies, departments, and dependencies, each with its own legal, tax, and financial systems. In Central America, the future political stability of several countries remains an open question.

Many island states, such as Montserrat and St. Vincent and the Grenadines, have virtually no resources other than cheap labor and sandy beaches, and no means of sustaining economic self-sufficiency. Others, such as Barbados,

Trinidad & Tobago, and Jamaica, possess developed private sectors but failing infrastructures.

The Caribbean Basin region includes the Central American countries of Guatemala, Honduras, El Salvador, Costa Rica, Belize, Nicaragua, and Panama, with a combined population of approximately 30 million. It also includes nearly 30 Caribbean island states with a combined population of approximately 18 million, but ranging in size from the Dominican Republic with 7 million people to Anguilla with a population of fewer than 5000.

Colonial ties persist in several Caribbean island states. Martinique, Guadeloupe, and St. Martin are not independent but are instead considered "departments" of France. British dependent territories consist of the Caymans, Turks and Caicos, Anguilla, Montserrat, and the British Virgin Islands. The U.S. Virgin Islands and Puerto Rico have territorial and commonwealth status (respectively) with the United States. Curacao, Bonaire, Sint Maarten, and, until recently, Aruba, remain Dutch parliamentary democracies grouped as the Netherlands Antilles.

Caribbean Basin countries have a few common traits, but also great diversity. Many suffer from slow growth and foreign exchange shortages caused by several factors, including low commodity prices for traditional exports—mostly agricultural products and natural resources.

Most countries in the region encourage export-oriented development strategies and actively seek foreign direct investment. Skilled and semiskilled labor is readily available in nearly all the countries. Many have international airports, deep-water ports, and infrastructures that are more fully developed than those in Africa, but still below par for developed nations. Electricity, telecommunications, and potable water are unreliable in many places. Virtually all countries have or are in the process of establishing free trade zone facilities.

On the other hand, vast economic differences exist between Caribbean Basin nations. Per capita GNP ranges from less than US$350 in Guyana to over US$17,000 in the Cayman Islands. National languages include Spanish, Dutch, French, and English—although English remains the common business language in all but Martinique and Guadeloupe.

This cacophony of languages and governmental units, variations in market size, and diversity of resources, restricts strategic market opportunities to those individual states that, for one reason or another, interest a specific foreign company. Nevertheless, because the United States and the European Community have defined the Caribbean Basin as an entity for purposes of trade and aid, a rationale exists for describing the region's trade and investment opportunities within a rather narrow band of political entities.

The balance of this chapter briefly analyzes opportunities with the following trading partners:

- The English-speaking Caribbean states forming the Caribbean Common Market (CARICOM), including Jamaica

- The Dominican Republic
- The special case of the Cayman Islands
- Puerto Rico and the U.S. Virgin Islands

Chapter 11 looks at market opportunities in the Central American countries of Costa Rica, Guatemala, and Panama.

Political conditions in Cuba and Haiti are too unsettled to offer market opportunities at this time, although they will probably open to trade before the end of this decade. When Fidel Castro's regime topples, Cuba could easily once again become the star performer in the region. Until then, however, Cuba holds little promise for either foreign investment or trade.

Even under pseudo-democratic rule, Haiti traditionally has been and still is the poorest and least desirable nation in the region for either trade or investment. El Salvador and Nicaragua still suffer the legacy of violent civil wars, although both are beginning to right themselves. Potential future market opportunities in these two countries were reviewed in Chapter 4.

The French and Dutch islands remain part of their respective mother countries, and trade and investment opportunities must be viewed in conjunction with those offered by France and the Netherlands.

Caribbean Basin Initiative

In 1983, the U.S. Congress passed the Caribbean Basin Economic Recovery Act, which included the Caribbean Basin Initiative (CBI). The CBI's specific purpose was to promote economic growth, stability, and diversification in the region through private sector investment and trade.

Original provisions limited the act to providing duty-free access to U.S. markets for CBI-produced goods and services. Now, however, the CBI has been expanded to include preferential treatment of U.S. exports to the region and special financing arrangements through Eximbank, OPIC, Puerto Rico's Section 936 program, and the Inter-American Development Bank.

The CBI program was set to expire in 1995 until Congress passed the Customs and Trade Act of 1990. This act, which includes the Caribbean Basin Economic Recovery Expansion Act of 1990, makes the CBI a permanent fixture of U.S. trade policy in the region.

This updated version, labeled CBI II, also includes a series of minor additions and deletions that recognize changing regional conditions. Further references to CBI include provisions of both the 1983 and the 1990 bills.

As of 1991, the following 24 countries qualified for CBI status:

Antigua and Barbuda	Haiti
Aruba	Honduras
Bahamas	Jamaica

Costa Rica	Montserrat
Dominica	Netherlands Antilles
Dominican Republic	(Curacao, Bonaire, Sint Maarten)
El Salvador	Nicaragua
Grenada	Panama
Guatemala	St. Kitts-Nevis
Guyana	St. Lucia
Haiti	St. Vincent/Grenadines
Honduras	Trinidad & Tobago
Jamaica	

Four additional countries are potentially eligible for CBI trade benefits, but have not as yet applied for entrance to the program: Anguilla, Cayman Islands, Suriname, and Turks and Caicos Islands. To qualify for admission to the program, countries must execute a Tax Information Exchange Agreement (TIEA) granting the IRS the right to examine records relating to trade transactions of U.S. companies.

Although petroleum, sugar, and tourism revenues have declined in the region, nonpetroleum and nontraditional exports have increased. Over time, this should provide a more balanced production and export base. Since 1983, nonpetroleum exports from CBI countries to the United States have grown at an average annual compound rate of 14.3 percent, or an accumulated 122.3 percent.

Exports of nontraditional products, such as apparel, winter vegetables, fruits, seafood, and wood furnishings, grew at an even greater rate. Apparel exports nearly tripled.

Regional exports using indigenous materials and skills are especially competitive. In addition to thriving tourism and data processing/keystroke industries, companies located in the Caribbean Basin have been most successful in exporting:

Apparel and other made-up textile items

Electronic and electromechanical assemblies

Handicrafts, giftware, and decorative items

Wood products, including furniture and building materials

Recreational items, sporting goods, and toys

Seafood

Tropical fruit products

Winter vegetables

Ethnic and specialty foods—sauces, spices, liqueurs, jams, confectionery items, etc.

Ornamental horticulture

Leather goods

Medical and surgical supplies

Footwear

Since the inception of CBI, many smaller companies have invested in virtually every one of the Caribbean island states, as well as all the Central American nations. According to the U.S. Department of Commerce, 789 new foreign exchange–generating investments in the region totaled an estimated $2.2 billion and created more than 142,000 new jobs.

Because of intense interest from the U.S. government in developing the Caribbean Basin's economic base to ensure political stability, virtually all federal agencies with responsibilities for the promotion of U.S. foreign trade or investment, as well as those commissioned to protect the environment and to further U.S. international policy, take an active role in promoting Caribbean Basin development. This includes financial and technical assistance, environmental protection measures, special market studies, labor training, and assistance for developing transportation and infrastructures. Table 10-1 presents key economic statistics for each Caribbean Basin country.

Caribbean Common Market

The Caribbean Common Market (CARICOM) was formed in 1973 under the Treaty of Chaguaramas to provide for duty-free trade between member nations. This applies to goods produced or manufactured within member nations, with certain classifications of goods being of regional origin. CARICOM also established a common external tariff for all goods coming into the common market. In addition, the organization arranged for an integrated system of fiscal incentives for both foreign investment and domestic industry, and executed double tax treaties between CARICOM members.

The basic idea behind CARICOM is to facilitate long-term general economic development of member nations, with a strong emphasis on creating jobs and reducing the region's external dependence. In addition to a substantial emphasis on the development of economic and social infrastructures (such as the University of the West Indies in Barbados), CARICOM sponsors the Eastern Caribbean Association of Commerce and Industry to promote trade and investment in the region and the Caribbean Development Bank (CDB) to facilitate financing of investment projects.

Membership in the CDB has been extended to Anguilla, the British Virgin Islands, the Cayman Islands, Turks and Caicos Islands, Colombia, Venezuela, Canada, and the United Kingdom.

A free trade framework agreement between the United States and CARICOM was executed in 1991.

Table 10-1.   Key Caribbean Basin Statistics

	Population	Per capita GDP (in US$)	Growth rate percentage	Unemployment rate percentage
CARICOM states				
Antigua and Barbuda	79,000	5,500	6.2	5.0
Bahamas	246,500	9,082	2.0	11.7
Barbados	262,700	5,054	3.5	18.0
Belize	219,700	1,187	6.0	15.0
Dominica	84,000	1,170	-1.4	10.0
Grenada	84,100	1,656	5.6	N/A
Guyana	764,600	350	-3.5	30.0
Jamaica	2,441,400	1,357	2.6	18.0
Montserrat	12,500	3,780	12.0	3.0
St. Kitts-Nevis	45,000	3,822	6.0	15.0
St. Lucia	150,000	1,200	6.0	20.0
St. Vincent/Grenadines	113,700	1,413	8.4	30.0
Trinidad & Tobago	1,300,000	3,338	-2.4	22.0
Non-CARICOM states				
Aruba	62,700	11,900	16.0	3.0
British Virgin Islands	12,300	7,715	2.5	N/A
Cayman Islands	26,400	17,227	13.0	-0-
Dominican Republic	7,240,800	950	0.6	30.0
Haiti	6,263,000	380	-1.5	50.0
Curacao	151,000	6,447	3.5	21.0
Sint Maarten	27,000	5,186	2.0	25.0
Central America				
Costa Rica	3,032,800	1,912	3.8	5.0
El Salvador	5,330,000	913	1.1	20.0
Guatemala	9,097,600	1,215	3.0	43.0
Honduras	5,259,700	960	2.1	25.0
Nicaragua	3,722,700	470	-5.0	25.0
Panama	2,314,400	1,925	3.0	25.0
United States affiliates				
Puerto Rico	3,300,000	6,060	7.3	15.0
U.S. Virgin Islands	110,000	8,717	N/A	3.0

SOURCE: Caribbean/Latin American Action, 1991, *Databook*.

The Organization of Eastern Caribbean States (OECS), consisting of Antigua and Barbuda, Dominica, Grenada, Montserrat, St. Kitts-Nevis, St. Lucia, and St. Vincent and the Grenadines, was established in 1981 as a subcommon market within CARICOM to promote trade and investment for its smaller member nations.

Contacting CARICOM, OECS, and the Caribbean Development Bank is a first step for foreign companies investigating investment or trade with member nations.

Foreign Direct Investment

The primary areas for foreign investment are sugar, apparel, handicrafts, tourism, infrastructure development and maintenance, light-assembly manufacturing, aquaculture, rum, furniture, and food processing. The Eastern Caribbean Investment Promotion Service (ECIPS) promotes general investments throughout the region and can be of enormous help in identifying specific projects and joint venture partners.

Financing is plentiful throughout the region. The Puerto Rican 936 program is now in full swing. U.S. Eximbank and OPIC, as well as the British Commonwealth Development Corporation, are very active in the region. Local branches of American and British banks handle normal trade finance. Financing for major infrastructure and local government-sponsored development projects can be obtained from local development banks, which in turn receive funding from the Inter-American Development Bank (IDB).

Tourism continues to be the predominant industry in most CARICOM countries. Hotel development projects have been substantial over the last four years. Even in more developed countries, such as Barbados, tourism accounts for more than 50 percent of GNP: in the Bahamas, it accounts for 70 percent. Although recessionary pressures from the United States, Canada, and Europe can directly affect this segment, the island states seem to have weathered economic downturns as well or better than developed countries over the years.

Foreign Trade

Major exports to the area vary with each country. Larger countries, such as Jamaica, Barbados, and Trinidad & Tobago, support a small but thriving manufacturing base that supplies a portion of domestic needs. Smaller states, such as Montserrat and St. Kitts-Nevis, have virtually no industry and import nearly all of their domestic needs.

Regional imports include: processed food, apparel, medical supplies and equipment, construction equipment and services, power-generating and distribution equipment, water purification and storage equipment, educational supplies, telecommunications equipment and services, building materials, frozen meats, basic computer hardware and software, security equipment, vehicles and parts, hotel and restaurant supplies and equipment, water sports products, building materials, chemicals, and fuels and lubricants.

Jamaica

Jamaica is a relatively highly developed nation compared to other CARICOM members. It has an active stock market in Kingston and a host of British, Canadian, and American commercial and merchant banks. The work force in the Kingston and Montego Bay areas is plentiful and skilled. Although, as in other island states, tourism remains a major industry, bauxite mining runs a close second.

Over fifty major companies from the United States and Europe have established businesses in Jamaica, including such well-known names as IBM, American Airlines, Nestle, W. R. Grace, and Sterling Drug.

Jamaica's main exports in addition to bauxite and alumina are sugar, bananas, citrus fruits, rum, cocoa, and coffee. It imports fuels, processed food, apparel, a variety of consumer goods, hotel and restaurant supplies, and equipment for construction, transportation, and light manufacturing.

The Dominican Republic

Representing the eastern two-thirds of the island of Hispaniola, the Dominican Republic (DR) has matured into a viable Caribbean trading partner, while neighboring Haiti continues along its road to oblivion. With seven million people, the DR represents the second-largest market in the Caribbean Basin, next to Guatemala.

Historically the DR has maintained close political and economic ties with the United States. It was occupied by U.S. troops for many years. Later, in the 1960s and 1970s, the spider web development of the giant Gulf+Western Corporation permeated the nation. Well over three hundred foreign firms operate businesses in the Dominican Republic, including many multinationals from the United States, Europe, and Japan.

Free Trade Zones

Foreign direct investment is welcome in the DR. A foreign company may freely repatriate profits and capital and own 100 percent of a Dominican business. Plentiful industrial free zones (IFZs) have become a major attraction for foreign companies. The DR government has found IFZs so beneficial in attracting foreign investment that it continues to open new ones every year. Currently, approximately thirty IFZs are in operation in various sections of the country. A few of the well-known U.S. companies currently operating in IFZs include Westinghouse, American Airlines, Warner Lambert, and GTE.

IFZs have many advantages, including duty-free import of raw materials, equipment, and goods destined for reexport; complete tax exemption for fifteen to twenty years; and the option to sell up to 20 percent of production output in the Dominican market. When combined with duty-free imports to the United States and Europe (under the Lomé IV Convention) and a minimum wage of US$0.56 per hour (including fringes) the advantages of locating in an IFZ usually outweigh the risks from the nation's ongoing political and social turmoil. Exports from the free zones total approximately US$850 million per year.

Nonfree Trade Zone
Foreign Investment and Trade

Outside the IFZs, business conditions are not as attractive. The nation's top corporate tax rate of 46 percent is one of the highest in the region. Foreign branches also pay a top rate of 46 percent, plus a 20 percent remittance tax.

Economically, the Dominican Republic has suffered from a combination of the U.S. and European recessions and internal political strife between the Reformist Party, the Dominican Revolutionary Party, and the Dominican Labor party, all of which hold commanding positions in the government. The nation's annual growth rate continues to be one of the lowest in the Caribbean islands. Its inflation rate, hovering between 40 and 50 percent, is one of the highest. And its per capita income of only US$950 ranks near the bottom. Unemployment at 30 percent hurts what could be a sizable domestic consumer market.

The DR suffers from an external debt burden of more than US$4 billion, a very high figure for a country this size, and the country is in arrears on interest as well as principal.

Primary exports from the Dominican Republic include sugar and sugar by-products, ferronickel, gold, silver, coffee, cocoa and cocoa by-products, and bauxite. Total annual exports range upward of US$1 billion, excluding those from IFZs.

The Dominican government has targeted four sectors of the economy for active promotion of foreign investment and trade: agriculture, mining, tourism, and free zones. High inflation rates and government price controls keep agricultural exports from being competitive in international markets, severely restricting the development of this sector.

The mining sector hasn't done much better, achieving a mere 0.2 percent growth in 1989. Progress in 1990 and 1991 was slightly better, but far from the growth that should be coming from a country rich in minerals.

As in prior years, free-zone business and tourism constitute the nation's major economic growth sectors. Tourism isn't restricted to hotels and resorts. The DR has actively solicited foreign investment in a spread of villa and condominium developments on the nation's north shore. The town of Puerto Plata now has airport facilities capable of handling any size commercial aircraft. Direct flights arrive from New York, Miami, and several European capitals. Government promotions point to 1992 as a banner year for tourism, as the country marks the five hundredth anniversary of the discovery of Hispaniola by Christopher Columbus.

Major imports to the DR consist of processed food, basic foods such as wheat and corn, animal feeds, fuels, industrial raw materials, machinery and equipment of virtually all types (especially power-generating and telecommunications), fabrics, pharmaceuticals, and chemicals. Excluding IFZ imports, the DR brings in about US$1.9 billion per year in foreign goods and services.

The United States remains the DR's major trading partner, although accusations of DR agents bringing child labor in from Haiti could alter this in the short-run.

The Cayman Islands

The Cayman Islands warrant special consideration when planning strategic market expansion in the Caribbean Basin. With zero unemployment and a population of only 26,000, it is the richest island state in the Caribbean. Its per capita GDP of more than US$17,000 approaches that of the United States.

The Caymans achieved such enviable status by being recognized throughout the world as a legitimate tax haven and offshore financial center, with political stability guaranteed by the United Kingdom. Its close proximity to Miami (460 miles south) and its affiliation with Britain have made the Caymans a favorite repository for companies and individuals from the United States, Canada, Europe, and Latin America.

Pragmatically, the Caymans are wide open to foreign investors. Profits and capital are freely repatriated. The island state has no exchange controls. Taxes of any kind are unheard of. And island banking laws provide tight security for foreign deposits and trusts.

Nearly all U.S. Fortune 500 companies have branches in the Caymans. All major international banks, insurance companies, and public accounting firms maintain offices there. Most international fund management firms operate from Grand Cayman.

In addition to attracting international businesses, Grand Cayman has become a major tourist spot for American and European sun lovers. The nation boasts one of the four best diving areas in the world.

Foreign Direct Investment

Space limits a full disclosure of the advantages of using the Cayman Islands either for banking, insurance, or trust needs or as a jumping-off site for other trade and investment in the Caribbean Basin. Briefly, however, here are the island state's pluses and minuses.

On the plus side, the Cayman Islands offer:

- Political stability unmatched in the region
- Security—in terms of physical plant, personnel, and bank deposits
- Confidentiality
- Zero taxes of any kind
- Excellent telecommunications
- No exchange controls
- A very pro-American atmosphere, with English the only language used throughout the islands
- Major insurance, trust, and banking facilities
- A very high standard of living

- Free import of components and equipment
- Outstanding electric power generation and distribution
- Efficient and honest (really!) customs officials
- Modern, developed infrastructure

On the minus side, it must also be said that the Cayman Islands have:

- A small population, with a resultant shortage of labor
- A very high cost of living (by anyone's standards)
- An erratic water supply during the dry season
- No eligibility for USAID, OPIC, CBI, or 936 programs
- A very small internal market

The best industries for direct investment, other than financial services, center on high-value products requiring low-labor content: cosmetics, security devices, small electronics products, research and development centers, computer software development, certain types of data processing, flowers (orchids), hybrid seeds and fruit trees, and seafood.

Seafood offers the highest potential for export growth. The waters around the islands are rich in every conceivable type of seafood, including an abundance of farm-raised turtles. The aquaculture industry has not caught on to any significant extent yet, but most assuredly will be a big winner in the future.

The best exports to the Caymans, in addition to all the supplies and equipment needed in the tourist industry, include: virtually all types of consumer manufactured goods; processed food; beverages; tobacco; petroleum products; a variety of machinery and equipment; vehicles and parts; building materials; and computers, peripherals, and spare parts.

The United States takes about three-fourths of Cayman exports. Another 9 percent goes to Europe, 3 percent to Japan, and 8 percent to other Caribbean nations. The Cayman Islands do not have any unemployment. Everyone who wants to work can find a job.

Because the Cayman Islands depend upon an international reputation as an offshore financial center and tax haven, the government has been extremely careful not to get mixed up in drug trafficking or money-laundering schemes. Although bank security and confidentiality are paramount to its reputation, any transaction suspected of being tainted is immediately opened and disqualified. Severe sentences are imposed on those caught in these nefarious activities.

More than five hundred licensed banks in Georgetown give the capital more banks per capita than any other city in the world. Of the top 50 banks in the world, 43 have staffed offices in Grand Cayman. The Caymans also boast the registration of more than four hundred insurance companies. The latest figures show more than 20,000 registered companies.

Clearly, the stable government, lack of taxes and exchange controls, and bank secrecy laws have provided shelter for forward-thinking companies from around the world—although most are American. Over 80 percent of the more than 500,000 annual visitors to the Cayman Islands come from the United States; many making the trip come to survey and manage their investments.

Virtually anyone from any country may open a bank account in the Caymans upon presentation of a reference letter from a home-country bank. For obvious reasons, however, banks in the Caymans will not accept large cash deposits. Funds may be deposited in U.S. dollars or other currencies by check, bank draft, or wire transfer.

Accounts earn interest at a rate quoted on receipt. With no exchange controls or reporting requirements, funds may be withdrawn at any time. They may also be converted into other currencies and freely moved in and out of the country.

Opening a Business in the Caymans

Cayman law requires that any corporation set up to do business in the Cayman Islands that is not at least 60 percent owned by Caymanians must obtain a license from the Caymanian Protection Board. This procedure is both costly and entirely up to the discretion of the board. Several broad exclusions exist, however. In general, a Cayman corporation need not obtain a license if its purpose is to enter into investments on behalf of a foreign person or company.

Puerto Rico and the U.S. Virgin Islands

Puerto Rico (a U.S. commonwealth) and the U.S. Virgin Islands (a U.S. territory) offer special advantages to American as well as to non-American companies. Citizens of both Puerto Rico and the Virgin Islands are also considered U.S. citizens. Both locations fall under the taxing jurisdiction of the IRS.

Travelers between the United States and Puerto Rico do not have to pass through U.S. customs, but those returning to the United States from the Virgin Islands do. Both send elected representatives to the U.S. Congress who are not entitled to cast votes, except in committee. Both locations fall under the U.S. federal court system and share in the U.S. postal system. Telecommunications are excellent, with direct dialing to and from the United States, Canada, and Europe.

Puerto Rico

With exports and imports totaling more than US$35 billion, Puerto Rico enjoys a volume of foreign trade greater than that of all other Caribbean nations combined and exceeding that of every Western Hemisphere country south of the U.S. mainland except Mexico and Brazil. To outward appearances, the island bears more resemblance to southern Europe than to Latin America. Four-lane superhighways carry thousands of late-model cars. Glass and steel office buildings form the center of clusters of modern shopping centers, new residential communities, and high-technology industries.

In many respects, Puerto Rico is the best-kept secret in the Western Hemisphere.

The modern era began in 1947, when the Puerto Rican legislature passed laws exempting profits made from goods manufactured in Puerto Rico from all island taxation. In addition to tax benefits, the commonwealth offers foreign companies competitive factory leases, labor-training incentives, a very high level of educated, skilled workers and managerial talent, and direct air and ocean shipping lines to U.S. and foreign markets. Since the 1950s, business and financial incentives have attracted millions of dollars of foreign capital under what Puerto Ricans fondly dub "Operation Bootstrap"—one of the most successful development programs in the world.

Initially the island state attracted labor-intensive industries: textiles, apparel, food processing, machinery and components, and paper production. The second phase focused on heavy industry, primarily oil refining and petrochemical operations. The third stage, in the late 1970s and 1980s, shifted to high-tech industries: pharmaceuticals, scientific instruments, electrical appliances, consumer electronics, computers, and medical products.

In 1990, the commonwealth exported US$19.3 billion worth of goods, of which 73 percent were high-tech products. American, European, and Japanese manufacturing operations have given Puerto Rico a distinctly international manufacturing flavor. Manufacturing now accounts for 40 percent of commonwealth GDP—compared to 20 percent in the United States.

Puerto Rico boasts a highly educated, skilled work force and a trained cadre of managerial talent. The average wage rate of US$6.06 compares favorably with US$10.96 in the United States. The country's very favorable tax climate—together with cash grants for employee training, government-paid leasehold improvements, and defrayal of equipment-transportation charges—offer foreign companies an excellent opportunity to penetrate not only Caribbean Basin markets but also those in the United States. As a U.S. commonwealth, Puerto Rico's political stability is assured for generations to come.

The commonwealth now stands ready to enter the fourth phase of its economic development: the stimulation of R & D projects and the continued pursuit of world-class excellence in manufacturing. In addition to hundreds of U.S. companies that find Puerto Rico an excellent Caribbean location, European and Japanese firms have begun to recognize the competitive advantages of commonwealth sites. Over the last four years European companies have invested more than US$500 million in Puerto Rican facilities and Japanese firms, a total of US$80 million. To date, Japanese interest has centered mainly on the tourist industry.

Puerto Rico also serves as the cornerstone of the CBI program. Through the Internal Revenue Service's Section 936 funding program, companies with operations in Puerto Rico use these tax-free funds to set up "twin plants" in qualified CBI countries such as Jamaica, Grenada, or the U.S. Virgin Islands. The program is similar to the Mexican–U.S. maquiladora program. The major difference between the two, however, is that companies can finance expansion with 936 funds at approximately 85 percent of LIBOR (London Interbank Offered Rate).

Projects eligible for 936 funding include new businesses or expansions in manufacturing, information processing, agro-processing, hotels, and tourism projects. This financing is also available for the development of roads, airports, telecommunications, and low-cost housing.

Table 10-2 presents key economic and trade figures for Puerto Rico.

Puerto Rico's principal industries are pharmaceuticals, food processing, electrical/electronic manufacturing, computers and software, scientific instrumentation, and apparel. Table 10-3 lists the commonwealth's major exports.

Table 10-2. Key Puerto Rican Statistics

	Statistics
Population	3.3 million
Size	3,400 square miles
Literacy	89 percent
Labor force	1.1 million
Unemployment rate	16 percent
GDP	US$21.5 billion
Inflation rate	3 percent
Total annual exports	US$19.1 billion
Total annual imports	US$14.6 billion

SOURCE: Puerto Rican Economic Development Administration.

Table 10-3. Puerto Rico's Major Exports*

	US$ billions	US$ millions
Drugs and pharmaceuticals	6.4	
Food products (excluding fish)	2.1	
Chemical products	1.9	
Electrical machinery	1.9	
Electronics/computers	1.8	
Professional and scientific instruments	1.2	
Apparel and textiles		797.9
Petroleum refining products		645.0
Fish processing		573.7
Leather and leather products		268.1

*As of 1990.

U.S. Virgin Islands

The U.S. Virgin Islands of St. Croix, St. John, and St. Thomas, commonly referred to as USVI, are located 40 miles east of Puerto Rico. With a population of only 110,00 spread between the three islands, the USVI depends upon Puerto Rico for much of its trade. Hourly commuter flights carry business people to and from Puerto Rico and between St. Thomas and St. Croix (40 miles to the south).

Rather than use free trade zones to attract foreign investment, the USVI government set up a series of tax and tariff incentives comprised of: a 90 percent exemption from local corporate income tax; a 1 percent customs duty rate for imported raw materials and component parts; and a 100 percent excise tax exemption for raw materials, component parts, machinery, and equipment.

On shipments to the United States, the Virgin Islands also enjoys unique duty-free advantages not shared by CBI nations or Puerto Rico. Any CBI-eligible product may be imported into the United States from the USVI free of duty—even if more than 70 percent of its value consists of foreign-dutiable components. Noneligible CBI products may be imported duty free from the USVI, provided that no more than 50 percent of the value consists of foreign dutiable components. In other words, products like leather goods and textiles, which are excluded from CBI privileges, may be imported duty free from the Virgin Islands.

In addition, a USVI producer may import a CBI country's eligible duty-free product containing more than 50 percent dutiable foreign materials, combine it with other non-CBI materials or components, and ship the finished product duty free to the United States, even though it may contain 80 percent dutiable materials.

Under the IRS Code's Section 936 program, American companies do not pay U.S. income taxes on dividends received from a USVI subsidiary. Tax exemptions and subsidies offered for from ten to fifteen years may be summarized as:

- 90 percent exemption from local corporate income tax

- 90 percent exemption from income taxes paid by resident stockholders on dividends received from the business

- 1 percent customs duty rate on raw materials and components (the standard rate is 6 percent ad valorum)

- 100 percent excise tax exemption for raw materials and components for processing and assembling goods or commodities

- 100 percent excise tax exemption for building materials, machinery, equipment, and supplies utilized in the construction, alteration, reconstruction, or expansion of physical plant or facilities

- 100 percent exemption from property tax and gross receipts tax

- Withholding tax reduction from 10 to 4 percent, with an additional 2 percent for reinvestment of at least one-half of otherwise repatriated dividends in eligible activities for at least five years

In addition, the USVI encourages very small manufacturers to produce tourist-targeted gifts, crafts, and other products with a variety of incentives and subsidies.

The USVI also qualifies under the General System of Preferences (GSP) from several countries—such as Japan and Canada—and may ship selected products duty free.

The USVI qualifies as a foreign country for American companies wishing to set up a Foreign Sales Corporation to achieve tax savings on export income. Every major FSC management firm has offices in the USVI, mostly on the island of St. Croix.

Somewhat surprisingly, non-U.S. companies have not taken advantage of the USVI location as much as American firms. Nearly all the incentives and benefits enacted by the USVI government apply to non-U.S. as well as to U.S. companies. Immediate access to the CBI program, 936 funds, and virtually all the U.S. aid and assistance programs offer unique export and investment opportunities not found elsewhere in the Caribbean—or in Latin America for that matter.

A politically stable government under the jurisdiction of the U.S. Congress, executive branch, and judicial system reduces the risk of foreign investment to near zero. Security protection provided by the U.S. armed forces further reduces the possibility of local or foreign power expropriation. The 1990 move by the U.S. army to protect St. Croix after Hurricane Hugo is a good example of the importance of such security measures.

11
Central America

Tips to Foreign Traders and Investors

1. Make Costa Rica a home base for trade in Central America. It has the most amenities to offer and is a great place to live.

2. Check out possibilities for education-related products in Costa Rica.

3. Be ready to pay off corrupt Guatemalan trade officials.

4. Locate a Guatemalan facility on either coast. STAY AWAY from the northern highlands where guerrilla bands hang out.

5. Don't bother with a local partner in Costa Rica. Conversely, in Guatemala and the rest of Central America, it's a necessity.

6. Use Panamanian offshore banks to shelter profits from international trade throughout Latin America.

7. Embassy offices in Washington

Costa Rica: (202) 234-2945
Guatemala: (202) 745-4952
Panama: (202) 483-1407

The Central American Common Market (CACM) consists of Costa Rica, El Salvador, Guatemala, Honduras, and Nicaragua. It was originally conceived in 1961 but disintegrated after minor conflicts between El Salvador and Honduras in the mid-1970s. The only segment of the agreement that remained functional was the Central American Bank for Economic Integration (CABEI), a variation of a common market/development bank.

During 1990–1991, member countries agreed to rejuvenate CACM as a means of participating in the current round of newly forming regional trading blocs. Many protectionist features of the original CACM have been eliminated and replaced by more cooperative measures. By the end of 1990, 95 percent of all tariffs between the member countries had disappeared.

Although it appears reasonable to expect the CACM to play a role in the development of free trade in the region, to date the highest marks for improved trade and investment climate must go to individual countries. One of the most progressive has been Costa Rica.

Costa Rica

Of all Central American countries, Costa Rica has enjoyed the longest tenure of economic growth and political tranquillity. It is often referred to as the "Switzerland of the Americas," maintaining the political structure and constitution adopted more than forty years ago.

A 95 percent literacy rate substantiates the importance placed on education. A common phrase used by Costa Ricans is, "Our teachers are our army. Our arms are our books." The absence of a standing army since 1949 testifies to the country's obsession with political tranquillity. More than 20,000 American retirees now call Costa Rica their home.

Costa Rica operates under the same three-tiered balance-of-power government as the United States, with an elected president presiding over the executive branch, an elected congress comprising the legislative branch, and appointed judges serving in the judicial branch.

With political stability and a highly educated work force, it's not surprising that many American, European, and Asian companies operate profitable facilities in the country. A good example is the U.S. electronics firm Conair Corporation, which recently shifted its US$10 million Costa Rican operation from simple assembly to more sophisticated operations, utilizing the range of workers' skill more fully. The company now builds its hair dryers from scratch in Costa Rica instead of importing parts for assembly. Another example is Motorola's Costa Rican operation, which recently won worldwide recognition for employee excellence.

Wages are higher in Costa Rica than in other Latin countries. The minimum wage rate, including fringe benefits, stands at US$1.07; higher than the US$0.56 per hour paid in the Dominican Republic and US$0.47 in neighboring Honduras, but substantially less than that paid for comparable work in the United States. Table 11-1 shows Costa Rica's key economic and trade statistics.

Costa Rica's major trading partners are the United States, Japan, Venezuela, Mexico, and Germany—in that order. Its principal exports include: bananas, coffee, plants and flowers, apparel, meat and fish, electronics, and pharmaceuticals. The country's major imports consist of equipment and machinery of various types, petroleum, and a wide range of industrial and consumer products.

In addition to labor advantages and political stability, Costa Rica attracts

Table 11-1.   Key Costa Rican Statistics*

	Statistics	
Population	3.0	million
Labor force	1.2	million
Unemployment rate	5.0	percent
Inflation rate	27.3	percent
Economic activity		
Industry	22.0	percent
Agriculture	19.0	percent
Commerce	17.0	percent
Total annual exports	US$1.45	billion
Total annual imports	US$2.00	billion
Foreign debt	US$9.50	billion

*As of 1989–1991.
SOURCE: Costa Rican Ministry of Trade.

many foreign companies to its active free zones. Approximately 130 foreign companies have located facilities in these zones, producing primarily electronics products and pharmaceuticals, and employing about 11,000 workers. The country offers seven privately owned free zones stretching from the Pacific to the Caribbean Sea.

Free zones offer investors: 100 percent exemptions from import duties and export taxes; independent profit and foreign exchange handling; 100 percent exemption from municipal and capital taxes for ten years; and 100 percent exemption from income taxes for twelve years, with a 50 percent exemption for a subsequent six years.

Foreign companies locating in free zones outside the capital of San José get even more benefits, including a 15 percent new-job bonus for the first five years, dropping by 2 points yearly thereafter. Rents vary by industrial park but average about US$3.25 per square foot.

Tourism is also catching on rapidly. The government hopes to make the tourism industry its largest foreign exchange earner. Costa Rica has a larger percentage of its land in national parks than any country in the Western Hemisphere, and its emphasis on ecotourism in 23 national parks is beginning to pay off.

Ex-president and Nobel Peace Prize–winner Oscar Arias is adamant about the necessity of Central America joining in the North American Free Trade Agreement between the United States, Mexico, and Canada. As he stated during his address at the University of Colorado in October 1991, Mr. Arias does not believe it practical for each Central American country to seek admittance individually. Instead, he urges that they petition for entrance as a group, perhaps through the CACM, but including Panama.

Since more than half of Costa Rica's trade is already transacted within North America, and all of Central America already qualifies under the CBI program, it appears that the region's inclusion in NAFTA is a foregone conclusion. When that occurs, foreign companies already located in Costa Rica will enjoy a significant trade advantage, not only in the Caribbean Basin, but in the rest of North America as well.

The Costa Rican trade commission is quick to point out the advantages to foreign firms of making direct investments in the country. (Most of these claims are very accurate—in contrast to similar claims by other Latin countries.) The Costa Rican advantages include:

- Peaceful democracy without military power
- A high literacy rate of 95 percent
- A well-educated work force
- An impeccably moderate climate
- A pleasant living environment
- No racial or religious problems
- An excellent telecommunications network
- Abundant water supplies and hydroelectric power
- Duty-free access to the United States under the CBI program

Guatemala

Guatemala is the largest country in the Caribbean Basin, with a population of 9.1 million and a GDP of US$7.5 billion. Its growth rate at 3 percent may not be spectacular, but for a country with a 43 percent unemployment rate such growth appears close to miraculous. The agriculture sector, accounting for 26 percent of GDP, employs about 60 percent of the country's population and generates nearly 75 percent of its exports.

Over the long term, the outlook for Guatemala's economy remains fairly optimistic. Significant economic reforms, especially in the areas of foreign exchange and interest-rate determination were enacted in 1990 in an attempt to make the economy more resilient and internationally competitive.

In contrast to other Latin countries, Guatemala's private sector dominates the economy, accounting for 90 percent of GDP. The government's participation in the productive process is limited to public utilities, a handful of development-oriented financial institutions, and a range of regulatory activities.

The nation's nine million people are divided into two distinct segments. *Ladinos* are those who, regardless of race or national heritage, have adopted Westernized customs. *Indigenas*, descendants of the Maya, are those who retain their distinctive vestments and preserve their own values and traditions. Most indigenas (42 percent of the population) live in rural areas and are excluded from the work force.

The nation's literacy rate is very poor by Latin standards. In rural areas it reaches a mere 28 percent, while in the cities it hits 72 percent.

Guatemala faces some very serious political and social issues that must be addressed quickly to meet the government's proclaimed objective of bringing the country into the international trade arena.

Aside from horrendously high illiteracy, the nation has three extremely serious problems:

1. A long-term insurgency by guerrilla bands operating as *banditos* from rural camps and preying on civilians

2. An abusive, violent, and often out-of-control military, seemingly intent on murder as a way of life

3. Severe environmental degradation, affecting forests, land, and water—as well as the population of Guatemala City, where the air is unbreathable.

In addition, the country's infrastructure in many areas has collapsed.

Although Guatemala does have a relatively sophisticated business class and a reasonably large pool of semiskilled and skilled labor, the nation's political and social problems tend to overwhelm any progress in governmental economic reforms. Foreign companies interested in Guatemala as a facility site should bear in mind that many political and social changes must take place before the country can be considered a viable, long-term prospect for foreign trade.

On the foreign trade front, exports hit US$1.6 billion in 1991, an increase of US$400 million over the previous year. Imports increased by the same amount to US$2.0 billion. Table 11-2 shows the breakdown by trading partner.

Table 11-2. Guatemalan Trading Partners*

	Exports in US$ millions	Imports in US$ millions
United States	387	605
Germany	86	102
Japan	27	102
Mexico	—	101
Italy	33	—
Netherlands	21	—
Saudi Arabia	20	—
Central America		
El Salvador	132	88
Costa Rica	71	55
Honduras	37	—
Venezuela	—	124
Others	386	423
Total	1,200	1,600

*As of 1990.
SOURCE: Banguat, Investors Service Center.

Guatemala's principal exports include: green coffee, sugar, bananas, cardamom, meat, raw cotton, petroleum, and light manufactured products.
On the import side, highest demand will be found in:

Fuels and lubricants

Building materials

Medical supplies and equipment

Air pollution control devices

Air conditioning and
refrigeration equipment

Agricultural machinery
and equipment

Agricultural chemicals

Computers, peripherals,
and software

Construction equipment

Food processing and
packaging equipment

Hotel and restaurant
products, and equipment

Machine tools and metal-
working machinery

Material handling equipment

Plastic materials, resins,
and production machinery

Printing and graphic arts
products and machinery

Process controls

Railroad equipment

Telecommunications equipment
and technology

Trucks, trailers, buses,
and parts

Automobiles and parts

Yarns

Panama

For years Panama has been famous (or infamous) for: the Panama Canal, managed by the United States; drug trafficking and political corruption controlled by Manuel Noriega; and banking secrecy. Under an agreement reached with then U.S. President Jimmy Carter, the Panamanian government will assume responsibility for managing the canal before this decade ends. Noriega rests comfortably behind bars, observing the parade of witnesses and lawyers at his trial. That leaves banking secrecy and the legacy of government mismanagement as the two overriding issues facing the current government of President Guillermo Endara.

As a tax haven and offshore financial center, Panama offers many advantages to foreign companies looking for banking confidentiality, tax-free status, and a strategically located site for trade with South America, the Caribbean Basin, and East Asia.

Despite the havoc wrought by General Noriega on Panama's international reputation as a reputable offshore financial center, nothing has really changed. Panama is still a U.S.–dollar country protected by bank secrecy laws. It is still free of any exchange controls. There is no income tax or corporation tax on foreign-source income.

Corporate profits fall into one of three categories, each handled differently for tax purposes:

1. Panamanian source income—taxed at rates ranging from 20 to 50 percent.
2. Export income for a free-zone company—taxed at rates from 2.5 to 8.5 percent.
3. Non-Panamanian source income—no income tax. Non-Panamanian, or foreign source, income includes: the invoicing of exported products from abroad; directing transactions abroad; distributing dividends abroad; and receiving interest, commissions, or fees from financial operations conducted abroad.

The advantages to corporate executives in using tax-haven bank accounts for their personal investments are obvious.

The Endara government is desperately trying to interest foreign companies in investing in Panama. A lengthy list of industrial incentives, investment incentives, and tourism incentives have been enacted, including exemption from all import and export duties, exemption from most income taxes, free repatriation of profits, open foreign exchange, and the beginnings of a stock market in Balboa.

Most foreign companies elect to set up facilities in the Colon Free Trade Zone, located at the Atlantic mouth of the Panama Canal. Currently, more that 1400 foreign businesses use Colon free-zone services for importing, warehousing, assembling, repacking, and reexporting a vast array of products. The range of products is wide, including electronic apparatus, pharmaceutical products, liquors, tobacco, furniture, clothing, shoes, and jewelry.

The Colon free zone is advertised as the "shop window" for South and Central America and has modern facilities in which companies may display their wares. In 1990, U.S. companies imported US$2.7 billion worth of goods to Colon and exported US$3.1 billion. Foreign companies also use Colon to supply products to other free zones in Latin America, such as San Andros in Colombia and Margarita Island in Venezuela. They also ship products direct to Caribbean Basin commercial centers, such as Aruba.

Outside the free zone, Panama's major exports are sugar, bananas, shrimp and sea products, coffee, apparel, and a small amount of petroleum products. About 45 percent of Panama's exports go to the United States; about 21 percent go to other Caribbean Basin countries; 28 percent go to Europe; and the balance is spread evenly among Mexico, South America, and Asia.

The country's main imports consist of food products, medical supplies and equipment, and fuel. The United States supplies about 40 percent; the Caribbean Basin, 23 percent; Mexico, 10 percent; Europe, 11 percent; and South American countries, 14 percent.

The looting that took place after the U.S. invasion in 1989 left store shelves bare of consumer goods. Although conditions have improved somewhat,

Panamanian residents still thirst for virtually every conceivable consumer product. The domestic market may not be flush with cash, but there can be little doubt that demand is extraordinary.

The country's infrastructure, such as it was, was also severely damaged by the U.S. invasion. President Endara is still looking for foreign investment to rebuild practically the entire infrastructure, not only in Panama City, but in the countryside as well. Japanese, Taiwanese, and South Korean companies are already hard at work building new shopping centers and development projects. Still, there is plenty of room for others.

PART 2

Europe, Africa, and the Middle East

12
Western Europe

Tips to Foreign Traders and Investors

1. Open a subsidiary or joint venture in Europe now to get a foothold in what will soon become Fortress Europe, where trade and direct investment will be difficult and costly for outsiders.

2. Keep a sharp eye on opportunities for trading military products and supplies when Europe rearms a unified military machine: negotiations have already begun.

3. Don't expect the advertised EC "single market" to be free from snarls: there will be plenty.

4. Use a European location as a jumping-off point to African, Soviet, Middle East, or South Asian markets.

5. Embassy offices in Washington

Belgium: (202) 333-6900
Denmark: (202) 234-4300
Finland: (202) 363-2430
France: (202) 944-6000
Germany: (202) 298-4000
Great Britain: (202) 462-1340
Greece: (202) 667-3168
Iceland: (202) 265-6653
Ireland: (202) 462-3939
Italy: (202) 328-5500
Luxembourg: (202) 265-4171

Netherlands: (202) 244-5300
Norway: (202) 333-6000
Portugal: (202) 234-3800
Spain: (202) 265-0190
Sweden: (202) 944-5600
Switzerland: (202) 745-7900
Turkey: (202) 387-3200

Led by the twelve-member European Community (EC)—Great Britain, Belgium, Luxembourg, the Netherlands, France, Germany, Italy, Greece, Denmark, Spain, Portugal, and Ireland—Western Europe continues its struggle to enter the twenty-first century as an economic power bloc. Although EC leaders decry the designation "Fortress Europe," fears of competition from giant American and Japanese corporations point to a very real possibility of there being future external trade barriers more severe than those in existence prior to the implementation of "Europe 1992." In fact, pressure within the EC is increasing to extract the most rigid barriers from each member and apply them en masse to trade with non-EC members.

In October 1991, agreement was reached by representatives of 19 European countries meeting in Luxembourg to form an even larger, more powerful economic bloc than the framers of the European Community envisioned.

All twelve EC members, plus the seven-member European Free Trade Association, frequently called EFTA (Iceland, Norway, Sweden, Liechtenstein, Austria, Finland, and Switzerland) reached an accord to link the two trade blocs in a European Economic Area (EEA). Only Turkey and the Eastern European countries are not included.

Under the agreement, the EEA, with a combined population of 374 million and 40 percent of world trade, would permit most goods to flow freely among all 19 members. Individuals could live, work, and offer services throughout the bloc. Capital movement will be liberalized. Scheduled to be implemented in 1993, the EEA will have a joint ministerial council and a court to settle disputes (however, the EC court objects to such sharing). Under the agreement, all EFTA member nations will adopt EC rules on company law, consumer protection, social policy, research and development, and environmental protection.

Only the first step has been reached in the formation of the EEA, however. Each member country must officially sign the agreement and achieve ratification by national parliaments—no easy task for nations such as Norway and Switzerland. This could prove a long, drawn-out process and 1993 is probably merely a dream at this stage. After all, the EC has been trying to reach agreement on common market rules since 1958. Members are still debating free trade provisions that are theoretically to be implemented in December 1992. In addition, the "no" vote from Danish citizens threw a clinker into unification plans adopted with the Maastricht Treaty.

Nevertheless, the political and economic clout resulting from a unified European trading bloc casts an ominous shadow for foreign traders.

The EEA agreement will likely increase the number of countries seeking admittance to the European Community, which is moving toward social as well as economic integration. Non-EC European countries have already lined up for admittance. Varying degrees of pressure from Sweden, Norway, Finland, Iceland, Switzerland, Austria, and Turkey to join the club will result in an even broader, more powerful trading bloc than Europe 1992—one that can be construed as an interim step to a full European common market.

As the Eastern European countries achieve free market status, their addition to the EC will round out the balance of Europe. Poland, the CSFR, and Hungary have already lined up. However, a split between Czech and Slovak republics could delay their entrance.

A Changing Role in World Trade

The enthusiasm for "Europe 1992" by member and nonmember countries alike bids fair warning to Western Hemisphere and Asia-Pacific companies that, notwithstanding GATT, the rules of global trade are due for major revision before this decade ends.

The precise nature of final EC tariffs, quotas, and other protective measures won't be known until after "E-day" (December 31, 1992). The general nature of trade with Europe is already evident, however, from the recent conflicts during the Uruguay round of GATT negotiations. Although disagreements between the EC and the United States over agricultural subsidies received the greatest press, other protective measures, such as the quotas placed on European production and sales of Japanese automobiles, have also surfaced.

Non-European companies have been scurrying for several years to solidify their position on the continent. European subsidiaries have been formed, joint ventures and other strategic alliances with European companies have been negotiated, and franchising agreements have been enacted.

American firms especially have begun reshaping internal operating policies to gain a perceived competitive edge in European markets. Giants like Bendix and 3M, along with smaller firms like RQV Products and East Coast Automation, have honed their quality procedures to meet Japanese standards. Dupont, Dow, Rohm and Haas, Toby Lane, and Clamox have embarked on studies to define the cultural differences in variant European markets necessary to modify product, packaging, advertising, customer service activities, and quality standards.

In 1958, the Treaty of Rome guaranteed freedom of movement for goods, services, capital and people for European companies and European citizens. To foster competitiveness in international trade, the EC has attempted to create a business environment that supports internal competition and encourages international trade. Thirty-four years later, many important issues remain unresolved.

One of the initial objectives of the EC was to implement uniform standards and regulations for all members. Presumably this would allow products that were manufactured to standards in one country to be marketable in all.

Objections from several corners now makes common standards—other than those affecting health, safety, and environment—an unworkable goal. Replacing national product standards with a set of Euro-norms would be a herculean task. Germany alone has more than 20,000 standards, France 8,000, and Britain 12,000.

A common market might eliminate cross-border tariffs and quotas but not cultural differences and technical variations in standards, such as building codes. To compensate, the EC is using the principle of "mutual recognition": standards developed in one European country would be accepted in another providing they meet basic uniform health and safety requirements. This means that global traders must continue to modify products to variant cultural tastes for each destination country.

Cross-Border Trade and Investment Legislation

In addition to the issue of standards, the EC has enacted or plans to enact legislation in three important areas affecting cross-border trade and investment.

1. Company Law.   In July 1989, the EC created the European Economic Interest Grouping (EEIG), a legal framework for companies from different countries to engage in cooperative cross-border trading within the EC by forming semipermanent joint ventures or subsidiaries.

EEIGs affect mostly small and midsize companies by allowing them to cohabitate within a legal framework while retaining their legal and economic independence. An EEIG is not a separate company. It consists of two or more companies from different countries joining resources, capabilities, and activities to further the goals of all participants. Profits are distributed periodically to all participants, none of which can have more than five hundred employees.

2. Mergers/Acquisitions.   The intent of these regulations is to protect EC companies, creditors, and employees in the event of a merger or acquisition. If a firm buys more than one-third of the shares of another firm, a proposal currently on the table would mandate the acquisition of all the shares. The acquirer must also notify target company employees of its intention to take over, the fate of the work force, and the amount of overall debt to be incurred. This "workers' rights" law enables target employees to block proposed mergers or acquisitions.

For larger takeovers, an EC directorate must review and approve or disapprove cross-border mergers or new-company startups with annual sales greater than US$1 billion.

The "EuroCompany" law, also on the drawing boards, permits joint ventures, acquisitions, mergers, and joint subsidiaries to be formed as a European Company with minimum capital of 100,000 ecus. EuroCompanies would have special tax credits, labor regulations, worker participation in corporate affairs, and protection of workers' rights in the event of closings or changes in overall corporate policies.

3. Unified Financial Markets. The European Monetary System (EMU), which created the European currency unit (ecu) as a common currency, went into effect in 1979. Much hoopla advertised that finally Europe could present a single currency in foreign exchange markets.

One consequence has been the liberalization of capital markets to permit cross-border issuance or purchase of bonds, securities, and other capital instruments. To reach unanimous agreement on the EMU, the European Commission grants "special exemptions" from time to time, permitting member nations to install temporary or sectoral controls. These exemptions are gradually being phased out over a transition period. Germany and the United Kingdom have abolished controls altogether.

Uniform accounting regulations for transnational banks have been established. The Second Banking Directive permits banks incorporated in one EC country to trade in all other EC countries. It also provides a minimum capitalization of 5 million ecus, supervision of principal bank shareholders, and a limit on their holdings of nonbank undertakings. Minimum standards for cross-border mortgages have also been established.

A series of directives affecting cross-border insurance companies including the winding down of activities, reinsurance, and single markets for life and automobile insurance—have been proposed: many have yet to be implemented.

Reciprocity between EC and non-EC banks remains a major unresolved issue—one that generated heated debate during the Uruguay Round of GATT negotiations. The EC finally agreed that non-EC banks established in an EC country could have access to the same European markets as EC banks—with one major proviso. EC banks must be allowed the same privileges in the non-EC bank's country of origin. To date, the United States, Japan, and other non-EC countries have not agreed to such reciprocity.

Hurdles for Foreign Traders

To the extent that trade or foreign direct investment in Europe looks strategically viable, companies must overcome six existing or proposed hurdles:

1. *Import quotas and tariffs.* Stringent import quotas and usurious tariffs remain in force in several European countries. The "harmonization" of the

most restrictive of these barriers for the entire EC could easily create a near-impenetrable Fortress Europe.

2. *Trade reciprocity.*   Unresolved subsidy and other issues during the Uruguay Round of the GATT negotiations leaves a high degree of uncertainty surrounding a variety of industries. Agriculture has received the most publicity, but others, including automobiles, steel, and electronics, are also affected.

3. *Local content.*   Many European countries currently require that foreign-owned local firms design products with a minimum amount of local labor, materials, or components.

4. *Company law.*   New, strict antitrust laws are on the drawing board in many countries and the EC itself. "Workers' rights" laws in Germany and other countries severely limit management flexibility.

5. *Tax ramifications.*   Several countries are currently considering changes in tax laws. Major anticipated changes in German capital gains regulations have stimulated small and midsize local companies to seek foreign parents. Table 12-1 lists 1991 tax rates.

6. *Standards and regulations.*   The original dream of uniform standards to permit single manufacturing facilities and quality standards for all EC countries remains unfulfilled. The "single-source, single-market" concept will not be realized in the foreseeable future.

Table 12-1.   Maximum Tax Rates*

	Percentages		
	Corporate income	Capital gains	Branch
Britain	35	35	35
Belgium	39	19.5	43
Denmark	40	40	40
Finland	23	23	23
France	34	19–25	34
Germany	50	50	46
Greece	46	46	46
Iceland	50	50	50
Ireland	43	30–50	43
Italy	36	36	36
Luxembourg	33	33	33
Netherlands	35	35	35
Norway	50.8	50.8	50.8
Portugal	36.5	36.5	36.5†
Spain	35	35	35
Sweden	30	30	30
Switzerland	10–27	0	10–27
Turkey	46	46	46

*† Municipal surcharge.
SOURCE: Ernst & Young.

On the Bright Side

Almost without exception, every country in Western Europe imports a large number of high-tech products (even Germany, with its substantial technical base). Although a wide range of high-tech products are needed, especially in Spain, Portugal, Greece, and Turkey, the hottest products for export to Europe are computer hardware and software and medical diagnostic and treatment equipment and supplies.

International database developer, Intellibanc Corporation of Torrance, California, identifies ten of the best world markets for both computer and medical technology exports. On the computer side, Sweden ranks fourth, Germany fifth, Finland sixth, the Netherlands seventh, and Switzerland ninth. For medical technology and supplies, Intellibanc ranks the United Kingdom first, followed by Germany second, Italy fourth, Switzerland fifth, and France seventh.

Imports of high-tech products by Portugal, Spain, Greece, and Turkey run the gamut from artificial respirators to computer-based production systems. Although in many instances a direct investment brings greater returns, smaller high-tech companies find that exporting is an easier and quicker method for penetrating European markets—at least for the present.

A Bursting Bubble?

The original concept of European political and monetary union seemed an ideal antidote to what some analysts referred to as "Euro-sclerosis." This nasty disease produces symptoms of low investment levels and rapidly rising labor costs. Many blamed the disease for the noncompetitiveness of European firms in such world markets as electronics and automobiles.

Today, Europe's business leaders are rapidly becoming disenchanted with the promises of "Europe 1992." Originally they had assumed that a Fortress Europe would create vast public and private European funds for megaprojects in research and development and infrastructure upgrading. Companies within the fortress would be able to combine resources and talent to meet the demands of European consumers and to compete in world markets. No one dreamed that EC openness would be extended to outside competition—especially to Americans.

To combat the Fords and the IBMs of the world, European firms have formed megacompanies through a flood of cross-border strategic alliances. FIAT of Italy joined France's Alcatel-Alsthom; Carnaud (France) and Metal Box (Britain) merged to form CMB packaging; Siemens (Germany) and GEC (Britain) jointly acquired Plessey.

Not to be outdone, American firms entered the joint venture fray. Eastman Kodak joined with Amersham International (Britain) to produce reagents; General Mills plans an alliance with Nestle to produce cereal for European consumers; IBM joined with Siemens in a telecommunications venture;

Cadence Design Systems (San José, California) and European Silicon Structures (London) will jointly develop software for electronics design systems; Turner International Industries plans to launch a venture with Turner Steiner (Brussels); Boston's Downer & Co. and 3i Corp. (London) will provide merger and acquisition services. The list is endless.

The easy part—the wheeling and dealing, the strategic alliances, the strategic plans—has been going on for several years. Soon government subsidized, protected, and in many cases grossly inefficient European companies will be thrown to the wolves of international competition. The chaos created by American deregulation of many industries during the 1980s looks mild compared to that facing European companies after 1992.

Intense pressure from business leaders is already mounting for government intervention to support Europe's agriculture, electronics, automobile, and aircraft manufacturing industries. The bulk of the intervention should come from public sector procurement orders, just as the American defense industry was supported by Department of Defense spending for more than twelve years.

Free trade sounds wonderful at cocktail parties; it becomes a deadening, and deadly, exercise when thrust upon unprepared private enterprise. The Europe 1992 bubble has indeed burst and massive changes can be expected in planned implementation of trading policies both before and after December 31, 1992.

To be sure, certain areas have already been notably improved. Most customs controls were shelved during 1991. Companies can ship anywhere in the EC with a minimum of customs delay and cost. Freight costs should be reduced by 10 to 15 percent when restrictions on *cabotage*—the right of foreign haulers to pick up and deliver goods within another country's boundaries—is abolished. Only Portugal, Greece, and Ireland still have foreign exchange controls in place.

Table 12-2.   Value-Added Tax Rates*

	Percentages	
	Standard	Luxury/higher
Ireland	23.0	
Denmark	22.0	
Italy	19.0	38.0
Belgium	19.0	25.0†
France	18.6	22.0
Netherlands	18.5	
Greece	18.0	36.0
Britain	17.5	
Portugal	17.0	30.0
Germany	14.0	
Spain	12.0	33.0
Luxembourg	12.0	

*As of March 1991.
† Plus 8 percent on selected goods.
SOURCE: UK Treasury; *The Economist*.

Table 12-3. Governmental Industrial Subsidies

	Annual average (billion ecus)	Per employee (000 ecus)
Italy	9.6	3.1
Germany	7.8	1.2
France	5.8	1.5
Britain	3.9	0.8
Spain	3.0	1.5
The Netherlands	1.0	1.4
Belgium	1.0	1.6
Greece	1.0	3.5
Portugal	0.5	0.7
Ireland	0.4	2.5
Denmark	0.2	0.7
Luxembourg	0.1	0.9

SOURCE: European Commission.

But such matters as gross inequities in the value added tax (VAT) (see Table 12-2), the policies affecting public procurement of goods and services, and the lack of a unified currency system leave much to be desired. Wide variations in industrial subsidies also rankle nonbeneficiaries.

For example, in spite of an enormous budget deficit, the Italian government spends an average of 9.6 billion ecus each year on industrial aid. That's an average per employee of 3136 ecus. Table 12-3 shows industrial subsidies from 1986 to 1988 as compiled by the European Commission.

Red Flag

In addition to the host of potential economic calamities on the horizon as the Western European business community scurries to comply with ill-defined rules established by EC bureaucrats, a sticky political issue has arisen. Faced with world criticism of the European Community's lack of participation in the Persian Gulf war, the EC's inept influence on Yugoslavia's disruptive civil war, and the withdrawal of most United States armed forces from Germany, a unified proposal by France and Germany has raised the globally unwelcome specter of a unified European military force.

The two countries proposed a 50,000-person force that they hope will be a precursor of a European army. Britain called the plan "useless and a threat to NATO." Many people throughout the world shudder at the thought of rearming a powerful and aggressive Germany, but at some point in the not-too-distant future, the world will have to face up to the inevitability of Europe defending itself.

The effect of such a military might on the economic stability of the region remains unclear. Defense contractors the world over, however, are already developing strategies to exploit the move.

Economic Convergence

Other major unresolved issues pose obstacles to the implementation of "Europe 1992." Two of the more serious problems are:

1. What to do about a common currency
2. How to further the development of the European Monetary System (EMU)

Little disagreement exists within the European Commission or elsewhere that the success of a unified financial system depends to a large extent on the economic convergence of member countries.

By economic convergence, the commission means that macroeconomic factors experienced by each member nation should be similar and within a narrow range of one another, so that if and when government intervention is needed—to stabilize a currency or to match competitive exchange rates—it will not disrupt the internal economic flow of the country.

Currently, EC member countries show a wide divergence, and EC leaders must somehow resolve how much divergence (or convergence) is acceptable and how many countries must meet the test to enact economic and monetary union policies.

Take inflation: a recent Dutch government proposal suggested that countries have reached acceptable convergence if their inflation and interest rates are within 1 to 2 percent of the rates of the lowest EC member.

The original seven countries that agreed to the exchange rate mechanism of a 2.25 percent band (Belgium, Denmark, France, Germany, the Netherlands, Ireland, and Luxembourg) generally meet the test. Current consumer price inflation ranges from a low of 2.1 percent in Denmark to 4.6 percent in the Netherlands.

Although Britain's inflation rate may fall below 4 percent, it would have to remain there for a couple of years to qualify. Italy and Spain at 6 percent do not qualify. Greece and Portugal are experiencing double digit inflation rates of 18 percent and 12 percent respectively.

Short-term (three-month) interest rates fall into a similarly wide band. Except for Italy and Spain (approximately 12 percent), Portugal at 13 percent and Greece at nearly 25 percent, other countries fall within Germany's low of 9.2 percent and Britain's high of 10.3 percent.

Budget deficits as a percentage of a country's GDP have actually been diverging for the last couple of years. The Dutch propose that this ratio should be less than 4 percent of GDP and public debt to GDP ratios no more than 60 percent of GDP (the current EC average). But Belgium, Germany, the Netherlands, Italy, Greece, and Portugal all have deficits greater than 4 percent of GDP. Ireland's public debt amounts to 113 percent of GDP and Italy is saddled with 110 percent.

Only three countries—Denmark, Luxembourg, and France—meet all three convergence measures.

Whether or not EC members will achieve acceptable convergence by the end of 1992 is open to question. Unacceptable convergence leaves the management of exchange rates and other facets of the EMS also up in the air.

The inclusion of EFTA countries in the EC either before January 1, 1993, or later brings additional confusion to the table.

From the perspective of a monetary union, community acceptance of applications from Eastern European nations could create an entirely new financial paradigm for EC planners to contemplate.

In any event, global trading waits for no country. Trade and investment move forward with or without European economic and monetary union. The question of convergence merely exacerbates already foggy strategies for non-EC companies.

Tentative agreement has been reached to set the date for Phase III of the economic and monetary union (EMU) when seven or eight countries (the number has yet to be agreed upon) can pass four tests of convergence when:

1. Inflation rates have fallen to the lowest EC level

2. Interest rates have fallen to the lowest EC level

3. Their currencies have a record of stability within the European monetary system

4. Their budget deficits are not excessive ("excessive" has not been defined)

Common Currency

A discussion of alternative methods of financing trade and foreign direct investment in Europe extends far beyond the scope of this book. For those interested in exploring the wide variety of financing options both in Europe and the rest of the world, *The McGraw-Hill Handbook of Global Trade and Investment Financing* provides as comprehensive an analysis as can be found anywhere.

In addition to trade finance and investment funding opportunities, Europe offers the potential for foreign traders to eventually eliminate exchange rate fluctuations, a major concern when developing strategies weighing market and investment alternatives. The EC plans to accomplish this with the introduction of a common European currency with the uncreative label "the European Currency Unit," or ecu.

Framers of the economic and monetary portions of the European Community visualized the eventual abandonment of national currencies in favor of the ecu, both for private and public sector use. The idea behind the ecu dates back to the regional formation of a European Monetary System (EMS). The EMS was to be divided into three phases.

Table 12-4.   World Foreign Currency Reserves

	Percentage of world reserves	
	1976	1990
US dollar	80	51
German D-mark	7	19
Japanese yen	1	9
Other currencies	12	9
Ecu	0	12
Total	100	100

SOURCE: IMF.

Phase I structured the initial arrangement of the EMS and its ground rules. Phase II is to be the formation of a European central bank, fondly referred to as EuroFed. EuroFed will utilize the ecu as the settlement and accounting unit for EC member governments and is scheduled for full implementation in 1994, with the creation of the European Monetary Institute. Phase III includes the full control by EuroFed of the monetary policies of the European Community.

By Phase III, the framers envision the ecu to have replaced all national currencies of EC member nations. No date has been set for this conversion.

The ecu is a weighted basket of the twelve EC currencies and is not legal tender at this time. However, it is playing an increasingly important role in international finance, especially as a replacement for U.S. dollar foreign exchange reserves. (See Table 12-4.)

To become a true international currency, the ecu must perform three functions. It must:

1. Serve as a unit of account for trade invoicing

2. Act as the means of payment for employees, purchased goods, operating expenses, debt service, etc.

3. Become the denomination of the stores of wealth for governments and private investors

To date, it has achieved modest success only in the third area, and then mostly for EC governments.

The U.S. dollar remains the favorite currency for trade invoicing and capital markets. In 1987, 42 percent of industrialized nations invoiced in U.S. dollars (the United States exported 22 percent of the total). The dollar accounts for an even bigger share of imports (50 percent). OPEC nations price oil sales in dollars, and many other nations price commodity exports to industrialized nations in dollars. With the advent of Europe 1992, the EC will be the world's largest exporter and importer, making the ecu more popular than in today's markets.

Caution Alert

Strategies of non-EC exporters and importers should make provision for dealing with the ecu in foreign exchange markets and in trade invoicing. The use of ecus in European capital-raising ventures is a foregone conclusion. It may be several years before full use of the ecu becomes a reality, but that time is inevitably approaching. While international trade experts do not believe the ecu will totally replace the U.S. dollar as a favorite unit of payment, they do believe it will be regarded on a par with the dollar.

Environmental Issues

Members of the European Community generally agree in principle that environmental regulation is better handled by the EC than by national governments. But agreeing to a common regulatory agency in principle is a far cry from accepting and acting on the agency's recommendations. The EC has taken environmental protection seriously, issuing green rules in increasing numbers. Yet member nations have been reticent to comply with European Commission directives.

The commission has no policing authority and can only act on infractions when it receives a complaint. In 1990 the commission received 480 complaints. Procedurally, the commission first asks the offending government for an explanation. An unsatisfactory answer brings a formal warning. After that, the commission issues a "reasoned opinion" that the government is in breach of EC law. As a last resort, the EC can take the offender to the European Court of Justice. An average of fifty months transpires between a formal complaint and a ruling by the court. The effectiveness of such actions is certainly suspect.

Take, for example, the case of a road-building program in northern Spain that is lowering the wetland table. An EC warning came in 1987. The court ruling was expected in early 1992. No one expects Spain to comply—assuming anything is left of the wetlands by that time.

Britain averages 125 complaints a year, not because the country is any dirtier than others, but because Britain harbors active environmental groups. Table 12-5 lists the breaches of EC green laws as compiled by the commission.

More than 75 percent of disciplinary proceedings involve birds, bathing water, drinking water, and "environmental-impact assessments" which governments have to carry out and publicize before approving big construction projects.

To date, EC environmental enforcement has been a joke. Without any teeth, EC laws can be as easily disregarded as complied with. The EC has not yet addressed the very severe industrial pollution evident in Eastern Europe. Automobile emissions are still a national concern as is the entire subject of waste disposal—both toxic and nontoxic. Recycling is not yet an issue.

Table 12-5.   Breaches of European Community Green Rules*

	Warning letters	Reasoned opinions	Court cases	Total
Spain	30	25	11	66
Italy	16	28	9	53
Greece	13	31	6	50
Belgium	3	17	10	30
Germany	1	18	11	30
France	9	13	6	28
Ireland	12	13	3	28
Portugal	8	15	1	24
Britain	12	9	2	23
Netherlands	5	15	2	22
Luxembourg	1	11	2	14
Denmark	2	2	0	4
Total EC	112	197	63	372

*Outstanding cases as of May 1991.
SOURCE: European Commission data.

Caution Alert

Although it is too early to assess the final structure of environmental regulations, it is not too early to begin preparing for constraints similar to those imposed in the United States—at least for laws pertaining to industrial waste and packaging material.

Franchising

Traditionally an American phenomenon, franchising began taking off in Europe during the booming 1980s. Many companies suffered severe setbacks during the learning process. A series of court rulings eventually wiped out legislative obstacles, and in the 1990s franchising has become one of the highest potential growth segments on the European landscape. Franchising has matured, as Chantel Zimmer-Helou, director of the French Franchising Association was quoted as saying in *World Link*, and is becoming more professional, more reliable, and of more value to the customer.

Although gross statistics remain sketchy, French franchising firms appear to be among the most aggressive in Europe. In 1991 there were seven hundred franchisers and thirty thousand franchisees operating in France. According to Ms. Zimmer-Helou this represents increases of 25 percent and 20 percent respectively over 1987 and clearly demonstrates the dynamic nature of franchising compared to the rest of the economy.

As in the United States, European banks look kindly on loans to franchise companies. Recognizing that returns on them come in better than on traded stocks, investors are also lining up to get in on the franchise boom.

France is far and away the market leader in European franchising, with more than 50 percent of the total EC market. Britain is second, with a highly developed internal market made up of domestic and foreign (predominantly American) franchises. France's internal market consists almost totally of French franchises.

The Netherlands and Belgium also sport well-developed franchise companies. Spain, Portugal, and Italy are beginning to show signs of franchising life. On the flip side, Germany, with its well-developed distribution system, remains immune to the franchising fever.

Companies with a yen to enter European franchising should find a lucrative market. The only caveat is to target market-sensitive products or services specifically adaptable to the country of choice.

Eastern Europe also has attractive possibilities. Franchising has always been an excellent development tool when financial resources are tight and a strong need exists to develop entrepreneurial initiative. The Hungarian government established a development fund specifically earmarked for franchising. Poland and the Czech and Slovak republics are also moving toward special funding arrangements to attract foreign franchisers.

13
The Best and Worst Western European Sites

Tips to Foreign Traders and Investors

1. If your firm is anticipating future entry into European markets, now is the time to move by purchasing an existing corporate shell.
2. Trade is still profitable with Germany, but don't waste time and effort searching for a facilities site. Too many uncertainties cloud Germany's financial future.
3. Within the EC, choose the Netherlands or Ireland for best investment incentives and least cost.
4. Pick non-EC site locations in Finland or Turkey for even better strategic advantages.

Companies already established in Europe will be less bothered by restrictive trade barriers or meeting new EC environmental regulations than those that wait until Europe 1992 is a reality. Therefore, it makes sense for non-European companies to seriously consider forming an entity in Western Europe as early as possible.

Starting from scratch, it takes from six to nine months to form a corporation. Purchasing a corporate shell already in existence in the country of choice is a more direct route and far less costly. Thousands of easily accessible European attorneys buy and sell corporate shells as a lucrative sideline. The total acquisition cost is relatively minor—about US$10,000—for a shell with a modest number of registered shares. Local attorneys also change the corporate name to suit the purchaser and file appropriate forms with government agencies.

The European attitude toward incorporation is entirely different from that in the United States. In America, anyone can form a corporation: it's a right. European governments impose stricter criteria and consider incorporating a privilege.

Forming or purchasing a corporate shell early in the game offers several advantages. Corporations can hold licenses and agreements with European companies. They are less expensive, easier to control, and faster to set up than joint ventures, mergers, or acquisitions.

Licensing through a European shell eliminates credit concerns for a parent company. Europeans generally feel more comfortable buying imported goods from a local company than from a foreign entity. A European shell can acquire another European company faster and with fewer legal complications than can a non-European company.

Once the decision is made to establish a shell corporation, another question must be answered: Which country offers the least cost and greatest competitive advantage? The results of a 1991 Ernst & Young survey which included replies from hundreds of companies can serve as a good starting point.

Here are a few of the answers:

1. *Telecommunications costs.*   The lowest are those in Belgium, Denmark, and the Netherlands.

2. *Labor costs.*   The lowest are those in Greece, Portugal, and Spain.

3. *Regional growth rates.*   The highest are those in Greece, Portugal, and Spain; the lowest are those in Belgium, France, and Germany.

4. *Property costs.*   The highest by far are those in London. Also high are those in Barcelona and Madrid.

5. *Corporate taxes.*   Ireland has the lowest tax rate, the fastest depreciation, and no withholding tax. Italy imposes the highest total tax burden. Britain has imputed tax credits (a guaranteed refund program) for U.S. investors.

6. *Quality of work force.*   The best educational systems are those in Ireland and Germany. The worst educational systems are those in Britain, Greece, Portugal, and Italy. Vocational training is best in Germany and Ireland.

7. *Labor laws.*   In Spain, one to three months' severance pay is standard for senior managers. In Italy and Portugal, the dismissal process is very time-consuming and costly. In Belgium, there are very few labor hurdles. Trade union strikes are quite likely in Britain and Italy, much less likely in Germany and the Netherlands.

The report also rates the top ten locations for various types of facilities. For a European headquarters office, Berlin, Brussels, and Copenhagen rank first, second, and third. The top three for manufacturing plants are Abrusi-Milise (east of Rome); Centro, Spain; and any place in Ireland. The best locations for research and development facilities are Brussels, Hamburg, and the Frankfurt region.

Any attempt to generalize must be regarded with skepticism, however. The best location for one company may be the worst for another. Nothing beats personal inspections and evaluations.

The following pages focus on those European nations that are doing things right to attract cross-border trade and foreign investment and that offer the greatest growth potential over the next ten to fifteen years. But first, factors leading to diminishing opportunities in what has been one of Europe's hottest markets—Germany—are worth reviewing.

Germany

The big story in Germany is the impact of the unification of West and East Germany on the internal German economy and on cross-border trading practices.

Foreign traders and investors have long known the advantages and disadvantages of West Germany. The strength of the D-mark, the abundance of skilled labor (a work force of 26 million) and management talent, technical proficiency, workers' rights, and access to important raw materials reflect the enormous success of the post–World War II rebuilding effort. Large and small foreign firms from Europe as well as North America and East Asia have been eminently successful in trade and investment with Germany.

One of the strongest features of German economic policy has been the separation of the German central bank, the Bundesbank, from governmental fiscal policies. As opposed to the objective of central banks in other developed countries, the primary mission of the Bundesbank is the containment of inflationary pressures on the country's monetary system. The continued strength of the D-mark in world trading provides ample evidence of the bank's success in this endeavor.

In early 1991, Karl Otto Pohl, who had led the Bundesbank through years of effective inflation-fighting measures, resigned. His replacement, Helmut Schlesinger, faced a very uncharacteristically German phenomenon: an inflation rate of 4.5 percent, the highest since 1982. Although modest compared with the British or American inflation rate over the last fifteen years, 4.5 percent was considered a near catastrophe, given that German monetary prudence had been known for holding inflation to 3.5 percent or below.

According to both German and OECD economists, the main culprit behind this shaking of the German financial system is the extraordinarily high and grossly underestimated cost of unification. Current estimates from German officials place the total cost in excess of DM500 billion over a five-year period.

This does not include the incalculable costs of cleaning up the pollution mess left by communist-run factories—a cost that will continue to escalate for years to come.

In addition, the Bundestag's move from Bonn to Berlin will require DM90 billion (US$50 billion), probably spread over a decade. So far no funds have been set aside for this move. By mid-1991, total public borrowing had soared to DM200 billion—nearly 8 percent of GDP—leading experts to predict the inevitability of another tax boost.

Caution Alert

The magnitude of these costs sends cold chills through the veins of global traders. One of the two financially strongest nations in the world, Germany faces at least a decade of extraordinarily huge national expenditures. This threatens to undermine not only prudent national business practices but the credibility of the D-mark.

Intelligent global traders will watch developments in Germany closely for signs of rising taxes, import duties (regardless of the EC), and restrictions on repatriation of foreign profits and capital.

The world has not seen the end of a financially strong Germany, but cracks are appearing. The euphoria of Europe 1992 may gloss over the ramifications of a weakened Germany on planned Phases II and III of the European economic and monetary union. Media hype may bring foreign investors and traders to the EC. But lest we forget, the entire underpinning of the European Monetary System rests on a strong and reliable D-mark—and hence, on a strong and stable Germany.

One indication of the German banking community's concern over the seriousness of the deterioration in the internal financial system is the advertising done by one of the country's largest banks, Commerzbank. During the latter part of 1991, the bank ran advertisements in international periodicals imploring the German government to face up to its fiscal responsibility by cutting the deficit and pursuing conservative, not expansionary, fiscal policies. The gist of the bank's plea was the need to increase public and private savings and to restrict wage increases as a means of generating additional capital for unification costs.

East German Privatizations

The experience of West Germany's BASF, the world's largest chemical company, exemplifies the difficulties encountered by firms jumping on the East German bandwagon. Thinking it had found a jewel in East Germany's once thriving chemical industry, BASF purchased Synthesewerk Schwarzheide (SYS) in October 1990.

Company officials report that since the acquisition, BASF has had nothing but trouble. Most SYS managers have been replaced with BASF people. These new managers are still trying to purge the staff of excommunist apparatchiks unwilling to cooperate with the modernization of the plant. BASF went so far as to rewire the old building, suspecting that it might be bugged.

According to the old SYS books of account, more than 20 percent of total costs during the communist reign were spent on the factory's outdoor swimming pool, creches, schools, a thirty-doctor hospital, and an abbatoir for SYS employees. It is costing DM100 million just to replace the scrubbers to clean up the company's power station (which also provides electricity for 1500 homes in the area), fueled by heavily polluting brown coal. These are but a sample of the problems faced by BASF—and it is a German firm taking over another German firm. One can only imagine the nightmare if BASF had been an American or a Japanese company!

Japanese firms have already given the cold shoulder to investing in East German firms. In June 1991, the president of the Treuhandanstalt, which had sold 2200 of the 8000 East German state-owned firms, met with Japanese business leaders in Tokyo, advocating tax breaks, generous German subsidies, and loans to foreign firms willing to purchase the balance of state-owned businesses.

Tadashi Ito, chairman of Sumitomo, summed up the Japanese response: "The progress of direct investment has not been satisfactory because of lack of infrastructure, environmental pollution, and lack of clarity over ownership." Other Japanese businessmen cited ill-trained workers, rising wages, and poor highway, telephone, and other systems as deterrents.

Red Flag

To attract much-needed foreign investment, it seems inevitable that the German government will have to offer guarantees against hidden property claims, environmental liability, and personnel layoff costs. To date, it has been unwilling to take this step.

It also seems inevitable that foreign investors will share in the cost of German unification. Like it or not, with a doubling of the federal budget, potential unemployment in East Germany (up to 80 percent by some calculations) and as-yet-incalculable environmental cleanup costs, Germany will look to the business community—national and foreign—as a primary source of funding.

The Financial System

On a more positive note, Germany offers global traders one of the most sophisticated banking and financial systems on the continent. Deutsche Bank, West LB, Dresden Bank, and a variety of smaller banks are easy to work with and provide every form of short-term trade finance and long-term loans. German banks, together with those in France and Britain, are knowledgeable and experienced in international finance and maintain branches throughout the world.

Once established on German soil, government-supported export credit and insurance is available through Hermes Kreditversicherungs-AG (Hermes). Although all Western European countries have export credit and insurance facilities, Hermes, along with the French Campagnie Française d'Assurance pour le Commerce Extérieur (COFACE) and the British Exports Credit Guarantee Department (ECGD), offer some of the broadest coverage. Hermes is receptive to export credit applications from any company located in Germany—national or foreign-owned.

Germany is also active in providing bilateral financial and technical aid to developing countries, primarily in Africa and Latin America. The German Finance Company for Investments in Developing Countries provides long-term loans, equity contributions, and guarantees for private-sector projects in developing countries. Companies investigating European trade or expansion in Africa find this a convenient source of funding. So far, at least, the stretching of government financial commitments has not materially affected this bilateral body.

The Netherlands

Although Brussels offers convenience to European Commission agencies and reasonably good tax and labor laws, the Netherlands is rapidly becoming a favorite location for the European headquarters offices of foreign companies. Belgium remains the favorite as a European distribution center, but the Netherlands offers a wider and better-skilled labor and management pool for manufacturing facilities.

The Dutch government actively solicits foreign direct investment. In 1978, it created the Netherlands Foreign Investment Agency (NFIA) to assist companies that may be interested in starting up European operations or expanding existing facilities. All services from NFIA are free of any charge.

Over the past ten years, NFIA offices in North America—Los Angeles, San Francisco, New York, and Ottawa—have helped more than 350 companies invest US$2.5 billion in Dutch businesses that created over 7600 new jobs.

After a company identifies its foreign investment objectives and Holland remains as a strong possibility, NFIA takes over. It organizes an exhaustive fact-finding trip for the company's executives, making certain that every facet of opening a facility gets addressed during the visit.

NFIA helps executives understand tax structures, regulations, availability of personnel, and research facilities. It also assists in learning language skills, defining access points to European markets, site-selection and cost comparisons. It identifies prospective business partners, helps arrange venture capital and other funding, and makes sure the company participates in the appropriate government-sponsored incentive program.

During 1989–1990, the organization assisted such North American companies as Smith Water Products Company, Access Innovations, Allen

Bradley, AMP, Biomedical Business International, International Bitstream, Caddock, CBS Records, OTC Group, Synoptics Communications, and Walker, Richer & Quinn, to mention a few.

Everything considered, NFIA does one of the best jobs of any European government agency in assisting foreign investors to get established.

Holland-based foreign companies also have access to the Netherlands Development Finance Company. This pseudo-government development bank provides feasibility-study financing and technical assistance for Dutch companies wishing to expand to or trade with developing countries. It handles projects in the agriculture, industrial, and finance sectors. Both equity and debt financing are available. Although Dutch residency is not required to obtain this assistance, it certainly helps to have at least a base of operations in the Netherlands.

Turkey

Of all the countries in Western and Eastern Europe, Turkey seems doomed to be the odd man out. Though for centuries it has been a bridge between East and West, its semi-alignment with old communist and radical Middle Eastern regimes, its remote location relative to the rest of Europe, and its age-old battles with Greece over Cyprus and other eastern Mediterranean islands have caused European companies (and North American ones to a lesser extent) to snub this pillar of stability in an otherwise hostile region.

Reassessing its role in international commerce, Turkey has enacted massive political and economic changes to bring it into line with Western needs. The most fundamental political change, of course, was indicated by its swift closure of the Iraqi oil pipeline when Saddam invaded Kuwait. If there were any doubts in Western minds about Turkey's political position, they were quickly erased. Turkey is now clearly aligned with the West.

Turkey's economy has been growing at a remarkable 9 percent clip. Recognizing the impact of diminished trade with the Middle East and the collapse of the Soviet Union, the country must now shore up its trade with the EC and Eastern Europe. In doing this, Turkey has a lot to offer traders and investors. Agriculture has bounced back after a dismal year in 1990. Foreign reserves are high—US$12 billion in 1991—as compared with a foreign debt of US$40 billion. National and business debt is manageable. Credit is plentiful. The Export Credit Bank of Turkey, Turk Eximbank, supports a range of buyer and supplier credit facilities.

Turkey's government has made a real effort to eliminate trade barriers of all types. Consumer spending is on the rise. The Istanbul stock market is thriving as liberalization makes foreign investment welcome. Traditional private and family-owned companies are now going public. Privatization of state-owned companies is moving ahead rapidly. Turkish banks are aggressively seeking foreign business with short-term trade finance and long-term expansion loans.

Caution Alert

On the downside, Turkey's current account balance has switched from a surplus to a deficit. Imports continue to outshine exports by nearly a two-to-one margin. Inflation continues in the 50 to 60 percent range.

Turkey provides an excellent location for tapping markets in the Middle East and the southern rim of the former Soviet Union. Its labor/management pool is talented and plentiful. The country's infrastructure is in place and functioning. Pollution hasn't reached the abominable levels of Eastern Europe. Its trade barriers are less obtrusive than those of Western Europe.

Situated seven hours from both Tokyo and New York, Turkey's developing offshore financial market offers intriguing possibilities. With or without the EC, market opportunities in Turkey should be substantially higher than those in Eastern Europe for at least ten to fifteen years.

Japanese companies have already spotted Turkey's potential, especially in automobile manufacturing. A country that imports 70,000 cars each year is bound to attract foreign investors. Although General Motors now produces its Opel Vectras in a factory near Izmir, and Peugeot recently started a plant in the same vicinity, Japanese manufacturers lead the way. Toyota and the Sabani Group have both opened new factories.

Imports of Japanese cars continue to soar, currently running about 50 percent of total imports. Eastern European cars (priced at the equivalent of four tires and a battery from a Western European manufacturer) account for 30 percent of imported automobiles. The balance is spread among the Italian, French, British, and so on. Turkey spent over US$600 million in 1990 on car imports. Clearly, enormous opportunities exist for foreign investment in basic automobile manufacturing as well as in the myriad automotive support industries, from parts to paint to tires.

Ireland

Ireland is rapidly becoming the darling of the EC (especially after its ratification of the Maastricht Treaty). Although external debt continues to absorb an unconscionable amount of GDP (113 percent in 1991), substantial progress in the government's fiscal and monetary adjustment policies is bringing it down from its peak in 1986 of 130 percent. Important statistics bear out Ireland's progress.

In 1986 the Irish economy had negative growth, investment was a negative 2 percent, and exports rose a meager 2.9 percent. In 1990, GNP grew at a brisk 4 percent, investment totaled 10 percent, and exports rose 10.7 percent. Today Ireland is one of the most buoyant, low-inflation countries in the European Community.

A series of innovative tax incentives and subsidies brought a stream of foreign manufacturing companies to this island nation. Ireland has now become a very competitive niche player in the EC in such high-tech industries as computer software design, electronics, and pharmaceuticals. With this base, the country is now striving to become a major financial services center for Europe.

The first step was the construction of Dublin's new International Financial Services Center. This facility, together with a maximum corporate tax rate of 10 percent for foreign companies and access to EC markets, has attracted foreign investment in such specialties as captive insurance, asset financing, and funds management. Dublin has already attracted more than 140 of the world's leading financial companies, including American International Group, Citicorp, Dresdner Bank, Commerzbank, National Westminster, Daiwa Securities, Mitsubishi Bank, Credit Lyonnais, and Barclay's.

Ireland boasts a substantial labor and management pool of English-speaking, highly educated, and highly motivated men and women, many of whom are computer literate. Inflation rates were running around 2.9 percent in 1990–1991 when Britain, Ireland's major trading partner, was suffering inflation in the 10 to 11 percent range.

Dependence on the British market has decreased markedly over the last three years. The costs of operating a headquarters or administrative office in Dublin are miniscule compared to similar costs in London or Zurich. In addition, Ireland offers several generous provisions for rapid depreciation of plant and equipment investments, further reducing tax burdens.

Exports approximated imports in 1991. The OECD forecasts a 1992 increase in exports of 6.7 percent and imports of 5.8 percent, which, if achieved, will enhance the nation's trade balance.

Caution Alert

The OECD warns that the recession of 1990–1992 has caused a slowdown in the Irish growth rate and an increase in unemployment. The high public-debt-to-GDP ratio remains a constant reminder of past follies, keeping economic growth far below the country's capabilities. The OECD places GDP at 2.25 percent in 1991, with a slight forecasted rise in 1992—both years down from 4.5 percent in 1990.

Although inflation should decline further, perhaps to below 3 percent, unemployment will accelerate (15.1 percent in 1992) from an already high level (14.7 in 1991 and 14.0 in 1990). A new three-year wage agreement went into effect at the end of 1990, establishing wage rate increases of 3.5 percent per year up to 1993, plus a potential 1 percent per year add-on at the local level.

According to the OECD the most serious threat to continued economic improvement is pressure from the European Monetary System that may force interest rates higher than anticipated. This in turn could affect both consumer and investor confidence.

Finland

Finland is another stepchild of Europe. Like its peripheral cousins Ireland, Portugal, and Britain, Finland regards Europe as if it were somewhere else.

Highly individualistic, prizing initiative and independence, Finnish managers are decision makers. They seldom follow the Swedish approach of seeking consensus before acting.

Although the Finnish population totals a mere five million, the country boasts a highly educated, technically skilled managerial and labor pool. Most managers have an engineering background. Finnish manufactured products are noted for their high quality. Abundant in natural resources, Finland depends heavily on foreign trade to support its economic growth. Throughout the 1980s combined exports and imports totaled 50 percent of GDP.

Forestry, including papermaking, remains an important industry, accounting for approximately 17 percent of production and more than 40 percent of exports. But during the last ten years other industries have become the largest employers and producers. These industries are centered in the mining and engineering sectors and include basic metals, metal products, instruments, and transport equipment, predominantly shipbuilding. Finland has been transformed from a mainly agrarian economy to a vibrant industrialized society.

About 60 percent of the labor force is employed in commerce, transport, and services, 30 percent in industry and construction, and 9 percent in agriculture and forestry. Finland leads the world in the manufacture of paper machines, forest-logging machines, rock-drilling equipment, and mobile telephones. Well-known American companies, such as Wilson Sporting Goods, MacGregor Golf Company, Leaf, Inc. (Milk Duds, Whoppers, etc.), Jamesbury Corporation, and Nordberg, Inc., are owned by Finnish companies. The world leader in mobile phones, Nokia, has formed a major strategic alliance with Radio Shack.

Although Finland is outside the EC, the issue of joining it has become a hot topic of debate within the country. Indications point to Finland being admitted in 1993. The Finnmark is already tied to the ecu currency basket.

Major Finnish exports are road vehicles and other transportation equipment (24 percent) and paper and related products (22 percent). United States exporters have captured 30 percent of the computer and peripherals market in Finland, estimated to be US$200 million. Other major imports to the country include electronic components, electronic industry production and test equipment, telecom equipment, business and office machinery, medical electronics, avionics and ground-support equipment, pollution-control equipment, medical electronics, and automotive parts and accessories.

Strategic Advantage

Finland continues to maintain close trading ties with many republics in the former Soviet Union. It is strategically located to serve as a base for trade with the Baltic states. A part of Sweden prior to 1917, Finland claims a Nordic heritage that makes it an excellent jumping-off point for trade with Scandinavian countries.

Caution Alert

Finns have a paranoia about losing their independence in anything, including their companies. Although all Finnish companies have the right to make any number of shares available to foreign ownership, even 100 percent, they are also permitted under company law to include restrictions on foreign ownership in their articles of association. This tact has allowed many companies to restrict foreign ownership to less than 20 percent.

In June 1991, a government committee recommended the abandonment of segregated foreign and domestic shares and encouraged companies to permit foreign ownership. To date, few have taken the bait. The Commission for Foreign Investments, a permanent body of the Ministry of Trade and Industry continues to review foreign applications case by case.

This same committee also recommended allowing foreigners to purchase property. Historically this was prohibited, unless the property was specifically related to a business. Foreigners have been totally prohibited from real estate deals, oil refining, mining, and basic forest industry production. Considering the Finnish propensity for independence, it seems doubtful that these recommendations will be implemented in full in the near future. Railways, airlines, postal and telegraph services, and trade in alcoholic beverages remain firmly under state control.

OECD Projections

Finnish output in 1992 is projected to be significantly weaker than in 1989–1991. Although export levels are holding in spite of the collapse of the Soviet market, imports have slackened considerably, thus improving the country's balance of payments. Business investment continues its steep decline, reflecting high interest rates and weakening profitability. Residential construction will contract even further. Unemployment is expected to increase throughout 1992.

On a positive note, the OECD projects a turnaround in the economy before 1992 ends. Strengthening exports and decreasing inflation will lead the way.

14
Eastern Europe

Tips to Foreign Traders and Investors

1. Stay away from joint ventures or other "partnership" arrangements that do not carry a government-backed, ironclad guarantee for protecting ownership equity.

2. Go slow. Demand hard-currency cash when exporting goods and services to the region. This means that the deal must be small, since very few customers have enough cash to pay more than $50,000 to $100,000.

3. Be sure to use irrevocable L/Cs confirmed by a bank in a hard-currency country and preferably with government-backed insurance.

4. Insist on government-backed political insurance for direct investments.

5. Stay away from countertrade deals unless in-house expertise and a ready market for exchanged goods both exist.

6. Avoid foreign trading companies at all costs: most are run by excommunist bureaucrats who practice favoritism and demand rake-offs.

7. Don't listen to so-called "expert" Western consultants, lawyers, or accountants, unless they can prove credentials from previous deals: many operate out of a textbook.

8. Hire a local "fixer" (also referred to as a "runner") to cut red tape, arrange meetings, and source customers, financing, materials, and labor.

9. Avoid a high profile: Westerners are still thought of as being wealthy capitalists, and locals know how to squeeze them.

The glow of new Eastern European markets—ready, willing, and able to absorb a plethora of Western goods and investment—is rapidly fading.

Poland, Hungary, and the Czech and Slovak republics, touted by overzealous media and Western bureaucrats as the next major opportunity for large and small companies alike, have all run into the staggering problems inevitable in a conversion from controlled to market economies.

Bulgaria and Rumania still aren't certain they want Western-style societies. Although stirrings can be heard, backward Albania remains locked in virtual isolation. Yugoslavia has split at the seams.

Disruptive sociopolitical roadblocks must be removed and dysfunctional economic infrastructures resolved before the majority of Western companies will find either markets for their goods or opportunities for direct investment. Aside from the necessity for rebuilding collapsing infrastructures, Eastern European governments—and to a large extent local business leaders—must come to grips with methods for establishing the basic ingredients of a modern market economy: institutions and rules within which society and free enterprise business can coexist.

In the more advanced countries—Poland, Hungary, and the Czech and Slovak republics—leaders are just beginning to debate ways to create the following:

- Property and contract laws and a legal system to enforce them
- The structure and supervision of banks and financial markets
- Tax codes and bankruptcy laws
- Laws governing employee rights—including unemployment, health care, and the arbitration machinery to resolve labor-management disputes

The less-developed countries haven't even begun to address these issues.

Lessons drawn from other developing countries don't apply in Eastern Europe. These nations are already highly industrialized. Elementary and secondary education systems are in place and functioning. Health care facilities are operable, although lacking modern technology and supplies.

A reallocation of resources remains the single largest problem to be overcome. People are working at the wrong jobs and producing the wrong goods at the wrong time and place. Massive privatization of state-owned industries must be accomplished before free market forces can reallocate workers, materials, and money. While Poland and, to a lesser extent, Hungary initially plowed forward relentlessly to transfer enterprises to private hands, little of any importance has been accomplished.

The horrific consequences of the industrial collapse in the former East Germany have caused bureaucrats and technocrats to rethink the privatization process. With the realization that two to three decades of dislocation, unemployment, and inflationary prices are the price to be paid for a quick conversion to free enterprise, Eastern European countries have backed away from their initial desire to privatize everything in sight.

The final collapse of the Soviet Union further aggravated foreign trade for Eastern Europe. All these countries relied to a greater or lesser extent on export and import trade with the Soviet states, even after they themselves had withdrawn from the communist bloc.

The result of this stumbling, start/stop approach to conversion has been varying degrees of economic hardship for each country, as demonstrated in Table 14-1.

Western Assistance

Nearly all economists, business leaders, and government bureaucrats in Eastern Europe as well as in the West agree that two conditions must be rectified to enable these countries to proceed with their conversion.

1. The West must provide adequate technical and financial assistance. Banking and financial systems in all Eastern European countries are in turmoil. Currency conversion has slowed to a crawl. Government debt is strangling self-help measures. Lack of experienced management in finance, banking, modern manufacturing techniques, and distribution prevents local firms—public and private—from functioning in a market economy.

2. Western trade barriers against Eastern Europe's goods must be lowered or abolished to permit the generation of foreign exchange. Although few goods produced in Eastern Europe meet consumer or industrial standards in the West, enough do to enable the beginning of cross-border trade. Without exports, these nations cannot generate sufficient foreign exchange to purchase much-needed imports.

Poland, Hungary, the Czech and Slovak republics, Rumania, and Bulgaria all belong to the International Monetary Fund (IMF), the World Bank, and the General Agreement on Tariffs and Trade (GATT). The IMF and the World Bank, as well as other multilateral and bilateral institutions, have diligently provided technical assistance wherever possible. But monetary assistance has been nil.

Countries belonging to the European Community (EC) were originally expected to take the lead, both in furnishing technical and financial assistance, and in opening their borders to Eastern European trade. Except for a pittance, this has not happened.

Some aid has flowed from the European Bank for Reconstruction and Development (EBRD); several Western European companies have formed joint ventures; and a handful of banks (mostly German) have established branches and joint ventures. However, none of this assistance has been sufficient to break the logjam.

Little Cooperation

Western European nations have been obstinate about opening their borders to trade with the East. Wrapped up in getting the EC off the ground and trying to

Table 14-1. Trade Comparisons in Eastern Europe

	Poland			Hungary			Czech and Slovak republics			Bulgaria			Rumania		
	1989	1990	1991*	1989	1990	1991*	1989	1990	1991*	1989	1990	1991*	1989	1990	1991*
Percentage change over previous year															
Real GDP	-0.2	-12.0	-3.7	-0.2	-3.5	-6.0	1.4	-3.1	-9.8	-0.4	-11.8	-19.8	-9.9	-10.2	-10.0
Industrial output	-2.5	-28.8	-5.7	-1.0	-10.0	-12.0	1.0	-3.7	-4.5	1.1	-10.7	-12.0	-2.1	-22.0	-20.0
Exports US$billions	15.6	18.6	18.6	10.9	10.8	11.4	14.3	13.5	13.7	7.9	6.4	6.1	6.1	3.5	3.2
Imports US$billions	17.4	14.7	18.8	12.4	12.6	11.3	17.1	19.0	16.5	10.0	8.9	6.5	3.8	5.2	3.9
Inflation percentage	251	684	80	17.5	28.2	36.0	1.4	15.0	40.0	6.4	26.3	200.0	1.1	27.0	130.0
Unemployment percentage	0.3	6.1	7.3	0.5	1.6	2.9	0.0	1.0	2.8	0.0	1.6	2.7	0.0	0.0	3.6
Trade balance US$billions	-1.8	3.9	-0.2	-1.5	-1.8	-0.1	-2.8	-5.5	-2.8	-2.1	-2.5	-0.4	2.3	-1.7	0.7
Exchange rate/US$	1,439	9,500	11,392	59.1	63.2	75.0	15.0	18.2	29.0	0.86	2.15	18.0	14.5	34.7	60.0

*Figures for 1991 are forecasted.
SOURCE: OECD, PlanEcon.

agree on cuts in massive farm subsidies to fit Uruguay-round GATT negotiations, Western Europe has given short shrift to the needs of their Eastern cousins. Busy worrying about protecting their own producers, not one country has relaxed its import restrictions on food, textiles, and steel—the three industries in which Eastern European companies feel they are most competitive. To date, the EC has provided a terrible example to the East of how a free market economy should operate.

The United States has been equally hesitant to provide significant aid or loosen trade barriers. Although the countries of Eastern Europe would much rather trade with their European neighbors than with the United States, they welcome assistance regardless of its source. But the United States has its own financial and banking problems. With the exception of a handful of multinational corporations and a smattering of smaller companies, American firms are more eager to open trading doors in their own hemisphere than to tackle the hornets' nest of Eastern Europe.

A Bright Spot

All is not bleak, however. On the plus side, private enterprise flourishes on the streets of Prague, Budapest, and Warsaw. Small shops proliferate. Vendors and customers can be seen on virtually any major thoroughfare. Hard currency is flowing into Eastern Europe from Western tourists and from relatives living in the West. Jeans, TV sets, Pizza Hut and MacDonald's restaurants, and Western food can be found in Poland, the Czech and Slovak republics, and Hungary. Bulgaria is actively promoting its image as the Eastern European equivalent of the Riviera.

These are mostly small businesses, to be sure. But they are privately owned, they are profitable, and they exhibit all the traits of Western small business. Market opportunities do exist for Western firms. Investment in local businesses, business startups, or joint ventures are all very much a reality for Western companies. The risks are certainly obvious, but so are the rewards for those companies willing and able to struggle through the long period of market conversion.

Hungarian exports to OECD nations rose 26 percent in 1990. Poland's jumped 44 percent. Many firms reported profits in 1990, adding to tax revenues. Granted, much of this resulted from sell-offs of inventory rather than from new production. But some markets are beginning to function.

So far, however, the expected flood of Western investment has been more of a steady trickle. New deals are announced daily, but the number of such deals doesn't even come close to what was expected. Western managers find Eastern European bureaucracy difficult to deal with and time-consuming. Uncertainty about the new laws that are being enacted daily works against the reaching of definitive business conclusions.

Massive amounts of foreign investment are desperately needed for Eastern Europe to rebuild its infrastructures and modernize its factories. Some Europe

Table 14-2. Net Inflow of Foreign Direct Investment

	US$ millions	
	1990	1991
Hungary	900	500 (First quarter)
Poland	200	370 (First half)
Czech and Slovak republics	100	200 (First quarter estimate)

SOURCE: Bain and Company.

watchers estimate that to achieve parody with its Western neighbors, Eastern Europe needs more than US$400 billion in new investment each year. Based on 1990 figures, that's two-thirds of total output. Such massive amounts are nowhere to be found. Optimistic estimates put foreign investment at a maximum of US$7 billion a year through 1995, plus another US$21 billion from multilateral aid agencies and banks.

Clearly, Eastern Europe must help itself with domestic savings. This is certainly not unusual. Based on World Bank and OECD studies, both developing and industrialized countries rely nearly 90 percent on domestic savings for investment growth capital. The success of internally generated capital depends entirely on the ability of an economy to transfer savings funds into productive investments. And that can only be accomplished with functioning banking systems, stock markets, and other financial services.

Good opportunities for Western investment do exist in consumer and capital goods, and especially in services. Although the region has experienced a severe recession, a modest number of investments in 1990 and a greater number of investments in 1991 have occurred. Table 14-2 shows the net inflow of foreign capital.

Table 14-3 shows the number of actual investments.

The Attractions of the Industrial Economies

Several short-term benefits attract investors to Hungary, Poland, and the Czech and Slovak republics:

1. All highly industrialized economies

2. A good cost-effective base from which to manufacture and export

3. Enormous potential gains in labor productivity

4. A low initial investment for operating companies

In the long term, as the economies of the region shake off the cobwebs of state control, pent-up demand for consumer goods of all types will flower. Also, as infrastructures rebuild, these countries will likely take their rightful places in the European Community, which provides non-EC investors an excellent entrée.

Table 14-3. Cumulative Foreign Direct Investment by Country of Origin

	Share of joint venture activity: number of deals as of May 1991	Value of FDI by percentage value of deals
Czech and Slovak republics		
Germany	861	85.1
Austria	831	–
Switzerland	197	–
Italy	134	15
United States	132	–
Other	739	–
Total	2894	
	Share of joint venture activity: number of deals as of May 1991	Value of FDI by percentage value of deals
Hungary		
Germany	1410	21.8
Austria	915	18.8
United States	610	40.6
Other	879	18.8
Total	3814	
	Share of joint venture activity: number of deals as of May 1991	Value of FDI by percentage value of deals
Poland		
Germany	981	29.2
Austria	200	5.9
Italy	131	5.2
United States	214	7.8
Sweden	256	8.7
United Kingdom	145	3.7
France	130	3.8
Netherlands	108	7.1
Other	638	28.6
Total	2800	

SOURCE: Bain and Company.

Each country has specialized skills to offer global traders. The Czech and Slovak republics boast a strong engineering capability. In Hungary, it's agriculture and foodstuffs; in Poland, heavy industry.

Most future foreign direct investments will be small rather than large deals. It will be far more common to see US$20 million investments than US$500 million ones. The reasons are clear: most state-owned companies large enough to attract large Western investors are so vertically and horizontally integrated that they do not fit the specialized mold of Western industry.

Adequate financial backing will also be hard to come by for large amounts of capital. Even though the EBRD has significant resources, the region's stock markets and banking systems are pedestrian. The clincher is that state-owned companies continue to be saddled with overregulation and labor giveaways—both incompatible with Western production efficiency.

For Western companies, Eastern Europe's attractions fall into four categories:

1. A huge pent-up market demand by the consumer and industrial sectors for a wide variety of imports

2. Relatively inexpensive and ready access to the European market, including the EC after 1992

3. A logical jumping-off point for manufacturing and distributing goods to South and Southeast Asia as well as the Middle East

4. A low-cost, ready supply of highly skilled labor and highly trained engineers, scientists, and technicians

The wide disparity in 1990–1991 hourly wage rates between Eastern and Western Europe can be seen in the following compilation by Bain and Company:

	Hourly Wage Rates in US$
West Germany	21.30
Italy	16.29
France	15.25
United Kingdom	12.42
Spain	11.60
East Germany	7.14
Czech and Slovak republics	3.02
Hungary	1.88
Poland	1.58

Even with these strong assets, however, the same two conditions that prevent rapid investment by major multinationals should deter small and midsize companies from moving too fast: ethnic instability, and confusion about ownership rights.

Until ethnic groups in the Czech and Slovak republics, Rumania, and Hungary resolve their differences, currency instability and political unrest will persist.

Until Western-style property, contract, and corporate laws are legislated and a judicial system is in place to enforce them, the risk of losing everything with the stroke of a pen escalates with each passing month.

It is equally important to recognize the long road that still lies ahead for the region before it can achieve a fully integrated market economy. From fifty years of war and communist rule these countries have inherited:

- A legacy of technical backwardness

- A communist elite that continues to manage most companies

- Unmanageable debt

- The absence of democratic traditions

- Ecological catastrophe

- A habit of dependency on government bureaucracy

- The simmering of age-old ethnic wounds and national rivalries

There is only so much help the West can contribute. Beyond that, these nations must develop self-sufficiency or face the specter of new dictatorships entering political and social vacuums.

The next five years will be the proving ground for Eastern Europe. The biggest unanswered question is whether the fortitude of the Polish, Czech, Slovak, Hungarian, Rumanian, and Bulgarian people can overcome the obstacles ahead and endure the social dislocations that are bound to occur before the trough is reached.

The latest forecast from Morgan Stanley shows national incomes plummeting in 1991—down 10 percent in the Czech and Slovak republics and 5 percent in Hungary (although Polish income is forecasted to increase 4 percent). Industrial output and investment follows national income. Employment drops over the next two years are forecasted to be 7.5 percent in Hungary, 8.3 percent in Poland, and 6.3 percent in the Czech and Slovak republics. Unemployment is estimated to peak at twelve million in all of Eastern Europe by 1994.

The West Steps Forward Cautiously

Financial assistance to resolve Eastern Europe's chronic balance-of-payment problem became a key objective of the international community in the early 1990s and will continue to absorb the attention of United Nations organizations and Western governments for years to come.

Five key regional and international organizations are entrusted with managing Western assistance. They are:

1. The European Community (EC) on behalf of the Group of Twenty-four (G24). G24 consists of the Group of Seven (G7) industrialized countries (the United States, the United Kingdom, Canada, France, Germany, Italy, and Japan); the balance of EC members (Belgium, Luxembourg, Denmark, Greece, Ireland, the Netherlands, Portugal, and Spain); the European Free Trade Agreement (EFTA) countries (Austria, Finland, Iceland, Norway, Sweden, and Switzerland); and Australia, New Zealand, and Turkey.

2. The European Investment Bank.

3. The European Bank for Reconstruction and Development.

4. The World Bank's International Bank for Reconstruction and Development (IBRD).

5. The International Monetary Fund (IMF).

Private and bilateral organizations also channel funds to Eastern Europe, although their decisions are predicated on a country's compliance with macroeconomic adjustments negotiated with the IMF.

From a political perspective the most important assistance to date has been Poland's agreement with the Paris Club of creditor nations to forgive US$33 billion, or 50 percent of the amounts owed these governments. This was a compromise between the 80 percent reduction requested by Poland and supported by the United States, and no debt reduction at all argued by Japan.

The London Club (private creditors) continues to be split, with the United Kingdom and the United States holding fast for rescheduling debt under the Brady Plan, and Austrian, German, and French banks willing to write off all or most of the US$10.6 billion debt.

Negotiations with Hungary and the Czech and Slovak republics are continuing at a slower pace but official opinion is that they will inevitably fall within the same lines as Poland.

In addition to debt relief, several steps have been taken to encourage trade through reduced tariffs or larger export quotas. Although EC countries lag in tariff reductions, the United States and other countries have granted most-favored-nation (MFN) status to Poland, Hungary, and the Czech and Slovak republics under the General System of Preferences. Various forms of technical assistance have been provided, such as advice about setting up banking and financial systems and steering macroeconomic policy under pluralistic democracy.

Humanitarian steps have also been taken: foodstuffs to Poland, foodstuff loans to Bulgaria, and similar loans and medical aid to Rumania. Formal "European agreements" on association with the European Community for Hungary and Poland carry a 1992 implementation tag. Each country, along with the Czech and Slovak republics, is also negotiating trade agreements with EFTA nations. Pollution-fighting moves are being addressed by the EC under the aegis of the PHARE (Pologne-Hongrie: Assistance à la Restructuration Economique) program.

Caution Alert

At times it appears that these assistance efforts have little effect. More time is spent negotiating than implementing. Many export tariffs and import quotas from Western nations remain in place despite promises of reductions by government officials. Western companies trading in the region continue to run up against financing and collection problems. Hard currency remains in short supply. Joint ventures with Eastern European companies, hampered by undefined contract laws and disputed ownership claims, often fall short of expectations. A go-slow policy remains the only sensible course, regardless of efforts by multilateral and bilateral organizations.

Affordable Funding

The *Wall Street Journal* quoted the chairman and chief executive officer of Credit Suisse First Boston, Ltd., as saying that, without financing to cover their enormous capital needs, "the economic outlook in these countries [Eastern Europe] will be so miserable that you'll face a mass migration of people."

Although the entire world will suffer if Eastern Europe fails to achieve market economies, thus causing a period of political and social instability, Western Europe will bear the brunt. A strong challenge faces government negotiators in reconciling Czech and Slovak ethnic differences. Yugoslavia has already blown apart. Thousands of Rumanians, Poles, Bulgarians, and Albanians have begun the trek to a better life in the West. Without rapidly improving conditions, thousands more can be expected.

Although strides are certainly being made in Poland, Hungary, and the Czech and Slovak republics, without adequate funding, the governments of these countries and the rest of Eastern Europe cannot hope to meet the massive capital demands market economies exact.

As previously described, a modest amount of funding is filtering in from the World Bank and the European Bank for Reconstruction and Development. In September 1991, the latter launched its first bond issue, totaling 500 million ecus (European currency units)—the equivalent of US$611.3 million. Although this will help finance specific projects, it falls far short of providing sufficient capital to meet the East's ongoing general needs.

A trickle of funding comes from trade and a bit more from Western hard-currency investments. Added together, however, these sources provide only a small portion of the funding needed to meet capital demands. Public borrowing is the only path available to shore up national economies sufficiently.

The obstacle these nations face, however, is that in the wake of Latin American and African defaults, syndicated bank loans are practically nonexistent. That narrows options to a single choice: public bond issues sold to institutional and private investors. The National Bank of Hungary has already gone this route, with a 200 million ecu issue.

Hungary had to settle for an interest rate about three percentage points higher than Western European government bonds, thus reducing net cash benefits.

Suggestions have been made that regulators allow institutions to allocate a small proportion of their funds—3 to 5 percent—to high-yielding Eastern Europe bonds. So far, this has not happened, and the problem of massive funding for Eastern Europe remains unresolved.

15
Poland

Tips to Foreign Traders and Investors

1. Don't invest in Poland without substantial private financial resources.
2. Join up with a Polish partner who has high-powered connections in government. Corruption in high places can be deadly.
3. Take advantage of Western financial aid programs to get hard currency for exports.
4. Go slow on both trade and direct investments. Conditions are changing weekly.
5. Embassy office in Washington: (202) 234-3800.

Of the seven Eastern European nations, Poland, with a population of 37.8 million and a labor force exceeding 17 million, initially attracted most of the international publicity because of its early decision to go for the "quick fix" to conversion.

After the fall of communism, the new Solidarity government inherited an economy that was on its back. The most pressing issues were hyperinflation and large-scale shortages of everything from food and clothing to industrial replacement parts and fuel. An enormous trade deficit depleted foreign exchange reserves. Unmanageable debt to Western public and private creditors sapped what was left of the financial system.

Leszek Balcerowicz, Poland's finance minister, answered the call by taking three bold initial steps:

1. Eliminating practically all price controls
2. Lowering trade barriers
3. Making the country's currency near-convertible

A program to privatize Poland's state-owned businesses was quickly implemented. In the early 1990s over 60,000 state-owned businesses were sold or leased to private investors. According to Poland's Foreign Investment Agency, 4800 licenses had been issued to foreign companies through 1991, generating total investment of US$670 million. Observers estimate that the private sector now accounts for as much as 40 percent of the nation's GDP.

Most of these private businesses, whether started from scratch, held over from the previous regime, or converted through privatization, are in retailing, distribution, and transport. Few heavy industries have left the government fold. Infrastructure plants also remain in state hands.

Although Western enthusiasm initially bolstered the government's announcement of fast-track privatization, government leaders, liberal opponents, and trade unionists debated the form and shape of the process for a year before anything happened. Debates about how fast the process should proceed, what value to attach to companies in the privatization scheme, and how to stimulate competition while keeping unemployment at a minimum, continue to delay finalized regulations.

Most agreed that to encourage competition, state monopolies should be split up before offering the segments for sale at public auction. The determination of market price proved more difficult. Shares were offered at three different prices: one for individuals, another for employees of the firm (who get 20 percent of the business at a 50 percent rebate), and another for those paying with vouchers. Foreigners end up paying the highest price.

The Polish government has been slow to move on privatization for fear of making errors. Speed of conversion, market price, and the dissection of state monopolies run the risk of bringing the privatization program to a halt, or at best, to keep the process at a snail's pace. Polish economists, such as Adam Gwiazda, professor of economics at Szczecin University, have expressed fears of a reversal in popular support for market economy conversion without radical changes in the government's privatization program.

Foreign Direct Investment

So far, joint ventures with Polish firms have been the choice of most foreign companies. German firms top the list at US$152.6 million. Investments from American companies are a distant second, totaling US$53.2 million. Swedish firms kicked in US$46.4 million.

The Polish government has taken steps to encourage foreign investment with a series of liberalization incentives. Most restrictions on foreign investment have been lifted. Foreign companies may set up and own subsidiaries or invest in Polish companies (up to 100 percent ownership). Foreign-owned companies enjoy a tax holiday for three years and exemption from import duties. Curbs on repatriating profits have been rescinded.

In mid-1991, agreements reached with several Western firms allowed

Poland to purchase much-needed equipment on favorable terms to begin the modernization of communications, transportation, and banking systems. Although multinational giants are already trading and investing in Poland, several smaller deals have also been concluded. The trend seems to point to a continued mixture of large and small companies for both export trade and direct investments.

For example, AT&T will upgrade Poland's telecommunications network for US$100 million. McDonnell Douglas is selling US$350 million worth of jets to replace crumbling Soviet planes. Unilever N.V. purchased 80 percent of the Pollena detergent company for a cool US$200 million—the largest acquisition by a Western firm to date.

Exxon Corporation's German affiliate announced a US$8.4 million investment in a joint venture to operate service stations. Gerber began making baby food specifically for the Polish market. PepsiCo and Coca-Cola waged a bidding war for investments totaling US$50 to US$60 million.

General Motors plans to invest US$400 million in the Polish auto industry. Pilkington (Britain) invested US$140 million in a joint venture with HSO Sandomierz to operate a glass factory. ABB, the giant Swiss gas turbine company, invested US$50 million with Zamech to build turbines.

On the other side of the fence, smaller companies are also making headway. Golub Corporation of Schenectady, New York, and Epstein Engineering of Chicago have contracted to build a financial center with the National Bank of Poland.

SerVass, an Indianapolis trading company, announced that it has invested over US$5 million in a new factory for its Polish subsidiary, giving it the capacity to produce 3600 Otake television sets a day. The company plans to put in another US$15 million to expand the facility.

Stanley Works of New Britain, Connecticut, intends to export pliers and other hand tools from a joint venture facility it negotiated with a Polish company.

The most promising industries for foreign investment are: machine tools, meters and measuring devices, lighting equipment, home appliances, furniture (both wood and metal), heating systems, and ventilating and air conditioning equipment.

Polish tax rates are much too high to sustain corporate development. Both the representative office and the corporate rates stand at 40 percent. Joint ventures benefit from a three-year tax holiday, but that's hardly enough compared to other developing countries. Look for revisions in Poland's tax code before the end of 1992.

Foreign Trade

Exports from Poland have also begun to take hold. Table 15-1 shows the major hard-currency exports for 1990. Total exports to the West totaled more than

Table 15-1. Selected Polish Industry Hard-Currency Exports*

	US$ millions	Percentage increase over 1989
Chemicals	900	58
Metallurgical products	1300	43
Agricultural products	400	40
Electroengineering	1800	22
Light industry	500	20
Food	900	18
Fuels and power	800	2

*For the nine months ending September 1990.
SOURCE: Polish Central Statistical Office; *The Economist.*

US$11 billion, a jump of 34 percent from the previous year. During 1992 this trend continues as privatization accelerates.

On the import side, demand for Western products by Polish consumers with a per capita income of US$4180 has escalated significantly, hard times or not. Western apparel, automobiles and parts, household appliances, entertainment and leisure products, even jewelry, sells well. The import of processed foods and fast foods has become a big business. Basic agricultural commodities are also in high demand. In addition, the following items must be imported, at least until Polish industry modernizes: computers, peripherals, and software; medical supplies and equipment; process controls; instrumentation; leather goods, including shoes; aircraft and parts; public transport vehicles and parts; pharmaceuticals; and various types of chemicals.

On the capital goods side, the country needs virtually every conceivable type of machinery and equipment: metal-working, plastic-conversion, packaging, transport, construction, food-processing, woodworking, telecommunications, power-generation and power-distribution. The rebuilding of Poland's infrastructure and the construction of commercial and residential buildings calls for a complete assortment of construction equipment, materials, and services.

Future Outlook

Leadership of the Polish government is in turmoil. Finance ministers, prime ministers, and other key bureaucrats come and go as if through a revolving door. A recalcitrant parliament remains controlled by communists.

The control exercised by Lech Walesea is questionable, although he is expected to continue to pursue policies that will allow Poland to compete in international markets and eventually join the EC.

Stringent austerity programs have not brought hyperinflation under control. Yet, the country's fragile economy has paid a high price for accomplishments to date. Industrial output and employment fell sharply in 1990 and 1991 and were still declining in 1992. Progress in selling over 7600 state-owned businesses, slated for private ownership under the privatization program, has been agonizingly slow. A mere 1000 went on the block in 1991. Many still awaited buyers a year later.

Red Flag

In addition to the 50 percent forgiveness of national debt by the Paris Club, the IMF has agreed to a US$1.7 billion adjustment loan, provided that certain internal conditions are achieved. Recognizing that many of these conditions cannot be met, Poland has asked for relief.

Although inflation hit 80 percent in 1991 compared to a hoped-for 36 percent, the government is under constant pressure to ease monetary restrictions and permit bigger wage increases in state-owned companies. Labor strikes are becoming commonplace. The Polish budget deficit is out of control. Corruption scandals and mounting recessionary problems are bringing the government's reform program to a screeching halt. This will have a major negative impact on trade and foreign investment.

Without substantially more assistance from Western European private industry, financial institutions, and government agencies, Poland's future as a market economy is at best questionable. Without cooperation from Western Europe to eliminate trade barriers against Poland's meager export program, there is little hope for sufficient hard currency to purchase much-needed infrastructure and industrial equipment.

A go-slow policy continues to be the most reasonable course for foreign investors.

16
Hungary

Tips to Foreign Traders and Investors

1. Don't be fooled by trade and investment promotions or media hype. Financial and tax incentives are a far cry from those of other developing nations.
2. Go with a local partner. It's essential to cut through red tape.
3. Prepare to deal with excommunist politicians who still demand payoffs and practice favoritism.
4. Stick with exporting until the country develops further. Now is not the time to invest in facilities.
5. Embassy office in Washington: (202) 362-6730.

Hungary was the first country in Eastern Europe to begin the conversion to a market economy. It continues to stay far ahead of the pack with visible results. Up to one-third of all businesses are in private hands—not as a result of privatization, but because they were already privately owned under the communist regime (although unrecorded as such by official government statistics).

The nation's financial systems were also functioning under the communist regime. A rudimentary stock market gave budding capitalists a head start on the rest of Eastern Europe as the old government gave way to the new. Trading level was very low, but at least it was functioning.

Hungary's banking system was also in modestly good shape. A central bank and several retail banks were not in the same league as those in the West, but at least they existed. When the communists left power in 1989, the country's monetary system was already working. By capitalist standards it was very elementary, but it was certainly way ahead of any other Eastern European monetary system.

Table 16-1.   Hungarian Exports by Destination

	Percentage of total US$ billions
European Community countries	32.2
EFTA countries	11.9
Soviet Union	20.6
Other Comecon countries	10.9
Other countries (including the United States)	24.2

SOURCE: OECD.

Foreign Trade

Over 50 percent of Hungary's exports now go to the West. The country managed to earn a remarkable US$9.5 billion hard-currency trade surplus in 1990. The main exports were processed foods, chemicals, agricultural products, a small amount of specialized machinery, and some consumer goods. Most of these exports went to Western Europe, and the trend continued in 1991 and 1992. Table 16-1 shows the breakdown.

Hungary may be the closest to a market economy, but with a population of 10.6 million it still needs to import a wide range of Western goods and services. Hungarian businesses look to their European neighbors to supply the machinery, equipment, raw materials, professional and financial services, energy, and modernization technology to get them up to competitive speed.

Although the range of imports is too broad to list inclusively here, the major goods and services include:

Specialty chemicals

Mining equipment

Fuel, primarily oil

Construction equipment
and services

Banking computer systems
and services

Agricultural equipment

Rail cars, buses, automobiles,
and spare parts

Aircraft and parts

Consumer household goods

Telecommunications equipment

Power-generating and distribution
equipment and products

Tobacco

Leather goods, including shoes

Beverages

Processed food

Medical supplies and equipment

Process controls

Foreign Direct Investment

Foreign investment may seem like a trickle in Poland and the Czech and Slovak republics, but in Hungary it is rapidly becoming a torrent. In 1990 it totaled US$1.25 billion, far more than any of its neighbors. Estimates place 1991 investment at between US$1.5 and US$2 billion. An even higher rate is expected in 1992. *The Banker* estimates that the percentage of foreign ownership in Hungarian businesses could top 15 percent by early 1992 and reach 20 percent by year's end. The current target established by the Hungarian government is 25 to 30 percent (compared to 40 percent in 1938).

Like other Eastern European countries, Hungary's government has enacted a series of economic reforms aimed at stimulating foreign investment. Although the forint is not convertible outside Hungary, foreign investors may repatriate profits and capital in hard currency to the extent that forint funds are sufficient to cover the transfer.

Hungary has some way to go, however, in the direction of liberalizing government regulations to be as attractive to foreign investors as it could be. As developing countries throughout the world have found, such liberalization is imperative in order to sustain foreign trade interest. Although price controls have been dismantled on a wide range of goods, they still exist on many others. The country has also lifted many trade barriers and regulatory restrictions on foreign trade, yet exchange controls remain in effect, as do import and export tariffs and special taxes.

Foreign companies may own up to 100 percent of Hungarian businesses, except in specific industries.

Red Flag

As in other Eastern European countries, Hungary's tax system does not encourage foreign investment. Certain staged tax reductions are available, based on foreign shares in Hungarian companies, but overall tax rates remain much too high compared to other developing nations. The corporate tax rate, the capital gains rate, and the representative office rate all stand at 40 percent. In addition, a variety of special provisions can increase these rates under certain conditions.

Although American businesses moved to invest in Hungary at a rapid pace in 1990 (led by the GE-Tungsram light bulb joint venture), investment trailed off in 1991. General Motors jumped in with US$150 million for a joint venture with Raba to build cars and engines. Ford built a new plant for US$80 million. Suzuki teamed up with Autokonzem to build cars to the tune of US$110 million.

Sanofi (France) joined Chinoin for US$80 million to produce pharmaceuticals. Oberoi (India) invested US$80 million with Hungarhotels to build and operate several hotels. Sara Lee and Compack joined in a US$60 million food processing venture. Ilwa (Italy) invested US$25 million with Salgotarjua Iron to produce steel. Watmoughs (Britain) joined Revai Printing in a US$7 million publishing company. And Bay Holding (Austria) kicked in US$11 million to join forces with Nyiregyhaza in construction projects.

The Hungarian-American Enterprise Fund has provided a major stimulant to American companies exporting to and investing in Hungary. As added encouragement to Western investment, Hungary advertises itself as the major trade conduit to the former Soviet Union.

Interestingly, Japan's interest in Eastern Europe has been slack, although Hungary remains the favorite target. So far, Japanese companies have invested a mere US$12 million in twelve joint ventures, compared to more than US$1 billion and several thousand joint ventures by American and Western European companies.

Caution Alert

All is not a bed of roses, however. Although slightly less than predicted, inflation hit 25 percent in 1991 and the OECD predicts a 37 percent rate in 1992. The OECD also forecasts another drop in GDP. Output has decreased twice as much as forecasted— down 8 percent in 1991. Privatization has been slow. Only half the five hundred shops offered for sale in the first six months found buyers. Hungary has over 10,000 small state-owned retail and service shops to dispose of.

The privatization of large firms is even further behind. Preparing these companies for sale has proven a herculean task. In addition, without a voucher system for Hungarian citizens, few locals are taking the bait. Only sales to foreigners show any sign of life. Finance Minister Mihaly Kupa hopes to transfer all companies to private ownership by 1994. At this stage, no one believes that will happen.

Hungary is the most heavily indebted country in Eastern Europe, with foreign debt accounting for 65 percent of GDP. Its currency is convertible for most business uses, but not for individuals (although the distinction is hardly ever enforced). Trade barriers have come down, but tariffs remain high on certain imports to protect national industries.

The experience of the Schwinn Bicycle Company of Chicago typifies the obstacles facing foreign investors. Schwinn joined the Csepel Works in a joint venture (Schwinn-Csepel), capitalized at US$2.1 million, to produce 275,000 bikes a year for export to Western Europe and North America. Schwinn chose the Csepel Works of this giant, state-owned heavy manufacturing group based on its reputation and cheap labor. The Institute for Energetics (also state-owned) was the third partner.

Negotiations were time-consuming, difficult, and tedious. The deal took more than a year to complete because there were no uniform procedures. Joint venture laws kept changing (and they still do). Neither lawyers, company officials, or government officials knew precisely what had to be done.

Shortly after the joint venture began production, Hungary's import regulations changed again. The cost of imported components skyrocketed—15 percent duty, 25 percent VAT, and a 2 percent handling charge. Lack of computers in the customs office meant five people working full-time to count and calculate.

The company had a guaranteed line of credit from a Hungarian bank and met all its payments on time. But suddenly new monetary policies forced the bank to cut the line 30 percent. Interest rates on long-term debt remain at approximately 40 percent. Some raw materials cost more than in the West. Energy costs have soared. Productivity remains low.

Although 175 of the 675 employees inherited by the joint venture have left the company, Schwinn still feels productivity is much too low and defects too high. Traditions and secrecy held over from the communist regime foster favoritism and intense politicking by management staffs.

On the plus side, domestic sales are doing well. The company has established a 55-shop dealer network. Advertising is unnecessary. No competition exists except from Soviet bikes that are made so poorly they fall apart.

Financial Services

Privatizing the financial services sector is moving at a faster clip. Half of Hungary's thirty-plus small banks are now partially in private hands. In addition, 16 foreign banks have opened branches, subsidiaries, or representative offices.

To date, none of the larger banks have a majority foreign ownership; and it remains uncertain whether the Hungarians will ever permit this to happen. A new banking law currently being drafted restricts foreign ownership to 40 percent for the entire banking system. Hungary's banking and financial sector is still extremely primitive.

Government regulators react to changing conditions with a constant barrage of new regulations—some favorable, some unfavorable. Although the conversion of the nation's financial system looks encouraging compared to other sectors, it still has a long way to go.

Six of the country's ten insurance companies are already partly or fully foreign-owned. Budapest's stock exchange is also fairly active, and sports a surprising range of foreign securities considering the low level of activity. Listings include Creditstalt and Girozentrale from Austria, and Nomura and Daiwa from Japan, as well as Credit Suisse First Boston, Banque Indosuez, and Banque de Paribas.

The Hungarian dream is to make Budapest the financial center of Central Europe. To this end, the international property developer Olympia & York has teamed up with Magyar Hitel Bank to construct an international financial center out of a midtown parking lot.

Future Outlook

Compared to other Eastern European countries, Hungary is politically stable. Although ethnic divisions exist, they are too small to have a major political impact on the future of the country.

Hungary has earned high marks from international bodies for the effectiveness of its austerity programs. The international financial community also ranks Hungary's privatization initiatives to attract foreign investment among the best.

With a work force of nearly five million and a comparatively high per capita income of US$6,000, Hungary's future market and investment potential should be as good or better than most of its neighbors.

There is little question that Hungary's economy is the strongest in Eastern Europe. The country leads the pack, thanks largely to two decades of so-called "goulash communism." To keep moving, however, Hungary needs a debt-forgiveness package similar to that granted Poland.

Although the outlook for trade with and investment in Hungary remains modestly optimistic, Western companies might keep in mind the difficult experience of Schwinn.

17

The Czech and Slovak Republics

Tips to Foreign Traders and Investors

1. Don't be misled by media and government pronouncements. The Czech and Slovak republics is a tough market to crack.

2. Delay direct investment until both the privatization program and ethnic disagreements are resolved.

3. Insist on hard-currency payments for export orders.

4. Beware of very high potential environmental clean-up liability if buying an existing business. The Czechs are learning from the West how to soak companies for everyone else's pollution problems.

5. Embassy office in Washington: (202) 363-6316.

The former Czechoslovakia, renamed the Czech and Slovak Federal Republic (CSFR), and now moving toward a permanent split between the Czech republics of Bohemia and Moravia on the one hand and Slovakia on the other, has moved slower than either Poland or Hungary toward a market economy. Although there is a substantial cadre of highly skilled engineering talent, it has not—so far at least—been converted into designing or developing exportable products. Prior to World War II, Czechoslovakia boasted one of the most progressive industrialized economies in Europe. After fifty years of totalitarian rule, factories are falling part, labor productivity is abysmal, and pollutants fill the air and topsoil.

Economic reform is progressing, albeit slowly. The Czech government freed about 85 percent of administered prices in January 1991 and more since. At the

Table 17-1.   External Debt in Eastern Europe

	US$ billions	
	Net debt	Net debt/export ratio
Soviet Union	51	1.5
Poland	41	3.0
Hungary	20	1.8
Bulgaria	11	4.4
Yugoslavia	9	0.4
Czech and Slovak republics	6	0.7
Rumania	1	0.2

*As of 1990.
SOURCE: Deutsche Bank; *The Banker.*

same time, the koruna was made convertible for businesses but restricted for individuals.

Private business has not become the major force that it has in Poland or Hungary. Czech officials estimated that in 1991 private business accounted for a mere 2 percent of GDP.

At the macroeconomic level, the Czech and Slovak republics have fared better than any of their neighbors. According to the IMF, total output decreased a mere 4 percent in 1990, compared to 28 percent in eastern Germany, 23 percent in Poland, and 5 percent in Hungary. The republics also boast one of the lowest national debts: at a mere US$6 billion, it is just 0.7 percent of exports. Only Rumania carries less external debt, as shown in Table 17-1.

Foreign Trade

The Czech and Slovak republics need modern technology as much as products and services. According to government trade officials, energy, pollution control, and communications industries are the prime candidates for foreign technology transfer.

Specific Western-made products are also in high demand. High-tech Western firms should concentrate on computers, chemicals, instrumentation and equipment for monitoring and controlling, state-of-the-art construction machinery, and research laboratory equipment. In addition, technology licensing and Western imports are in high demand in the petrochemical, textile machinery, and television production industries. Markets are also ripe for cigarettes and candy.

The country's 15.7 million population boasts a per capita income of US$7900. This is the highest per capita income in Eastern Europe.

As in many other underdeveloped countries, air, water, and ground pollution are major headaches. Czech trade sources claim that imports of products and services for environmental cleanup and protection will be given high priority.

Medical supplies and equipment are also sorely needed. Hospitals and clinics are at least thirty years behind in diagnosis and treatment equipment. Disposable supplies are in very short supply, and in many cases nonexistent. Professional medical services also need significant upgrading.

Import and export barriers have been lowered somewhat, although relatively high tariffs remain in place for many imports deemed necessary to compete with local goods.

Since most businesses of any size are state-owned, the same bureaucratic hang-ups and corruption exist here as when selling directly to government agencies. On the plus side, government businesses have access to hard-currency reserves, so payment for imports should not be a major problem.

Foreign Direct Investment

There is no restriction on the percentage of foreign ownership of Czech companies. Local companies, including those owned by foreigners, may sell shares to the public and list them for trading on the Prague (or Bratislava) stock exchange. Through 1991, however, the exchanges were still in the formative stage.

The Czech and Slovak republics government has identified transportation, environmental cleanup and protection, chemicals, light industry, energy, telecommunications, metallurgy, tourism, and financial services as high priorities for foreign investment. Other, more specific industries offering excellent opportunities include: machine tools, earth-moving equipment, shoes, textile products, glassmaking, and wine.

Privatization continues at a snail's pace. About 6000 small shops have been sold at auction. The government hopes to sell another 11,000 as soon as possible. Nearly all these small businesses have been sold to Czech and Slovak citizens or returned to previous owners. Foreign investment has moved agonizingly slowly. Very few stakes have been sold in large state-owned companies.

A few large foreign investors have stepped forward, however. Germany's Volkswagen plans to spend US$6.1 billion over the next ten years to rebuild the Czech car manufacturer Skoda. The deal is worth nearly 10 percent of the entire Czech gross national product. By the year 2000, Volkswagen hopes to be selling 500,000 Czech-made cars throughout Europe.

CBS from France has invested US$175 million with Tourinvest to build and manage several hotels. Linde of Germany has invested US$196 million with Technoplyn to produce industrial gases. US West, in partnership with Bell Atlantic, has kicked in US$80 million to develop and build telephones and switches. Siemens (Germany) has invested US$11 million with Tesla Karin to begin a telecommunications venture.

Although the newly formed (1991) Czechoslovak-American Enterprise Fund has begun to attract smaller companies, to date the United States is a distant fourth in the number of joint ventures (and 60 percent of them involve less than a US$17,000 investment). American companies continue to look, however. In 1991, Prague was home to sixty American company representative offices.

In an effort to speed up conversion, the government plans a massive privatization program in 1992 using the voucher system for residents. Vouchers are being distributed to every adult citizen to exchange for stock in state-owned companies. The government is also trying to handle precommunist property-restitution claims.

According to the finance ministry, Western companies hoping to bid on Czech firms or to regain property lost before the communist takeover should move quickly to insert their bid or claim. Interested companies should send representatives to Prague and first contact the factory or ministry that oversees the enterprise. If the answer received is, "the company has already been purchased," the finance minister urges interested parties to contact him directly.

According to the finance minister, by the end of 1992 all companies will have been privatized except for schools, training academies, "strategic industries," health groups, and transport and telecommunications ventures. The minimum investment is US$100,000. Forty-one factories are also slated for liquidation. Foreign companies may purchase up to 80 percent of privatized businesses, with 20 percent reserved for citizens.

Except for those companies being auctioned, foreign investors must submit applications and business plans to the finance ministry. They will be evaluated using various factors, including who else is bidding, what investment will be put into the company, and the quality of the business plan.

Caution Alert

Indications from business leaders and potential entrepreneurs in Prague are that the voucher system will be only modestly successful. Lack of short- and long-term internal financing is the major stumbling block.

Predictions from the international business community suggest that the same absence of ownership regulations and contract laws as in Hungary and Poland will hinder any significant foreign participation in privatization efforts here.

Since privatization rules remain in a state of flux, two agenda items concern Western investors. First, will the regulations that are eventually passed prohibit foreign owners from instituting immediate, wholesale layoffs? To date, privatization agreements have been mandated to include such a provision.

The second question involves an environmental issue: will privatization agreements require foreign firms to clean up toxic waste remaining from previous state ownership? No one can hazard a guess, but if the United States and Western Europe are any indication of what could happen, investors should keep a wary eye on potential environmental liability.

Future Outlook

The biggest worry is the continuing tension between Czechs and Slovaks, which will probably lead to a "Velvet Divorce." On the economic front, the collapse of trade with the Soviets has hurt both exports and imports. Unlike Poland and Hungary, the Czech and Slovak republics had no private sector before the "Velvet Revolution" in 1989 and were more insulated from the West. President Vaclav Havel's promise to privatize over 4500 companies in 1991 and 1992 seems very optimistic. Foreign investors like the country's highly skilled work force but worry about the political situation.

Perhaps the best approach is the one used by Chiquita Brands International. Faced with an undeveloped market, Chiquita plans to use the next few years to build a distribution system and test-market its premium bananas as consumers grow wealthier and more discriminating.

Although Chiquita has been in Czechoslovakia for several years, it has always operated through a foreign trade organization, which until recently had a monopoly on trade with the West. Chiquita is dissatisfied with this approach and feels comfortable going it alone, using the test-market concept to expand slowly.

Another major concern is the extent to which the Czech or Slovak governments will enact additional tax and other investment incentives. To date, incentives have been meager and the tax system remains very outdated. The top income tax rate for corporations is a blistering 55 percent. Even the rate for companies with foreign equity ownership greater than 30 percent stands at a whopping 40 percent, as does the representative office rate. The potential for special dispensation upon application to the Ministry of Finance merely adds to the possibility of large payoffs to government officials

On top of income taxes, businesses with foreign equity ownership pay a 50 percent payroll tax on their gross payrolls. Firms that do not match their salary raises to changing government standards are socked with up to a 200 percent penalty. The current standard triggering the maximum penalty is salary increases more than 3 percent over the previous year. It's hard to visualize a better way to destroy worker initiative and productivity than restricting wage increases to less than 3 percent in the face of runaway inflation!

Currency conversion rules are more favorable. The koruna may be converted internally at the State Bank of Czechoslovakia, but not outside the country's borders. Foreign firms may repatriate profits and capital by converting to hard currency through the same bank.

Tax treaties have been signed with most European countries but not with the United States.

All things considered, the Czech and Slovak republics have a long way to go to be of significant interest to foreign traders or investors other than large multinationals with internal resources and staying power. Eventually, assuming the absence of civil strife, the republics should settle down. Until then, however, the risks to foreign companies appear to far exceed the potential rewards.

18
Backward Countries in Turmoil

Tips to Foreign Traders and Investors

1. Stay away from direct investment in Bulgaria, Rumania, and Albania.
2. Export to them only with both commercial and political risk insurance and hard-currency L/Cs.
3. Embassy offices in the United States:

   Bulgaria: (202) 387-7969
   Rumania: (202) 232-4747
   Albanian Mission to the United States (New York): (212) 249-2059

Foreign trade and investment with Bulgaria, Rumania, and Albania must be regarded as the highest risk endeavors in Eastern Europe or the former Soviet Union republics.

Civil war has thrown the former Yugoslavia into turmoil. Deep family hatreds on both sides will not be settled by a temporary truce or United Nations peacekeeping forces. Temporary lulls bring optimism, but hardly enough to risk business investments.

Bulgaria and Rumania remain locked in medieval social cultures. Both countries, but especially Rumania, face a herculean task of rebuilding decimated industrial bases inherited from former communist bosses. Bulgaria hopes to develop its tourist trade and become an Eastern Europe "Riviera," but has a lot to do to clean up its act before foreign visitors will be attracted. Shifting leadership makes the Rumanian government so unstable that the beginnings of long-term economic rehabilitation programs have become mired in political squabbling.

Albania remains a lost cause. Historically the poorest country in Europe, Albania became only poorer under its strong-arm dictators. For the foreseeable future, the country will attract only very high-risk ventures in trade or investment.

As with Hungary, moves toward a free-market economy in Bulgaria, Rumania, and Albania were started by reformed communists. Unlike their Hungarian counterparts, these excommunist officials retained power after near-free elections. Since then, widespread unrest in Bulgaria and Albania has led to multiparty coalition governments. Rumanians still cannot decide what form of government they want.

Bulgaria

The caretaker Bulgarian government, headed by lawyer Dimiter Popov, claims to be committed to radical IMF-backed reforms. These include decontrol of prices, removal of subsidies, a reduced budget deficit, a squeeze on credit and consumer spending, currency convertibility, land reform, and privatization.

A major restructuring of the banking system is also planned. Beginning in 1990, the government installed a two-tier system. It consists of eight sectorial banks spun off from the National Bank, and the planned formation of sixty small private banks. The entire system remains in a very weak condition, however, and is grossly undercapitalized. At some point banking, along with the entire financial system, must be overhauled if the country hopes to compete in world markets.

In 1991, the Bulgarian government launched its free-market conversion, opting, like Poland, for immediate rather than gradual changes, but on a much reduced scale. Except for 13 "essential" food items and public transport, prices were freed. The government unified the exchange rate and allowed it to float. Convertibility remains very limited, however, and wholly within the country.

Privatization is on the drawing board but has not started. Over 100,000 very small mom-and-pop private businesses have been started—20,000 in 1991 alone.

Restrictions on imports and foreign investment have been partially lifted, but tariffs are still much too high to stimulate foreign trade. Ownership laws and repatriation rights remain very foggy.

Red Flag

The biggest problem facing the Bulgarian government is finding a way to reduce an unmanageable level of foreign debt. If this is not achieved, hyperinflation is just around the corner.

Any major rollout from the government's economic reform program is expected to take ten to fifteen years. Output continues to decline well beyond 10 percent per annum. Food shortages are widespread. External debt-service payments are not being met. Very little hard currency exists, even to pay for much-needed energy imports.

Except under very unusual circumstances, Western companies will find better and more immediate opportunities elsewhere. As the political situation stabilizes and basic reforms take hold, conditions should improve. But this is not the time to venture into this country.

Rumania

Prior to communist rule, Rumania was predominantly an agricultural society. Communist leaders transformed the country into a maze of heavy industrial plants, and in the process created one of the world's worst cases of industrial pollution. Rumania's factories are totally outmoded and its labor efficiency ranks below that of most industrialized countries. Technical skills are abominably missing. With the exception of Albania, Rumania is now the poorest country, with the lowest living standards in all of Europe.

The country has virtually no external debt and labor is pitifully cheap. But the country has few other assets.

By mid-1991, a team of young technocrats were following the directions set by prime minister Petre Roman, who took command when president Ceaucescu's regime was toppled in 1989. The reform program included a two-stage price liberalization, reforms of the tax system, new labor and social laws, a foreign investment law, encouragement to private businesses, and the creation of a two-tier banking system, including the partial write-off of uncollectible loans.

It also included a privatization program for state-owned companies and agriculture involving the free distribution to employees of vouchers totaling 30 percent of equity in state enterprises. This "shock therapy" approach won the support of the IMF.

Caution Alert

In October 1991, Roman's regime was toppled. A former finance official, Theodor Stolojan, was designated prime minister, and he pledged to keep the reforms moving. This post-coup government acted to underpin a market-oriented economy, and moved the currency close to convertibility. It also scrapped subsidies and freed most prices. A 200 percent increase in prices within ten months was a primary cause of the riots that had led to the coup. Although the new prime minister has vowed never to let that happen again, only time will tell.

Rumania's political turmoil stalled at least US$750 million in foreign loans, including US$300 million from the World Bank.

Red Flag

Insufficient food production—which has declined 20 percent since the end of communism in this previously agricultural nation—continues to aggravate an unstable political environment. Shortages continue to be widespread.

Very little foreign investment or trade has found its way to Rumania. Its currency is still not convertible. Stringent trade controls remain in force. Although a privatization program began in August, the October coup disrupted sales. Over 50,000 private businesses have been registered, mostly one- or two-person service businesses. Prudent Western managers have adopted a wait-and-see attitude.

Albania

The caretaker government of Ylli Bufi is trying to open the doors of a previously sealed-off economy under former Communist Party boss Enver Hoxha. According to the IMF, output is falling drastically, the trade deficit is growing, and food shortages are acute. Although the new government has made overtures to forge links with the IMF and the European Community, little has yet been accomplished.

According to the U.S. Department of Commerce, the best prospects for trade with Albania include computer hardware and software, process controls, instrumentation, chemicals, energy-conservation processes and equipment, and consumer goods. But trade of any type assumes that somewhere hard currency can be found—not an easy task.

Western companies have not yet begun to explore seriously either trade or investment possibilities in this extremely poor, politically unstable country. Formal diplomatic relations with Washington still do not exist. Lacking formal embassy recognition, Albanian officials use the Albania Mission in New York as the point of contact with U.S. companies interested in establishing trading ties.

19
The Commonwealth of Independent States (Former Soviet Union)

Tips to Foreign Traders and Investors

1. Put investment plans on hold, with or without joint ventures, until central government authority in one form or another is restored.

2. Don't believe forecasts from anyone about when economic order might be restored: no one can be sure where the floor might be or when it will be reached.

3. Conduct trade with government agencies, state-owned companies, or private businesses only with letters of credit backed by hard-currency reserves.

4. Check out black market exchange rates against Gosbank quotes.

5. Beware of ruble conversion if and when republics introduce their own currencies.

The August 1991 coup attempt and subsequent breakup of the Soviet Union sent government officials, economists, and business leaders back to the drawing board. The speed of internal changes begun before the coup under Mikhail Gorbachev's *perestroika* (economic restructuring) accelerated mercilessly. Thousands of entrepreneurs working newly privatized farms and small businesses saw their incomes rise beyond expectations. With money to spend, they clamored for goods and services but found only empty shelves and closed doors.

Leaders of industrialized nations have found this phenomenon difficult to understand, much less cope with. Traditional Keynesian recessions, now common in North America and Western Europe and becoming more frequent in East Asia, stem from a slackening in the demand for goods and services. Overburdened with debt, facing increased credit shortages and escalating unemployment, consumers are unable to keep up the buying pace of better days. Fearful of even more severe economic privation in the future, they refrain from spending and hoard those resources they currently possess. Companies cannot sell their goods and therefore cannot pay their bills, leading to further collapse. But eventually, pent-up demand takes over, credit loosens, and spending once again stimulates companies to rev up their production facilities.

The Soviet Union, now renamed the Commonwealth of Independent States (CIS), faces a reverse situation. With incomes soaring and privatization of agriculture and small business taking hold, demand flourishes. Consumers and companies have money to spend but few goods or services to spend it on. Contrary to Western experience, this is a supply recession, or depression. For a variety of reasons, raw materials and finished goods have disappeared from supply channels. Factories, waiting for deliveries to produce products, have become idle. This in turn has crippled their customers, making it impossible for the production chain reaction to occur.

The uniqueness of the Soviet experience has caused more international concern than depressions in other countries. Experts have no prior experience to draw on. Traditional remedies won't work. Those that might work can only be guessed at. Much to the consternation of world leaders and global traders, it seems that the Soviet solution must inevitably be found through trial and error, necessitating much confusion and pain before the economy reaches its nadir and begins an upward climb.

One might presume that companies from industrialized countries could solve supply shortages merely by shipping the republics goods and services they need. That certainly is easy enough to accomplish, and many Western and East Asian companies are chomping at the bit to start exporting. It is the other side of the coin that stops them. How can Soviet companies, consumers, or government bureaus pay for these goods and services with an inconvertible ruble and hard-currency reserves at rock bottom?

A smaller country possessing a smaller population base and fewer natural resources would not attract such expert international attention. The CIS, however, has both a large and diverse population and an abundance of natural resources—including oil. Companies from both the East and the West expect enormous market and resource opportunities in many of the republics and therefore expend vast amounts of time, energy, and money strategizing the most opportune trade and investment approaches. Inevitably, the region's dysfunctional financial system presents a hurdle too high to jump.

As a prelude to developing trade strategizes, it is appropriate to review both the microeconomic conditions and the macroeconomic factors that traditionally determined the Soviet government's monolithic role in trade and investment decisions, the allocation of resources, and the ability of customers to acquire and pay for goods and services. This must be contrasted with today's situation, in which the social, cultural, ethnic, and political forces of twelve newly independent republics all demand attention and must bear heavily on any decision involving the reconstruction of the region's domestic and international trade.

As a framework for assessing these matters intelligently, the balance of this chapter will look at deterrents and opportunities as they relate to: central government issues, financial issues, and environmental issues. The chapter will then examine the market demand and resource availability resulting from the postcoup breakup into independent republics.

Central Government Issues

It is entirely possible that as the former Soviet republics struggle for mutually satisfactory means of integrating their economies and political institutions, the region could plunge into an economic snake pit akin to the Great Depression.

The causes of the current economic mess—with all its potential for disaster—may be debated by economists and academicians for decades, and certainly pose an interesting subject for intellectual dialogue. In the business world, however, we are more concerned with the future than the past: historical blame is only relevant to the extent that it helps strategize future trade and investment moves.

Every economy needs reliable, functioning mechanisms and institutions to match the production of goods and services with their consumption. Under communist rule, the central government filled the void by dictating production quotas and allocations. State-owned factories, distribution systems, banks, and mines took orders from the Kremlin. Although certainly inefficient, central control permitted the economy to function with some semblance of order. Now the region (country?) is shifting toward a market economy.

Even if the centrally controlled mechanisms and institutions had not been dismantled by inept reforms and the country's breakup into sovereign republics, they would not have been capable of functioning in a free market environment. A market economy matches market demand and producer supply through an integrated web of functioning (and *functioning* is the key) distributors, wholesalers, financial institutions, and investors. Free prices are set by market demand. Usable money must be available. Property rights and contract law must be in place. And last but certainly not least, a stable governmental structure must be in operation to protect, adjudicate, and legislate.

So far, the new CIS does not have these characteristics any more than did Gorbachev's Soviet Union.

A second element disrupting market conversion is the lack of consensus among the republics about resource allocation through interrepublic trade. The Baltic states traditionally shipped 50 percent of their output to other republics. The Russian republic, with over 50 percent of the population, exports nearly 20 percent of its output to other republics.

The debate is inflamed by the Kremlin's policy of allocating exclusive production capability to specific republics. For example, all commuter rail cars are made in Latvia. The Ukraine has enormous nuclear energy capability. Russia owns more than 90 percent of the region's oil production, while Kazakhstan has most of the oil reserves. Uzbekistan (third-largest in population) and Kazakhstan (fourth-largest in population) have substantial minerals but little manufacturing capability. Table 19-1 shows the magnitude of interrepublic trade for 1988, the latest year for which there are published statistics.

Without a workable agreement among all the republics, it is difficult to see how and where interrepublic trade will function in the future.

At the macro level, economic problems existed long before either the coup or perestroika. Under central planning, most production and distribution decisions were made administratively at government centers. However, consumers paid for goods and services with money, received income in money, and saved money.

In a market economy, sellers raise prices when too much money chases too

Table 19-1. Interrepublic Trade*

	Exports and imports as percentage of each republic's output	Total imports and exports (ruble billions)
Turkmenistan	75	7.9
Armenia	58	7.7
Moldavia	51	9.8
Estonia	51	5.7
Latvia	50	9.1
Belorussia	50	32.4
Lithuania	50	11.7
Tadzhikistan	48	5.0
Georgia	48	10.7
Kirgizia	48	5.5
Azerbaijan	46	11.7
Uzbekistan	45	20.6
Ukraine	30	83.1
Kazakhstan	30	22.0
Russia	10	138.3

*As of 1988.
SOURCE: National Statistics; *The Economist.*

few goods. In a centrally planned economy wherein misallocated production capacity is causing severe shortages, buyers hoard cash, buy precious metals or goods with resale or barter value, or add to their savings deposits.

When there is a parallel market (like the one that has existed in the Soviet Union since the days of perestroika) funds leak into that market, pushing up its prices. To some extent such leakage encourages additional supplies—but rarely enough to eliminate a "money overhang."

When conversion to a market economy begins, a burst of inflation creates social apathy as incomes are distributed by prices and wages at different rates (prices always exceeding wages, thus causing inflation dislocations). The implementation of perestroika created panic buying and hoarding in the Soviet economy.

However, according to the deputy chairman of Gosbank (the Soviet central bank), cash income represented only 10 percent of total expenditures throughout the economy. Under Gorbachev, government deficit financing was the primary inflation stimulator. The government used its own credit to grant indiscriminate and unsecured low-interest loans for investment in excessive inventory and long-term capital projects that would not be economically viable at market prices. Households continued to build excess monetary balances; business losses continued to be covered by state loans and the printing of more money.

The Supreme Soviet passed several inept reform packages, many with conflicting objectives whose originators were bureaucrats unfamiliar with the rules of market economics. They proclaimed the transition to a market economy as a national policy without providing the tools to make it happen. The result was confusion, conflicts of jurisdiction, and, most serious, uncertainty on the part of consumers and business leaders. In November 1990, Deputy Prime Minister L. Abalkin predicted that a full-fledged market economy would take a complete generation to develop. He was probably being conservative.

Consumer prices rose about 55 percent in the first six months of 1991, leveled out briefly, then continued escalating. Foreign debt was estimated at US$70 billion at the end of 1991. The twelve republics' trade surplus with the outside world was nil, and the OECD projected that a trade deficit beginning early in 1992 would escalate rapidly.

The CIS, or any subsequent entity, needs all the help it can get from the West and East Asia—way beyond the billions of dollars and credits already in the pipeline from the United States, the European Community, and Japan. The region must look to the West and Japan for loans, guarantees, joint ventures, and increased purchases of equipment and advanced technology—each desperately needed to patch up a deteriorating infrastructure and modernize factories.

The perception of Ronald L. Sloberg, an economist and manager of the risk-policy division of Security Pacific Corporation, is that instead of clarifying future opportunities, the coup discouraged foreign investors. It proved the volatility of the Soviet Union, which in turn gave marginal investors second thoughts about proceeding.

The oil industry is a good example of an entire sector in distress. It desperately needs help to drill, produce, refine, and distribute oil and its derivatives. Collapsing industrial equipment and outmoded technology leave enormous oil reserves untapped. Before the coup, U.S. oil companies planned to invest about US$5 billion in the Soviet oil industry. Chevron alone was negotiating a billion-dollar deal to develop the Tengiz oil field near the Caspian Sea. Some experts predict that if that deal is culminated, it could be a catalyst for other Western investors.

Caution Alert

Such a prediction seems optimistic, given the lack of unity among the republics and the absence of a unifying central government policy. If the republics are to survive in any integrated form, some type of federalization must eventually occur. Until then, most companies seem willing to wait it out and redirect their strategies to other, more stable global markets.

Two other elements muddy the assessment of trade and investment opportunities:

1. The absence of reliable methods for accumulating economic data
2. The extraordinary inability of the republics' governments to come up with workable reform packages

Blueprints for reforming the economy are no sooner issued than discarded as unworkable. Producing, revising, synthesizing, and dumping economic plans creates an aura of gross uncertainty—definitely the wrong environment to attract serious foreign trade and investment. The command economy is dead; the market economy, nowhere in sight.

Investing time and resources without a reasonable expectation of when and how the political and social fabric will mend takes unusual foresight and a gambling nature—not qualities noted in business leaders. Nevertheless, 280 million people are clamoring for everything from TV sets to hamburgers, shoe polish to movies, computers to automobiles. For those companies willing to take the risk, the CIS presents a gold mine of market opportunities, some of which may be realized in the short term, but most of which, only over the long haul.

Official figures released by the state committee for statistics prior to the coup, although certainly incomplete and probably grossly optimistic, placed GNP for the first six months of 1991 10 percent below that for the comparable period the year before. Industrial output was down 6 percent and agriculture output down 11 percent. Prices were reported to be 58 percent higher than those for the previous year, although the chairman of the committee placed the jump at 110 percent.

Forecasts from Soviet (now Russian) economists are becoming gloomier by the week. The deputy head of the interim committee charged with running the economy, predicted a 1991 GNP 17 percent below that for 1990. Anders Aslund, a respected Sovietologist, forecasts a 20 percent drop. Another deputy prime minister and economist told the news agency Interfax that inflation is running 2 to 3 percent per week—240 to 365 percent per year. That's hyperinflation by anyone's book. Other forecasts place the combined budget deficits at 270 billion rubles—a staggering 25 percent of GNP, and climbing.

The frightening part of this whole scenario is that the economy's fall resulted from the decay of the planning system, not the response to market forces. That is why no one can intelligently judge where the floor might be or when it will be reached. Meanwhile, politicians debate which of the competing reform plans they should try next.

Red Flag

Foreign trade with Soviet and republic central governments and companies collapsed near the end of 1991. The oil industry is in terrible shape: as a result, oil exports, the main source of foreign exchange, have suffered a severe blow. This has led to a drastic decrease in imports—close to 50 percent. Lack of imports have made the bottlenecks in domestic output that much worse.

State finances are out of control—the result of the republics' holding back tax revenues from the Soviet central government, thus forcing external debt to balloon.

Many joint ventures that once looked attractive have stagnated. Foreign direct investment for all except very large investors has dried up, even though 100 percent foreign ownership is permitted.

Financial Issues

In practical terms, the internal financing of foreign trade and investment has totally collapsed. Vacillating reform policies have left the banking system in ruins. Under communist rule, foreign traders could be assured of getting paid within thirty to forty days with hard currency from importer accounts at Vnesheconombank, the Bank for Foreign Economic Affairs (the official foreign trade bank).

This cash payment system has broken down. As part of the economic reform program, state-owned businesses were allowed to handle their own foreign exchange transactions, passing foreign currency through Vnesheconombank. As a result, Vnesheconombank continued to meet its commitments while state businesses fell further behind. In mid-1991, these companies owed between US$4 and US$5 billion in overdue bills for imports of hard-currency goods.

Although bank privatization should eventually lead to more flexible foreign exchange transactions, the current atmosphere remains chaotic. Privatized banks are lining up against Vnesheconombank to handle foreign exchange—just as reform plans get going to decentralize the system for foreign currency auctions.

Red Flag

Western companies have quickly learned that, at least for the moment, trade is better handled through letters of credit backed by hard-currency reserves than through open accounts. They have also learned that if letters of credit are not available, sales should not be concluded.

The Moscow Stock Exchange has opened, although it is set up to trade shares that do not yet exist in privatized companies. The Moscow Commodity Exchange is a more serious venture. It is functioning, although traders consider it more of a bazaar than a commodity exchange by Western standards. Companies use it to sell above-quota output and to search for scarce supplies. Plans call for specialization in oil, construction materials, and grain, and for trading five days a week rather than the current two. With the many uncertainties arising from republic independence, however, the timing remains indeterminate.

Government leaders and businesses can expect little help from Western banks. When Mikhail Gorbachev came to power, Western banks couldn't wait to lend to the new regime. It didn't take long, however, to recognize that, as with everything in the Soviet Union, what you see is not necessarily what you get.

Long before the 1991 coup, alarm bells were going off in the boardrooms of lending banks that had leaped before they looked. Most of these banks are in Western Europe, predominantly Germany, France, Italy, and, to a lesser extent, Britain. Worried about the Soviet Union's US$60 to US$70 billion in net foreign debt, many banks cut their exposure.

Even though gross foreign debt nearly doubled between 1986 and 1989 and the proportion of Soviet debt held by commercial banks rose from 50 to 66 percent, some Western banks remained confident that they could cope. In April 1989, Gorbachev allowed 15,000 Soviet enterprises to trade abroad. The banks, assuming that loans would be implicitly guaranteed by the Soviet government, obliged with new credits. Then the axe fell.

As overdue payments to Western firms began piling up, eventually hitting US$6 billion, Vnesheconombank denied responsibility for debts it had not specifically backed. In October 1990, a presidential decree ordered all enterprises engaged in foreign trade to pay 40 percent of their 1991 profits into a central fund that would be used to pay off the arrearages.

The result? Companies merely salted away more in illegal foreign bank accounts and reported less profits.

This Soviet version of flight capital finally convinced the remaining Western banks that the country had become a basket case. Once they realized the full

Table 19-2.   Commercial Bank Loans Outstanding to the Soviet Union/CIS

	US$ billions
Germany	21.9
France	5.5
Japan	4.5
Italy	4.5
Austria	3.3
Britain	3.2
Switzerland	3.0
Netherlands	2.1

NOTE: Banks in Finland, Belgium, Sweden, Spain, and the United States each hold loans of less than US$1 billion.
SOURCE: BIS.

extent of their mistake, they all began bailing out. It is now nearly impossible to obtain trade credit from any Western bank.

Through 1991, the pile of overdue bills was hardly dented, even though imports were slashed by 50 percent. This, in turn, has taken an additional toll on major Eastern European and Finnish trading partners.

Table 19-2 shows the amount of outstanding Soviet or CIS loans from commercial banks, using the latest 1991 figures available from the Bank for International Settlements.

It should be noted that much of the German lending was backed by German government guarantees. French banks weren't as prudent, getting a mere 15 percent guaranteed, thus exposing themselves to US$4.8 billion (about the same exposure as German banks).

Another financial problem now faced by the republics is the near exhaustion of foreign currency reserves. The chairman of Vnesheconombank reported to the World Bank and the International Monetary Fund that the nation's reserves were "close to zero." He also reported that the central government held 240 tons of gold reserves worth about US$2.7 billion and that figures were still being compiled on the amount held by the republics.

Although gold reserves have been tapped already to counter negative private credit, further sales could destroy the world gold market, creating even more havoc in international financial circles.

Red Flag

It is quite clear that without a massive infusion of Western aid, the republics will plunge into a classic, less-developed-country balance-of-payments crisis similar to that experienced during the 1980s in Africa and Latin America. If and when that happens, all bets are off about the timing or even the desirability of tapping either CIS markets or resources.

Caution Alert

Early on, foreign traders traveling to Moscow became cognizant of a thriving black market in rubles. The black market's success at offering a rate of 30 rubles to one U.S. dollar encouraged the government to abandon efforts to hold currency auctions to set the rate at which tourists could buy rubles. Instead, the Gosbank set the ruble-dollar rate at 32, undercutting the street price. Tourists immediately flocked to the banks.

This new rate applies to foreigners living in the CIS as well as to local citizens buying money to travel abroad.

Official Aid from the IMF

Prior to its breakup, the Soviet Union applied for full membership in the IMF to avail itself of another avenue for financial bailout. The United States opposed the request on the grounds that the Soviets should move further toward a market economy and a convertible currency before joining the 155-member organization. This excuse was nonsense. The IMF charter does not forbid members with planned economies: both Rumania and Yugoslavia have been members for several decades. The real reason for the U.S. position, backed by several other rich countries, is more convoluted.

The immense capital demands from Eastern Europe and Latin America are draining IMF coffers. To increase country contribution quotas, governments that account for 85 percent of the total quotas must approve national funding. The United States is committed to 20 percent of the total, and therefore its approval is crucial. But with the horrific deficit in Washington, Congress's reluctance is understandable. Table 19-3 shows the IMF contribution quotas for the top ten contributors.

Each country has a quota equal to the subscription it pays to the IMF. The subscription also determines its voting power and the amount it can borrow. Quotas are based on a complicated formula that weighs GNP, trade, and

Table 19-3. IMF Contribution Quotas for the Top Ten Contributors

	US$ billions	Percentage of total
United States	35	20
Japan	11	6
Germany	11	6
Britain	10	5
France	10	5
Saudi Arabia	7	4
Italy	6	3
Canada	6	3
Netherlands	5	3
China	5	3

SOURCE: IMF.

official reserves. The CIS is probably fourth behind the United States, Japan, and Germany in terms of GNP, but its external trade and reserves are low, thus reducing its likely quota. If admitted, it could probably get about the same as France or Britain: about US$10 billion.

But calculating the quota size for a new entrant is just the beginning of the problem. Other quotas may have to be reset, juggled, and the balance of power can shift. The last resetting ended in three years of squabbling between France and Britain.

To get in, the CIS would have to pay about 25 percent of its subscription in hard currency, the rest in rubles. It would also have to disclose accurate information about its economy, gold reserves, and foreign exchange reserves, and allow IMF official access to review its policies.

Late in 1991, the IMF granted the Soviet Union "associate" status, giving it access to IMF's advice, but not money. Which entity, if any, will fill the shoes of the now dismantled Soviet Union remains unclear.

Why Worry about Esoteric Financial Issues?

One might well ask the question: why is all this financial background germane to doing business with the CIS? The answer is threefold:

1. Without a freely convertible ruble and a foreign exchange system that permits payment in hard currency, foreign traders must rely on guarantees from CIS banks. Without a stabilized banking system capable of backing a buyer's credit with guarantees, no foreign bank or export credit agency will provide trade finance.

2. Without sufficient government-held foreign reserves, national currency convertibility cannot be assured.

3. Without foreign exchange reserves, a country's only source of financial aid is a multilateral agency such as the IMF. Since a country must comply with IMF-dictated economic standards to qualify for aid, a company that ignores the critical role of IMF scrutiny runs a huge risk of jeopardizing its strategies for developing new markets and resources.

More than anything else, the CIS needs foreign private investment and management to resolve the many obstacles in its path to establishing a market economy. But foreign companies will not invest unless they can be assured of the free repatriation of profits and capital in hard currency. To give this assurance, the country needs an exchange rate that is both convertible and stable.

Practical roadblocks to Western support of the ruble have already been discussed. In addition, free aid is a blank check to as-yet-unqualified and perhaps untrustworthy officials from Russia and other republics.

Several tentative market-based solutions have been put on the table by officials from the IMF, the European Commission, the U.S. government, and influential leaders in the international banking community. To date, all have been rejected by the Russian republic, and without Russia's endorsement, no other republic seems willing to step forward.

Environmental Issues

The CIS republics face two massive environmental challenges. The first is to clean up the horrific mess left by seventy years of environmental neglect. The second is to protect the environment from further degradation. Since it is impossible for any of the former Soviet republics to accomplish either objective on its own, both avenues offer enormous opportunities for foreign firms.

Although the old central government had stringent environmental control laws on the books for decades (far more stringent than those existing in the United States or Europe), virtually no attempt was made to enforce them. The costs of the environmental cleanup have not even been estimated, but will certainly run into the hundreds of billions of U.S. dollars. Nor has anyone attempted to project the time schedule for such a massive cleanup, although environmentalists gingerly talk about three to five decades—if ever.

This environmental crisis is not merely a concern of ecological activists. It contributes directly to the region's near-hopeless economic situation. By the time the Chernobyl disaster is fully accounted for, the total bill is expected to top US$350 billion—14 percent of 1988's GNP.

Russian environmentalists conservatively estimate that industrial pollution and natural resource degradation costs continue to run more than 17 percent of GNP—annually. Environmental protests from the Soviet people over the last few years have forced the closing of hundreds of factories that produced such critical goods as medicines, paper products, and heating equipment. Millions of acres of contaminated farmland have been removed from agricultural production, contributing to food shortages throughout the country.

As Western nations have already learned, the only feasible way to stop ecological degradation is to utilize private sector capital investment for environmentally safe production facilities, waste disposal, and advanced agricultural technology.

Market opportunities for foreign companies focused on environmental cleanup and the production of ecologically safe products are even more abundant in the CIS than in Eastern Europe. The widespread damage is even more severe in the CIS, and virtually every facet of the economy needs new technology and equipment.

Take pollution from industrial production as a prime example. In 1989 the Soviet State Committee for the Protection of Nature issued a report stating that air pollution in 103 cities housing 50 million people was 10 times worse than that allowed under Soviet standards. In addition, 16 communities experienced air pollution levels 50 times the standard. Air pollution has not improved since 1989, and many cities have become much worse.

According to Hilary F. French, noted environmental author and senior researcher at Worldwatch Institute, industrial by-products that cannot be pumped into the air in the CIS are randomly dumped into lakes, streams, rivers, and inland seas. Industrial discharges, plus untreated sewage and agricultural runoff, have contaminated most of the region's inland waterways and seashores. That includes Lake Baikal, the world's largest body of fresh water, which supplies 80 percent of the commonwealth's fresh water needs.

Throughout the countryside, indiscriminate dumping of hazardous waste has polluted millions of acres of rich farmland. Statistics are scarce, but according to J. D. Peterson, in his report, "The State of the Environment: Solid Wastes," dated May 1990, more than half the republics' 6000 landfills do not meet old Soviet standards. Over 75 percent of the landfills in Uzbekistan, Georgia, Moldavia, Latvia, and Turkmenistan are not in compliance.

According to J. D. Peterson's June 1990 report, "The State of the Environment: The Land," land degradation has become a major deterrent to raising agricultural productivity. More than 1.5 billion tons of topsoil are eroded each year, accounting for production losses of between US$31 and US$35 billion annually.

Inappropriate fertilizers and pesticides take a further toll, causing costly and dangerous health problems. In 1987 it was found that 30 percent of foods contained concentrations of pesticides dangerous to human health. In some areas, half the food supply was contaminated.

As with air pollution, land degradation can only be stopped by the investment of foreign capital and technology.

Other environmental disasters include faulty irrigation practices, which have drained two-thirds of the commonwealth's fresh ground water supply. Forests are ruined by acid rain and overharvesting; in the Russian Far East, nearly 25 percent of timberland has been lost. The nuclear disaster at Chernobyl forced plans for thirty nuclear power plants to be abandoned or shelved indefinitely.

Ms. French reports that the former Soviet Union, which covers about 12 percent of the earth's land mass, is responsible for 19 percent of the carbon dioxide emissions that are causing global warming, 13 percent of the chlorofluorocarbons that are depleting the ozone layer, and 20 percent of the sulphur dioxide emissions that are causing acid rain.

An Opportunity for Smaller Firms

The big question facing foreign companies is how to tap this enormous environmental market when the region's ruined economy has sapped hard-currency reserves. Although media coverage has been minimal, several international bodies have stepped forward with financial and technical assistance earmarked for environmental cleanup and technology to prevent future degradation.

At the intergovernmental level, bilateral agreements on scientific and technical cooperation once existed between the Soviet Union and ten countries. The Scandinavian governments plan to finance pollution-control equipment to stop emissions from two nickel smelters near their borders that are causing acid rain. The European Community, working jointly with Russian and Ukrainian agencies, is trying to structure a nuclear safety program. The U.S. government has promised to help fund a center for promoting energy efficiency.

Although public sector funding is important, it barely scratches the surface. Massive doses of both public and private capital are needed to make a dent. Smaller foreign firms can utilize creative countertrade arrangements or, when the financial system opens once again, normal trade finance.

The CIS environmental problem is so severe, however, and the cleanup cost so immense that the development of environmentally safe technology must fall to public institutions or large transnational corporations capable of raising capital on the open market. When and if such dedication will be forthcoming remains to be seen. Time will tell.

Meanwhile, market opportunities remain for smaller firms producing virtually any environmentally related products or services. Now is the time to plan for the strategic entrance to this very lucrative market, even though actual participation may have to be delayed until financial issues get resolved.

20
Opportunities in the CIS Republics

Tips to Foreign Traders and Investors

1. Trade only with businesses in Russia and Ukraine for the foreseeable future.

2. Seriously consider Western-oriented entrepreneurial businesses that can generate hard currency.

3. Stay away from Western "experts" in Soviet trade. Most have little or no hard-core experience and don't know what they're doing.

4. When the financial system stabilizes, check out the potential for exporting environmental protection technology and equipment in joint venture with Western contractors.

5. Insist on Western government commercial and political risk insurance for all exports or direct investments.

6. Embassy office of the Russian republic: (202) 628-7551.

In 1991 the international community witnessed the breakup of one of the four largest, most heavily populated trading areas in the world. Although several years will pass before the full ramifications of the Soviet political and economic disunion are fully known (some world leaders estimate twenty to thirty years), global traders must assess market openings and competitive resource availability as opportunities present themselves.

Companies wishing to tap a market of more than two hundred million people and a landmass rich in oil and other minerals as well as agricultural commodities must develop strategies from available data (skimpy as it may be) and informative projections. To wait for the full stabilization of political and economic institutions is to yield competitive advantage.

The Commonwealth of Independent States (CIS) consists of all former Soviet republics except the Baltic states of Lithuania, Estonia, and Latvia, which won their independence after the August coup and have no plans to join any form of union with any ex-Soviet republics.

When the CIS was formed, the republics agreed to abandon any semblance of central government from Moscow or anywhere else, although Kiev was selected as the titular site of centralized commonwealth activities. Being the largest state, Russia assumed the United Nations seat of the former Soviet Union, along with several other functions of the former central government. However, no pretense was made that the Russian government was a successor to the Kremlin.

While such an economic union was a prerequisite for Western aid, the exact provisions of the commonwealth agreement will be negotiated among the republics for several years to come. In general terms, preliminary provisions call for a single monetary and banking system, coordinated customs rules and tariffs, and cooperation in energy, transportation, and communications.

Proposals were also introduced to permit the republics to have their own currencies and control their own national budgets. Ukraine first announced that it would introduce its own currency, then acquiesced to a common ruble.

Caution Alert

Reform economists claim that the introduction of separate currencies by individual republics could lead to economic catastrophe. Foreigners should keep a close eye on further developments in this area, as well as on the impact such national currencies could have on any form of centralized banking system.

Should separate currencies be introduced, the big unanswered questions are how and when each republic would build regional exchange reserves and achieve currency convertibility.

An economist with extensive Soviet experience, Michael Claudon, of the Geonomics Institute in Vermont, has been quoted as saying that the breakup into republics will make the economic collapse worse in many ways, but will also give some republics the freedom to follow their strong desires for a market economy as fast as they can. It is his opinion that separate states will advance much quicker in the conversion process than the Soviet Union could have done as a whole. For obvious reasons, the U.S. government, World Bank, and the International Monetary Fund disagree.

Ranking the Republics for Trade and Investment

What many believe to be the most thorough analysis of the twelve republics to date was released by Germany's largest bank, Deutsche Bank. Portions of this analysis that relate to strategies for foreign traders are as follows:

1. Three republics have significant economic potential: Ukraine, the breadbasket of the region; Russia, with its vast reserves of oil and other miner-

als; and Georgia, which boasts one of the most efficient "business" economies in the region. (The breakaway Baltic states are also highly industrialized.) Although Russia has the natural resources, Deutsche Bank rates it behind the Ukraine and Baltic states as an economically viable entity.

2. Five republics have moderate economic potential: Belorussia, which is highly industrialized but resource-poor; Kazakhstan, which is mineral rich but ethnically divided; Moldavia, which is close to Europe and partially tied to Rumania but has few natural resources; and the Caucasus republics of Armenia and Azerbaijan, which are both politically unstable and without industrial bases.

3. The bank found that the four Central Asian republics of Uzbekistan, Turkmenistan, Kirghizia, and Tadzhikistan have no potential as independent economic entities. They are all dependent on external sources for all types of finished goods. They have virtually no capacity to earn hard currency with their own resources and products.

Deutsche Bank attempted to rank the republics by economic potential for trade and investment using nine different variables:

- Degree of industrialization
- Mineral resources
- Agricultural production
- Hard-currency earning capacity
- Level of education
- Business-mindedness
- Proximity to European markets
- Homogeneity of population
- Infrastructure

The bank put the Baltic states of Latvia, Lithuania, and Estonia, which refuse to join the CIS or any other Soviet-related economic union, second, third, and fourth behind the Ukraine as potential trade and investment partners.

The following summarizes the characteristics of the twelve republics comprising the Commonwealth of Independent States and forms an outline for appraising market opportunities and resource availability. Much of this information was compiled by Bruce Larrick for the *Philadelphia Inquirer*. The balance was derived from Deutsche Bank, the *New York Times,* the *Statesman's Yearbook,* the Associated Press, Reuters Wire Service, and the *World Almanac.*

The European Republics

1. Ukraine (Deutsche Bank ranking: 1)

Ukraine's 233 thousand square miles (an area slightly smaller than Texas) is home to 54.1 million people. Referred to as the breadbasket of the region because of its huge wheat production, Ukraine also grows large amounts of sugar beets, tobacco, fruit, and vegetables. The Donat Basin is heavily industrialized and boasts large deposits of coal, oil, natural gas, and iron ore. The two most important industries are chemical processing and machine tools.

2. Russia (Deutsche Bank ranking: 5)

With a population of 148 million spread over 6.6 million square miles (nearly twice the area of the United States), Russia controls over 75 percent of the landmass of the former Soviet Union, 50 percent of its population, and 70 percent of its total economic output. Its major industries include steel, oil production, chemical processing, electrical power, aerospace, farm equipment, agriculture, oil, coal, and other mining.

3. Belarus (formerly Belorussia) (Deutsche Bank ranking: 7)

This republic, with 10.1 million people living in 80 thousand square miles (about the size of Kansas) is highly industrialized, with a broad manufacturing base and skilled workers. Major industries include heavy machinery, machine tools, appliances, farm equipment, steel, cement, textiles, leather, glass, and timber. Agricultural commodities are predominantly livestock and dairy products.

4. Moldavia (Deutsche Bank ranking: 9)

Comprising 13 thousand square miles (about the size of Massachusetts and Connecticut combined) and 4.2 million people, Moldavia is closely tied to Europe. Light manufacturing is mostly limited to textiles and electrical equipment. Winemaking contributes substantially to the economy. Small quantities of tobacco, fruits, vegetables, and grains make up its agricultural base. Moldavia has virtually no minerals, timber, or energy sources.

The Caucasus Republics

5. Georgia (Deutsche Bank ranking: 6)

Georgia is comprised of 27 thousand square miles (about the size of West Virginia) and 5.3 million people. It has virtually no self-sufficient industry or natural resource base. It does have coal and manganese mines and small facilities for steelmaking and textiles. Winemaking, silk, grains, tea, grapes, and tobacco make up the balance of the economy. Seaports on the Black Sea encourage tourism.

6. Armenia (Deutsche Bank ranking: 10)

Armenia's 11 thousand square miles (about the size of Maryland) and 3.5 million people mine copper, zinc, aluminum, molybdenum, and marble, and grow cotton, fruits, grapes, olives, and grains. Textiles and cement comprise the only manufacturing.

7. Azerbaijan (Deutsche Bank ranking: 11)

Azerbaijan has very little industry in its 33 thousand square miles (about the size of Maine), although some steel, electrical equipment, and chemicals are produced. The republic has modest mineral resources in oil, iron ore, cobalt, copper, lead, and zinc. Agriculture, timber, and fishing make up the balance of an economy that supports 6.9 million people.

The Central Asian Republics

8. Kazakhstan (Deutsche Bank ranking: 8)

This republic is comprised of 16.5 million people and one million square miles (twice the size of Alaska). It is important to the region for its extensive mineral deposits of coal, oil, iron ore, copper, lead, and zinc. It has an agricultural base consisting of grains, tobacco, cotton, and livestock.

9. Uzbekistan (Deutsche Bank ranking: 12)

Uzbekistan is the most important republic in Central Asia and consists of 173 thousand square miles (comparable to California) and a population of 19.6 million. It supplies the entire CIS with 67 percent of its cotton needs and 50 percent of its rice. It also has an industrial base consisting of steel, automobiles, farm equipment, electronic equipment, and textiles.

10. Turkmenistan (Deutsche Bank ranking: 13)

Turkmenistan is basically a nomadic republic consisting of 188 thousand square miles (larger than California) and 3.5 million people. It has modest mineral deposits of coal, sulfur, salt, and gypsum. It also manufactures carpets.

11. Kirghizia (Deutsche Bank ranking: 14)

Another poor, primarily agricultural economy with a small manufacturing base in light machinery and chemicals, this republic's population of 4.2 million lives in a 77-thousand-square-mile area (close to the size of Nebraska).

12. Tadzhikistan (Deutsche Bank ranking: 15)

This very poor agricultural region of 54 thousand square miles (about the size of Illinois) supports five million people. Its only major resource is a hydroelectric plant.

Foreign Direct Investment

During 1990, joint ventures with Soviet companies stirred the hearts and minds of American, European, and Japanese executives. In response to the government's privatization of state-owned businesses, and to the new entrepreneurial spirit permeating Soviet business, large and small foreign companies jumped on the perestroika bandwagon, eager to partake of apparently enormous untapped markets and resources.

Chevron attempted the biggest American-Soviet joint venture in history to develop the rich Tengiz oil field. Ford set up a joint venture dealership in Dnepropetrovsk, 250 miles southwest of Kiev in Ukraine, and planned a second one in Tallinn, 200 miles west of St. Petersburg. It also planned service centers in Moscow and St. Petersburg.

Bell Atlantic signed an agreement with Belle Mead International Telephone, under which Bell Atlantic would build and run a mobile cellular phone system in Moscow. Belle Mead was one of two companies chosen by the Soviet Ministry of Communications to provide the service. Many smaller firms from the United States and Europe executed joint ventures with Soviet partners.

Red Flag

Two years later, with the economy deteriorating and republics declaring independence, U.S. business interest has ground to a halt. "Things are on hold," according to Margaret H. Chapman, director of U.S.–U.S.S.R. trade programs for the American Committee on U.S.–Soviet Relations, a Washington organization that for years pushed for greater investment in the Soviet Union. European and Japanese companies have also pulled back just at the time when the CIS needs foreign investment more than ever before.

Conditions have become so ragged that private economists and U.S. government officials claim it is no longer possible to supply an up-to-date list of joint ventures and other investments. Apparently the records were moved from Moscow to the republics, where no one was prepared either to analyze or file them. It's anyone's guess when this mess will be straightened out.

Only about US$3 billion has been invested by Western companies in joint ventures or business startups since the doors opened in 1987. However, many of those have taken hold and are beginning to develop into viable businesses. Arkady Volsky, president of the Scientific Industrial League, which represents about 75 percent of all state and private businesses, claims the private sector already employs more than twenty million people in cooperatives and nonstate, market-driven enterprises. While state production fell 12.5 percent during the first half of 1991, Volsky notes that output from cooperatives and joint ventures rose by 3.8 percent.

Clearly, when the market reopens, Western oil firms will be the first to jump in, simply because hard currency can be earned and cashflow will secure financing. Furthermore, it is likely that foreign investors will stick to Russian and Ukrainian market opportunities rather than venture into the unknown Caucasus and Central Asian republics.

Aside from oil companies, U.S.–based grain giant Cargill has searched for more than a year for a joint venture partner. Other food companies, large and small, are also interested, believing that scarce commodities and high consumer demand foretell enormous opportunities. Still, no one is in a hurry, including Cargill.

Mining and refining of industrial and precious metals is another major industry that should attract substantial foreign investment. Traditionally, the former Soviet Union exported 50 percent of the West's palladium supply and 11 percent of its nickel needs. According to the best Western guesses, this makes the region the world's largest or second-largest producer of all the major refined metals except tin. (See Table 20-1.)

The same holds true for precious and minor metals. The CIS is the world's largest producer of palladium (67 percent). It is second only to South Africa in world platinum output (25 percent), and second in rhodium production, with 33 percent of world output. It is third in gold production (behind South Africa and the United States) and either first or second in the production of chromium, vanadium, manganese, magnesium, titanium, and mercury.

Table 20-1. World and Soviet Metal Production

	Million tons		
	World total	Soviet production	Exports to West
Aluminum*	18.1	2.3 (2nd)†	0.3
Copper‡	10.9	1.3 (2nd)†	0.1
Lead‡	5.9	0.7 (2nd)†	0.02
Tin*	0.2	0.02 (4th)†	N/A
Zinc‡	7.2	1.0 (1st)†	0.01
Nickel‡	0.9	0.2 (1st)†	0.1
Iron ore*	973.0	236.0 (1st)†	N/A

*As of 1990.
† Soviet ranking in world production.
‡ As of 1989.
SOURCE: World Bureau of Metal Statistics; *The Economist*.

Table 20-2. The Top Ten U.S. Exports to the Soviet Union*

	US$ millions
Corn	1078
Wheat	543
Animal feed	338
Fertilizers	201
Meat	99
Computers	72
Butter	68
Textile and leather machinery	62
Oil seeds	61
Tobacco	47

*As of 1990.
SOURCE: U.S. Census Bureau; U.S. Department of Commerce.

Table 20-3. The Top Ten U.S. Imports from the Soviet Union*

	US$ millions
Silver and other platinum metals	336
Oil (not crude)	331
Radioactive materials	103
Inorganic chemicals	47
Alcoholic beverages	26
Uranium and related ores	25
Pig iron, iron powder, etc.	24
Tractors	20
Artwork and antiques	19
Crude animal materials	11

¹As of 1990.
SOURCE: U.S. Census Bureau; U.S. Department of Commerce.

Foreign Trade

Notwithstanding the political and economic turmoil, and even though new deals are at a virtual standstill, Western companies already established in the region continue trading, and new entrants stand in the wings waiting for openings. Table 20-2 shows major exports from the United States to the Soviet Union. Table 20-3 shows major imports back to the United States for the year 1990.

Entrepreneurial Opportunities

In addition to oil, agriculture, basic foodstuffs, and mining, several entrepreneurial opportunities appear ripe for the picking as soon as the political situation stabilizes and financing channels open. Although certainly not inclusive, the following businesses generate hard currency (scarce as it may be), mostly from foreign travelers and companies. Many can be initiated from outside the region's boundaries, giving companies a toehold for future trade.

1. *Dual retail stores.* McDonald's is a prime example. One store sells for rubles, another for hard currency, which can be repatriated. Ruble income covers local expenses of both stores.

2. *Advertising and public relations.* Local advertising or public relations firms that specialize in helping Japanese and Western companies promote their wares can demand payment in hard currency outside the CIS.

3. *Quick-print services.* Small, quick-print shops, popular in the United States and spreading to Europe, are virtually unheard of in the CIS. They can be opened either as independents or as franchises (like the pioneer Alphagraphics). The same dual ruble/hard-currency arrangement as in retail shops applies here.

4. *Travel agencies and tours.* As Western and East Asian tourists flock to Moscow and the Caspian resorts, local tours and tour guides are much in demand, as are multilingual travel agencies. Foreigners and some locals pay for tour bookings and travel arrangements in hard currency.

5. *Soviet arts and crafts.* These can be imported to the United States and other Western countries duty free. Articles can be purchased in rubles and sold for hard currency.

6. *Satellite telecommunications and other office services.* Offices of foreign companies desperately need state-of-the-art office services. Reliable international telephone and fax services are especially needed. Foreign companies pay in hard currency.

A few other ideas for niche markets that can generate hard currency include: arranging production sites for Western filmmakers; booking Western entertainment groups; law, accounting, and consulting services for foreign companies; technology licensing; and the booking of CIS entertainers for Western or East Asian performances.

The CIS is one of the few trading areas of the world where the composition of market demand, resource availability, and competition encourages direct investments in entrepreneurial businesses in preference to straight export trade. The unusual supply-side depression (described in Chapter 19), which has produced an oversupply of money in the hands of consumers, coupled with the lack of official hard currency to pay for imports, gives impetus to spending for locally produced goods and services.

Clearly the same is not true for major equipment purchases or commodities. Large capital equipment must be imported because no local capability exists. Similarly, without local conversion facilities, only export markets exist for mined commodities such as platinum and oil. As the door opens to multinationals, capital goods will eventually be manufactured locally and CIS markets will be found for minerals.

21
Africa

Tips to Foreign Traders and Investors

1. The biggest near-term advantage of an African direct investment is as an immediate, low-cost entree to trade with the European Community through the Lomé Convention agreement.

2. Concentrate on export markets in the English-speaking West African nations of Nigeria (which has 75 percent of the region's population and economic activity) and Ghana, and in the francophone countries that guarantee hard-currency convertibility through the CFA franc.

3. Watch for the right timing and then make direct investments in South Africa. It will eventually become the best strategic location on the continent.

4. Stay alert to serious payment problems from soft-currency areas.

The phrase "Out of Africa" aptly characterizes the way that for generations the developed world viewed the dark continent, and to a large extent still does. For two centuries, the European excolonial powers—Britain, France, Belgium, Germany, Italy, and the Netherlands—plundered Africa's natural resources and antique treasures, delighting in taking as much as they could "out of Africa." Before and during that time, slave traders from the United States and Saudi Arabia wantonly transported young men and women "out of Africa."

As colonialism faded and the patron rulers returned home, the world's superpowers used Africa as their whipping boy to support Cold War aims, shoveling weaponry and mercenaries to African dictators for local wars that would keep the United States and the Soviet Union "out of Africa." In righteous rage over apartheid policies, the world powers opted to move investment "out of South Africa."

Today, when all but 16 African nations have either converted to democratic governments, have scheduled elections, or have promised to do so in the near future, the same industrial powers, intent on coping with their own recessionary problems and growth policies, largely ignore the potential of this vast continent. Large and small companies elect to stay "out of Africa," while opting for more obvious Third World trade in Asia and Latin America.

The African continent is home to 46 separate countries. Nearby archipelagoes hold another five. These 51 independent nations account for almost one-third of the membership of the United Nations. They boast natural resources unmatched in variety and abundance by any contiguous landmass in the world except North America. Labor is inexpensive and abundant. Consumer and industrial demand for imported basic goods and services exceeds that in many other developing markets. Infrastructures need to be built, agribusiness developed, health care and education provided, and shelters constructed, none of which can be accomplished internally.

Why then, when Africa offers such enormous market and resource opportunities, has the outside business world shunned the dark continent? Why not follow the lead of European colonial patrons and superpowers? Why not take profits "out of Africa" instead of merely staying "out of Africa"?

The primary reasons appear to be fourfold:

1. A general ignorance of African political structures and tribal cultures which in turn tends to escalate business risks

2. Unreasonable trade barriers erected by African governments which practice corruption at a level surpassing that experienced by Western traders in other Third World countries

3. A history of government expropriation of property and bank accounts belonging to Western corporations

4. A critical lack of hard currency to pay for imported goods and services

Of course, real or imaginary barriers at the local level also contribute to unacceptable trade conditions: racial unrest in South Africa, anarchy in Somalia, famine and civil strife in Ethiopia and the Sudan, Moammar Gadhafi in Libya, armed revolt in Liberia, and the brutal Marxist dictatorship of Mobuto Sese Seko in Zaire.

Lack of hard currency, however, supplemented by rigid import and foreign investment barriers, continues to be the overriding deterrent to increased American, European, and Japanese trading interest in the region.

Slowly but surely, small amounts of hard currency are beginning to flow. Multilateral aid agencies, development banks, European public and private financial institutions, and local banks partially owned by international banking institutions are struggling to right Africa's near-impossible currency debacle. But the road is long and bumpy.

The regional development bank, Banque Africaine de Developpement

(African Development Bank), headquartered in Abidjan, Côte d'Ivoire (Ivory Coast), remains all but immobilized by the 1991 local civil uprising and lack of funds. Economic reforms must precede serious IMF and World Bank funding.

Social structures must be rebuilt to ensure at least a modicum of stability in labor skills and management talent. Corrupt bureaucracies must be replaced by civil servants willing and able to mesh the demands of the elite minority with the needs of the poverty-stricken majority. Abrasive bureaucratic procedures, import licensing, and quotas must be relaxed to permit the import of vital goods and services. And restrictions on foreign ownership of businesses and the repatriation of profits and capital must be revised to entice foreign investment.

To date, steps to resolve these issues have been only modestly addressed by a minor number of African states. In a report commissioned by the United Nations for the General Assembly's special session to hear the pleading of Africa's case in September 1991, the following conditions were revealed:

- Since 1985 real GDP (excluding South Africa) grew by a meager 2.3 percent. However, since the population grew faster, per capita GDP declined 0.7 percent, increasing the number of Africa's abject poor.

- Measured in constant prices, the net flow of money to Africa hit US$23.6 billion in 1990, down from US$24.6 billion in 1986, even though foreign aid rose 4 percent.

- Bank loans and export credit dried up.

- Inept private sector managers and muddled bureaucrats "do as much to stifle growth as misguided subsidies and five-year plans."

- More than half of Africa's countries still depend on one or two commodities for 70 percent of their export earnings.

- Between 1978 and 1990, donor governments wrote off loans to the poorest African countries worth about US$7.6 billion. Yet those poor countries still have unmanageable debt levels.

Trade Opportunities in West Africa

In the face of seemingly insurmountable odds, representatives from several African states continue to solicit trade and foreign investment from around the world, citing enormous market demand for imported goods and services, and labor and natural resource availability for foreign-owned factories.

In conjunction with the 1991 U.S. General Assembly special session on Africa, two ambassadors, Ansoumane Camara of Guinea and Charles Gomis of Côte d'Ivoire met with U.S. government and private industry trade officials to push trade opportunities in Africa. Camara announced that all Guinean state-owned businesses have been turned over to private ownership or liquidated. Guinea has a population of only seven million, but is among the world's biggest exporters of minerals and metals, primarily bauxite and alumina, which account for 95 percent of the country's export earnings. Gold, diamonds, manganese, and uranium are also exported.

Gomis assured audiences of Côte d'Ivoire's new political and economic stability, stating, "The key to our growth has been the emphasis on free market." He also noted that the United States is Côte d'Ivoire's largest trading partner after France and that his country is the world's largest producer of cocoa and the third-largest producer of coffee. The ambassador informed audiences that Côte d'Ivoire subsidizes foreign investments in food processing and mineral processing, among others. Full foreign ownership is allowed, although the government prefers joint ventures.

In 1990, U.S. companies exported US$200 million to Côte d'Ivoire and US$141 million to Guinea. Imports from the two countries were US$78 million and US$43 million, respectively.

Total U.S. exports of goods and services to Africa (excluding Egypt, Morocco, Tunisia, Algeria, and Libya) topped US$4.1 billion, of which US$1.7 billion went to South Africa and US$550 million to Nigeria.

Imports hit US$12.7 billion, with Nigeria accounting for the lion's share at US$6.0 billion, followed closely by South Africa at US$1.7 billion.

With such a small manufacturing base, African countries other than South Africa must import virtually everything they consume. Basic human needs are not being met in many countries and conditions are substandard in others, creating a need for products and services in health care, infrastructure construction, transport equipment and parts, agriculture, and food processing. Rice, wheat, fertilizer, automobile parts, aircraft parts, cigarettes, and clothing are especially critical imports.

Future Hope

With the help of their mother country, France, 13 West African nations have formed a monetary union to ensure adequate supplies of hard currency. Seven francophone members of the Economic Community of West African States (ECOWAS)—Benin, Burkina Faso, Côte d'Ivoire, Mali, Niger, Senegal, and Togo—together with Cameroon, the Central African Republic, Chad, Comoros, Congo, and Gabon, all use the CFA franc as their currency. The CFA franc is pegged to the French franc at FF 1 = CFA 50. Guaranteed by the French treasury, the CFA franc is fully convertible into hard currency. ECOWAS members also share a central bank, the Central Bank of West African States.

The English-speaking West African states of Nigeria, Gambia, Sierra Leone, Liberia, and Ghana, and the Portuguese-speaking states of Cape Verde and Guinea-Bissau also belong to ECOWAS. Each group has its own monetary union.

In addition to monetary stability, the major purpose in forming these common markets was to liberalize trade between the countries. To date, a few barriers have fallen, but not many. Still, it's a step in the right direction, and foreign companies seriously considering Africa should look at these West African states first. Nigeria, which accounts for 75 percent of the ECOWAS population and a comparable share of the region's economic activity, is the most appealing.

One interesting feature of a direct investment in an ECOWAS country is that it provides an automatic entree to trade with the European Community under the Lomé Convention agreement. Lomé grants duty-free entrance to the EC for most of the group's exports.

In addition, several ECOWAS nations qualify for the U.S. Overseas Private Investment Corporation (OPIC) programs, as well as for aid from the African Development Bank (ADB) and the World Bank. Recent projects aided by the ADB include updating the computerized systems at several ports of entry and the expansion of Nigerian processing plants.

The most likely countries for foreign direct investment now and for the foreseeable future are Nigeria (which boasts the only viable domestic market), Côte d'Ivoire, Togo, and Ghana.

Trade Opportunities in Southern Africa

Now that South Africa is entering the postapartheid era, business leaders from its neighbors—Angola, Botswana, Mozambique, Namibia, Zambia, and Zimbabwe—are breathing a sigh of relief. With industrialized South Africa in the lead, Southern African leaders announced at a 1991 roundtable meeting in Switzerland that they hope to transform the region into another Southeast Asia by the early part of the twenty-first century.

If that is to happen, most agree that South Africa must lead the way. South Africa's economy accounts for almost 20 percent of the entire continent's GNP and 40 percent of its industrial output. Although much of South African industry is state-owned, the country boasts a vibrant private sector of internationally competitive companies. In addition, an unregulated informal sector accounts for between 20 and 30 percent of the nation's GNP.

South Africa is also the only country on the continent with a sophisticated, working urban infrastructure and a strong financial sector.

On the downside, the nation has an overabundance of crime, an alienated youth, shattered families, and widespread illiteracy—all traceable to three factors:

1. The effects of international sanctions

2. The enormous cost of the bureaucracy needed to administer apartheid

3. A large, underskilled work force

As the white government and black political factions struggle to create a replacement for apartheid, joint committees are working on the implementation of a free market system. Regardless of the specific programs for redistribution of wealth that the two sides eventually agree upon, and the details of the economic reform package necessary for its achievement, most believe that South Africa's economic future will be vibrant.

Foreign investment has always been welcome in South Africa, according to Kent Durr, minister of trade, industry, and tourism. Strategically, the country is ideally suited to serving not only Southern African markets but all of the countries bordering the Indian Ocean. This Afro/Asian littoral of more than two billion people is within easy shipping distance. Within this area South African companies clearly have competitive advantage in business infrastructure, natural resources, labor, geographic position, business culture, and financial and management expertise.

With the further demise of apartheid conditions, the infrastructure of vast segments of the country must be rebuilt. Enormous amounts of imported goods and services will be required in the development of: roads; electric-power generation, transmission, and distribution; schools; hospitals; living accommodations; communications; and water distribution.

Foreign suppliers as well as foreign investors in infrastructure projects, agribusiness, and food processing should find substantial market opportunities in South Africa. Although the nation must still resolve serious political and cultural problems, the time is rapidly approaching when South Africa could become the commercial jewel of the dark continent.

22

Israel and the Arab Middle East

Tips to Foreign Traders and Investors

1. Take a close look at the many advantages for trade with Israeli state-owned companies.

2. Use Israel as a direct route to trade with the European Community.

3. Carefully check out any individual or company "partner" when doing business in Arab countries. Many are very reputable; some are not.

4. Be prepared for stiff competition from American and European firms for construction- or petroleum-related projects throughout the region.

One positive result of the Persian Gulf war was the bringing together of Israeli and Arab representatives for the first time to negotiate a sustainable peace accord for the region. Although it will probably be many years before the world sees the final results of these ground-breaking negotiations, it seems clear that a peaceable Arab-Jew coexistence will strengthen, not only the political stability of the region, but market opportunities for foreign trade as well.

The lessening of tensions and consequent lessening of the emphasis on military might will have a decided impact on companies' decisions regarding trade or direct investment in Israel, as will the following developments:

1. The 1985 U.S.–Israel Free Trade Area (FTA) agreement

2. Israeli trade liberalization policies and privatization programs

3. The continued influx of Jewish emigrés, primarily from the former Soviet Union

4. The 1992 electoral overthrow of the Likud Party and the choice of Yitzhak Rabin as the Labor Party's new prime minister.

The United States is Israel's most important trading partner. Since the execution of the FTA, U.S. companies have exported a wide range of products. Although military hardware has received the most press, a variety of other products are also in high demand. Some of the best are: consumer goods of all types, including a wide range of luxury and high-tech items and clothing; machine tools; construction and transport equipment; pharmaceuticals; computers and software; telecommunications equipment and supplies; medical diagnostic and treatment equipment; and electronics. Under the FTA nearly all these goods can be exported to Israel duty free.

U.S. companies are also the predominant source of foreign direct investment. According to the Israeli Trade Center in New York, the average annual direct investment by more than two hundred American companies exceeds US$325 million. Many have found the highly skilled Israeli work force ideally suited to high-tech electric and electronic assembly operations. Motorola and several other multinationals operate facilities in Israel, as do a multitude of smaller companies.

In addition to its highly educated and skilled work force, the country boasts a large cadre of qualified management personnel and a significant number of scientists and technicians. Russian emigrés are adding to the numbers in both categories daily.

Israeli research and development facilities are among the best in the world, affording excellent product development opportunities at substantially less cost than in the United States or Europe.

All international trade is conducted in U.S. dollars. A variety of aggressive tax and other incentives are offered by the Israeli government. All business documents are in English, and most Israel businessmen are fluent in the language.

Probably the most important advantage to locating a facility in Israel is that the country enjoys free trade with the European Community. This affords entry for American companies and others not privy to such access from their home country.

The Israeli Trade Center lists the following Israeli products as being available for export from the country:

agricultural machinery and equipment	food
apparel, footwear, and accessories	furniture
arts and crafts	health care products
automotive parts and accessories	computer software
avionics and airfield equipment	electronics and communications
books, printing, and stationery	equipment
building materials and supplies	fashion and home textiles

certain types of industrial machinery
    and equipment
jewelry
safety and security products

solar energy products
toys and games
teaching aids and sports
    equipment

Arab Markets: Opportunity or Mirage?

While Latin America, most of sub-Saharan Africa, Eastern Europe, the former Soviet republics, Pakistan, and, to a lesser extent, India are moving toward one form or other of elected democratic rule and market economies, and even China is reaping the economic benefits of capitalist markets, the Arab states represent the last bastion of feudalism. The gap between "haves" and "have-nots" is larger in the Arab Middle East than it is nearly anywhere in the world.

While some countries boast modern skyscrapers (Saudi Arabia), a thriving tourist industry (Egypt, the United Arab Emirates, and Oman), and large metropolitan areas with an abundance of small shopkeepers (Tehran, Cairo, Beirut, Damascus, Jeddah, and Riyadh), the region cannot by any stretch of the imagination be considered a hotbed of free markets. Ruling royal families and strong-armed dictators have been the prime beneficiaries of the region's oil wealth, while hundreds of thousands of the peasant and bedouin underclass live at subsistence levels.

As an adjunct to its dysfunctional markets, the region's dedication to Islamic fundamentalism makes any radical change in its political paradigm and any uplifting of the underclass very unlikely in the foreseeable future. Such a status quo places severe constraints on the volume and diversity of foreign trade, as well as on foreign direct investment, regardless of the extravagant oil wealth. (There are, of course, noted exceptions.)

In addition to the wide disparity of wealth between rulers and ruled, there exists a widely shared distrust of non-Islamic Westerners. This phobia emanates from Pan-Arabic loyalty, or *qawmiyya,* one of whose rules is that decisions about anything must be by consensus. *Qawmiyya* means loyalty to a larger sense of Arab nationhood, a loyalty that is supposed to transcend the borders imposed on the Arabs by Western imperialism.

Prior to the Persian Gulf war, qawmiyya was pervasive and jeopardized more than one trade or investment transaction between an Arab government agency and a Western company. Nearly all foreign trade and investment is conducted from the Arab side by one or more government agencies or bureaucrats. Private enterprise does not flourish.

Since the Persian Gulf war, conditions have changed somewhat. Qawmiyya now plays a lesser role, and country nationalism, or *wataniyya,* is more pronounced. This has not affected the belief in consensus decisions, however, which remains a central tenet of Islamic fundamentalism. Conducting

Western-style business in such an environment is still fraught with peril; contracts, pricing, quality, delivery, and payment schedules retain a degree of mystery to all but the most adept Western traders.

Arab Market Opportunities

The region has a very small manufacturing base and depends nearly entirely on foreign imports to sustain an increasingly high-tech urban society. Nor does the region have a sustainable agricultural base, making imported foods and chemicals critical to survival.

Locally produced capital goods are virtually nonexistent and transport, communications, power generation and distribution, water purification and distribution, and construction equipment must all be imported. Health care supplies and equipment, automobiles, aircraft, spare parts, hospitality-industry supplies and equipment, and building materials are other excellent prospects for exporting to the region. The intense desert heat makes air conditioning equipment and related spare parts highly lucrative markets.

Even before the Persian Gulf war—and certainly after its end—by far the best market opportunities have lain in the following areas: petroleum production, refining, and transport; infrastructure development; and military supplies and hardware. The Kuwaiti oil fires have created a whole new industry for specialists. Environmental cleanup after the war damage will be a thriving market for years to come. However, competition from foreign multinational engineering and construction companies is fierce in all these key industries.

Computer systems for the banking industry and offshore financial centers are also a hot market in Saudi Arabia, Bahrain, and the United Arab Emirates (UAE), all of which are trying to develop more sophistication in financial services industries.

Caution Alert

Local labor is practically nonexistent in the Arab gulf states of Saudi Arabia, the UAE, Oman, Dubai, and Kuwait—especially for construction work and building-trade skills. In the past, labor was imported from Jordan, Egypt, Yemen, and as far away as Pakistan and the Philippines. By siding with Saddam Hussein, Palestinians made themselves no longer welcome in the region and this has created a more severe labor shortage than before the war. Foreign contractors would be wise to make arrangements for sufficient labor prior to entering into any construction contracts.

Professional services are also very much in demand throughout the area. Although an increasing number of young people are seeking professional education and training abroad, the relatively small educated population makes importing foreign professional skills an essential ingredient for economic and social development. Health care personnel, financial experts, consultants in virtually every field, and educators are desperately needed. With no shortage of hard currency, the pay is usually very good: however, living accommodations don't usually measure up to Western standards.

Caution Alert

Arab states offer virtually no tax incentives to foreign companies. All income earned within the country is taxable. Compared to other trading regions, the rates are high, topping out at 45 percent for corporate income and capital gains in Saudi Arabia. The top foreign branch tax rate is also 45 percent. "Supply only" contracts are normally exempt. Rates in other countries are comparably high.

Most Arab governments require foreign companies to team up with a local partner, often a well-connected individual, for any direct investment, regardless of the industry or project. This can be a very expensive proposition for smaller companies.

PART 3
Asia-Pacific

23
Northeast Asia: Japan

Tips to Foreign Traders and Investors

1. Stay away from *keiretsu*-controlled markets.
2. Go after markets for top-of-the-line Western-style consumer goods.
3. Arrange financing with Japanese sources for closer ties.
4. Modify export products and packaging to meet Japanese market tastes.
5. Negotiate intellectual property protection with the appropriate government agency before entering Japanese markets. Without this protection, proprietary products will be copied.
6. Embassy office in Washington: (202) 939-6700.

A truism often overlooked by overzealous promoters of global trade is that very few companies have the financial resources, key personnel, or time to sell their products or services in every viable international market. The world is too big, competition too intense, resources too scarce, and markets too specialized. To be realistic, growth strategies must focus on those markets with the best combination of reasonable access, least cost to penetrate, and best expansion potential—in other words, markets that offer the best return on investment; the biggest bang for the buck.

The other side of the coin—resource cost and availability—also enters the equation. Few companies have the wherewithal to source money, labor, or raw materials throughout the world. Prudent strategies call for choosing those sources that yield the least cost, best delivery, and highest quality to meet specific market needs.

Although a few companies have the luxury of spanning the globe for both resources and markets, most do not.

The presence of formal and informal trade barriers further complicates global strategies. Although debate rages over the advisability of tripolar trading blocs—Europe, Asia-Pacific, and the Americas—each major power is moving in that direction. The additional probability of intraregional trade expanding to the detriment of panglobal trade cannot be dismissed lightly.

As the world leader in GNP growth and financial resources, Japan plays a major role in any company's growth strategies. Much has been written and spoken about the enormous potential of Japanese markets, closely guarded from the outside world by subtle and not-so-subtle barriers. Less has been said about Japan's role in a tripolar world, although there can be little doubt that it will be the focal point of any Asia-Pacific bloc. No authority speaks of abundant raw materials or natural resources in Japan: they just don't exist.

Strategically speaking, foreign companies must weigh the high cost of entering Japanese markets, the lack of immediate natural resources, and the pure aggravation of penetrating culturally dissimilar markets, against the returns that may be realized. With limited resources, personnel, and time, companies must also weigh the opportunities in Japan against those from other, less costly, less-competitive world markets that offer immediate proximity to materials and labor as well as reasonable access to domestic or export customers. And of course, the positioning of a facility in Japan to serve as a foothold in an Asia-Pacific trading bloc must be included in any intelligent evaluation.

Obviously similar considerations relate to trade and direct investment in Japan's neighbor, South Korea. There, the added dimension of political instability and the ramifications of a possible merger with North Korea further complicate market strategies. The fact that South Korean financial conglomerates and manufacturing companies are turning away from further domestic, European, or American investments to other, less-costly, and better-positioned Southeast Asian nations may cast doubt on the advisability of foreigners bucking the trend.

Nevertheless, both Japan and South Korea do offer potentially lucrative trade in some areas and bear serious evaluation in any global strategy.

Caution Alert

The saying that "all's fair in love, war, and business" aptly applies to Japanese companies. Quick to sense Americans' penchant for things foreign (as well as Americans' simultaneous fear of any foreign "occupation" of U.S. industry, which they equate with loss of jobs), Japanese companies hire well-positioned, and in many cases very well-known, Americans to serve as promoters of Japanese companies and trade. Much of the media hype about the enormous advantages for American companies of exporting to or investing in Japan comes from these hired ambassadors. The same holds true to a lesser extent for South Korea.

Other well-meaning American executives have had good experiences in Japan and

South Korea and firmly believe that American and other foreign companies can also succeed in these markets.

Caveat emptor!

Here are some recent quotes favoring Japanese trade:

- Ira Wolf, director of government relations in Japan for Motorola, says, "The Japanese market can be incredibly attractive." Urging companies to move quickly in exploring the Japanese market, he continues, "Do it now; the longer you wait, the more expensive it will be."

- William Farrell, executive director of the Japan chamber of commerce, notes that the government-funded Japan External Trade Organization has "shifted significant resources to promoting imports."

- Paul Muther, vice president and general manager of the First National Bank of Chicago, says of the South Korean market, "There's a potential for an avalanche of demand."

But before jumping to the conclusion that either Japan or South Korea is the best place to reap returns, an evaluation of competitive and market conditions is in order.

Opportunity or Mirage?

Even more than is true of the United States and Europe, the economies of America and Japan have become so intertwined over the past 15 years that it is practically impossible to separate them. A recession or growth period in the United States materially affects Japanese companies; likewise, a recession or growth period in Japan impacts American businesses. Given that fact, it's easy to understand why the governments of both countries are working hard to keep the peace between each other's business communities.

After a series of bilateral negotiations between trade representatives in 1990 and 1991, a few more doors have opened to U.S. companies. Not many, but a few. Cultural chasms separate the two countries and continue to reflect material differences in the conduct of business.

Probably the biggest difference, and the one that foreigners and especially American companies have difficulty competing against, is the Japanese custom of *keiretsu*. A *keiretsu* is an interlocking group of businesses in diverse sectors that share ownership and resources. Typically, a keiretsu consists of a trading company that is responsible for worldwide marketing and distribution, a manufacturing company that produces a wide range of products, and a financial institution that provides domestic and international financing for the group.

Most keiretsu are massive conglomerates—Mitsubishi, Sumitomo, Mitsui, Marubeni, and so on. The trading company, or *sogo shosha*, is at the apex of a keiretsu. In addition to conducting foreign trade on their own behalf, trading companies provide worldwide market intelligence and marketing expertise to the manufacturing and financial arms. The nine largest trading companies control the distribution of more than half of all Japanese imports and exports. Only foreign companies that are very large or resource-rich can successfully bypass the sogo shosha.

Manufacturing companies in a keiretsu have a distinct advantage over foreign competition in both domestic and worldwide markets. Without diverting valuable resources to marketing activities, manufacturers can devote their entire attention to improving manufacturing processes and product lines. They can devote resources to R & D projects that would otherwise go to marketing and promotion. With financing from well-heeled commercial and investment banks at their disposal, they need pay little attention to raising working capital or expansion funding.

In domestic markets, smaller firms proliferate in the business landscape. Here again, however, close ties to banks and tightly knit distribution companies give them a substantial competitive edge over foreign interlopers.

These monopolistic characteristics promote an economic environment that is a far cry from the open, free market economies of the United States and (to a slightly lesser extent) Europe. To enter such an arena and compete effectively, foreign companies must have vast resources, close political ties to Japanese ministries, an affiliation with one or more power-broker partners within Japan, and support from their home-country government. Large multinationals have all of these. Smaller companies seldom have even one.

Market Opportunities for Foreigners

Specialty-niche markets are the best shot for new entrants—markets that for one reason or another Japanese companies choose to ignore or are blocked from entering. Avon, for example, has done very well selling cosmetics door-to-door in Japan. McDonald's and Coca-Cola, with their unique, worldwide images, have been successful. Specialty pharmaceutical and chemical companies have done well, although most non-Japanese firms in this field are giants such as Dupont, Grace, and Upjohn.

Other products that foreigners successfully bring to Japanese markets include: specialized telecommunications equipment, uniquely designed electronics components, forest products, medical services and devices, transportation machinery, and automobile parts. Westernized consumer products have definitely caught on with this population of 120 million. Apparel, jewelry, housewares and appliances, sporting goods, health foods, recreational equipment and services, and pet foods have been especially well received.

Foreign companies involved in certain service businesses have also been successful. Product design, market research, advertising and promotion, management consulting, health care, consumer finance, specialty insurance, and data communications are hot markets, with lower domestic competition than many others.

Caution Alert

The cost of doing business in Japan often shocks newcomers. Operating costs, on average, are up to twice those in the United States and one and one-half times those in Germany. Wages, employee benefits, and facilities costs are the worst. Japan has limited natural resources; most raw materials, therefore, must be imported. The further expense of purchasing, shipping, delivery, and import tariffs adds to both product and packaging costs.

Four other major obstacles must be overcome by foreign suppliers, whether exporting to Japanese markets or investing in facilities.

1. *Technical advantage.* The technical advantage North American and European companies have had in many product lines is vanishing quickly. The classic case is the semiconductor industry. At first Japanese companies captured the memory market; now they control the entire industry. Another example is the onetime superiority of U.S. development and manufacture of sophisticated military hardware, software, and support technology. Japanese companies now share leading-edge technology in partnership with U.S. companies in a series of joint ventures.

2. *Captive exports.* The proliferation of Japanese direct investments in the Americas and Europe has changed the face of export competition from these regions. Japanese-owned companies in the United States, for instance, compete directly with U.S.-owned companies for products exported to Japan. Since Japanese companies or joint ventures have direct access to domestic financial and distribution systems, foreign-owned companies are at an increasing disadvantage when exporting to Japan.

3. *Japan, Inc.* Japanese domestic companies and consumers are not as fascinated with foreign-made products as Americans are. Local PR has been extremely effective in convincing Japanese consumers to "buy Japan"—much more effective, in fact, than similar programs have been in the United States and Europe. If domestic buyers have a choice between imported and locally made products, they choose the latter hands down.

4. *Copycat skills.* Japanese application engineers made their mark in world markets by copying products designed in America and Europe. Although pure R & D efforts are accelerating, the Japanese propensity for copying remains strong. Without mutually agreed, specific barriers to copying, imported products soon lose their company of origin and are copied by Japanese companies for local production.

The Japanese government also maintains strict control over which industries foreigners may enter. The construction industry, in which foreign companies have been prohibited from bidding on local projects, is a prime example. This tight control loosened somewhat as a result of Japan—U.S. trade negotiations. Foreign companies may now bid on projects in excess of US$60 billion— airports, bridges, port facilities, roads, tunnels, and so on—but local biases still exist.

The most important criteria for foreign success in Japanese markets are first, that the specific product or service being offered is needed in Japan, and second, that the management of a foreign company knows how to play the Japanese culture game. The first is obvious. The second relates to the typically Western philosophy of maximizing short-term gains.

Caution Alert

Short-term objectives are diametrically opposed to Japanese business custom: companies with such strategies should stay out of Japanese markets. The cost of entry, competition, and overcoming cultural barriers cannot be mastered in the short term. Typically it takes a foreign company four to six years to break even with a Japanese investment. It also normally takes two to three years to break into an import market.

Economic Trends

The 1989–1992 worldwide recession, especially in the United States, and a concurrent global credit shortage have braked the booming Japanese economy. When coupled with falling stock and property values, massive shake-ups in Japanese financial institutions, and a changing government philosophy that supports increased intraregional trade, economists and trade officials forecast near-term national growth of under 3 percent. They also predict a major shift in Japanese investment from the United States and Europe to China and Southeast Asia.

The Japanese government's tight-money policy intentionally reined in the economy. The twelve-month growth in industrial output dropped to 0.7 percent in late 1991, compared to 7 percent at the start of the year. Housing starts and auto sales both plummeted. Many conglomerates reported declining profits. Meanwhile, wages through the third quarter of 1991 jumped a fantastic 14.5 percent, boosting the annual increase to 6.5 percent. Comparable wage increases amounted to 2.3 percent and 2.9 percent in the United States; 9.3 percent and 7.0 percent in Germany.

A poll of 14 professional forecasters conducted by *The Economist* put Japan's 1991 annual growth at 4.2 percent and 1992's at 3.0 percent, the latter being about the same as that expected in the United States. OPEC forecasts Japan's 1992 growth at 3.5 percent, based on economic conditions in early 1991.

Table 23-1. Japan's Demand, Output, and Prices

	1988	1989	1990	1991	1992
Percentage increase					
Private nonresidential fixed investment	14.8	15.6	13.8	6.9	4.4
Total domestic demand	7.6	5.7	5.8	3.6	3.6
Exports	10.7	15.0	10.7	4.5	6.5
Imports	21.3	22.1	11.7	5.0	7.0
GNP	6.2	4.7	5.6	3.5	3.5
Inflation rate	-0.1	1.8	2.4	2.5	2.1
Unemployment rate	2.5	2.3	2.1	2.2	2.3

SOURCE: OECD.

These recessionary pressures halted the six-year investment boom by Japanese public and private sectors, as can be seen in Table 23-1.

The key to Japan's extraordinary growth during the 1980s was capital investment. Fueled by cheap money, double-digit business investment has accounted for over half the increase in GNP since 1986. But as Table 23-1 shows, that boom is over. The government's optimistic Economic Planning Agency forecasts a growth in business investment of 5 percent in 1992 (against OECD's 4.4 percent). Salomon Brothers forecasts a 4 percent growth for the next fiscal year, continuing the decline.

Internal credit availability is a major factor in decreased private investment. The combined deficits of nonfinancial companies hit 9 percent of GNP in 1991—clearly an unsustainable level. Bank lending is now constrained by the Bank for International Settlements guidelines and by mounting bad debts. The stock market plunged in 1991 and 1992 and continues to be sluggish. Financing large investments has become impossible, and firms are shelving plans for further development.

With a continued slump in the stock market, Salomon's Tokyo office warns that during 1992, when early-1980s warrants and convertible bonds become due, holders will not want to convert to equities. This will force companies to raise cash to buy them back—further dampening fixed investment prospects. Several automobile and electronics firms announced investment cuts in excess of 4 percent. Sony plans cuts of 20 percent to 30 percent in 1992.

Despite these gloomy predictions, Japan's economy is far from flat, and recovery will come much quicker there than in either the United States or Europe, although perhaps not with any more vigor. Several positive factors are at play:

1. Many Japanese companies still boast excess cash reserves. They borrowed cheap funds during the 1980s to boost liquidity, and the total of cash, deposits, and short-term securities is still equivalent to 1.6 months of sales. This is well above an average of 1.2 in the first half of the 1980s, although below the 2.0 average in 1990.

2. Part of the slowdown in bank lending results from a diminishing demand for funds rather than a lack of supply. Many companies are using their own cash reserves, instead of borrowing at what they consider to be exorbitant interest rates.

3. As much as 10 percent of capital investment during the late 1980s and early 1990s went into land speculation. That bubble has now burst. But a halt to land investment has no direct impact on the GNP measure of capital investment.

4. Only one-third of capital investment in recent years has added to production capacity, leaving plant utilization at a very high level. Most investment went into labor-saving equipment or R & D.

Many industrialized countries would be happy with a GNP rise of 3.5 percent. In Japan, however, a drop from the 5 to 6 percent range left businessmen clamoring for an easing of monetary policy. The Bank of Japan responded by shifting from inflation control and dropping its discount rate (the inflation rate was down to 2.7 percent at the end of 1991).

For all its fantasy land values, the Japanese economy is unlikely to experience anything like the recession in the West—at least not in the foreseeable future. It certainly won't crash-land. Recovery from the 1991–1992 slowdown, however, may be much more gradual than the business community would like. Analysts from Jardine Fleming believe that the Japanese economy is just catching its breath en route to its next big surge.

Trading Companies: Can Foreigners Compete?

Japan's nine largest trading companies are the spiders at the center of the nation's global economic web. Given their control of over half of Japan's exports and two-thirds of its imports, it is very difficult for small or midsize foreign companies to enter the Japanese market without assistance from one of these leviathans. Regardless of the much-publicized efforts by the U.S. Trade Representative to break down Japan's trade barriers, a near-monopoly on foreign trade forces foreign companies to compete at higher-cost levels than local firms. Only by adopting a very long-term strategy do foreign firms stand a chance of effectively competing. And such a long-term strategy requires a substantial investment without commensurate returns for many years.

The key to any effective market strategy is to understand one's competition. Therefore, it behooves foreign companies to understand the magnitude of power exerted by these trading companies or sogo shosha.

Each sogo shosha acts as the eyes and ears abroad for the whole keiretsu group of interlocking companies within its family. It spots market and product trends, market gaps, and direct investment opportunities. It also selects those products and services offered in world markets that can best be utilized by its keiretsu at home. In this way trading companies not only control which products are exported from Japan (and to which markets), they also cast a major influence over the choice of goods and services to be imported.

Sogo shosha managers are some of the best Japan has to offer. The cream of Japanese college graduates are attracted to these highly visible organizations. These trading companies maintain a presence in out-of-the-way corners of the globe, permitting opportunities for travel. They reward specialists rather than generalists, moving people into new jobs every five to seven years, rather than every two to three years, as is common in Japanese domestic companies.

A few signs point to a lessening influence by trading companies. The gross profit margins of the nine largest have slumped over the past 15 years to 1.3 percent on sales of US$900 billion, down from 2.2 percent on 60 percent of this volume in 1977. The non-keiretsu giants, Honda, Toyota, and Sony, have become successful multinational competitors and set up their own export networks, reducing the portion of total Japanese exports handled by the big nine trading companies.

As a defensive move, the trading companies are changing their posture, going upstream into mining and manufacturing and downstream into retailing. Dropping their image as pure traders in areas where high-volume and low-margin commissions dominate, the sogo shosha have shifted to more financially sophisticated holding companies. They are becoming more like merchant banks than market-oriented traders.

Mitsubishi represents a prime example of this successful strategy. It invests in the securities of companies with which it has a business relationship as supplier, customer, or credit provider. It then exerts a substantial influence over the company's operating decisions. In return, Mitsubishi reaps dividend income and trade business. In 1991, affiliates in which Mitsubishi had major stakes contributed 20.6 billion yen (32 percent) of the company's total profits.

Exerting a major impact on Japan's trade, Mitsubishi groups account for 19 percent of the imports of coking coal, 12 percent of the imports of steam coal, 16 percent of the imports of iron ore, 40 percent of Japan's manufactured exports, and all of the exports of Mitsubishi Motors. Mitsubishi is Japan's largest oil importer, representing 20 percent of the country's total needs. The company is the predominant importer of liquefied natural gas from Malaysia and Brunei.

The company also owns a 48 percent stake in Kentucky Fried Chicken of Japan (nine hundred outlets). It has major investments in medical electronic equipment, British food wholesaling, and American fast-food packaging and chemicals. Its 1991 annual report lists 144 "principal" subsidiaries in fuels, machinery, information systems, metals, food, chemicals, and textiles. Mitsubishi's main investment criteria is a return on investment of five percentage points over the host country's inflation rate.

Other major trading companies, such as Sumitomo, Mitsui, C. Itoh, Marubeni, and Nissho Iwai, boast equally far-flung empires and are major competitors for foreign companies trying to enter Japanese markets.

Clearly, strategies calling for trade with Japan must reckon with these trading companies. Some foreign companies find that a joint venture with one of them is the only way to penetrate Japanese markets. Others have tried this route and given up, citing favoritism and price cutting between local competitors as the prime reasons for failure.

Growing Domestic Markets

As the Japanese culture gradually becomes more attuned to international mores and the domestic economy evolves along the lines of other industrialized countries, market demands are also shifting.

Japan will soon have the oldest population in industrialized countries. By the year 2025, nearly a quarter of Japan's population will be over 65 years old. After a lifetime of prudent savings, many retirees will be looking for a wide array of goods and services to take care of retirement needs and enhance a leisurely lifestyle. Medical equipment and supplies head the list. Leisure-time products and services, personal care products, travel accommodations and accessories, and recreational products and facilities are a few examples of expanding markets.

The labor shortage is reaching acute stages in many Japanese industries. This brings an increasing number of women into the work force and puts a greater amount of income at their disposal. Workplace clothing and accessory markets will expand markedly. The demand for household goods will increase. Toys of all types will boom. Financial services and leisure-time activities geared to women, as well as personal care products, are other examples of markets that will expand to meet this huge consumer segment.

The younger generation is beginning to reap the labor-saving benefits of high-tech products. More time is being spent at home, on vacation, and away from the workplace. Western-style entertainment has already become big business and will grow. Fancy consumer goods, convenience items, and fast-food items—both in restaurants and for home consumption—are taking center stage. Products that Americans take for granted are now infiltrating the lifestyles of young, working Japanese men and women.

Even American-originated mail-order businesses are catching on, and telemarketing is growing in popularity as a means of reaching a greater number of consumers.

Foreign firms that try to service these markets should recognize that as Japanese affluence increases, so does consumer sophistication. Markets demand high-quality goods and services—in many cases higher quality than is demanded in similar markets in Europe and North America. Japanese buyers have also become very price conscious. The practice of selling imported goods at higher prices than those of local producers won't fly anymore. The same price comparisons made by American consumers are being made in Japan.

Many foreign-made capital goods and construction services still have a ways to go before becoming accepted and competitive. In many cases, capital goods manufactured locally continue to outdistance foreign imports in quality, price and, most important, acceptance by Japanese industry. Although competitive bidding has been partially opened to foreign construction firms, the policy of limiting the market to mammoth government-sponsored projects keeps smaller subcontractors from competing. This may change, but in the foreseeable future, most domestic construction projects will continue to go to Japanese or South Korean firms.

Foreign Direct Investment

Exporting is certainly one way to penetrate Japanese markets. Large foreign companies have achieved modest success, although the powerful sogo shosha preclude smaller, lesser-known firms from competing seriously. Those bent on capturing Japanese markets usually do better by establishing a presence in Japan—either as a manufacturer or as an importing and distribution center. As with other industrialized countries, foreign companies have a better chance of being perceived as long-term players if they have a local presence. It also adds credibility to their marketing efforts.

Two reasonable possibilities exist for a direct investment: a branch office or a locally incorporated subsidiary. Branch offices are certainly less expensive to set up. U.S. companies save taxes by including losses from foreign branches in their corporate tax returns. Usually, however, subsidiaries do better because of the image of permanency they project to Japanese markets.

Japanese taxes are about the same for foreign branches and subsidiaries. Subsidiaries also limit the parent company's liability. In addition, because Japanese customs officials are usually more lenient toward customs valuations for permanent Japanese companies than for foreign branches, importing materials and products is easier and less expensive.

A stock corporation in Japan is called a *kabushiki kasisha* or just KK, and is the form usually chosen for the subsidiary of a foreign company. A KK is similar to American corporations or British "limited" companies. Shareholders are not liable for company activities. Ownership and management are separated. The KK has a perpetual life.

Only one class of stock is needed for a KK, although at least one-fourth of its authorized shares must be purchased at the time of incorporation. The registration tax is .007 percent of the paid-in capital, with a minimum of 150,000 yen. Minimum capital of 400,000 yen, or about US$3000, is required. Loans from the parent can be used to fund the subsidiary's working capital and expansion needs, although interest payments to a foreign parent, along with royalty payments, are subject to a 10 percent withholding tax.

In 1991, the minimum cost for establishing a KK ran about 800,000 yen including all taxes and fees. Corporate income tax rates are 28 percent of income up to eight million yen and 37.5 percent on the excess.

Although no law requires Japanese participation in management, most foreign companies find it essential to have a Japanese national either on the board of directors or in a key management slot. The reasons are the same as those in any foreign country. In the long run national managers more than make up for the extra cost—if for no other reason than their ability to smooth the way through bureaucratic mine fields.

Foreigners must have at least a ninety-day visa to enter Japan. They must also have a posting visa to live in the country. This is granted for three or six months, one year, or three years. The visa requires that the amount of trade to be conducted by the subsidiary be "substantial" (undefined) and that the person either run the KK or be employed as an executive or department manager.

A Stepping Stone to Asia-Pacific

As Japan leads the Asia-Pacific region toward the formation of an economic trading bloc, positioning will become an increasingly important strategic consideration for tapping this immense market. Japanese companies, including the big nine trading companies, are already turning away from further investment in North America and Europe. They recognize that both trade and natural resources within the Asia-Pacific region offer far greater long-term opportunities at far less cost and competitive risk.

By the end of 1990, Japanese companies had invested US$17.4 billion in the "Four Tigers" of East Asia (Hong Kong, Taiwan, South Korea, and Singapore) and an additional US$3.6 billion in Malaysia, Thailand, the Philippines, and Indonesia, according to Baring Securities in Hong Kong. During the early 1980s, Japanese companies focused on shifting heavy manufacturing to East Asian countries to exploit lower labor costs and plentiful raw materials. Over the past few years, they have concentrated on financial services, distribution, and retailing, as well as on heavy construction.

Recently, Japan has been making investments in China and is beginning to accelerate its trading ties there. Late in 1991, the Japanese government announced the formation of a Sea of Japan economic zone to help improve shipping and other transport facilities in the region (which includes the Russian Far East and northeastern Japan). Government aides also announced plans for accelerating trade and investment in the northern provinces of China and in Mongolia.

Foreign traders can be relatively certain that this trend toward regionalism will continue. For all the reasons previously discussed, Japanese markets may be unattractive to foreign firms, either for trade or direct investment. However, an established presence on Japanese soil will provide foreign firms with an opportunity to utilize vast Japanese financial resources and trade contacts in moving into Asia-Pacific markets along with Japanese companies. That reason alone may be enough to develop a strategic direct investment.

Caution Alert

Although Japan certainly offers a direct entree to Asia-Pacific markets, other countries provide the same opportunity at substantially less cost. Entree to China can be achieved through Taiwan or Hong Kong; to Southeast Asia, through Singapore or one of the "Little Dragons" (Thailand, Malaysia, and Indonesia); to Australia and New Zealand, either directly or through one of the Pacific island locations. Granted, none offer the financial resources of Japan, but cost and competition are significantly less also.

24
South Korea

Tips to Foreign Traders and Investors

1. Invest in South Korea only as a long-term strategy to tap north Asian markets.
2. Keep close watch on Korean unification opportunities.
3. Join forces with a *chaebol* for exports or imports.
4. Concentrate on products for the older population, women, and youth.
5. Pick environmental cleanup and protection products for the best big-ticket markets.
6. Guard product designs carefully and introduce only "father generation" products. Either Korean firms or Japanese competitors will copy state-of-the-art technology.
7. Don't try to finance anything in Korea except exports out of the country.
8. Embassy office in Washington: (202) 939-5600.

South Korea is trying hard to become more like Japan every day. Even though Japan's decade-long brutalization of Korea ended in 1945, its economic influence there is still very much in evidence. The Japanese approach to business and its array of production skills are admired by South Korean businessmen. This is more easily understood when one considers the cultural similarity between the two countries, dating back hundreds of years. Still, these close business ties continue to be overlooked by foreigners who are trying to begin trade or make direct investments in the country.

South Korea's version of the Japanese keiretsu is the huge, monopolistic *chaebol*. For decades, an authoritarian, interventionist government worked closely with chaebol to develop the electronics, steel, and automobile industries. Companies were supported with a variety of direct and indirect subsidies. Very high tariffs prevented foreign imports from competing.

South Korea's Economic Planning Board (EPB) has evolved into the same kind of superministry for determining the future of the economy as Japan's Ministry for International Trade and Industry. It accomplishes this goal by feeding local and foreign capital into favored companies through a variety of mechanisms that include preferential financing, tax incentives, and protectionist trade barriers.

The main purpose of the monopolistic chaebol is to develop and produce products for export, not local consumption. A similar policy built up the Japanese economy after 1945. The relative openness of the U.S. market to foreign goods has provided the chaebol the same opportunities as those exploited by the Japanese keiretsu. The five chaebol that control South Korean commerce are:

	1990 sales in US$ billions
Samsung	41
Hyundai	39
Lucky Goldstar	24
Daewoo	18
Sunkyong	11

SOURCE: W. I. Carr.

Cheap labor has been crucial to South Korean development. It has been kept cheap by repressive government policies that forbid strikes, decertify trade unions, and use military and police force to prevent workers from reorganizing. Such policies have produced a 58-hour work week, the industrialized world's highest accident rate, and a working class that even today remains impoverished compared to that of Japan, Hong Kong, or Singapore.

Per capita income remains the lowest of the Four Tigers—approximately US$4900 in 1989, compared to US$7500 for Taiwan, US$10,700 for Singapore, and US$10,900 for Hong Kong. Forecasts for 1992 indicate approximately the same spread.

Violent worker and student demonstrations have led the government to ease up on repressive labor policies. This in turn has led to increased wage rates, as in the other Tigers. Per capita income has risen 15 percent per year from 1989 through 1991. Now much of South Korean heavy industry has moved to Southeast Asia and China, where wage rates remain at depressed levels. As a substitute, the government encourages the import of high-technology industries and technology transfer. Japanese companies have been quick to invest in the former and reluctant to relinquish the latter.

Japan remains South Korea's number-one trading partner and presents other foreign firms with a highly competitive challenge. Trade officials from

Table 24-1. Key South Korean Economic Statistics*

	Statistics
Population	42.8 million
GDP	US$233.9 billion
GDP growth	12.4 percent
Unemployment rate	2.5 percent
Inflation rate	9.0 percent
Exports as percentage of GDP	28.0 percent
U.S. exports	US$17.0 billion
Real effective exchange rate (1980–82 = 100)	85.3

*As of 1990.
SOURCE: KOTRA; IMF; World Bank; U.S. Department of Commerce.

the Korea Trade Center (KOTRA) willingly admit that whenever a U.S. company opens a market in South Korea, Japanese competitors quickly exploit it. They also admit that the main reasons why Koreans buy from Japanese firms in preference to other foreign competitors is that the Japanese give good after-sale service. Most other foreign firms do not. Another criticism leveled at foreign competitors, and especially at American firms, is that they seem reluctant to adopt products and services unique to Korean markets.

South Korea has intentionally reduced its trade barriers for non-high-tech products with the aim of making Korean manufacturers more efficient and internationally competitive. Imports from Japan caused a trade deficit of US$8 billion in 1991. Imports from the West weren't even close.

Table 24-1 shows the country's key economic statistics.

Foreign Trade

Despite publicly announced preferences for Japanese goods, South Korean trade officials actively solicit trade with U.S. and European companies. They cite a population of 43 million people and growing per capita income in making their case for South Korea as a viable market for foreign imports, and U.S. trade officials go along.

The South Korean government is trying hard to attract U.S. exports. Tariffs have been drastically cut, quotas eliminated, and trade missions to the United States instructed to purchase billions of dollars worth of American-made goods. Korean exports to the United States dropped 5 percent in 1990: U.S. exports to Korea increased 7 percent.

But despite these signs of trade cooperation, conditions within the country are not as rosy. Foreign companies find that their merchandise is often removed from storekeepers' shelves; that there are "special" tax audits of foreign firms located in South Korea and of Korean firms buying foreign products; and that foreign firms can expect general harassment, both by government bureaucrats and by workers' organizations.

In 1990 the South Korean government launched a campaign condemning the purchase of luxury items—mostly foreign-made luxury items, of course. Threats of enforcing Section 301 sanctions emanate periodically from Washington, but to date, they have not been taken seriously. However, the Korean Trade Commission points out that it has investigated more than seventy complaints by foreign companies of unfair trading practices. No penalties; just investigations.

Nevertheless, the U.S. Department of Commerce insists (?) that strong Korean demand should encourage U.S. exporters. Commerce officials push exports of industrial raw materials, heavy machinery, factory automation, electronics, high-technology scientific products, and pollution-control equipment.

KOTRA recommends the following high-demand items as attractive for foreign companies: medical equipment, machine tools, chemicals, logs and lumber, scrap metal, telecommunications equipment, industrial process controls, auto parts, and coal.

KOTRA has also announced that mammoth construction projects have been opened to bids from foreign contractors for a new international airport near Seoul, as well as for high-speed rail lines, highways, ports at Pusan and Kwangyung, and refineries.

Foreign Direct Investment

Regardless of encouraging hype from national trade bureaus, South Korea has never been overly receptive to foreign direct investment. Despite reluctance on the part of government bureaucrats and chaebol to allow foreign firms equal competitive footing, several such firms continue their South Korean investment efforts—albeit at a radically decreasing rate.

Companies from Japan and the United States (in that order) have been the main investors. In the early 1990s, however, investment from both nations tapered off. U.S. investment was just over US$300 million in 1990, bringing the total to US$2.3 billion. Japanese private investment was cut in half, to US$236 million, reflecting the diversion of Japanese investment to lower-cost areas in Southeast Asia and China.

The South Korean hotel industry and the banking sector took the biggest hits. Investment in the chemical, electronics, and machinery industries actually increased slightly.

Compared to other East Asian countries outside of Japan, the South Korean direct investment climate is not good. Tax incentives do not compare with those offered in the other Tigers or in Southeast Asia. The top corporate income tax rate for both domestic and foreign-owned corporations, including branches, is 34 percent. Capital gains are taxed at 25 percent. Foreign investments that qualify under the Foreign Capital Inducement Act get several tax breaks:

1. A 100 percent tax exemption for the first four years of the business, plus a 50 percent exemption for the following two years

2. A 50 percent reduction on taxes payable on dividends on shares acquired by the foreign company

3. A 50 percent exemption from acquisition and property taxes on properties acquired by the foreign company

4. A 100 percent exemption on royalties received from high-technology contracts for five years

To qualify for any of these incentives, a company must receive specific permission from the South Korean Ministry of Finance.

Except in "high-priority industries" (which the government keeps redefining), labor and lease subsidies are virtually nil. The lack of support from the South Korean government, coupled with rapidly increasing labor costs, makes the nation significantly less desirable for investment than other, equally strategically situated countries.

The one attraction that South Korea has over its East Asian neighbors is its location at the north end of the East Asian arc. To the extent that trade develops with Mongolia, Manchuria, North Korea, or the Russian Far East, South Korea is the place to be for optimum advantage.

Korean Unification

With the dismantling of the Soviet Union, the gradual restoration of peace between Indochina and the rest of the world, and China's first halting steps toward a market economy, North Korea remains one of the few communist holdouts left in the world. Since the Korean war ended in 1953 (without an official peace treaty), North Korea has been committed to overthrowing the South Korean government by force. It has also supported worldwide terrorism—especially against South Korea—and has developed nuclear armament capabilities.

Long considered one of the world's most volatile powder kegs, the Korean peninsula is at last moving toward unification with the long-term goal of disarmament and the withdrawal of American troops from the south.

North Korea is not an especially large market, although it certainly has potential. In 1990 its economy shrank for the first time according to South Korea's National Unification Board. Gross national product contracted 3.75 percent to US$23.1 billion, which represented a reversal from a 2.4 percent growth in 1989. The board cited low productivity, outdated facilities, power shortages, and sluggish trade as the main reasons. Foreign trade fell 4 percent from a year earlier to US$4.64 billion.

In an effort to stimulate its new interest in joining the world community, the North Korean government created its first free economic zone. Located in the northeast part of the country, in North Hamgyong province, the free zone is 240 square miles in size.

According to government sources, substantial incentives have been set up to attract foreign companies to invest in facilities in the area. Among the most beneficial is preferential treatment in setting up joint ventures and coproduction facilities. However, since "preferential treatment" from the North Koreans can mean practically anything—not necessarily fitting Western definitions of what is advantageous to private enterprise—foreign companies have not begun a stampede.

After a pledge by the two prime ministers to work toward ending forty years of confrontation, representatives from the two Koreas reached agreement on an historic rapprochement. Foreign observers have become convinced that Korean unification will bring problems and opportunities of so great a magnitude that they will dwarf those created by German unification.

There can be little doubt that unification will change the economic face of South Korea and strongly impact trade and foreign direct investment. The nature of the changes remains uncertain, but at a minimum, a united Korea will present interesting possibilities as a door to Northeast Asia.

It would not be surprising if such unification creates a market of sufficient size and attractiveness to interest Japanese companies in using the peninsula as the cornerstone of a regional trading bloc. Japan desperately needs resources and space that Korea can provide. It also needs a direct, offshore entree to the eastern Russian and northern Chinese markets. Foreign companies that can afford to implement a high-risk investment strategy might find themselves more strategically located in Korea than farther south.

Future Problems

South Korea's future as a viable trading partner for Western firms is becoming increasingly murky, in part because the government and the Korean people are so committed to maintaining their high growth rate. This commitment has become an addiction, and to feed it, Korean companies and the nation as a whole must remain competitive in world markets. But to accomplish this they need to turn inward to solve four serious conditions, any one of which could effectively check further growth.

1. Outmoded National Infrastructure

The nation's infrastructure requires a massive injection, not only to deal with future demands, but also to cope with existing congestion. The streets of Seoul are nearly impassable, with six hundred new cars each day joining the already-clogged arteries. Telephone lines are jammed. The Seoul international airport cannot handle existing traffic. Electric power generators shut down periodically. Ports are clogged.

The director of planning for the Korea Development Institute, Kim Jong Gie, estimates that the government will have to spend at least US$10 billion a year between 1991 and 1996 just to stop things from getting worse.

2. Environmental Pollution

South Korea's chaebol have completely ignored environmental destruction on their path to high-speed industrial growth. Polluting emissions from coal- and oil-burning smokestacks fill the air. Factory emissions of sulfur dioxide are five times those permitted in Los Angeles. Drinking water is contaminated by industrial waste. At midday, Seoul's decibel level is nearly intolerable.

History has shown that during industrial revolutions people will put up with horrendous living conditions as long as they feel that their economic situation is improving. History has also shown that once people stop believing they are benefiting from economic growth, their tolerance for terrible living conditions diminishes. In such situations, the stability of a nation that has neglected its social structure (without which there could be no growth) can collapse.

3. Poorly Developed Financial System

The third problem is financial. Gross domestic saving totaled approximately 33 percent of GDP in 1990, an extremely high rate when compared to the OECD average of 20 percent. The big question is how efficiently these savings can be channeled into the economy. A paradox throughout East Asia is that the fastest-growing economies have the least-developed financial systems.

To fuel an ever-increasing demand for short-term capital, "informal" markets have sprung up—often commanding interest rates in excess of 25 percent. The biggest chaebol carry massive amounts of debt. When Samsung's electronic subsidiary pushed into semiconductors, it took on debt amounting to seven times its net worth, a move reminiscent of the American LBOs of the 1980s, which are now going under in the 1990s.

Government trade surpluses in the latter half of the 1980s permitted a restructuring of the nation's financial system. Instead, government bureaucrats closed their eyes to protect their own positions. The current account is now running constant deficits. Seoul's stock market continues to operate like a gambling casino, as the nation's banking system stutters through one mishap after another.

4. Underdeveloped R & D Capabilities

The last, and in many respects the most serious, problem facing the nation's growth dreams is the underdevelopment of its R & D capabilities. This is not to say that South Korean companies don't pour billions of dollars into R & D projects: they do. Nor does it mean that South Korea lacks qualified technical brainpower: it doesn't. What it does mean is that South Korea is at the same stage in its technological development as Japan was in the 1960s when Japanese engineers amazed the world by their ability to copy other products— but not to develop many on their own.

Technology is moving so rapidly, especially in electronics and computer industries, that the only way South Korean companies can hope to learn new technologies fast enough to turn out competitive new products is to get that technology from competitors in Japan, Germany, and the United States. This they try to do through joint ventures and foreign investment. To date, they are finding competitors less than eager to share new technology until the next generation is ready to be introduced—which keeps Korean firms playing copycat.

Until Korean firms develop sufficient homegrown scientific talent, the playing field will remain unlevel. Progress is being made, but it will take many years to form a sufficient Korean cadre of young scientists and technicians to compete in worldwide R & D markets.

Of course, every problem creates an opportunity. This is certainly true in South Korea. Leaving aside the unification issue and the myriad problems— and hence opportunities—that it will create, the resolution of infrastructure, environmental, financial, and R & D problems leaves the door open to foreign companies with the resources and skills to step in. At some point the South Korean government, backed by the chaebol, will find it expedient to look to the outside for assistance. Strategically positioned companies should have the inside track.

25
China

Tips to Foreign Traders and Investors

1. Outside the SEZs, make direct investments only if resources are sufficient to gamble on very-long-term returns.
2. Invest in outlying areas of free-zone provinces rather than in overcrowded SEZ cities.
3. Make direct investments in Hong Kong or Taiwan as the best way to access China's markets.
4. Once established in a SEZ, move to a free-zone province for cheap labor.
5. Use a Chinese presence as an entree to currently forming East Asian trading blocs.
6. Embassy office in Washington: (202) 328-2500.

One of the last hard-line communist countries, China continues to confound the world. Extremely restrictive measures designed to enhance state control over the country's social and economic activities have failed to stem the tide of reforms begun in the 1980s.

The dichotomy of purpose shown by China's hard-line leaders can best be understood as a coupling of their undying devotion to personal power (achieved through repressive social and political policies), and their desire to partake of the money, goods, and services lavished on a market economy. While political and ideological repression continues unabated, economic reforms move forward (*despite* Beijing's policies, not because of them), pressing China toward a position as an ever-more viable trading partner.

The government's attitude toward economic development since Tiananmen Square sheds light on the potential for future trade, but also leaves many unanswered questions. Prior to 1986, the country's trade deficits stimulated foreign credit, which fueled a rapidly growing economy. After June 1989, international leaders placed a credit embargo on China. With total debt of US$45 billion and access to new credit denied, China's hard-liners were forced to shift the trade deficit to a surplus overnight to meet the nation's foreign debt obligations.

The government started by imposing strict controls on imports. Factories were ordered to produce to maximum capacity without regard for consumer demand. Tight wage freezes and other state controls caused domestic demand to sag, but intentionally produced excess inventory fueled exports. According to Chinese figures, exports increased 18 percent to US$62 billion, while imports decreased 10 percent to US$53.4 billion, creating a US$9 billion surplus.

The trade imbalance, coupled with a traditional surplus on nontrade items, swelled foreign reserves. This enabled hard-liners to maintain intransigent political policies in spite of the credit embargo. Over strong congressional objections, President Bush renewed China's most-favored-nation status in June 1991, allowing China to increase its trade surplus with the United States to more than US$10 billion.

The hard-liners also managed to keep foreign direct investment from declining after Tiananmen Square. From a total of US$3.4 billion in 1990, new foreign capital contract commitments increased to US$12.3 billion in one year, making both investments and commitments about the same as those in 1989. Internally, the government shifted its fixed investment priorities to state-owned energy-related and transportation enterprises, leaving any increase in production capacity to foreign companies.

The agricultural sector enhanced China's resurrection. In 1990, the country experienced its highest grain output in history. Cotton and linseed oil production also hit new highs.

A Brighter Future?

As 1991 began, government planners claimed victory over the 1989–1990 recession, citing the prior year's 5 percent growth in GNP—nearly all accounted for by good crop harvests and reviving industrial production (a 6 percent growth, excluding village industries) in the fourth quarter.

Despite output gains, labor efficiency and productivity continue to be a major headache for Chinese industry, particularly in state-owned firms. Productivity in these firms increased a mere 0.8 percent in 1990, largely accounting for a 58 percent decrease in profits. Although official state statistics reported a 2.6 percent unemployment rate (excluding underemployment in rural areas), some experts believe the real rate runs between 5 and 6 percent.

The figures in Table 25-1, compiled by government bureaus, clearly reflect both the devastating economic affect of Tiananmen Square and the severe

Table 25-1. Annual Percentage Change in Selected Indicators

	1988	1989	1990	Forecasted for 1991
Gross national product	10.9	3.6	5.0	5.7
Net material product	11.3	3.3	4.8	5.4
Industrial output	20.8	8.5	7.6	7.7
Agricultural output	3.9	3.1	6.9	4.0
Gross fixed investment	23.5	-8.0	4.5	10.0
Value of retail sales	27.8	-7.6	1.9	9.0
Retail price index	18.5	17.8	2.1	7.8
Value of exports	20.5	10.6	18.1	6.4
Value of imports	27.9	7.0	-9.8	11.0

SOURCE: State Statistical Bureau, *Statistical Yearbook of China 1990; Report on National Economic and Social Development in 1990.*

impacts of subsequently tightened central government controls over the business sector.

Chinese economic officials summarize their accomplishments as:

1. A government austerity program that has stopped inflation (2 percent in 1990 as compared to 17.8 percent in 1989)

2. Increased agricultural production

3. Expanded foreign exchange reserves, resulting from the conversion of a trade deficit to a surplus

4. Priority investments in energy and transportation

These same bureaucrats point to a nation poised to resume growth and eager to increase world trade. Perhaps.

Caution Alert

Several questions remain unanswered that impact short- and long-term market strategies:

■ *Politically, will hard-liners allow a market economy to develop, with prices, production priorities, and wages determined by market supply and demand factors, or will their repressive political policies once again jeopardize foreign trade?*

■ *How much of China's economic progress reflects current market-oriented trade policies and how much is merely a holdover from pre-1989 trends, which of course will eventually turn down?*

■ *Do the most lucrative strategies call for foreign direct investment, cross-border trade through exports and imports—or a combination of the two?*

- *What impact will the 1997 takeover of Hong Kong have on foreign trade and investment?*

- *How soon will the Republic of China (Taiwan) and the PRC merge markets and resources?*

Red Flag

Perhaps the biggest unknown at this time—but also the major influencing factor on long-term trade and investment—is the role China will play in the rapidly forming Asia-Pacific economic trading blocs.

Faltering Foreign Direct Investment

Despite bureaucratic optimism, foreign direct investment in China has taken a real beating since Tiananmen Square. During the 1980s, Western companies, especially those from the United States, jumped at the opportunity to invest in Chinese manufacturing facilities, hotels, and retail establishments. Large and midsize firms were attracted by China's vast market potential, unlimited cheap labor, and abundant natural resources. Countertrade deals were struck overnight. The U.S government couldn't do enough to encourage the trend.

Japanese companies also took the bait, and China became the second-most-popular avenue for overseas investments after Thailand. Many companies were willing to accept low profit margins or even losses from their Chinese operations because they wanted to be in on the ground floor when the economy converted to free markets.

Then, suddenly, the Tiananmen massacre cast a dark shadow on the future of these grandiose plans. The withdrawal of most-favored-nation (MFN) status for two years, the clampdown on foreign activities by Chinese hard-liners, and derogatory world opinion forced many foreign companies to pull up stakes and go home.

American direct investment dropped from US$2.3 million in the first half of 1989 to US$889,000 for the same period in 1990. Nearly all of this direct investment had been committed prior to Tiananmen. The bureaucratic haggling that marked the history of American Motors' showcase Jeep factory further shook business confidence. Occidental Petroleum announced its intention to sell its 25 percent interest in an open-pit coal mine in Shanxi province, up to then the largest single investment by an American firm in China.

Major revisions in the tax structure have further discouraged foreign investment. Tax breaks granted to foreign companies by provinces and municipalities have been abolished. Foreign firms must now withhold tax on the unofficial second salary they usually have to pay to motivate Chinese employees. (The state employment agency takes 80 percent of their regular wages.) These tax increases have destroyed many of the low-cost advantages of being in China in the first place.

Tax rates and regulations for domestic firms are not made public. In 1991, foreign joint ventures paid a tax of 33 percent on both income and capital gains, while wholly foreign-owned subsidiaries and branches paid 50 percent. Tax holidays or rate reductions apply to the following:

- Joint ventures in manufacturing with an operating period of at least ten years

- Joint ventures and foreign companies engaged in manufacturing in SEZs and other special development zones

- Export-oriented and technologically advanced joint ventures and foreign subsidiaries or branches

- Infrastructure projects in the Pudong Development Zone scheduled to operate at least 15 years

The Chinese government also seems to be doing everything in its power to undermine domestic companies. After June 1989, the government insisted on the return of Communist Party–faithful "commissioners" to each factory. In effect, two bosses now try to run each company—one charged with business affairs, the other with forcing employee adherence to hard-line communist rules.

In addition, the Beijing government has tightened foreign borrowing by domestic companies and centralized the supervision and approval of such loans. The new rules limit foreign-currency loans to projects that fit the government's industrial policies, variable though they may be. The new rules also limit borrowing to government-approved financial institutions and authorized industrial and commercial ventures.

By 1991, foreign borrowing by domestic firms stood at US$24.19 billion, or 46 percent of the nation's total foreign debt.

China's Needs

China's import requirements are not much different from those of other developing nations. Modern technology tops the list. At least twenty years behind in the education and training of a technical and scientific cadre, China's only hope of entering the modern age is to purchase technology from Japan and the West.

China sorely lacks modern management techniques. The imposition of Communist Party commissioners on factory management has stymied the further development of homegrown managers. The assimilation of effective management styles from Japan and the West into Chinese cultural mores will be necessary to jump-start the economy once again.

Chinese industry also desperately needs state-of-the-art manufacturing and testing equipment. Much of the machinery imported during the early 1980s is beginning to wear out. Although a domestic machine tool industry has begun to form, it has a long way to go to meet the modern manufacturing and quality requirements demanded by international markets.

Finally, the country's financial system must be modernized and upgraded to handle domestic banking and capital needs, as well as to effectively manage the nation's foreign exchange.

Without question, command economy rules from current Beijing hard-liners prevent both the public and private sectors from fully utilizing such market economy fixtures. Nevertheless, by permitting foreign imports to flow through SEZs and coastal provinces, especially in Cantonese sectors, the government has opened the door to foreign technology and support mechanisms.

Western and Japanese companies are already exploiting this opening. Some venture into production-sharing arrangements with Chinese firms. Others use the path of least resistance, through Hong Kong and Taiwan. Regardless of the approach, and despite hard-liner crackdowns, the import of goods, services, and foreign investment continues.

Does Stability Exist?

In addition to tax changes, political uncertainty, and the extreme difficulty Westerners have in coping with Chinese superstitions and xenophobia, two primary concerns stand out as deterrents to an acceleration of Western investment, at least in the short run. By far the biggest problem is the belief that the Chinese government does not want a fully competitive, market economy. It wants to keep businesses on a short leash, which it can tighten when it sees fit, then loosen again when additional foreign credit is needed.

Outward appearances (and few Americans, if any, have insider knowledge) indicate that as long as the bureaucratic power structure isn't threatened and money continues to flow into government coffers, semifree enterprise will be tolerated. Many foreign executives believe that the diminution of either condition will create further "remedies" against private enterprise.

China's shaky cash position is a second major concern. According to several China experts, even if the original goal, set in the 1980s by China's then-powerful reformers, of achieving a per capita GNP of US$800 is met by the year 2000, it would still only bring the economy up to the level of Nicaragua or Yemen, certainly not thriving marketplaces.

Red Flag

Chinese cheap labor certainly entices Western companies. On the other hand, cheap labor does not breed thriving markets; and abundant natural resources do not ensure their availability to private enterprise. Many companies are finding that investments can be made elsewhere at less cost, yielding much higher returns with less aggravation.

At the same time, foreigners are finding lucrative opportunities in the Special Economic Zones (SEZs) specifically designed to encourage foreign investment. Even without direct investments, foreign companies continue to profit from pure trade transactions. Trading companies do especially well with facilities in SEZs and with joint venture agreements with local producers.

SEZs allow the duty-free import of components, manufacturing and test equipment, technology, and a variety of other goods. Finished products from SEZs can then be sold in domestic markets or exported. Tax breaks, lease incentives, and a variety of subsidies have led to a flood of investment by offshore companies.

As long as foreign reserves hold out, exporting to SEZs makes sense and can yield significant returns.

On the flip side, Chinese manufacturers continue to produce an array of consumer and industrial products for export. North American markets, and to a lesser extent European markets, remain flooded with low-priced (and many times low-quality) Chinese goods. In many respects, imports from China rival both the price and quality of Japanese imports of twenty years ago. Exports from SEZ manufacturing sites to Asia-Pacific markets are also picking up.

A U.S. Trading Partner

American traders remain concerned that China will lose its MFN status. According to *China Business Review,* removal of MFN status would increase the price of China's top 25 exports to the United States by nearly 40 percent, significantly reducing their competitiveness. Although these goods fall into a variety of tariff classes, tariffs would rise from 8.8 percent to 50.1 percent on average.

Exporting to China (outside of the SEZs) remains a difficult undertaking because of the severe tariffs, quotas, and other restrictions against most imports. Even with adequate foreign reserves, the Chinese government continues to prevent open trade. This is especially painful to U.S. producers, many of whom stand ready, willing, and able with a variety of export products. If permitted to ship, such exports would help the United States lower its enormous trade deficit with China. This deficit of more than US$10 billion is second only to that outstanding to Japan.

As a trade-off to President Bush's personal determination to maintain MFN status, the U.S. Congress in mid-1991 exacted a promise to seriously consider sanctions under Section 301 of the 1974 Trade Act. Subsequently, U.S. Trade Representative Carla Hills began proceedings against China's unfair trade practices. Section 301 allows Ms. Hills to "investigate" China's trade practices for up to a year. If these practices are still deemed unsatisfactory at the end of that period, retaliatory measures may be taken.

Ms. Hills's office suggests that it will seek sanctions equivalent to the trade deemed lost by American exporters because of China's market barriers.

Typically, such sanctions amount to 100 percent import duties on selected items. Ms. Hills was reasonably successful in prying open Japanese markets using the same threat, and observers are betting on her success with China also.

While such actions encourage smaller traders, giants like Boeing are quaking. China has orders for 44 planes with Boeing totaling US$2.7 billion. A Chinese Embassy spokesman declined comment on whether China might target Boeing as a result of U.S. action. Boeing officials think it will.

The United States is China's biggest export market, especially for textiles, footwear, and toys. U.S. imports from China rose from US$4 billion in 1985 to US$15 billion in 1990. Meanwhile, exports from American firms have remained in the US$3 billion to US$5 billion range.

Miracle on the South China Sea

In 1979, China's leader, Deng Xiaoping, introduced two major reforms that would change the face of Maoist China. The first restored the family as the main unit of the farm economy and let the market set most farm prices. Rural income doubled in six years, creating a constituency within the political system that, to date, refuses to let reforms die, and a solid entrepreneurial base for future economic growth. One can only surmise the success Mikhail Gorbachev might have had if he had used these two legs as a foundation for perestroika and glasnost.

The second major contribution from Deng's reforms, also sorely lacking in both the Soviet Union and India, was a partially open door to foreign trade and investment that established world price discipline in small segments of the economy. Not willing to risk the "perversion" of China's entire soul by Western capitalism, the government selected specific areas along the South China Sea coast for the experiment. These provinces were the first to be liberalized. Then 14 cities were given the status of "coastal open cities." Extra freedoms and tax breaks were created to attract foreign trade and investment there.

Many northern coastal areas have benefited from this partial freedom. South Korean and Japanese companies have set up shipping and other subsidiaries in Liaoning (once Manchuria) and Shandong, across the Yellow Sea from Korea. Shanghai regained much of its old glamour by attracting investments from companies representing most trading countries.

The greatest benefits, however, have come to the southern provinces, arcing from Hainan Island in the far south, through Guangdong (adjacent to Hong Kong), Hunan, and Fujian province opposite Taiwan. This is where the "special economic zones," or SEZs, were located, with greater privileges still.

All SEZs have experienced a remarkable economic boom, but the town of Shenzhen, across the straits from Hong Kong, has grown the most. From a sleepy fishing town of 100,000 people, the city has expanded to a city of two million inhabitants, with a skyline of steel and glass, massive traffic jams, a per capita GDP of US$2000 a year, and a plentiful supply of prostitutes. The annual increase in trade and investment, as well as industrial output, tops 40 percent.

The province of Guangdong, within which Shenzhen is located, experienced increased industrial output of 15 percent per year during the decade of the 1980s. Its principal products, toys, shoes, and clothing, account for one-third of all China's exports.

Exports from Guangdong increased 25 percent in 1991. Foreign goods and services are in abundance; no empty shelves will be found in Guangzhou (once Canton), the provincial capital. Businessmen flock to a plethora of restaurants and night spots—unheard of in China's heartland. High-rise apartment blocks and office buildings dot the horizon. The same type of Westernization can be found in other SEZ cities.

Dating back to tribal days, China has been separated by culture and language into a rural, militaristic Mandarin population in the north and an independent-minded, trade-oriented Cantonese population in the south.

The Beijing government appears willing to put up with economic freedom for the Cantonese as long as the south continues to grant bureaucrats the skimming that lines their own pockets, and poses no threat to the political supremacy of the ruling elite. Whether or not conditions will change when Hong Kong reverts in 1997 and the Taiwanese reclaim their long-lost birthright is anyone's guess. But the clock keeps ticking and very soon answers will begin unfolding.

Both risk and trade advantage will accrue to foreign companies over the next eight to ten years as the economies of Hong Kong, Taiwan, and China become enmeshed. Already, Taiwanese companies invest over US$1 billion a year in mainland China, and Hong Kong businesses account for one-third of all foreign direct investment there. One can only imagine the immense trading power that might be created by harnessing the combined manufacturing potential of China, Hong Kong, and Taiwan with the financial and technical resources of Japan and the heavy-industry sophistication of South Korea.

When young, market-oriented bureaucrats replace the aging oligarchs in Beijing, and the China-Japan-Korea trading bloc is formed, foreign companies with an established presence will be likely winners. The political risks associated with investing in mainland China can be substantially mitigated today by addressing the existing potentials in both Hong Kong and Taiwan, as examined in the next two chapters.

26
Hong Kong

Tips to Foreign Traders and Investors

1. Use Hong Kong as a financial center and administrative headquarters for China-Korea-Japan trade.
2. Check out Hong Kong as a reexport center for goods produced in China.
3. Set up a local facility now to tap opening China markets.
4. Consider investment in China's Guangdong province as an alternative.
5. Keep financial exposure to a minimum until after 1997.
6. Beware of intense competition from U.S., Japanese, and Hong Kong firms. Newcomers are not always welcome.
7. Watch out for Chinese export products made with prison labor. Product design and materials may not meet international safety and health standards.

The British lease on the land beneath Hong Kong expires in 1997. British and Chinese negotiators have gone at it for more than a decade, trying to reach an amicable accord. Britain wants to preserve access to its last East Asian outpost, partly to pacify British pride, and partly as an economic entree to one of the world's largest markets. China, on the other hand, wants to savor Hong Kong's immense capital reserves and technology and to use it as a stimulant for the rest of the nation. Beijing's leaders also want to reunite Hong Kong's Chinese population with what it believes to be true Chinese culture.

Those, at least, are the publicly announced objectives of each side.

Hong Kong residents and businesses are caught in the middle. The treaty negotiated between Britain and the PRC leaves the door open for Beijing to enforce its power and way of life. Although China has agreed to leave all Hong Kong business and personal laws untouched for fifty years—until

2047—and assures residents that existing freedoms will not be diminished, many regard such statements as hollow promises, for obvious reasons.

Many middle class residents and business people have already left, most of them emigrating to Australia and Canada and taking their capital with them. Several major businesses have relocated their legal domicile. The investment banking house Jardine Fleming moved to Bermuda, the parent of Hong Kong and Shanghai Banking Group has moved to London. Many smaller firms have also decided not to play the wait-and-see game.

Conversely, Hong Kong is not becoming a ghost town. According to Hong Kong resident and New Jersey native John Kamm, past president of the American Chamber of Commerce in Hong Kong, 75 percent of the businesses polled in a recent survey indicated plans to stick it out. Only 13 percent said they were moving for certain. The balance hadn't decided.

Shifts in Economic Development

Economically, Hong Kong has seen many changes over the last twenty years. Most have resulted from the assimilation of the Hong Kong and mainland China economies. The distinctly Cantonese capacity for conducting business in a market economy and for independent social derivatives is very different from the communal party line emanating from Beijing. These independent Cantonese characteristics have blended nicely with the British market heritage of Hong Kong.

The result has been a melding of the mainland Cantonese economy and culture with Hong Kong's, permitting the colony to move from a dependence on adjacent provinces for foodstuffs and water supplies to an integrated business community. Today, the economies of Hong Kong, the Portuguese island of Macau, and the southern part of adjacent Guangdong province are closely intertwined and can be aptly characterized as a Cantonese economy.

Although China's reformers welcome expansion plans as much as hard-line conservatives fear it, both sides agree on the inevitability of a much larger and economically stronger Hong Kong in the future. From its colonial perspective, Britain sees expansion as threatening the stability of the territory.

Hong Kong firms have already expanded their role in the Chinese economy with large direct investments. They also serve as the main source of Chinese trade, dominating several SEZs; China has in effect turned these SEZs over to them to manage, in a role similar to that emerging for Taiwan.

The Hong Kong dollar is the currency of choice throughout Guangdong province (approximately the size of France); Hainan is considering formalizing it. Shenzhen's emerging stock exchange is patterned after Hong Kong's and looks to it for support. Business leaders hope to merge expertise in basic sciences from Guangdong province with Hong Kong's superior strength in marketing and finance to create a dynamic, export-oriented manufacturing region.

As its functional role expands, the Chinese government plans to extend Hong Kong's geographic area. Visa requirements have already been abandoned for Hong Kong residents visiting Shenzhen; plans call for the reverse to happen in a couple of years. Tight travel restrictions remain in effect at Guangdong's borders, however, preventing China's impoverished masses from swamping the province. In essence, Beijing plans to extend Hong Kong's borders to meld with those of the province, thus demonstrating to foreign executives the area's unlimited opportunities.

Current Foreign Direct Investment Potential

For decades, foreign firms used Hong Kong as a cheap-labor manufacturing location. Goods produced in Hong Kong could be found in stores and shops around the world. Practically any labor-intensive product could be made cheaper in Hong Kong and sold in world markets at lower prices than goods from any other manufacturing site.

Today, the mix of a rapidly escalating demand for labor to meet the industrialization of the colony and a finite labor supply have jacked up wages to the point where they can no longer be considered low by world standards. Increased labor costs, skyrocketing rents, and the opening of Guangdong province (and especially the SEZ in neighboring Shenzhen) have caused a massive shift in manufacturing from the tiny colony to the adjacent mainland. Eighty percent of the colony's manufacturing companies have now moved to Guangdong, where they chiefly produce low-end toys, plastic goods, and electronics.

Several Hong Kong firms have extended their investments far beyond the coastal zones. In 1991, these companies accounted for one-third of the total US$12 billion worth of foreign direct investment in the PRC.

In Shenzhen, foreign firms find abundant cheap labor, plentiful low-cost facilities, and, because of special concessions from Beijing, a proximity to mainland markets. Today, Hong Kong firms employ more than two million people across the border in China. Such relocations permit the territory to concentrate on becoming a world-class financial services center, a hub of high-tech development, and an administrative headquarters for virtually every major firm trading in East Asia.

Companies from the following countries were the major investors in Hong Kong through 1989:

	Investment capital in US$ million
United States	1190
Japan	1100
China (PRC)	407
United Kingdom	282
Australia	154

SOURCE: Hong Kong Department of Industrial Statistics.

Even with the international outrage over the Tiananmen massacre and the uncertainties surrounding the 1997 PRC takeover, many American firms continue to be optimistic about Hong Kong's future as a trading outpost. More than nine hundred U.S. companies have facilities in the territory—double the number five years ago. Virtually every Fortune 500 company is represented, as are hundreds of small and midsize firms.

The biggest attraction is Hong Kong's very active financial sector, which provides a safe haven for offshore capital. Indeed, for many years, a goal of the Hong Kong administration has been to build the colony into one of the world's mightiest offshore financial centers. The stability of the Hong Kong dollar in world financial markets (see Table 26-1) gives the colony a distinct advantage over other East Asian centers in Singapore and Indonesia. In addition, most international legal and accounting firms have offices in Hong Kong to service the needs of foreign companies and individual investors.

Citibank has maintained a presence in Hong Kong for decades and recently headed a syndication to fund the US$1.4 billion development of a new Hong Kong airport and refurbished port facility, labeled Port and Airport Development Strategy (PADS).

Two other well-known American firms have also made recent headlines with major investments. Motorola opened a new semiconductor chip-manufacturing plant to service the Asia-Pacific market. Waste Management International acquired a 70 percent interest in a consortium with a multimillion dollar contract to build and operate Asia's first chemical-waste treatment facility.

Meanwhile, Japanese companies have not been idle. Even though American firms edged in as top investors in 1989, Japanese companies poured US$5.3 billion into the colony during the four-year period 1985–1989. This makes Japan the biggest cumulative investing country by far. Japan is represented by 92 banks and controls 40 percent of the retail trade, led by the huge Yaohan department store.

Cross-border investment from South Korea, Taiwan, Singapore, Thailand, and Malaysia has also shown a significant increase since the mid-1980s.

Table 26-1. Hong Kong Economic and Trade Statistics*

	Statistics
Population	5.8 million
GDP	US$69.2 billion
GDP growth over 1989	2.2 percent
Unemployment rate	1.8 percent
Inflation	10.0 percent
Exports as percentage of GDP	116.0 percent
Real effective exchange rate (1980–1982 = 100)	99.1

*As of 1990.

SOURCES: Hong Kong Department of Industrial Statistics; IMF; World Bank; Morgan Guaranty Trust Company.

Hong Kong's attractive tax structure also draws foreign firms. Although conditions will certainly change after 1997, the current corporate income tax rate of 16.5 percent on both subsidiaries and branches is the lowest in the region. A foreign company located in Hong Kong (but not carrying on business in the territory) is not taxed at all, even for income derived from Hong Kong sources such as interest, dividends, or stock market gains. Furthermore, a Hong Kong business is not taxed on income sourced outside of Hong Kong.

Exporting from Hong Kong

Hong Kong also serves as a major export outlet for goods produced throughout China. Approximately 15 to 20 percent of Hong Kong's exports to the United States are in fact reexports from the PRC. Washington trade officials predict an increase in these exports to possibly one-third of Hong Kong's total. The U.S. Department of Commerce reports the following comparison of U.S. trade with Hong Kong to that with China directly:

	Trade in US$ billions—1989	
	Hong Kong	China
U.S. imports from	9.7	12.0
U.S. exports to	6.3	5.8
U.S. trade deficit	3.4	6.2

A 1991 documentary shown on American television stirred the hearts of the American public and awoke U.S. trade officials to the fact that all is not as it seems in trade with China. The documentary, filmed in part by undercover operatives in the PRC, identified the substantial production capacity being supplied by forced labor in Chinese prisons. When queried on camera about the destination of goods produced in these Chinese versions of slave-labor camps, a ranking Chinese official emphatically denied that any of these goods were being exported—insisting that everything produced by prison labor was marketed domestically.

Caution Alert

Theoretically the Chinese are right. These goods generally are not exported by the PRC directly to Western markets. Instead, they are shipped to a third-party country, where in many cases they are relabeled and then exported by the neutral nation. Such is the role of Hong Kong. The exact proportion of Hong Kong reexported goods that fall into this category is unknown, but trade officials now estimate that a very high percentage of the shoes, clothing, and toys in Western stores that are labeled as having been made in Hong Kong or Taiwan have actually been made in Chinese prisons.

It should be noted that the United States and most other industrialized nations refuse to allow goods to be imported that are produced by slave labor, prison labor, or any other officially repressed group. Yet the U.S. government is doing nothing to prohibit these transshipment imports from Hong Kong.

Exporting to Hong Kong

Western firms generally find it more expedient and less costly to service the Hong Kong market (and, via Hong Kong, the Chinese market) by establishing a local final-assembly or distribution facility in the colony. This is certainly not a necessary prerequisite for trade, however. Companies from North America and Europe have exported to Hong Kong for years directly from their home bases.

Whether imported or produced locally, certain goods and services are in greater demand than others. According to the U.S. Department of Commerce, the highest demand now and for the foreseeable future is for the following goods and services:

- Computer equipment and software designed to service the growing banking and financial services market
- A variety of plastic products usable in high-end manufacturing
- Office furniture, equipment, and supplies to service the development of foreign and local office facilities in Guangdong province and the Shenzhen Special Economic Zone
- Specialty textiles, especially designer fabrics and clothing
- Oil and gas equipment for resource development in China
- Pollution-control equipment and products to deal with the increasingly severe air and water pollution problems in and around Hong Kong
- Medical equipment and supplies
- Processed foods and agricultural commodities for consumer use
- Engineering and contractor services to handle a continuing building boom in coastal provinces and the PADS

Future Outlook

Putting aside the unknown ramifications of the 1997 takeover, Hong Kong poses an interesting strategic dilemma for Western companies. Short of experiencing extensive war damage by the PRC—which no one anticipates— Hong Kong's business infrastructure will probably remain intact to support its offshore financial center. Although emigration continues, the likelihood of a substantial brain drain of technically sophisticated managers seems remote. No one questions the strategic geography of Hong Kong as a trading center with access to virtually any Asia-Pacific market. (These factors alone indicate the desirability of locating facilities in the territory.)

Although Japanese firms presently control the automobile and retail markets, the growing affluent population will undoubtedly take warmly to competition from other companies. Strategically, both these industries are in the high-growth category and could offer interesting competitive possibilities.

It is also worth considering the long-term effects of the integration of Hong Kong into China when the aging Beijing hard-liners die off or lose power. The Chinese people who represent a large majority of Hong Kong residents have for centuries been pragmatic realists. Their resiliency is well documented throughout ancient and modern history.

As Baroness Lydia Dunn, Chairman of the Hong Kong Trade Development Council, aptly put it during an interview with *World Link*, "If we do not want China to interfere in our affairs, we must not interfere in what they are doing, irrespective of how we feel about the policies that they pursue. So there is a sense of realism, which is quite clear even among our budding politicians."

Potential foreign investors would do well to heed the cautionary tone in Ms. Dunn's words. While Hong Kong offers significant trade and investment opportunities, the potential for a conflict in ideologies could easily make the venture unwise at this time. On the other hand, foreigners willing to put their ideologies aside could find Hong Kong a gold mine.

Caution Alert

Foreign investors should be aware, however, that nothing changes very fast in Chinese politics. While it seems fairly certain that hard-liners will eventually disappear, it could be several years in the future, and even then, no one can be sure what unwelcome tactics new leaders might dream up.

The strategy employed by foreign companies as well as by the native Hong Kong business community must be to keep Hong Kong a viable business conduit for future trade with China. As Ms. Dunn comments, "The most important thing for Hong Kong is that we must at all times maintain our prosperity and stability, because only when we are prosperous and stable can we be useful and valuable to China."

A further long-range consideration that cannot be ignored relates to Hong Kong's role in Chinese trade after the formation of the inevitable Asia-Pacific trading bloc. Japanese companies have already positioned themselves in the northern centers of Liaoning and Shandong and continue to invest heavily in Hong Kong. Western traders might well decide that a tactical risk in Hong Kong now will provide a worthwhile strategic entree within the next decade.

As Lu Ping, director of China's Hong Kong and Macau Affairs office has stated, "Hong Kong is bound up with its Motherland. It will serve as a bridge, channel, and window between China and the rest of the world, and play its unique and positive role in China's development in the next century."

27
Taiwan

Tips to Foreign Traders and Investors

1. Don't be overly enamored of Taiwan's growth statistics; the political situation there is a powder keg.

2. First establish an export program to open doors for investment. Then consider a Taiwanese facility for exporting to China via Hong Kong.

3. Don't bother trying to develop strategies for using Taiwan as a low-cost source of imports to the West. Those days are long gone.

4. Coordination Council for North American Affairs: (202) 895-1800.

Taiwan (which prefers to be called the Republic of China or ROC) provides the second leg of the consolidation of Chinese trade opportunities. Whereas Hong Kong's future political affiliation is already established, that of Taiwan remains in a state of limbo.

The island's 22 million residents are proud of their achievement during the 42 years since Chiang Kai-shek's men were driven off the mainland and took "temporary refuge" in Taiwan. Today, no one questions that the island state has advanced to become one of the five main economic powers in the Asia-Pacific region. Although Taiwan's GDP per capita of US$7500 still lags behind that of Hong Kong and Singapore, its growth of nearly 380 percent since 1980 far overshadows that of the other three "Tigers."

The PRC's loosening of travel restrictions and investment opportunities, plus its imminent takeover, has left the Chinese population of Taiwan scrambling for identity.

Politically, the ruling Kuomintang (Nationalist Party) is being forced to come to grips with one of the ironies of democratic rule: the embarrassment that free elections so frequently bring to the incumbent party. But the key issue that democratization has brought to the front is not merely awkward, it is downright explosive: should the island state declare itself independent of the communist China mainland? The answer may very well hold the key to future foreign trade and investment opportunities in Taiwan, and therefore is worthy of a brief review.

The Politics of Freedom

The question of independence revolves around the island nation's 42-year-old claim that the Republic of China is the rightful China and the People's Republic of China is the interloper who stole the mainland during the Maoist revolution. In 1972 the United Nations felt enough was enough and awarded the U.N. seat originally designated for China to the PRC. The international political community went along, and Taiwan became a renegade—an island without a country, as it were.

Although official trade relations have long been operative between Taiwan and the international business community, Taiwan is still not recognized as China, has no seat at the United Nations, and is not a signatory of the General Agreement on Tariffs and Trade (GATT).

Lately, the Democratic Progressive Party (DPP), the Taiwanese opposition party, has opened old wounds by calling for a plebiscite referendum vote to designate the Republic of Taiwan a separate country, independent of any claim or ties to the mainland. For most of the past 42 years, such advocating of independence was a capital offense; it remains an act of sedition. Yet it has been impossible to stop such talk. After all, Taiwan is fast becoming a democracy. The first freely elected National Assembly, the island's constitution-writing body, came into being toward the end of 1991.

Meanwhile, across the straits, Beijing's leaders agree with the Kuomintang that Taiwan and the mainland belong together as one China. Over the years, the PRC has consistently said that it would use force to stop Taiwan from becoming independent. It recently reiterated its threat when China's president Yang Shangkun stated in true Confucianist style, "Those who play with fire will be burned to ashes."

Taiwan's government is as nervous as China's, yet it does not want to lose its hard-won democratic credentials abroad by shutting down the DPP. The people of Taiwan, pragmatic as ever, recognize the long-term loss that independence would bring—not to mention the potential armed conflict that would inevitably destroy their prosperous island. Opinion polls show little support for the plebiscite.

Nevertheless, China's leaders remain concerned. With Hong Kong, Tibet, and several other discontented cities and provinces to deal with, a breakaway by Taiwan could initiate a disastrous domino effect.

The impact of Taiwan's political machinations on foreign traders and investors should not be taken lightly. Strategically, Taiwan offers as much or more to foreign companies over the long-term as Hong Kong. Too many have already invested too much in the island state to walk away. And too many depend, for their competitive edge in the world marketplace, on imports from and exports to Taiwan to abandon a good trading partner.

The Economy

Taiwan has always exhibited the resiliency of its primarily Chinese inhabitants. Yet the country's rapid recovery from the severe economic turbulence of 1990 surprised even its staunchest advocates. The booming 1980s affected Taiwan as positively as they did its neighbors South Korea and Japan. The crash in 1990 was even more severe.

The cash generated by years of huge current-account surpluses coursed through the economy like running sand, lifting the price of assets—especially property and stocks—to absurd limits. The Taipei Stock Exchange became known as the gambling casino of the East, with stock prices escalating wildly and out of control. The number of stockbrokers increased tenfold, so that at one point there were two brokers for each listed company. The Taipei index rose from 1000 in 1987 to over 12,000 in February 1990. Citizens resigned from their normal jobs to spend days gazing transfixed at screens in brokers' offices. Capital investment as a ratio to GNP fell.

Money supply tripled from 1985 to 1989, while real GNP rose a mere 30 percent. Consumer-price inflation remained steady at around 4 percent, but wild asset values more than made up for that. Eventually, the market crashed, with the index falling 80 percent. The year 1990 saw the money supply shrink. GNP rose 5.1 percent, its smallest increase since the worldwide recession of 1982. Table 27-1 shows the economic status of Taiwan in 1990.

The economy bent, but did not break. Throughout 1991, Taiwan economists boasted that money supply, consumer prices, and stock prices remained at low levels. Exports, on the other hand, increased 14 percent in the first seven months and industrial production rose 6 percent. Current forecasts call for a steady 6 to 7 percent economic growth for the next five years.

Table 27-1. Key Taiwanese Economic and Trade Statistics*

	Statistics
Population	22.0 million
GDP	US$164.7 billion
GDP growth over 1989	5.2 percent
Unemployment rate	1.8 percent
Inflation	3.4 percent
Exports as percentage of GDP	40.0 percent
Real effective exchange rate (1980–1982 = 100)	94.0

*As of 1990.
SOURCES: Taiwan Department of Trade; IMF; Guaranty Trust Company.

Although the government plans a massive public works expenditure of 300 billion New Taiwan dollars (US$11.1 billion) during the 1991–1996 period, economic growth is coming from an unusual, though very pertinent source for the moment. The 14 percent export growth was not achieved by increases to the United States—whose deficit with Taiwan fell by 20 percent. Neither was Japan much help, with its surplus with Taiwan increasing by 20 percent. The source of export growth that surprised much of the international business community came from Hong Kong.

Taiwan's exports to the colony doubled during the period to US$6 billion. Practically all these exports were destined for mainland China, not Hong Kong, consumption.

For years Taiwan produced inexpensive toys, shoes, and clothing for export to Western markets. Cheap labor and low overhead led Western companies by the thousands to set up manufacturing facilities on the island. Now those days are gone. Labor and overhead costs have shot up, forcing the economy to turn to high-tech production and financial services.

Since the PRC is now the low-labor, low-overhead producer in East Asia, it only makes economic sense for Taiwan to provide the raw materials and intermediate components to be turned into finished product on the mainland—and Hong Kong becomes the broker location. Since officially, Taiwan and the PRC aren't speaking to each other—much less trading—all trade between the two countries must pass through an intermediary nation, in most cases Hong Kong.

Increased mainland dependence on Taiwanese investment and trade makes Taiwan even more pragmatically independent, and this worries the Kuomintang. Nevertheless, business-minded Taiwanese continue to trade and invest in response to market signals, not ideologies.

Foreign Direct Investment

As with South Korea, Taiwan was originally targeted by Japanese companies as a prime source of cheap labor and manufacturing expenses. Over the years, Japanese firms kicked in US$2.6 billion of the island state's total foreign direct investment of US$5.9 billion. As Taiwan became a huge domestic market with well-fed, eager-to-buy consumers, heavy manufacturing companies left the island and Japanese retailing and distribution services moved in, the better to service the cash-rich middle class.

Meanwhile, spurred by the government's active encouragement and a scarcity of land, Taiwanese manufacturing companies have been moving offshore to more lucrative sites in Southeast Asia and mainland China. The Taiwanese government has implemented a program to dip into its US$70 billion foreign reserves for U.S. dollar loans of up to 80 percent of startup costs for overseas ventures. Since 1988, nearly 60 percent of the US$2.3 billion invested by Taiwanese companies offshore has gone to Malaysia in search of cheap labor.

Now, however, the tables have turned. China is fast becoming the location of choice for strategically sensitive Taiwanese companies. The most important single contribution to the recent increase in China's foreign capital has been an inflow from Taiwan of more than US$1 billion, more than half of which went to nearby Fujian province. By the end of 1990, 877 Taiwanese enterprises were registered in Fujian, with an authorized Taiwanese capital share of US$1.8 billion.

Undoubtedly, a good part of this investment was attracted by the same cheap-labor factors that draw investment to Malaysia. But another, and perhaps more pronounced, reason is that Taiwanese business people are looking to the future, when Taiwan and China will be one. Such a toehold on the mainland would then serve a very real purpose, not only for island-mainland trade, but for enjoying the benefits of a trading bloc.

In addition to accountable investments in Fujian province, billions have been invested in Guangdong province through shell companies in Hong Kong. The official tally counts US$1.3 billion. Unofficial sources place the total in excess of US$3 billion.

Executives of foreign companies would have to be blind not to see the significance of these dramatic shifts in local investment decisions. Although Taiwan has for years been the manufacturing domicile for subsidiaries from America and Europe, the winds of change are rapidly converting Taiwan from a producer site to a prime distribution, retailing, and financial location.

The same arguments advanced in support of Hong Kong as a strategically advantageous regional administrative and trading center apply to Taiwan. And the same reasons apply when it comes to establishing an East Asian presence in anticipation of China's position as the focal point of a massive and powerful trading bloc.

Taiwan's government has determined that the future of the island state (exclusive of its relationship with a market economy China) lies in bringing its status up to that of a world-class trading partner. To do this, it plans to invest the previously mentioned NT$300 billion in refurbished infrastructure projects, human resources, and research and development.

On the R & D side, the government plans to increase research and development spending from the current 1.64 percent to 2.5 percent of GNP by the year 2000, according to the National Science Council. Currently, the private sector provides 52 percent of overall R & D expenditures and the government foots the balance. However, Taipei plans to require businesses to shoulder 70 percent of the total R & D costs by the year 2000.

Such a massive push for technology and high-tech products bids well for foreign companies active in these areas. Surely even a 30 percent kicker from the government is better than most home-country governments provide—certainly more than is available in the United States.

Taiwan's tax structure can't compare to that of Hong Kong. Both domestic corporations and foreign branches are subject to income tax rates of 25 percent, capital gains rates of 25 to 35 percent, and withholding and remittance taxes of 10 to 35 percent. A foreign subsidiary is treated practically the same way as a domestic corporation, with no significant tax incentives.

Foreign Trade Opportunities

According to Lin Yi-fu, deputy director of the Board of Foreign Trade, the government is eager to decrease its trade surplus and increase imports from its major trading partners—specifically the United States. To this end, the Trade Action Plan, introduced in 1989, has been aimed at reducing the surplus by 10 percent a year. Taiwan's export diversion program (to Southeast Asia and Europe) reduced the U.S. trade deficit by nearly 24 percent in 1990. Now it is time to begin increasing imports.

The Trade Action Plan also reduced the average nominal tariff rate from 12.6 percent in 1986 to 9.7 percent in 1989. No further reductions occurred in 1990. In 1991, the government introduced a bill to reduce tariffs to 8.9 percent, and until the bill took effect, temporarily reduced tariffs on 75 items. Excessive tariffs remain in effect for agricultural goods, however.

The same long-range strategic difficulty exists for Taiwan as for Hong Kong in regard to determining the best products to export to the island, versus producing them in a local facility. Here are a few suggestions, as published by the America Institute in Taiwan (not necessarily in order of priority):

Power plants, including gas turbines
Scientific instruments
Telecommunications equipment
Industrial process controls and instrumentation, electronic and thermal
Semiconductor manufacturing equipment
Equipment for food processing, hotels, and restaurants
Medical and pharmaceutical products
Computer equipment
Automated production equipment
Transportation equipment and services
Building supplies and materials
Aerospace and aviation equipment
Pollution-control products and equipment

Taiwan and Hong Kong are both viable entrees to the Chinese market. Western firms will find it less costly, faster, and much easier making their entrance through these back doors than directly to China. Fortune 500 firms have plowed the rough ground in China and many have been turned back. Firms of all sizes and many industries have exploited Hong Kong and Taiwan markets and resources for years. Now conditions have changed.

Strategically, the greatest future benefits for trade and investment lie in China, not in its outposts. Learning from the mistakes made by the multinationals on the mainland and positioning entrance through one of the Four Tigers could smooth the way toward a firmly established trade presence.

28
Southeast Asia: Singapore

Tips to Foreign Traders and Investors

1. Get in on Southeast Asia's low-labor costs and natural resources to compete with the Japanese, South Koreans, and Taiwanese.

2. Stay away from the Philippines for now. Political and financial institutions there are in disarray.

3. Keep an eye on accelerating political turmoil in the entire area.

4. Establish an administrative facility in Singapore as a strategic location for reexporting to Asia-Pacific markets.

5. Utilize Singapore's sophisticated financial sector and port facilities.

6. Singapore's embassy office in Washington: (202) 667-7555.

During the second half of the 1980s, the Southeast Asian "Little Dragons"—as media pundits refer to Thailand, Malaysia, and Indonesia—took off like the earlier generation of the "Four Tigers." Singapore also took a gigantic step, moving from the status of an island outpost to that of a major financial and high-tech center.

The Little Dragons grew on a diet of expanding world trade and relatively open access to rich American, European, and Japanese markets. When world oil prices normalized after the Persian Gulf war and America slid into a prolonged recession, world traders wondered if the Little Dragons had met their waterloo.

Not so, say the region's businessmen, economists, and government officials. Granted, low oil prices and an American recession hurt; but this was just the type of breathing space the region needed to assimilate five years of extraordinary growth. A slight slowdown in trade and investment was welcomed as a time to adjust and rethink future economic plans.

Whereas South Korea, Taiwan and, to a lesser extent, Singapore have depended primarily on trade with the United States for their extraordinary growth, the Little Dragons took a different direction. Thailand and Malaysia export roughly equal amounts to the United States, Japan, and Europe. Indonesia exports twice as much to Japan as to America—mostly in the form of raw materials.

Although exports of components to Japan suffer when Japanese exports to the United States decline, the labor-intensive, less-complex finished products from Southeast Asia are likely to be close to recession-proof. Everyone needs clothing, shoes, can openers, and screwdrivers. Purchases of yachts from Taiwan and transport ships from South Korea can be put off.

Foreign direct investment in Southeast Asia has also taken a different turn. During their growth years, South Korea, Taiwan, Hong Kong, and Singapore depended on capital invested from the United States, Britain, and other European powers. Now, officials believe that their alignment in productive capacity within Asia has gone too far to be reversed. Japan's labor-intensive products, for example, can only compete in world markets with those from South Korea and Taiwan by being produced offshore with significantly cheaper labor than that available at home. Therefore, Japanese companies lead the pack in investing in Southeast Asia, where labor is typically one-third the cost of that in South Korea or Taiwan.

Not to be outdone, Taiwanese and South Korean companies have followed suit. Investment from the three countries has been the driving force in the growth of both Thailand and Malaysia. Furthermore, local firms, in partnership with Japanese, Korean, and Taiwanese firms, have opened vast new markets. Over a three-year period, while world trade was expanding annually by 13 percent, exports from Thailand were increasing by 31 percent; from Malaysia, by 23 percent; and from Indonesia, by 15 percent. It's no wonder that profits from companies located in the region are mushrooming.

The one losing member of the Association of South East Asian Nations (ASEAN) is the Philippines. Already deeply in debt from the Marcos reign, wracked by internal political turmoil and guerrilla warfare, ravished by earthquakes and typhoons, and economically devastated by the pullout of American bases and expensive oil imports, the Philippines continues to teeter on the brink of social dissolution—or at best, national bankruptcy.

The Sultanate of Brunei, rich in oil reserves, and with Japan as practically its only customer, has been the clear winner. Long the world's richest man, the Sultan of Brunei becomes even richer with each barrel of oil.

Oil has also been good to Malaysia and Indonesia, both rich in reserves. The jack-up of world prices stimulated both economies to new heights in 1991. Meanwhile, Thailand's flexible and vigorous private sector has been quick to exploit even the smallest opening in world trade. When the Persian Gulf war began, the country's prime minister, Chatichai Choonhavean, exhorted the country's businessmen to sell fruit juices to American troops in the desert.

Political Stability in Southeast Asia

The only certainty in Southeast Asia is that the region's politics, economies, and social structures will not remain constant. Traditionally, this region has been a hodgepodge of alliances and rivalries, although never divided into opposing armed camps. The big shift in regional politics occurred several years ago, when the Soviet Union and China decided to end their old quarrel.

Unlike Eastern Europe, long dependent on the Soviet economy and mired in the quagmire of Cold War politics, Southeast Asia's reaction to the end of Soviet influence has been much less dramatic. To be sure, cessation of hostilities between the United States and the Soviet Union has caused ripples in the social fabric and economic planning of the region, and the overall situation will be slower to change than that in Europe. Changes are inevitable, however, and could be explosive.

Thailand, Malaysia, Indonesia, and Singapore remain the most economically developed nations in the region and offer the greatest trade opportunities. The other half of Southeast Asia—Vietnam, Cambodia, and Laos—originally designated as Indochina, offers long-term trade opportunities, but for the moment is sorting out a political jigsaw puzzle. Near-medieval Burma (now called Myanmar) is a good place to avoid for a long time.

Some analysts believe East Asia could evolve into another Middle East. While United Nations forces try to maintain order in Cambodia, the makeshift ruling body of government officials and leaders from five guerrilla factions could conceivably relapse into armed conflict, reigniting the country's devastatingly disruptive civil war. In the South China Sea, disagreements over the ownership of the oil-rich Spratly Islands could inflame hostilities between one or more of many combatants: Vietnam, Taiwan, the Philippines, Malaysia, China, and Brunei. The Spratly Islands, like the Paracels farther north, straddle sea lanes vital to each country, as well as to Japan.

Also farther north, Japan and China continue to dispute the Senkaku Islands. Japan and Russia are at odds over the Russian-occupied Kurile Islands. Throughout Southeast and Northeast Asia, nations dispute choke points and trade routes vital to the economic interests of each.

Will East Asia become another Middle East powder keg costing foreign companies billions in damaged or confiscated investments and severing trading ties with the West? Although the odds are not high, the possibility does exist.

As proven time and again, oil buys weapons. Singapore, Taiwan, and South Korea each have the industrial base to make plentiful weapons for their own use and for export. (See Table 28-1.) Indonesia, Malaysia, and Brunei have just

Table 28-1. Defense Spending at 1988 Prices and Exchange Rates

	1989 amount in US$ millions	Percentage increase over 1980
Japan	29,350	46
India	9,030	63
South Korea	8,030	63
Taiwan	6,346	42
Indonesia	1,876	-7
Malaysia	1,725	2
Singapore	1,414	91
Philippines	708	-11

SOURCE: SIPRI; *The Economist.*

as plentiful reserves of oil. Such a combination, when mixed with the hoard of money for defense modernization resulting from the rapid economic growth of the region, could lead to both political and military escapades.

In all the Southeast Asian countries except Malaysia and Singapore (which continue the British tradition of keeping the army and government separate) the armed forces play a major role in politics. In early 1991, a military coup in Thailand toppled the elected civilian government. Myanmar (formerly Burma) is ruled by a military regime with an army of 270,000 that may soon be increased to 500,000. In the Philippines, Corazon Aquino (who decided not to run for reelection in 1992) survived at least seven attempted coups by renegade army officers and periodically put down armed rebellion from guerrilla thugs.

In Thailand, the Philippines, and Indonesia the armed forces assume the right to intervene in politics if the government displeases them. More than half the members of Thailand's legislative assembly are military men. Indonesia's President Suharto is a general.

An aggressive China waiting in the wings has publicly acknowledged that if it had the wherewithal, it would exercise the power in the region that it feels it ought to have. Leaders in natural-resource poor, but increasingly voracious Japan have already changed the constitutional prohibition against an offshore army. The postures of both China and Japan add fuel to smoldering embers in Southeast Asia.

Cambodia and Laos are too broken to contribute to potential unrest in the foreseeable future. Burma is in the same boat, although its abundant natural resources look inviting for long-term growth. Hence its participation in regional unrest cannot be totally ignored. Although one of the poorest nations in the world, Vietnam does attract French and other European and Japanese direct investment, which could bring it further economic growth and thus participation in the region's restructuring.

Looking to the future, it appears that Western traders have plenty to worry about when strategizing long-term affiliation in Southeast Asian markets.

Notwithstanding potentially unsettling conditions that might arise in the future, several countries in the region offer enormous opportunities for foreign companies to tap growing markets, abundant natural resources, cheap labor, and strategic positioning. The most promising among them are Singapore, Malaysia, Thailand, and Indonesia.

Probably the biggest market opportunity throughout the region is in the construction industry. Mammoth infrastructure and commercial projects are either underway or will be started in the next few years. Mr. Sanjoy Chowdhury, an economist at Merrill Lynch, estimates that between now and the year 2000, Asia's fastest-growing economies will spend over US$1 trillion on building infrastructure.

Singapore's Star

Singapore was originally founded in 1819 as a trading outpost by the British East India Trading Company. Its deep-water port and strategic location at the tip of the Malay peninsula gave it access to important shipping lanes between Europe and China. This trading heritage has not been lost on its modern-day rulers. The nation continues to be committed to free trade.

In many respects, Singapore offers the most stable, long-term trade advantages of any country in East Asia. In addition, the nation has evolved from a strategic trading port to a world-class financial center, offering foreign companies a vital link to Asia-Pacific markets and resources.

In 1961, the Singapore government created the Economic Development Board (EDB) with the specific mission of transforming the island state from a trading port into a modern, diversified economy. To accomplish this end, the EDB implemented a comprehensive program to spur local investment in manufacturing and service industries by offering assistance aimed at improving productivity and product quality. The board also helped foreign investors complete feasibility studies, identify joint venture partners, locate local suppliers, and arrange financing.

In the mid-1980s, the EDB undertook to promote Singapore to American, Japanese, and European multinational companies as the ideal location for regional headquarters and Southeast Asian manufacturing facilities. The government's program offered tax concessions and other financial incentives, as well as low-cost, long-term leases on facilities. A large number of foreign companies took the bait.

Early foreign investments were attracted by low wages, stable politics, and a functioning infrastructure. One of Singapore's most significant advantages to foreign companies today, other than its tax and financial incentives, is a developed, workable infrastructure. Singapore's communication links, reliable electric power, and functioning transport system are unique in this part of the world.

Like several other Southeast Asian nations, Singapore experienced profound economic growth during the 1980s, averaging 7 to 9 percent per year. In 1991

Table 28-2. Key Singaporean Economic Statistics*

	Statistics	
Population	2.7	million
GDP	US$34.3	billion
GDP 1990 growth	8.5	percent
Unemployment	2.0	percent
Inflation	3.5	percent
Exports as percentage of GDP	91.0	percent
Imports from United States in 1990	US$9.5	billion
GDP per capita in 1989	10,740	
Real effective exchange rate (1980–1982 = 100)	81.1	

*As of 1990.
SOURCES: IMF, Singapore Ministry of Trade; World Bank; Morgan Guaranty Trust Company.

its economy slowed to about 5 percent; 1992 growth is forecasted to be in the 5 to 6 percent range. Table 28-2 shows the nation's key economic statistics.

Caution Alert

Although Singapore's economic growth, along with that of the other "Four Tigers," has been the envy of other world governments, for the first time in a decade the inflation rate is enough to trouble both the nation's leaders and foreign traders. From 1983 through 1988, it hovered around 1 percent. Since then it has steadily inched up to nearly 5 percent.

Granted that 5 percent is a far cry from the hyperinflation of many developing nations, it is higher than the average (4 percent) for the seven largest OECD countries that buy most of Singapore's exports. If inflation cannot be halted, it will inevitably erode Singapore's export competitiveness, not only in Western markets, but also in Japan, Australia, and China.

Direct Investment Opportunities

Low wages and manufacturing efficiency are no longer Singapore's main attractions. The rapid growth of the economy and a limited labor supply have pushed manufacturing offshore to lower labor-cost areas in Malaysia and Indonesia.

The Singapore of today has evolved far beyond a Southeast Asian outpost. It has a fully functioning offshore financial center, with every major international bank, fund manager, and brokerage house represented. It boasts a highly educated pool of technical and managerial talent. It is rapidly becoming a center for the development and manufacture of electronics and information technology. These two industries now account for more than 40 percent of Singapore's manufacturing output.

Singapore offers a wide range of tax incentives. Although the basic corporate and branch income tax rate of 31 percent applies to both locally generated income and offshore income returned to Singapore, a plethora of exemptions also apply. Special tax reductions and exemptions are granted to:

- Approved financial institutions
- "Pioneer" companies (those developing new industries)
- Postpioneer companies for a period of ten years
- Expansion of existing manufacturing facilities
- Expansion of service companies
- Exporting companies
- New plant investment
- Warehousing and service companies engaged in exports
- International consultancy firms
- International trading companies
- Multinational headquarters generating service income
- Foreign exchange transactions
- Trading activities involving foreign suppliers/customers

The government's twin objectives of developing a high-tech research and manufacturing base and a center for financial services is paying off. NYNEX, Data General, 3M, and Hewlett-Packard are but a few of the major firms that have set up shop in Singapore. The government continues to invest heavily in infrastructure and university education programs, while the EDB encourages foreign and local firms to invest in R & D ventures such as computer software and systems design.

The development of the biotechnology industry is also receiving a major push from government quarters. As a key element in Singapore's long-range plans to become a high-tech development and trading center, the government instituted a program to fund specialized labor training and joint university/industry research programs. It also established a US$45 million investment fund to attract biotechnology investments.

The strategy behind this primary shift from the status of a pure trading center to that of specialization in financial services and high-tech development is to position Singapore as the world's representative for the long-term growth of the entire Asia-Pacific region. To meet this objective, however, several obstacles must be overcome, not the least of which are a scarcity of research technicians, a nearly complete lack of local markets, and high operating costs.

If Singapore's high-tech products are to be exported (and, with the absence of a local market most will surely have to be), potential foreign investors will find that high operating costs could easily make their products noncompetitive in world markets. An example of how fast operating costs can escalate can be seen in the 15 to 20 percent increase in wages and the jump in professional compensation of 25 to 30 percent for the year 1990 alone. Rents, electricity, telecommunications costs, and living expenses are also accelerating out of control.

Despite Singapore's vast potential, such rapid cost increases are causing many foreign corporations to reevaluate their strategies for locating or expanding in the island state.

As an answer to the high-cost problem, Singapore, Malaysia, and Indonesia, all located within easy reach of each other, have developed what is locally referred to as the "Triangle of Growth." This triangle encompasses Singapore, Malaysia's Johor province (a thirty-minute drive across the causeway), and Indonesia's Batam Island. The idea is to relocate labor-intensive facilities to Johor and to Batam Island's five-hundred-acre industrial park, where labor costs are still as low as Singapore's were a decade or more ago.

Electronics manufacturers who, up until the latest round of cost increases, were happy to take advantage of Singapore's technical and infrastructure base, are now moving to Johor province. Labor costs aren't as low there as on Batam Island, but they are significantly lower than those in Singapore.

Singapore's ministry of trade hopes that foreign companies will be attracted to this triangle because it offers the best of both worlds: access to Malaysian and Indonesian cheap labor and abundant natural resources; and Singapore's political stability, strong financial base, and pool of managerial talent. Many are taking the bait. Others have deferred their decision, awaiting the outcome of political reshuffling in Indonesia and Malaysia and the potential upheaval caused by China's 1997 takeover of Hong Kong.

Export Potential

Excluding Japan, Asia has 22 million households with annual incomes over US$5000, according to Hong Kong's Pacific Rim Consulting Group. The group's predictions call for a doubling of households by the year 2000. In 1980, Asia (again excluding Japan) represented 4.7 percent of world markets. By 2000, that figure will be 10.6 percent.

American and European exporters will find this expanding market hospitable for three primary reasons:

1. The pure numerical expansion of Asian consumers outside of Japan will force an increased share of world production to the region.

2. As global manufacturing shifts to Asia, so will worldwide demand for an increasingly sophisticated production capability requiring computers and other high-tech equipment.

3. As Asian economies grow, consumer tastes will change. Demand will in-

crease for such luxuries as automobiles, appliances, Western clothing, and entertainment, along with all the products and services to support such tastes.

With the likely inclusion of Taiwan and Hong Kong in China's economic sphere of influence (to the detriment of Western traders), and with South Korea becoming increasingly dependent on Japan for financial and consumer markets, Singapore remains the only industrialized East Asian nation stable enough to warrant serious trade and investment consideration.

Exporters with strategies to exploit Northeast Asian markets will find Singapore a logical and relatively safe alternative for reexport to its northern competitors. Exporters looking for an entree to Southeast Asian markets will find Singapore's developed financial and distribution systems safer and easier to use than those in neighboring Indonesia, Malaysia, or Thailand.

In addition to imported goods and services needed for neighboring markets, the U.S. Department of Commerce lists the following exports as likely to succeed in Singapore's domestic markets:

Biotechnology products

Oil and gas equipment

Hotel equipment and supplies

Telecommunications equipment, supplies, and services

Computers, peripherals, and software—especially for scientific use

Electronic components and equipment

Medical and health care equipment and supplies

A variety of top-of-the-line consumer products

Professional and technical services, especially in financial and research segments

The Politics of Progression

In some respects, Singapore's economic and trade potential appears overwhelming, an obvious choice for foreign traders. Beneath the economic miracle, however, lie the smoldering embers of social discontent that could emerge as a major deterrent. Before they jump at the chance to seize Singapore's obvious potential, foreigners would do well to analyze the broiling social conflict evident in the nation's political system.

Perhaps more than any other factor, Singapore owes its economic miracle to the iron-handed rule of Prime Minister Lee Kuan Yew, who retired at the end of 1990. During the brilliant Mr. Lee's 31-year tenure, Singaporeans readily gave up certain freedoms in return for a standard of living that has now surpassed Spain's. Younger residents, unaware of the country's earlier poverty and seeing only the steel and glass skyscrapers and Western influences, are now agitating for a change of style, a chance to think for themselves.

The main item of contention is the Internal Security Act, a colonial relic left over from British rule. This series of laws gives the government the power to detain suspected subversives indefinitely and without trial.

In addition, public meetings are banned, unless the organizer first gets a government permit. Compulsory military service for young men is still required. Recent minor relaxations include the lifting of a ban on jukeboxes and the permission to show soft-porn "erotica" movies in the nation's theaters. But the latter freedom will probably be reversed under the government's new "committee to review censorship."

Another issue breeding discontent is a feeling on the part of a growing number of people that the government is run solely for the "eggheads" who do well on exams and then proceed to important government posts. Also, the government's official promotion of Mandarin angers the island state's substantial Chinese population, most of whom are Cantonese. On top of this, the nation's constitution can easily be changed by parliament—and consequently by the party in power, since that party is parliament.

Caution Alert

Although organized opposition to the ruling People's Action Party has not yet materialized in sufficient strength to overthrow Mr. Lee's handpicked successor, Goh Chok Tong, it makes sense to keep a close eye on how soon the much-needed freedom reforms get implemented. With democratization spreading through Eastern Europe and the former Soviet republics, and eventually to China, it's just a matter of time before social unrest will damage Singapore's economic growth pattern—and hence the desirability of this location as a prime Asia-Pacific outpost.

Red Flag

Notwithstanding potential disruptions caused by social unrest, Singapore's biggest threat to continued prosperity lies in the failure of the Uruguay Round of GATT negotiations. The country relies on trade with Europe, the United States and, to a lesser extent, Japan, to sustain its growth. When regional trade blocs are formed in Europe and North America, Singapore's global trade routes will be severely restricted. Whether regional trade within the Asia-Pacific bloc will compensate is questionable.

29
Malaysia

Tips to Foreign Traders and Investors

1. Make appropriate "political" connections before entering this market.
2. Beware of racial tension and violent demonstrations.
3. Tap Malaysian natural resources and cheap labor for domestic production as well as exportable products for Western and Asian markets.
4. Export Westernized consumer goods and technology to Malaysia.
5. Don't try Islamic banking without previous ties.
6. Embassy office in Washington: (202) 328-2700.

Originally part of the British Empire, Malaysia gained its independence in 1957 and has never looked back. Although the nation retains British models for most internal structures and systems, changing patterns are dominated by the overwhelming position of an extensive Chinese population in commercial affairs and the predominance of native Malays in government roles.

In 1971, the Malaysian government implemented what was referred to as the New Economic Policy (NEP) aimed at poverty eradication and a redistribution of wealth—and power—between the native Malay population and the Chinese. The NEP deliberately discriminated in favor of Malays. The government proclaimed a massive affirmative action program giving native *bumiputras* (Malays and indigenous groups known as "sons of the soil") preference in everything from contracts, to government jobs, to cut-rate stocks, to overseas scholarships. The avowed goal was to transfer 30 percent of total equity in the nation's businesses to the Malay population by 1990. In fact, 20 percent was achieved.

Critics of the NEP claim it inflamed the racial resentments it was supposed to defuse; that it fostered political patronage; and most important, that it created a class of mediocre Malay businessmen whose only talent was for making friends in high places.

The NEP did stifle foreign direct investment and served as the rationale for extending government control over the economy. The severe recession of 1984–1985 probably saved Malaysia from this desultory policy.

Faced with dropping world oil prices (the country's main export), a decline in GDP, and rising unemployment, the government's only viable policy was to shelve the NEP and actively court foreign investment and technology. By the end of 1986, restrictions on foreign investment were essentially dissolved, incentives were created to attract foreign investors, and the private sector was given the leading role in driving the economy.

Red Flag

Although government crackdowns have stifled overt rebellion, racial tensions still run at a fever pitch. Foreign companies can expect further disruption to production lines and increased political favoritism. Foreigners will do well to make appropriate political connections prior to establishing trade relationships or making direct investments.

Trade Policies

Malaysia's success story since 1986 is well documented. The government's pragmatic attitude toward a market economy unencumbered by political expediencies has become a shining star in the Southeast Asia business community. Domestic production rose from 5.2 percent in 1987 to 9.5 percent in 1990. After a brief slowdown in 1991, the pace once again accelerated in 1992. Malaysia, along with its neighbor Thailand, is the strongest economic performer in Southeast Asia, according to the Asian Development Bank.

In 1990, foreign direct investment topped US$3.1 billion, the bulk of it coming from Japan and Taiwan. Prime Minister Mahathir announced in a speech to the Malaysia Business Council toward the end of the year that by the year 2020 Malaysia is "to become a fully developed country." To achieve this goal, the economy must grow at a 7 percent annual clip over the next thirty years, quite an achievement by anyone's standards.

Several hurdles must be jumped to achieve this objective:

1. Malaysia is woefully short of technology in virtually every field. The current strategy looks for assistance from Japan.

2. If trading blocs develop in North America and Europe, Asia-Pacific must do the same. The proposed East Asian Economic Group is one solution. Malaysia must play a crucial role in structuring the rules for intraregional trade.

3. The infrastructure must be developed to support this high rate of growth: such development currently lags behind Singapore by a substantial margin.

4. Privatization of state-owned businesses must become an integral part of a restated NEP.

5. Most importantly, political and social discontent among Malays, Chinese, and Indians must be ameliorated. Malaysia is Southeast Asia's most racially mixed nation. Malays, most of whom are Muslims, make up 57 percent of the country's population of 18 million; Chinese comprise 32 percent; Indians, 11 percent.

Trade and Investment Opportunities

Malaysia's per capita GDP is a very respectable US$2305, well above the US$2000 benchmark that defines a "newly industrialized country," commonly referred to as a NIC. (In comparison, Thailand's booming economy produces a per capita GDP of only US$1418.) Since 1987, real growth in the country has topped 9 percent annually.

The convoluted Malaysian tax structure, though not a deterrent to foreign investment, doesn't help much either. Corporate and branch income tax rates at 38 percent are much too high to stimulate growth. Although the country has no capital gains tax, it does impose a sliding scale tax (from 20 to 5 percent, depending on the holding period) on gains realized from the sale of real property or shares in a closely held company that owns real property. It also imposes a tax of 20 percent on interest income and 15 percent on royalties. Foreign companies are treated the same as Malaysian; the place of incorporation is of no relevance.

Certain minor tax incentives apply to depreciation and capital allowances for new plant and equipment, agricultural plantings, roads, bridges, farm buildings, and forestry. To partially offset these incentives, the government imposes a sales tax of 5 to 15 percent on goods and contractor services.

Nontax incentives are somewhat more enticing. Malaysia has a liberal exchange control system that applies uniformly except to Israel and South Africa. Nonresidents are free to make direct and portfolio investments and repatriate dividends, profits, and capital. Foreign-controlled companies may borrow up to M$10 million from all sources in Malaysia, provided that 60 percent of such borrowing is from Malaysian financial institutions. Foreign borrowing in excess of M$1 million, however, requires government approval.

Foreign direct investment still pours into the country. In 1990 alone, Japanese firms invested US$660 million. U.S. semiconductor companies invested US$240 million, and plans call for another US$760 million over the next three years. Thanks to such investments, Malaysia is the world's largest exporter of semiconductor chips.

The country is also rich in a variety of natural resources. It is the world's leading producer of rubber, palm oil, and commercial hardwood. Its oil reserves rival those of Indonesia. Abundant resources and cheap labor have made Malaysia the second-most-prosperous nation in the region—behind only Singapore.

The country's exports reflect this preponderance of natural resources. Since gaining independence, Malaysia has concentrated on exporting raw materials and semifinished products in rubber, tin, iron, hardwood, textiles, copra, food oils (principally palm oil), rice, and pepper.

Within the last ten years, however, industrial production has climbed. Today, Malaysia ranks among the top exporters of semiconductors, room air conditioners, radios, and other electronic products, according to the government's ministry of trade.

The conversion of its natural resources to finished product has made Malaysia the world's largest exporter of rubber gloves, including surgical gloves. Most iron ore is now converted to steel prior to export. Rice, palm oil, and other agricultural products are now processed into food products for export.

Foreign executives are also happy to see a rapidly developing cadre of managerial technocrats. Over 15,000 Malaysian students now study at U.S. universities, making them one of the ten-largest contingents of foreign students. A lesser number are studying in European schools.

The most lucrative products for export to Malaysia fall into four categories:

- Equipment to manufacture labor-intensive products

- Mining, oil, and gas equipment

- Western-style clothing and consumer products (primarily for Kuala Lumpur)

- Medical equipment and supplies

Most of these products arrive from Europe and other Asian countries, although exporting companies in the United States are beginning to make a dent.

Construction equipment and services are also needed for major infrastructure development of highways and railroads, power stations and transmission lines, and gas pipelines.

Although an increasing number of affluent consumers in Kuala Lumpur demand Western-style goods, most importing remains focused on the equipment and technology necessary to sustain and expand production capability.

Trade finance is easy to arrange through banks in Kuala Lumpur. With more than adequate foreign reserves, hard-currency payment is seldom a problem.

In addition, Islamic banking plays a predominant role in financing internal expansion. Central bank governor Jaffar Hussain plans that by the end of the decade, the country will see "a comprehensive Islamic financial system" running parallel with the conventional one. Perwira Habib Bank, Malayan Banking, and Bank Bumiputra are toying with the idea of setting up "Islamic counters," although through 1991 none had taken the plunge. Foreign companies with Islamic ties will likely find ample internal financing through this rapidly growing channel. Non-Islamic companies are not welcome.

30
Thailand

Tips to Foreign Traders and Investors

1. Stay away from Thailand until the political situation there clarifies.
2. Beware of intense competition from Japanese companies already established in the country.
3. Take a close look at reforestation opportunities once the government stabilizes.
4. Concentrate on exports for now.
5. Investigate good construction opportunities in infrastructure projects.
6. Embassy office in Washington: (202) 483-7200.

Thailand's history dates back generations to monarchal rule by the king of Siam (the country's former name). In 1932, absolute monarchy was abolished and the nation began its long trek to democratization. It is the only country in Southeast Asia that has never been colonized. Many of its internal systems and infrastructure, including its legal system, are modeled after British versions, however.

B. T. Bangsberg of the Third World–oriented Compass News Features Agency of London writes that the fragile coalition of the fractious blocs now ruling Thailand after the 1991 coup faces two major short-term hurdles: "a loss of crucial military approval" and "a slow deceleration of the country's astonishing economic boom."

That may be so, but before Thailand can adjust to changes in Asian and world trade and resume its previous growth pattern, the government and the people must come to grips with the propensity of Thai army generals to interfere in the running of the country whenever the mood suits them. The nation must return to its path toward democratization and resurrect some semblance of a stable ruling party. Without both, foreign companies will surely pull up stakes for more secure surroundings and trade, taking a huge chunk of the country's prosperity with them.

A Question of Stability

By almost any economic measure, Thailand has succeeded admirably. The economic rules it follows may diverge from those of other nations, but it's hard to argue for a different course. For 25 years, the Thai economy has grown by at least 4 percent annually; during the past ten years, the rate has hovered at around 10 percent per year. Literacy and life expectancy rates continue to rise, while disease and infant mortality rates decrease. By most standards except per capita income, Thailand is already rivaling South Korea, Taiwan, Singapore, and Hong Kong in national prosperity for its 55 million inhabitants.

But strategies for foreign companies looking for long-term investments and trade demand more than a thin veneer of potentially short-term national prosperity. Prosperity based on fragile underpinnings can dissipate like dunes in a hurricane.

The Asian "Four Tigers" have achievements in four areas that must also be attained by Thailand if it is to match their economic sustainability. These achievements are:

1. A high savings rate

2. A strong, Confucian-like attachment to discipline and hard work

3. A high degree of political stability—notwithstanding the thorny issue of student riots in Seoul and the unknown consequences of Hong Kong's 1997 takeover

4. A government dedicated to permitting the market to function relatively easily and without government interference

Thailand has yet to prove its proficiency in any of these areas, although the vaunted goal of reaching such plateaus provided Thai generals with the justification to roll tanks into Bangkok in 1991 and oust the first prime minister to be elected there in twelve years.

The army justified its actions with reference to:

- A Chatichai government in which corruption was so rife it had given democracy a bad name

- A disintegrating social fabric

- A reassessment, by foreign countries, of Thailand's viability as a locus for trade and investment

All of which appeared to be true. Foreign investors applauded the coup in the hope that the corrupting influences that had begun to dismantle the economy could be put to rest.

The generals promised everything foreign businessmen wanted to hear:

- An amended constitution to eradicate vote buying and attract better qualified politicians
- An election within six months to return the country to parliament
- A fierce campaign against government corruption
- A restructured civil service to reduce political interference in the business community

Red Flag

The results? An amended constitution to preserve the military's influence and rampant rumors of military theft and corruption.

While East Asian companies don't seem to mind military dictatorship—Japanese, Taiwanese, and South Korean investments continue to flow into Thailand—Westerners are taking a second look. An unstable military-influenced government, coupled with rampant environmental destruction of the forests in the north and apparently sanctioned drug trafficking in the Golden Triangle adjacent to Myanmar are not conditions supportive of profitable, long-term investment.

An Economic Miracle or a Threat to Long-Term Growth?

Peeling away the media hype of a miracle economy ripe for exploitation by foreign traders, one finds a country headed for deep and long-term trouble— unless, of course, radical steps are taken quickly to correct its deficiencies. The following key economic indicators from the Thai Board of Investment demonstrate the souring economic trends being experienced in Thailand.

	1988	1989	1990	Estimated for 1991
Real GDP growth (percentage)	13.2	12.0	10.0	8.5
Population (million)	55.0	55.9	56.7	57.6
GDP per capita (US$)	1084	1236	1413	1661
Exports (percentage growth)	33.9	27.7	15.7	20.0
Imports (percentage growth)	46.6	29.8	27.4	24.0
Current account deficit (in US$ billions)	-1.65	-2.54	-6.10	-7.50
Inflation rate (percentage)	3.8	5.4	6.0	6.0 to 7.0

Recognition of Thailand's current problems assuredly must influence a company's long-term strategies for involvement in the country. While firms engaged in construction projects, pollution-control products, or educational support services might find the current Thai dilemma appealing for both investment and trade, those in other industries might be encouraged to develop East Asian strategies elsewhere.

Economic Deficiencies

During the 1970s, Thailand's economy grew at an average rate of nearly 10 percent, eclipsing that of either Taiwan or South Korea. Massive construction projects in and around Bangkok, some stalled in a partly finished state, others ready for occupancy, and still others clamoring for more materials and manpower, give ample proof of the nation's fixation on growth. But by the end of 1990, the red-hot economy boiled over. The clearest symptom is a current account deficit of US$8 billion, reflecting the continuing emphasis on imports over exports.

Underlying this is a US$5 billion trade deficit with Japan alone. In addition to cars, the country has gone overboard in importing production machinery from Japanese companies, theoretically to begin churning out products for eventual export. This policy appears optimistic. Most Japanese factories in Thailand are barely meeting domestic demand and will continue importing parts and components from their home base for several years to come.

The country has been able to live with this substantial trade deficit because capital inflows from foreign investment have more than balanced the outflow for goods. Now, signals indicate that this trend has reversed.

In 1990, the Thai government liberalized foreign exchange laws. Bank borrowing by Thai companies surged. And then foreign investment stagnated.

A lack of liquidity has led more than one developing nation to the brink of bankruptcy. Furthermore, U.S. companies can certainly vouch for epidemic private sector bankruptcies that have resulted from overextended credit. Thailand's public and private sectors appear to be headed in this direction.

Weak Infrastructure

The Thai infrastructure is not sufficient to support long-term growth. Half of Thailand's GDP is produced in or around Bangkok, with an infrastructure geared to the 1960s. The city needs new roads, a public transportation system, a few million telephone lines, and a sewer system that works at least most of the time.

Environmental Degradation

The environmental havoc wrought by sustained rapid growth and a devil-may-care government has made Bangkok as polluted as Mexico City. The difference is that in Mexico City the government is beginning to address the problem of dirty air and rancid water. In Bangkok, pollution has gone unnoticed.

In addition, the deforestation in northern Thailand has already caused extensive erosion, making the formerly fertile land unfit for agriculture or grazing. The social impact of the nation's environmental degradation will eventually erode worker capability and health and could easily result in apathetic indifference—not conducive to investment in productive enterprises.

Education Shortcomings

The most serious problem confronting the country's long-term growth prospects is lack of education. Less than 28 percent of the nation's youth go on to secondary education, although most of the population attains literacy through primary schools. The elite, of course, have done well and sport an abundance of doctorates. It's the large middle segment that is missing.

One indication of the low level of Thai education is the complaints from Japanese managers that they cannot find workers capable of resolving problems on their own initiative. Lack of secondary education for local managers, more than any other factor, directly affects the ability of foreign companies to prosper in Thailand.

Trade and Investment Opportunities

Companies intrigued by the potential for further growth in Thailand despite the nation's political instability and socioeconomic problems will find a well-diversified economy hungry for products and services in virtually any industry.

Agriculture is still the biggest sector and tourism accounts for most of the nation's foreign exchange. However, the industrial base is well diversified, from heavy industry and cement to plastics and computer hardware. Food processing and packaging are growing industries. Programs are under way to improve Thailand's scientific and technological capabilities, but the country still needs to import much of its technology.

The lingering construction boom in Bangkok and the soon-to-be-developed outlying areas desperately need construction equipment and services. Foreign construction firms are more than welcome to participate. In fact, foreign participation is a necessity, since Thai construction companies lack modern equipment and state-of-the-art know-how.

According to Thai trade officials, vast infrastructure development programs will be started within the year, both in Bangkok and in the outlying areas. Telephone systems and services, road-building equipment, school and hospital products, and electricity-generating and distribution equipment must come from foreign firms.

Thai consumers, especially in Bangkok, have more sophisticated tastes than are normally found in developing nations. Demand is rising for such consumer goods as personal care products, Western-style clothing and accessories, and recreational products and services.

In addition, a strong market demand exists for several other categories of products and services, whether imported from abroad or produced locally. The highest demand can be found for:

- Construction services (residential, commercial, industrial, government) along with appropriate construction equipment.

- Food-processing and packaging machinery. No local manufacturers exist to sell quality food, beverages, and household goods to increasingly affluent consumers.

- Medical equipment and supplies.

- Avionics, ground-support equipment, aircraft parts and supplies. There are no local manufacturers, although companies from Japan (and to a lesser extent Italy) offer stiff competition.

- Computers, peripherals, software. There is strong competition from Japan, but also increasing market demand.

To improve the image of Thailand's ruling junta for the 1991 worldwide meeting of the World Bank and the IMF in Bangkok, the Thai Board of Investment published a public relations circular encouraging foreign participation in the Thai economy. One of the major thrusts was to identify those areas targeted by the government for substantially increased foreign investment. They are:

- Engineering and supporting companies to upgrade the country's manufacturing sector to high-technology production. (The list ranged from companies engaged in metal-working to those providing testing and R & D services.)

- Infrastructure development, including electricity generation, roads, the extension of the expressway to the Bangkok airport, mass transit, a three-million-line telephone system, and port development and management.

- Advanced value-added agro-industry and biotechnology firms.

- Environmental clean-up and protection products, equipment, technology, and management.

Tariffs on imported machinery and equipment have been lowered from 20 percent to 5 percent in an attempt to encourage foreign suppliers. However, plans to reduce tariffs on certain raw materials have been delayed, according to the Board of Investment.

The Thai tax structure is nothing to brag about. Corporate and branch income tax rates of 35 percent (30 percent for Bangkok Stock Exchange companies) and rates of 20 to 25 percent on interest, dividends and royalties are noncompetitive. Foreign companies should not expect to receive any special tax incentives for investment.

One bright spot on an otherwise dim Thai horizon is that, as the doors of Indochina and Myanmar open to foreign investment and trade, Thailand-located firms will be strategically positioned to get a head start on both trade and investment opportunities.

31
Indonesia

Tips to Foreign Traders and Investors

1. Proceed with direct investments very cautiously.

2. Be ready to tap enormous natural resources (including oil) through joint ventures with local conglomerates when openings occur.

3. Keep an eye on strategic opportunities in forest products and consumer goods as markets clarify.

4. Plan to export products and services for reforestation programs when the timing is right.

5. Join forces with a local partner who has good political connections. A clever partner can cut through bureaucratic corruption and also signal opening market opportunities.

6. Embassy office in Washington: (202) 775-5200.

Indonesia's first postindependence leader, President Sukarno, faced a major task in his new country: that of creating a national identity for the archipelago's 170 million disparate peoples. But while achieving modest success, he suffocated the economy. Only state-run firms were allowed to develop the rich store of natural resources in this 3000-mile-long, 13,700-island nation. Oil, gas, rubber, and timber sustained a population that spoke three hundred different languages. Agriculture is still the biggest sector of the economy, with rubber, oil, palm, coffee, sugar, and bananas heading the list of products.

Indonesia didn't give birth to a private sector until after the post-1965 rise to power of Sukarno's successor, President Suharto. Concentrating on resource-based industries as well as on manufacturing, literally thousands of small, family-run businesses began transforming themselves into the omnipresent conglomerates visible today throughout the business community.

Suharto's administration concentrated on import substitution—the same approach as that used in Mexico during generations of government-spurred development.

The Indonesian government went one step further, however, and pressured the growing firms to concentrate on export promotion rather than on domestic markets. Government-sanctioned monopolies were set up with subsidized import licenses and special export permits.

By the 1980s, the government determined that it could no longer rely on the domination of a few select monopolies to increase economic growth. Most of these giants were owned and managed by Indonesians of Chinese origin. Though representing a mere 3 percent of the country's inhabitants, the Chinese in effect controlled the economic livelihood of the nation.

The concentration of such power in so-called "nonindigenous people" and their government protectors eventually raised the ire of the public. The people demanded change. Defusing racial and social tensions became President Suharto's primary objective. As oil prices fell in the mid-1980s, an opening developed for the government to effect major reforms through the deregulation of the economy.

To date, the financial sector has benefited most from deregulation. The Jakarta Stock Exchange remains a magnet for foreign funds. Private commercial banks were granted foreign exchange licenses. Joint ventures with foreign banks spawned a whole new financial services industry. Freeing the financial sector before deregulating trade led to a massive disequilibrium in the economy. Too much money was chasing too few goods. Stock and property values soared. Inflation skyrocketed. The government responded with tight monetary policies.

Further deregulation of industry and trade is desperately needed to bring Indonesia into line with regional and foreign competitors. Today's young entrepreneurs must be satisfied, as the older generation was twenty years ago. Indonesian trade officials admit that the most important step now is to create an atmosphere of more open domestic competition.

Very few Indonesian companies have an international flavor. As monopolies with captive markets, they have never been forced to become domestically competitive. Rather, Indonesian companies achieve what competitiveness they do have through currency devaluation, government export promotion schemes, subsidies, cheap labor, and a wholesale exploitation of natural resources. Without improving their production efficiency and quality standards and developing increased value-added products, Indonesian companies cannot hope to compete in world markets.

Domestic competition is the key to achieving these results. Without a viable, competitive domestic and international market presence, the country will remain dependent on the export of oil and other natural resources and the hope that its burgeoning tourist trade (especially in Bali and Lombok) will continue to flourish.

Table 31-1. Indonesian Exports, 1986 through 1990

	US$ billions		
	Oil/gas exports	Non-oil/gas exports	Total exports
1986	8.3	6.5	14.8
1987	8.5	8.6	17.1
1988	7.7	11.5	19.2
1989	8.7	13.5	22.2
1990	11.1	14.6	26.7

SOURCE: Indonesian Investment Coordinating Board.

Table 31-1 shows the important role that oil and gas exports continue to play in Indonesia's foreign trade. Other exports include rubber, palm, timber, coffee, sugar, and bananas, as well as a small amount of nonagricultural goods.

In addition to government-sanctioned monopolies, the absence of an educated work force and a labor supply in excess of available jobs further limit Indonesia's growth potential. More than two million people enter the labor market each year, and capital-intensive conglomerates offer few new openings. Per capita income runs approximately US$500 per year—one-third that of Thailand and one-fourth that of Malaysia. As surplus labor pushes up unemployment, social pressures build, placing the nation of islands precariously close to populist upheaval.

More than 80 percent of job seekers have only a primary school education. Only 2 percent go on to university. Lack of skills prevents both the public and private sector from taking advantage of much-needed technology transfer. It also prevents the country from advancing beyond the export of commodities and products built with low-cost labor.

Foreign Direct Investment

Even with these obvious deficiencies and the government's stranglehold on industry, foreign companies have been quick to seize Indonesia's abundant natural resources and exploit its extensive and cheap labor base. The Indonesian work force is ten times the size of the work force available in Malaysia. Wages are a small fraction of those in South Korea and Taiwan. Natural resources exceed those in neighboring Thailand. And to date, political stability exceeds anything the Philippines can offer.

Japanese firms, noted for their long-term approach to cornering resources and capturing markets, have been the leaders in Indonesian investment. However, the combined investment from the Four Tigers—South Korea, Taiwan, Hong Kong, and Singapore—exceeds even that of the Japanese. European and American firms have so far found Indonesian waters too treacherous for major commitments.

Undeveloped domestic markets and low per capita income cause most foreign firms to invest in export-related businesses. Local conglomerates, recognizing their inability to compete internationally on their own, welcome joint venture arrangements. Japanese and German automakers (Toyota and BMW) are prime examples of foreign companies that have gone the joint venture route. Privatized banks are also very active in forming allegiances with foreign rivals.

The ten largest Indonesian conglomerates are:

1. Salim
2. Astra
3. Sinar Mas
4. Djarum
5. Gudang Garam
6. Lippo
7. Dharmala
8. Jan Darmadi
9. Mantrust
10. Damatex

Caution Alert

The rise or fall of a foreign joint venture in Indonesia frequently depends on the contacts the local partner has in government circles, as well as on its status in the business community. If the wrong minister gets appointed to a related position, the domestic company will suffer and drag the joint venture with it. Clearly, foreign firms must carefully watch the shifting political fortunes of joint venture partners.

Table 31-2 shows cumulative foreign direct investment for the 25 years ending 1990. Table 31-3 breaks down this investment by business sector.

Red Flag

So far the protection of intellectual property has received little emphasis from the government. New laws are being considered, but foreign firms must continue to regard intellectual piracy a major problem. Computer software, pharmaceuticals, copyrights, and chemical formulas have shown particular susceptibility to piracy. In fact, several foreign companies in these fields have been pressured to dilute their equity holdings in deference to illegal competitive products.

Foreign trade with Indonesia is still difficult. Special levies, fees, high tariffs, and bureaucratic kickbacks continue to dissuade many foreign firms from exporting to the country.

Table 31-2. Cumulative Investment Commitments by Country of Origin

	US$ billions
Japan	9.65
Hong Kong	3.73
Taiwan	2.30
United States	2.20
Netherlands	1.96
South Korea	1.86
Germany	1.85
Singapore	1.00
Australia	.86
United Kingdom	.73
Others	12.53

SOURCE: Indonesia Investment Coordinating Board.

Table 31-3. Cumulative Investment Opportunities by Business Sector

	Percentage
Manufacturing	71.3
Mining	8.4
Services	6.9
Trade and Hotels	5.3
Agriculture	3.6
Other	4.5

SOURCE: Indonesia Investment Coordinating Board.

The Indonesian tax structure does nothing to encourage foreign investment, either. Corporate income and capital gains tax rates at 35 percent apply to any company incorporated or *domiciled* in Indonesia. Furthermore, such companies are taxed on worldwide income, regardless of their country of incorporation. Branches of foreign companies, however, are taxed at 35 percent only on Indonesian-source income. Indonesia also imposes a value-added tax ranging from 10 to 30 percent.

On the other hand, profits and capital may be freely repatriated. No foreign exchange controls affect repayment of loans or the remittance of dividends, interest, or royalties.

Those firms willing to live with these formal and informal barriers find growing market demand in the following products/industries:

- Infrastructure development, including construction equipment

- Tourism, especially in Bali, and, to a lesser extent, in various sites on Java

- Pollution-control equipment and products targeted at markets in Jakarta

- Financial services

- Educational supplies and services

- Medical and other high-tech equipment, although consumer markets have not developed sufficiently to exploit consumer electronics

- Basic consumer goods in Jakarta, primarily Western clothing and entertainment products and equipment

Eighty percent of Indonesia's population claims Islamic roots. As the nation develops, this will have a strong influence, both on the types of goods sold domestically and on the conduct of business relationships.

Foreigners should also be alerted to the intense competition from the Japanese and from Four Tiger companies and joint ventures already flourishing—especially in the financial and key export sectors.

Potential Reforestation Opportunities

Indonesia's rain forest covers 386,000 square miles—comparable to the combined areas of France, united Germany, and the three Benelux countries. Local logging companies are rapidly depleting this valuable resource. World Bank calculations indicate that in forty years Indonesia's virgin forests will all be gone.

Watching the decimation of Thailand's hardwood forests and the consequent soil erosion that destroys valuable farmland, Indonesian bureaucrats began to search for answers. No one wants to lose the nation's biggest foreign exchange earner after oil.

The government's first step was to set aside 121 million acres of forest for nature conservation and watershed protection. The export of raw logs is banned. Heavy taxes are levied on the export of sawn timber. A reforestation fee levied on logging companies was increased from 11 cents to 29 cents a cubic foot. In 1991 the government fined one of the world's biggest logging companies, Barito Pacific, US$10 million for failing to log selectively.

Although helpful, none of these steps has done much to slow continuing deforestation. One monitoring move currently under consideration is to bring in Société Générale de Surveillance (SGS), a private Swiss company that previously ended corruption at Indonesia's ports, to make sure that loggers abide by the regulations.

Another step under consideration is to invoke incentives for companies to take a long-term view of their logging practice. In Indonesia this means 35–50 years, the time it takes the more valuable forms of tropical hardwood to regenerate. Currently, twenty-year concessions go to political cronies at no charge. They then subcontract cutting to small operators.

A third scheme calls for reforestation with fast-growing eucalyptus and albizia trees which could be continually harvested for the pulp and paper industry. The economics of such a program make little sense, however: the world already has more than enough pulp and paper producers in Scandinavia and Asia.

Regardless of the eventual steps taken by the government, it seems certain that measures to curtail deforestation and create some form of reforestation program will be enacted. This will mean the importing of sophisticated logging and processing equipment, technology to preserve and replenish forests, and a variety of support goods and services, none of which are available locally. With the government behind such programs, tariffs and other barriers will likely be lowered or abandoned completely.

Japanese and South Korean firms are already positioning themselves for these new export and investment opportunities. European and American firms capable of producing appropriate technology and equipment might do well to consider similar strategies.

32

India and Pakistan

Tips to Foreign Traders and Investors

1. Unless there are extenuating circumstances, stay away from trade or direct investment with either India or Pakistan for now. The risks are too great, the returns too meager.

2. Check out Pakistan in a few years. If the economy stabilizes and the politics settle down, market opportunities will open.

3. Before making a direct investment in either country, get a local partner who knows the political ropes.

If the African continent is a tough nut to crack for foreign companies, the Indian subcontinent is more like a rock. Like so many other Third World countries, India has for years tried to evolve into a self-sufficient economy, to no avail. Subjugating their inherited British version of democratic socialism to a religion-based caste system, India's leaders have been eminently successful in destroying their industrial market base and agricultural wealth. They have proven beyond a doubt (as have their northern neighbors in the former Soviet Union after whom many of India's government policies have been patterned) that economic protectionism does not work.

Like many Latin countries during the "lost decade" of the 1980s, the Indian government borrowed heavily in world capital markets to finance its import substitution policies, without regard to the ability of its industrial base to generate sufficient revenues for repayment. By the end of 1990, its foreign reserves had dwindled to less than six weeks' supply. Between a dire shortage of hard currency and stringent protectionist barriers to foreign trade, it is not surprising that in 1989 foreign direct investment was only US$180 million—practically unbelievable for a country of India's size and natural resources.

In 1991, after shipping more than 65 tons of gold reserves to European banks as collateral to loans, and with only a few days' supply of foreign currency reserves remaining in the treasury, India won its appeal to the IMF for a balance-of-payments standby loan.

European and Japanese companies have begun to filter back, but American firms are still giving India a wide berth.

Aside from the currency problem, the main reasons for disinterest are the very strict government policies specifically designed in the 1960s to keep foreign investment out. Major changes have not yet occurred. The government has, however, lifted its foreign investment restrictions for certain projects and now allows its universal 40 percent foreign ownership rule to be broken on a case-by-case basis.

Much remains to be done to attract foreign companies, however, especially American firms whose current interest in Asian trade lies primarily with China and the Southeast Asian nations. The bureaucratic procedure for getting approval for investment projects is still time-consuming and costly. Exclusion from the 40 percent foreign ownership ceiling is still based on the purely arbitrary judgment of minor bureaucrats. And India's tax structure, obviously designed to penalize foreign investors, needs drastic revision.

A top corporate tax rate of 40 percent is increased by a surcharge of 15 percent if income exceeds Rs75,000 (approximately US$10,000 to US$20,000). The branch income tax rate stands at a whopping 65 percent and branch capital gains are taxed at between 45.5 percent and 58.5 percent. The government does not offer foreign investment tax incentives of any significance.

In certain areas, the government requires foreign investors to set up joint ventures or license their technology to local firms. The only type of direct investment that seems to make sense in such an environment is a facility that is 100 percent export-oriented. In such cases the government may allow up to 25 percent of the production to be sold domestically. Several large American companies have taken this bait. Motorola, Blue Star, Corning, Gillette, Lever Brothers, and Digital Equipment all have started joint ventures. Most smaller companies still prefer other markets.

According to Indian trade officials, the best industries for foreign investment are: telecommunications (especially for infrastructure development); consumer electronics (such as integrated circuits and semiconductors); computers (though several purchasers of domestically made ones claim that they don't hold up); and medical equipment.

Indian Trade Opportunities

Foreign direct investment may be an unwise choice, but exporting to India holds at least some promise. Of the country's eight hundred million population, three hundred million live below the Indian government's own definition of poverty, and millions more barely exceed it. In many outlying areas, however, television has introduced Western-style tastes. Consumer demand is beginning to foment, even though most of the population cannot afford such purchases.

A fairly large elite class of consumers does exist, however. Many of the upper class have been educated at American universities; others, locally. They have the same taste for designer clothes, high-tech gadgetry, and luxury items as consumers in the United States, Europe, or Japan.

According to the U.S. Department of Commerce, foreign companies willing and able to penetrate India's extensive import barriers, either through a local partner or through bureaucratic connections, will find market opportunities in: computers and software; food-processing and packaging equipment; chemical and petrochemical plant machinery and equipment; pumps and valves; power-generation, transmission and distribution equipment; medical instruments and equipment; leather-products machinery; oil and gas field equipment; alternate energy services; mining and excavation equipment; and consulting engineering services.

Caution Alert

India's main trade goal is to import sufficient technology to sustain its protectionist policy of self-sufficiency. Companies involved in technology transfer, either through export or direct investment, should be alert to potential intellectual piracy.

The United States was India's leading source of exports in 1990–1991. The leading components of the US$2 billion worth of sales were machinery, organic and inorganic chemicals, professional and scientific instruments, artificial resins and plastic materials, iron and steel, and nonferrous metals. After the United States, the nearest competitors were Germany (US$1.3 billion), Japan (US$1.2 billion), the United Kingdom (US$1.1 billion), and the Soviet Union (US$980 million).

Pakistani Trade Opportunities

India's northern neighbor, Pakistan, is at least making an effort to right an economy which has been seriously disturbed by twenty years of poor central planning, bureaucratic corruption, and violent ethnic groups. As opposed to India, Pakistan's government has thrown open its doors to foreign investment and hung a "For Sale" sign on many of its state-owned factories and financial institutions.

Attracting foreign investment is crucial to the country's survival. In 1991, Pakistan lost more than US$600 million in foreign aid in a wrangle with the United States over its nuclear arms program. At the same time, remittances from workers in the Gulf states were way down. The need for social services, which simply don't exist in many areas, is escalating rapidly: Pakistan's population has doubled since 1970 and now stands at 113 million inhabitants—three-fourths of whom cannot read.

In fact, Pakistan's economy is in shambles. Infrastructures crumble. Factories stand idle. Roads are impassable. Health care is nonexistent for the majority of the population and food is scarce. Communications are poor and power generation is erratic. Currency reserves are shattered, and foreign trade, skimpy.

On the plus side, Prime Minister Nawaz Sarif unveiled in 1991 what the Ministry of Industries called a "dramatic series of bold, ground-breaking economic and financial reforms that earlier administrations had often promised but never delivered."

Economic reforms are being implemented in three areas:

- Deregulation
- Privatization of state-owned companies
- Incentives to encourage foreign direct investment and foreign trade

Virtually all restrictions on foreign exchange transactions have been lifted for both foreigners and nationals. Endless clearances and permits for practically all industrial undertaking have been eliminated. Foreign investors can set up shop anywhere in the country. Banks are being revitalized with free currency exchange privileges.

Since its breakaway from India in 1947, most of Pakistan's assets have been in the hands of or controlled by a handful of wealthy families. During the 1960s, a study found that 22 families controlled 80 percent of the country's industry. During the 1970s, Zulfikar Ali Bhutto attempted to change this by nationalizing everything from banks to steel companies. Entrepreneurial families merely found opportunities in other countries. One enterprising entrepreneur with money, Agha Hasan Abedi, founded the Bank of Credit and Commerce International (the now infamous BCCI) and ran his worldwide empire with other Pakistani entrepreneurial managers.

Caution Alert

With the denationalization of industry and banking, wealthy families are reinserting themselves in Pakistan's business and financial community. Foreign investors would be wise to link up with such a partner to eliminate the risk of bureaucratic interference and potentially violent interruptions from warring ethnic groups.

Although tax rates remain high—50 percent for corporate income, capital gains, and branches—a variety of exemptions have been implemented as incentives to foreign investment.

In addition to the reduction of (and in some cases complete elimination of) bureaucratic permission for imports and exports, there has been a material reduction of tariffs and quotas.

According to the Ministry of Industries, excellent markets exist for foreign imports of: infrastructure development equipment and services; health care professional services, equipment, and supplies; financial-services computer systems and software; food-processing equipment; agribusiness supplies and services; transport equipment and spare parts; and a wide range of Western-style consumer electronics and clothing (for elite upper-class consumers only—the rest of the population is too poor to buy anything!).

Despite avowed efforts by the government to convert to a market economy, much of Pakistan remains in a state of war. The state's huge unions continue to exert enormous pressure. Warring tribal groups proliferate in the provinces. Arms shipments and guerrillas continue to move in both directions across the Afghan border. Skirmishes with India and Kashmir go on unabated. And cultural schisms between native Sindis and people who migrated to Karachi from India after partition have not been resolved. While the government's efforts to attract foreign investment and trade are certainly admirable, their success remains in doubt.

33
Pacific Basin: Australia

Tips to Foreign Traders and Investors

1. Don't be fooled by media accounts that depict the government's socialist policies as detrimental to trade: they aren't.

2. Get the lay of the land by exporting before confronting union problems with a direct investment.

3. Target high-tech industries that have less union labor.

4. Don't be detoured by the shaky economy. It's getting better.

5. Use local financing through Australian banks.

6. Establish a strategic position now to gain advantage in intraregional trade.

7. Embassy office in Washington: (202) 797-3000.

Long considered the sleepy Pacific outpost of the British commonwealth replete with a heritage of transported prisoners, cowboys, koala bears, and beaches, Australia is finally coming into its own as a viable trading partner. As the land of sheepherders, cattle ranches, and its own peculiar brand of socialist protectionism, New Zealand is following Australia's lead into the modern trading world. Even Pacific island states in Polynesia, Melanesia, and Micronesia are showing signs of economic life.

While the world's attention focuses on the enormous economic opportunities in Japan, China, the Four Tigers, and Southeast Asia, the near-forgotten nations of the Pacific Basin clamor for attention. This is a shame, because non-Asian-Pacific nations have a lot going for them.

Rich in natural resources and possessing settled populations that are not only in cultural harmony with the West, but are also crying out for the world's goods and services, Australia, New Zealand, and Oceania represent a gold mine of trade and investment possibilities. Japanese and other East Asian companies have long since discovered this gold mine. But except for a few multinationals, in Australia, the bulk of Western traders have been slow to explore it, dismissing the region as too remote.

On the flip side, several unresolved issues tend to detract from the region's full economic potential. Traditional dependence on British aid and trade works to isolate Australia and New Zealand from the rest of the world. Their enormous distance from Europe and North America makes transport costs high. Decades of socialistic governments, dedicated to preserving protectionist policies, dissuade smaller Western companies from seeking direct investment opportunities.

The Pacific island states also have drawbacks. The vast expanse of the north and south Pacific makes travel and shipping among these nations, and between Oceania and the rest of the world, costly and cumbersome. A strong dependence on old colonial ties for financial aid, a low population base, and inferior infrastructures keep many of these island states in the backwaters of global trade. Island states with traditionally small consumer markets prevent large companies from stepping forward.

Most nations in Latin America, the Caribbean, the Middle East, and East Asia have learned that a shrinking world necessitates entrance into the global community. Evidence suggests that the best way to achieve true independence is through a growing economy. And developing nations are realizing very quickly that the fastest and most permanent way to build their economies is through global trade. Slowly but surely, Pacific Basin countries are awakening to the same reality: that they must, one way or another, develop international trading partners—not only with Japan and other East Asian nations, but with Europe and the Americas.

Australia is the largest and by far the most populous country in the region. With 17 million people and abundant natural resources, it offers the most immediate and the best market opportunities.

The Land of Opportunity

A two-pronged approach characterizes Australia's effort to become a major world manufacturing power and the gateway to Southeast Asia.

First, given its strategic location within the Asia-Pacific trade belt, Australia needs to attract investment and trade from Japan and the Four Tigers—while trying to overcome a deep-seated cultural bias against anything Japanese. (Although cultural biases existed long before 1940, they flowered during World War II, with millions of Australians killed defending their homeland from Japanese invaders. Populations of many countries have long forgotten the animosities generated by World War II, including many Americans. Many Australians, however, continue to harbor a deep-seated distrust and hostility toward Japan.)

Second, Australia needs to encourage and improve its trading ties and foreign direct investment from the rest of the world. In this effort, it is being remarkably successful.

Foreign Direct Investment

Foreign direct investment has risen from just over US$2 billion in 1985 to more then US$12 billion in 1989. According to the Conference Board, companies from the United States are now providing the greatest thrust, placing more deals in Australia than in any other Asia-Pacific nation and replacing Japan as the number-one investing nation. Fifteen new U.S. manufacturing projects were started in Australia during 1990, three times more than the average of the previous three years.

Table 33-1 shows a few of the major U.S. companies that made direct investments in manufacturing in Australia during 1990.

According to the U.S. Department of Commerce, total direct investment by U.S. companies has doubled over the last twenty years. Investments from Taiwan, Japan, and Hong Kong also continue to accelerate. The combination of a massive restructuring of the economy and falling asset values has provided the impetus for global companies to begin looking at Australia as a viable long-term trading partner.

Recognizing the opportunity window, government officials have begun active promotion programs to lure foreign capital and technology. Their main

Table 33-1.   New U.S. Players in Australia*

	Type of investment		
	Joint venture	New business	Acquisition
Arvin Industries	X		
Borden, Inc.			X
Coca-Cola Co.			X
Conagra, Inc.	X		X
Du Pont Co.			X
Federal Mogul			X
H. J. Heinz		X	
Manville Corp.			X
McGraw-Hill Inc.			X
Mobil Oil Corp.			X
Naico Chemical Co.			X
Outboard Marine Corp.			X
Tyco Laboratories			X

*During 1990.
SOURCE: Investment Australia.

message trumpets an English-speaking Western culture, abundant natural resources, and skilled workers.

Caution Alert

Foreign companies considering an Australian facility should be careful to get competent advice about the country's tax structure. It is as complex as that in the United States. Tax rates are not low, hitting 39 percent for corporate and branch income, as well as capital gains. Australian tax laws continue to reflect socialist attitudes toward private enterprise. Very few tax incentives are available for foreign companies other than an exclusion for non-Australian source income and modest incentives for R & D projects. A sales tax of from 10 to 50 percent is levied on the sale of goods. Employers pay a 47 percent tax on all noncash employee benefits. Payroll taxes run 3.95 to 7 percent.

Government officials prefer to accent the positive, however, ignoring the oppressive tax structure in promotional spiels. Their main emphasis is on trade potential.

As an official from the Australian Trade Commission in Canberra boasts, the country is known throughout the world as a producer of farm products and mined resources. These have, in fact, been the main export products for decades. Now the government is trying hard to change this image, to promote the nation's ability to manufacture quality products as its primary export strategy. To achieve this, the government is trying to attract foreign investment in two primary areas:

1. Industries that add value to indigenous raw materials, such as fiber processing and minerals—turning wool and cotton into textiles and raw ore into fabricated metal

2. High-technology industries, such as biotechnology, aerospace, and medical diagnosis and treatment

The government's current promotion efforts include extensive advertising of:

- Tax incentives for research and development programs
- Assistance in matching foreign with local joint venture partners
- A skilled work force
- The best telecommunications system in the Asia-Pacific region
- A fully developed infrastructure

The nation's strategic location as a jumping-off point to Southeast Asia adds to its possibilities. Although the government has a way to go to dispel Australia's reputation for constant labor strife, rigid centralization, and a closed, protected domestic market, a recent restructuring of tariffs and quotas substantially enhance the country's image as a "new opportunity" for foreign investment.

Foreign Trade

For decades, the government kept out world trade with protectionist barriers, which in turn fed progressive rounds of wage and price hikes. With formal tariffs ranging upward from 30 percent, national companies could charge double the prices of those from abroad without fear of competing imports. This made most Australian companies totally immune to international trade pressures and therefore noncompetitive in world markets.

In an effort to broaden Australia's economic base, the government started reducing tariffs in 1988. Most now range from 10 to 15 percent. Between 1993 and 1996 the government plans to bring all tariffs down to a single 5 percent rate. Tariffs in several industries will not be included, however. Automobiles, trucks, clothing, textiles, and footwear will receive much less severe cuts, even though these industries need import competition the most.

Although this sounds like a grand scheme, it really isn't very spectacular. Other barriers are far more insidious than tariffs. Antidumping laws, "voluntary export restraints" (VERs), health and safety standards, quotas, environmental safeguards—all of which masquerade as national safety and security measures in the United States—are far more effective protective tactics than pure tariffs. In fact, to obtain support from the business community for its tariff reduction package, the government issued assurances that it "will not allow unfair competition from dumped imports to damage local industry."

Australia's primary trading partner is Japan, although close links also exist with South Korea and Taiwan. Asian trading partners absorb more than half of Australia's exports and account for one-third of its imports. However, stimulated in part by the strength of the Australian dollar, the government now actively solicits trade with the United States and Canada.

During 1991, the Australian dollar gained 4 percent against the U.S. dollar, which itself was relatively strong. Of all the world's currencies, only those of Australia, Singapore, Canada, Taiwan, and Japan gained against the U.S. dollar—and of these, Australia headed the list.

Traditionally, the nation's major imports have been industrial machinery, farm equipment, transport equipment, chemicals, petroleum and petroleum products, metal goods, textiles, and specialty clothing. The United States accounts for the largest share of Australia's US$30 billion import market, at about 22 percent. Japan is a close second at 21 percent.

Although a population of 17 million (about two-thirds the size of Canada) doesn't provide a huge consumer market, Australians are generally well-educated, sophisticated buyers, eager to acquire the same consumer products as Americans or Europeans.

Future import products that look especially attractive include computer hardware and software, medical supplies and equipment, industrial machinery, aerospace products, and virtually all Western top-of-the-line consumer products. The tourist industry is also booming and offers excellent opportunities for foreign investors.

The country's major exports include wheat, coal, wool, petroleum products, meat, dairy products, and special metal products.

The issue of agricultural subsidies continues to plague trade relations with the United States. The sharpest thorn concerns wheat subsidies, a major export commodity for Australia, the United States, and Europe. Foreign exporters of any agricultural products are advised to develop strategies that recognize the "great global wheat debate."

Under the Export Enhancement Program, the U.S. government guarantees or subsidizes up to 98 percent of the export value of wheat. Asia is Australia's biggest wheat market and the United States is actively encroaching on it with unfair trading practices according to Australian officials.

In 1991, U.S. companies sold wheat to China at US$75 a ton—when the unsubsidized world price was US$125. Earlier in the year the U.S. sold wheat to Algeria at US$65 a ton—of which US$64.55 was subsidized! Europe's exporters are doing the same thing as the Americans, often with even greater subsidies, if that's possible. Unsubsidized farmers in Australia, like those in Canada and Argentina, continue to raise loud objections.

Such international subsidies have contributed significantly to a decline of Australia's wheat exports—20 percent since 1985. Although agricultural subsidies were a major item in the Uruguay Round of GATT negotiations, nothing of substance has been resolved.

Australia's major agricultural products, in addition to wheat, are barley, oats, corn, hay, lamb, beef, sugar cane, dairy products, wine, fruit, and vegetables.

Deterrents to Economic Growth

The government has made significant progress toward bringing Australia into twentieth-century global trade by strengthening its internal economy. However, two of the nation's biggest economic problems have been left untouched: the authoritarian control of the labor market by unions, and the large number of nationalized industries.

Australia supports more than three hundred trade unions, many with a miniscule membership and all eager to make their mark. Typically, several unions are represented in one company. When the time arrives to negotiate new contracts, a company must deal not with one, but with several, sometimes obstreperous unions—a situation not unlike that in the United States during the early days of trade unionism.

Union dominance of such important areas as the automobile and truck industries has in effect prevented major companies from introducing automation as a cost-savings and quality-enhancement measure. Australia's motor industry is only about one-third as automated as that of the United States, Japan, and Europe.

The huge public sector is even more inefficient. According to OECD reports, the output per worker in Australian public utilities was less than half that of the average worker in its 24 member nations. Since state-owned companies account for more than one-fourth of Australia's nonhousing investment—compared to 10 percent in the United States and Japan—the gross labor inefficiency in the public sector filters straight through the entire economy.

Australia's economic malaise, though lessening, continues to hamper international trade. Unemployment rose steeply to near 10 percent in 1991. Bankruptcies among small businesses are pervasive. Inflation remains locked in at an unmanageable 7 percent.

The recession hit Australia like a ton of bricks in 1990, with real GDP dropping 3.5 percent in the second half of the year. The government responded by cutting interest rates eight times, from 18 percent in 1989 to roughly 10.5 percent by mid-1991. Surprisingly, exchange rates remained relatively stable.

Recent OECD projections show unemployment peaking at 10 percent, inflation remaining close to that experienced in other OECD members, and foreign debt as a percentage of GDP increasing slightly. The Australian Trade Commission forecasts that inflation will experience a slight decline in 1992.

Australia's net external debt was just under A$130 billion at the end of 1990, or about 35 percent of GDP. This compares to the approximately A$50 billion and 23.8 percent of GDP five years earlier. The country's current account ran a deficit of A$14.3 billion and is projected to improve to A$13.6 billion in 1992. Australia is the sixteenth-largest U.S. trading partner.

Although a highly regulated Australian economy faced potential national collapse ten years ago, a reshuffling of government priorities since then has begun to have a salutary effect. Over the past seven years the government has enacted corporate tax cuts, reduced import and export tariffs, abolished exchange controls and interest rate controls, and deregulated financial markets. Reduced government spending has started to bring the nation back to fiscal prudence.

Privatization

The Labour Party always presented itself as the voice of the Australian working man. The result, after more than a century of Labour Party maneuvering, is a hodgepodge of absurdly restrictive work practices and a culture of pervasive lassitude. Restrictive labor policies have led Australia from a status as the world's richest country (per person) at the start of this century to one that barely ranks in the top thirty in 1992.

It is not surprising that with the Labour Party's popularity having fallen to below 22 percent, radical steps can now be taken to slaughter many of the party's sacred cows. One of the first to go, in mid-1990, was the right of the jobless to receive endless unemployment benefits.

Next came a planned sell-off of many of Australia's state-owned companies and entire industries. One of the first moves in this direction was the part-privatization of the state-owned Commonwealth Bank (which was Labour's first step into public ownership 79 years ago).

Forty-nine percent of the state-owned airline Qantas and all of Australian Airlines were the next to go. The government then opted to sell parts of state-owned Telecom and to allow a private sector competitor access to its satellite network. The Bank of New South Wales also went on the block.

Although the number of state-owned companies that will eventually be included in the government's privatization program remains uncertain, Australian trade officials seem optimistic that the program will continue until the country's industrial base becomes competitive once again.

Market/Product Demand

Australia is Asia-Pacific's third-largest economy behind Japan and China. It boasts the second-largest per capita income, lagging only behind Japan. The United States accounts for a lion's share of the nation's US$30 billion import market, with more than ten thousand U.S. companies exporting goods and services to Australia. Nearly eight hundred have subsidiary operations in the country.

With Australia's economic horizon shifting rapidly from Europe to Asia-Pacific and North America, its potential to rival the EC has been enhanced. The Free Trade Agreement between Australia and New Zealand and assured entrance into the currently forming Asia-Pacific trading bloc significantly expand market potential beyond the nation's meager domestic markets.

Best Markets for Foreign Trade

The greatest opportunities for foreign exporters over the next several years are in those product lines deemed by the government to be essential for the nation's advance into the next century; specifically, high-value-added items in manufacturing and services, such as information processing, communications, and biotechnology. State-of-the-art computer software and hardware are highly sought-after imports. Hardware capable of running on the country's Integrated Services Digital Network (ISDN) is in high demand, as are software and hardware for industrial process controls.

The government marked the aerospace industry as a prime target for development, especially in the general aviation segment. Avionics, propulsion, and structural assemblies offer the highest potential for foreign exporters.

The export of medical equipment and instruments offers additional opportunities. In 1992, the government estimates a 40 percent growth in this market. Japanese and American exporters control the lion's share, although at this growth rate, plenty of room exists for others.

The Australian government estimates that the import market for industrial machinery exceeds US$500 million and is likely to grow rapidly as Australian industry becomes more competitive in world markets.

In addition to these prime markets, foreign companies find a ready demand for such diverse products as advanced ceramics, agricultural and construction equipment, building supplies, food processing, hospitality services, genetic engineering, industrial process controls, factory automation, telecommunications equipment, printing and graphic arts, and oil and gas field equipment. It should be noted that regulations require a 30 percent offset against many imported goods purchased by the government and the military.

Best Markets for Foreign Direct Investment

For decades, the Australian government discouraged foreign direct investment by demanding strict adherence to many unnecessary and unreasonable rules laid down by the Foreign Investment Review Board (FIRB). Most of these rules have now been abandoned, except in relation to matters of national security.

In addition to passing the FIRB hurdle, foreign investors in the past have been subjected to substantially higher tax rates (historically 49 percent, now 39 percent), inflation rates, and transport costs than those imposed by other Asia-Pacific nations. Add unmanageable labor costs and union work rules, and it's easy to understand the reluctance of smaller companies to undertake an Australian investment.

Still, with such outstanding market opportunities, an increasing number of small and midsize companies are taking the plunge, with the expectation that global competition will force continued changes. Textile manufacturing, basic metal products, and chemical processing offer good direct investment opportunities. Petroleum drilling, refining, processing, and distribution, as well as coal mining and processing, offer additional possibilities. Australian industry officials recently began a push toward enticing foreign investment in waste management projects.

Australia's sophisticated manufacturing sector, which contributes approximately 18 percent of GDP, produces a wide range of products for worldwide export. A few of the more prominent items are garments (especially woolens), agricultural products (primarily wheat and other cereals, sugar, beef, poultry, mutton, and lamb), electronics, household appliances, base metals (nonferrous metals and iron ore), precision instruments, plastics, coal and coke, and refined oil.

The country is a net exporter of energy, with massive reserves of coal, uranium, fossil fuels, and natural gas. Federal and state governments control all exploration and development of these natural resources. All shipping fleets and, until recently, airlines are owned by the government.

Japan remains Australia's major export market, accounting for 21 percent of agricultural exports, 40 percent of mineral, fuel, and metals, and a whopping 65 to 75 percent of all iron ore and coal exports.

34
New Zealand

Tips to Foreign Traders and Investors

1. Check out the current status of unions and welfare system before investing. They have driven out more than one foreign company.

2. Establish trading contacts through exporting before making direct investment.

3. Use local banks for financing.

4. Seriously consider a New Zealand facility as an entree to Australia and the Pacific islands. New Zealand is cheaper than Australia.

5. Embassy office in Washington: (202) 328-4800.

As a small market of 3.3 million people, situated at the foot of the globe, New Zealand doesn't excite much enthusiasm among North American or European traders. Being at the low end of the OECD growth league doesn't help much either. While every other industrialized economy has boomed over the past 15 years, New Zealand's output is no higher now than in 1985, despite the most radical free market reforms of the century. To add insult to injury, the economy suffered the worst recession in 1991 of any OECD country. Has New Zealand's experiment with free markets failed, or is this merely the bottom of the economic trough?

To understand New Zealand's resource and market potential, one must turn back the clock to 1984, the year the Labour Party won the national election from the ruling National Party of Sir Robert Muldoon. In 1984, New Zealand was the most regulated, protected, and therefore distorted economy of any capitalist nation.

The government tightly controlled wages, prices, interest rates, and the foreign exchange rate. Intentionally high tariffs kept imports out. As a result,

Table 34-1. Key New Zealand Economic Statistics

	Percentage change				
	1988	1989	1990	1991	Forecast for 1992
Private consumption	2.4	1.5	-1.0	-1.3	1.2
Government consumption	3.4	0.2	0.4	-2.9	-4.6
Gross capital investment	-0.2	9.3	4.7	0.8	-0.5
Exports	4.7	-2.3	6.4	2.0	5.0
Imports	-1.6	15.2	3.7	-1.0	2.0
GDP	2.4	0.2	1.2	-0.4	1.0
Consumer prices	8.1	6.3	6.1	4.0	3.0
Unemployment rate	5.6	7.1	7.8	9.3	10.0

SOURCE: OECD.

national investment fell to all the wrong industries. High taxes and a generous welfare state destroyed any incentive to take risks or work hard.

The nation's GDP per head descended from the second-highest among the 24 OECD countries in 1950 (after the United States) to the nineteenth by 1980. New Zealand was the nearest thing to a planned economy outside Eastern Europe.

When finance minister Roger Douglas entered office with the Labour Party, reformers went berserk. They combined strict monetary and fiscal discipline with the first steps toward a free market economy. This was the most comprehensive free market reform program ever undertaken by an OECD country.

The government tightened fiscal and monetary policies to squeeze out inflation. Wages and prices were set free. The financial system was deregulated. Government subsidies became a thing of the past. State owned companies were suddenly privatized. Trade barriers were lowered. The entire tax structure was revamped, making New Zealand's the least distorted tax system in the OECD. Probably most important of any reform, the government cut loose the central bank, giving it full independence—a step only Germany has dared to duplicate.

Seven years later the lessons learned by New Zealand bear close attention from foreign companies so eager to jump into Eastern Europe and the former Soviet Union. It is certainly true that the country's reform policies beat inflation, knocking it down from 18 percent in 1985 to 5 percent in 1991. But the price paid has been staggering.

The economy has been essentially stagnant for seven years, while unemployment continues to climb, as shown in Table 34-1.

A Stagnant Economy Arises

Another indication of New Zealand's stagnant economy is the fact that in 1990, its GDP was 3 percent lower than it was in 1985; during the same period, other OECD countries grew an average of 18 percent. The current account deficit remains a very uncomfortable 6 percent of GDP.

The lesson to be learned here is not that free market reforms failed, but that the government didn't go far enough. It tackled the easy problems, not the difficult ones that have kept foreign investors away from New Zealand for decades.

The government did virtually nothing to eliminate the restrictive practices and centralized pay award system in the labor system that suppress pay differentials and prevent wages from adjusting to market conditions. Further, the government closed its eyes to the need for reductions in the lavish welfare state. It refused to address the urgent need for a reduction in the budget deficit. Unfortunately, these are the same omissions being committed by most Eastern European nations today.

New Zealand's incomplete reforms caused two imbalances that substantially increased the cost of converting to free markets. First, loose fiscal policy, coupled with tight monetary policy (also currently practiced in the United States) distorted interest rates and foreign exchange rates, placing disproportionate strains on the financial health of private industry.

Second, an attempt was made to revitalize private industry while maintaining social welfare policies that encouraged employees to become dependent on the state. Only Sweden has higher unemployment benefits compared to average wages. With liberal unemployment benefits, many workers in New Zealand are better off drawing government checks than working. This, in turn, drains key employees from the labor market.

In 1991–1992, the government finally began corrective measures. A task force set about reducing government expenditures. The first step was to cut unemployment pay by 10 percent. Compulsory trade unionism has been outlawed. The centralized pay award system has been abolished.

These are certainly steps in the right direction. Even with an end to the welfare state, however, New Zealand economists reckon that the economy will not be truly on track until the late 1990s, and then only if rich nations (i.e., the United States and the European Community) liberalize farm trade by reducing the farm price supports that allow farm products to be sold at less than cost.

Foreign Trade

Agriculture accounts for 70 percent of New Zealand's exports. At world market prices, New Zealand food producers would have little difficulty competing. The country's dairy and meat farmers are probably the lowest-cost producers in the world.

Between the enormous agricultural subsidies granted by the United States and European Community countries and the very restrictive import quotas imposed on agricultural products to the EC, consumers are forced to pay much higher prices for homegrown products than they would for New Zealand imports.

Moreover, both the EC and the United States consistently overproduce. When governments purchase farm products, they turn around and dump them on world markets at depressed prices. New Zealand farmers are left out in the cold, just as Australian wheat producers are. New Zealand is the only OECD country that does not subsidize its agricultural sector at all.

The New Zealand market for foreign imports is very small compared to Latin America or Southeast Asia, which is why most multinationals have not bothered with it. This leaves the door open to smaller firms willing to service smaller markets. According to New Zealand trade officials, several interesting opportunities exist for foreign products, primarily in consumer goods and high-tech products.

Most consumer markets are relatively sophisticated. Personal care items, specialty clothing, and security systems are good bets for foreign exporters.

Computer hardware and software products do well, especially in insurance and banking sectors, which are becoming increasingly sophisticated. The popularity of local area networks and multiple work stations is accelerating rapidly.

Specialty apparel goods, such as swim wear and casual sportswear are in high demand. Demand for services businesses is picking up as the economy stabilizes. Foreign management consultants, for example, find a ready market. Travel services are also booming.

On the industrial side, food-processing machinery and office equipment and supplies are good markets. Computer-based manufacturing control and scheduling is coming into its own, as is sophisticated instrumentation for quality control and testing in the food-processing industry. Telecommunications equipment, electric power stations, and airport support equipment are all needed to further the development of the country's infrastructure.

For the most part, import licensing has been abandoned. Import controls now cover a mere 5 percent of products. The government plans even further reductions by the end of 1992.

Foreign Direct Investment

Foreign direct investment offers greater opportunities than exports. The government encourages foreign companies to set up facilities in practically any part of the country. The repatriation of profits and capital is unrestricted. The New Zealand Ministry of Trade suggests that viable industries for foreign investments are forestry, agriculture, food processing, tourism, transportation, and light manufacturing.

Although the corporate income tax rate of 33 percent is certainly an improvement over the previously usurious 53 percent, it is still too high. At 38 percent, the foreign branch rate is much worse and is another example of the socialist measures designed to keep out foreigners. In addition, nonresidents pay a withholding tax on dividends of 30 percent, and a tax of 15 percent on interest and royalties. Generally, New Zealand offers no tax incentives to foreign investors. However, foreign companies may own 100 percent of New Zealand companies.

Now that New Zealand's financial system has been deregulated, adequate trade and investment financing can be arranged. Interest rates, however, are still above Western standards. The recently rejuvenated Bank of New Zealand is a good place to start and welcomes foreign inquiries. The three smaller banks—Trust Bank New Zealand, ASB Bank, and NZI Bank—are also good possibilities.

One feature of New Zealand trade that is especially attractive to foreign companies is direct access to other markets. New Zealand and Australia have a free trade agreement, making products produced in one country duty free in the other. Also, New Zealand is the transportation and trading center for most of the Polynesian island states and some of those in Melanesia. Companies interested in expanding in these areas could combine their island markets with those of New Zealand and Australia.

Changes in government policy toward labor and welfare suggest an opening of the economy to a level of international trade heretofore unthinkable. Several foreign companies from Singapore have already recognized the change. Their direct investment soared to NZ$1.43 billion (approximately US$820.1 million) in the first half of 1991, nearly matching the amount for the entire previous year.

Trade and Direct Investment from U.S. Companies

Paradoxically, the governments of the United States and New Zealand have been at odds for more than six years. Here are two countries with a common culture, similar legal systems, the same language, and a history of strong trading ties that for six years haven't talked to each other. The reason? New Zealand's ban on visitation by nuclear powered or nuclear armed ships. For years, New Zealanders have been publicly hostile to continued French nuclear weapons testing in the South Pacific, a reasonable objection, considering the country's proximity to nuclear fallout.

Refusing to accept such a desire for national security from a country whose out-of-the-way location holds very little military importance to the United States, President Reagan declared a kind of quarantine. Washington effectively suspended New Zealand from the ANZUS (Australia, New Zealand, United States) Security Alliance. New Zealand was a friend, but no longer an ally.

Virtually all government-to-government contact was suspended. The U.S. government blackballed New Zealand, treating the nation as it did Cuba, North Korea, and Yemen. The United States abandoned joint training exercises, logistics support, and preferential sales of arms and equipment. Shared intelligence was halted.

Except for military sales, commercial affairs were not included in the quarantine, but trade and direct investment suffered, thereby forcing New Zealand to turn more and more to its neighbor Australia. This in turn hastened the free trade agreement between the two nations.

In 1990, the conservative National Party won the national election in a landslide, and relations with Washington began to mend. Although full defense and intelligence ties will not be restored until New Zealand lifts its nuclear ban, public opinion polls indicate that this is not likely to happen in the near future. Nevertheless, U.S. companies should not hesitate to open trade or make investments in New Zealand for fear of reprisals from Washington. The bomb has been defused, probably permanently.

35
Pacific Island States

Tips to Foreign Traders and Investors

1. Pick an island and a product line and start exporting. This is a dynamite area for smaller companies that don't like competition.

2. Stick with very basic products. The islands import nearly everything.

3. Check out U.S.–affiliated islands, especially the Federated States of Micronesia, for the best financing and tax breaks for direct investment.

4. Use tax-haven islands to shelter income.

5. Do not invest in Fiji, Papua New Guinea, Nauru, and much of French Polynesia for the next few years. The outcomes of political and social changes there are too uncertain.

6. Look into tourist-support industries and food and beverage distribution as very hot markets.

Mention Pacific islands and images of palm trees, sandy beaches, diving spectaculars, and quiet, relaxed respites from the rigors of life come to mind. People dream of retiring to a small Pacific island, or sailing to one, or perhaps vacationing on one, and many actually take the plunge. But foreign trade? Not likely. Direct investment? Never!

In fact, many of the tiny island states that populate the vast Pacific Ocean (and are frequently referred to as Oceania) support the same market demands for goods and services that are found in North America, Europe, or Japan. Infrastructures need to be built; students taught; health care given; leisure time filled; food and beverages supplied; and tourists catered to. Very few goods and services are produced locally. Nearly everything must be imported, including skilled professionals, managers, and workers.

Politics and Culture

Oceania consists of 22 political entities. Prior to the two world wars, the Pacific islands were colonial outposts of Germany, Spain, and Japan. After World War II the region was carved up among six colonial powers: Australia, France, New Zealand, the Netherlands, the United Kingdom, and the United States. In all the island states, colonial legacies are very evident in such matters as government structure, education, legal systems, and trade development. A few have elected to remain dependent on their colonial parents. Others have opted to become independent. Still others have chosen the status of self-governing nations in free association with former colonial powers. Table 35-1 shows their political status.

The Pacific islands were originally settled between 2000 and 5000 years ago by three distinctly different cultures, all originating in what is now Southeast Asia. The ancestors of the Polynesians ventured furthest east and settled generally in French Polynesia, the Cook Islands, New Zealand, Tonga, Niue, the Samoas, Tuvalu, Wallis & Futuna, Tokelau, the Line Islands, Pitcairn Islands, and Hawaii. This entire area is generally known as *Polynesia* (meaning "many islands").

The ancestors of the Melanesians settled in Fiji, New Caledonia, Vanuatu, the Solomon Islands, Papua New Guinea, and West Irian (now part of Indonesia). This area is referred to as *Melanesia* (meaning "dark-skinned islands").

The ancestors of the Micronesians settled in what is obviously now called *Micronesia* (which means "tiny islands"), north of the equator. Micronesia encompasses the Gilbert Islands, Nauru, the Caroline Islands, the Marshall Islands, Palau, Guam, and the Northern Marianas Islands.

Political institutions in Oceania are generally stable, although changing local conditions and demands for modernization are causing strains in several island states.

The language of government and commerce throughout Oceania is either English or French, depending on heritage. Culturally, however, virtually every island state has its own language. Countries such as the Federated States of Micronesia (FSM) include more than a thousand islands and use hundreds of distinct languages.

All commerce, transportation, communications, college level education, and foreign aid reflect former colonial associations. For example, even though the FSM is an independent nation and now has a seat in the United Nations, U.S. aid finances nearly all its trade and infrastructure development. Also, the FSM remains part of the U.S. Postal System.

Table 35-1.   Political Status of Oceanian States

	Year independence was achieved	Former colonial owner/ruler
Independent		
Tonga	1970	Britain
Fiji	1970	Britain
Tuvalu (formerly Ellice Islands)	1978	Britain
Solomon Islands	1978	Britain
Kiribati, which includes the Line Islands and the Gilbert Islands	1979	Britain
Vanuatu (formerly New Hebrides)	1980	Britain and France
Nauru	1968	Australia
Papua New Guinea	1975	Australia
Western Samoa	1962	New Zealand
Free Association		
Cook Islands	1965	New Zealand
Niue	1974	New Zealand
Marshall Islands	1986	United States
Federated States of Micronesia, composed of the Caroline Islands (includes the states of Yap, Chuuk [née Truk], Kosrae, and Pohnpei)	1986	United States
Continued Dependence		
Palau		United States
American Samoa		United States
Northern Mariana Islands		United States
Guam		United States
French Polynesia, which includes Tahiti, the Society Islands, the Tuamotu Archipelago, and the Marquesas Islands		France
New Caledonia		France
Wallis and Futuna		France
Pitcairn Island		Britain
Tokelau		New Zealand
Several small atolls scattered throughout Polynesia		New Zealand

SOURCE: World Bank, U.S. Department of Commerce, University of Hawaii.

Foreign Trade

In terms of diversity of market opportunity, Oceania holds more promise for foreign traders than many developing nations currently attracting worldwide publicity and hence foreign investors and traders. Smaller companies find less competition, stronger market demand, and wider market diversification in Oceania than in much of Eastern Europe. They also find very few formal or informal trade barriers, active home- and host-country assistance, and a usually friendly population eager to learn about and participate in the international community.

The Pacific islands also have obvious trade disadvantages. The sheer vastness of the Pacific Ocean makes transporting goods cumbersome and costly. Except for Papua New Guinea, individual island states have very small populations, making their markets and labor pools equally small. With the exception of Fiji, Papua New Guinea, and Nauru, very few islands have significant supplies of natural resources other than undersea minerals.

The high-tech revolution hasn't hit the islands yet, nor has heavy industry. However, once foreign traders overcome the peculiar difficulties associated with transporting goods over vast distances to tiny markets, they find eager markets awaiting a wide variety of basic goods and services.

On the consumer side, high-demand markets include processed food; fresh fruits, vegetables, and meats; ice cream; beer, wine and liquor; hand tools and power tools; automobiles, auto parts, and gasoline; light bulbs; radios, TVs, VCRs, video and audio tapes, and stereo equipment; pleasure boats and outboard motors; fishing and diving gear and accessories; furniture and appliances; shoes and basic Western clothing; personal care products; and virtually every other type of basic consumer product.

High demand also exists for medical equipment and supplies, microcomputer hardware and software, books and educational supplies, building materials, telecommunications equipment and supplies, electric power-generating equipment, water drilling and purification equipment and products, hotel and tourism equipment and supplies, construction equipment and machinery, light manufacturing machinery (primarily for assembly operations), agricultural equipment and supplies, livestock and poultry, and aircraft parts.

These island states must also import a wide variety of services. In highest demand are medical professionals; lawyers; bank and insurance managers; public health and administration professionals; management and engineering consultants; and educators at all levels.

Infrastructure development is just beginning on many islands and contractors are desperately needed in virtually every specialty.

Since very few islands possess natural resources beyond those needed to sustain their domestic populations, exporting is not a big business. Nauru does have significant phosphate deposits and generates most of its GDP from such exports. A small amount of fish and sponge exports emanate from several islands. Papua New Guinea, with a population of four million, exports copper, gold, copra, coffee, cocoa, timber, and tea—but not in large quantities. Fiji exports several products, including sugarcane and gold.

Foreign Direct Investment

It's easy to see from the long list of imported products that foreign direct investment is needed in virtually every industry. Most investment to date has come from Asian countries, led by Japan and South Korea (primarily in the area of infrastructure construction).

Since 1987, annual direct investment from Japanese companies has averaged about US$100 million. Most of this has gone into hotels and other tourist facilities. A smaller proportion has gone into fish-processing plants, retailing, light manufacturing, and mining. Visitors to Guam and Saipan (Northern Marianas) will swear that they are in Japanese rather than American territories.

Electronic and Industrial Enterprises, the huge Japanese conglomerate, has been the heaviest investor to date, with over US$7 billion invested in the Pacific region (including Australia and Hawaii). Companies from Singapore, Taiwan, Hong Kong, and South Korea have also made substantial investments, especially in the larger island states of Papua New Guinea and Fiji. Malaysian and Thai companies are now getting into the act.

Western firms have pretty much ignored the region. Strategically, this could be a big mistake. Even with relatively small markets, positioning in the low-cost, hungry Pacific islands will bring companies in direct line with outposts for exploiting markets in Australia and New Zealand to the south and East Asia to the west. The cost of getting established in the islands is significantly less than in any of the larger Asia-Pacific markets. The region's important telecommunications lines, shipping and air routes, and territorial economic zones for exploiting seabed minerals, fish, and other sea life, provide a bridge between West and East. Most important for smaller firms, financing can be arranged through colonial aid packages.

Colonial Aid

Despite the grandiose development schemes advocated by many island leaders, the fact is that these states are desperately poor. The culture of many of the islands reflects living and social conditions reminiscent of the eighteenth century and before. Autocratic clan chiefs rule small villages with an iron fist. Infrastructures are primitive, education practically nonexistent, and job opportunities negligible. The emigration of young people to former colonial powers is on the increase.

Each of the colonial powers continues to provide financial assistance to its island wards. Much as island leaders hate the idea, they are dependent on foreign aid to maintain a subsistence standard commensurate with twentieth-century demands. Tuvalu is the extreme case. Nearly the entire income of the island comes from aid. In contrast to other regions, Pacific island states have not had any problem getting their former colonial bosses to pay up.

Britain and Australia have second thoughts about letting their possessions go their own way. Japan probably feels a bit of nostalgia for the thousands of islands it once ruled. The United States seems to harbor a guilt complex about its destruction of the islands during World War II. Peace Corps Volunteers continue to play major roles in America's former and present possessions of FSM, Palau, Northern Marianas, and Guam.

Table 35-2 shows a sampling of the 1989 foreign aid that went to Oceania and indicates how much these states rely on tourism.

Table 35-2. Foreign Aid and Tourism as a Percentage of GDP*

	Percentage	
	Foreign aid	Tourism
Tuvalu	100	-0-
Vanuatu	60	18
Kiribati (1988)	42	10
Cook Islands	40	30
New Caledonia (1988)	38	8
Tonga	38	10
Solomon Islands	30	2
Western Samoa	28	20
Papua New Guinea	25	-0-
French Polynesia	25	10
Fiji	2	20

*As of 1989.
SOURCE: OECD; Tourism Council of South Pacific; *Europa.*

Since many island states have very little or no income of their own, most imports and foreign direct investment projects are financed through foreign aid packages. Although the Asian Development Bank helps, most of the aid comes from colonial powers. As long as they trade or invest in their former wards, foreign companies based in the United States, Britain, France, Australia, or New Zealand should have little difficulty arranging all the financing required through their home-country aid agencies. As in the rest of the world, companies from Japan and the Four Tigers can easily arrange financing from their home ports.

Special-Case Islands

Several Pacific states offer unusual tax or market opportunities and are worthy of consideration as Pacific outposts. All have politically stable governments. Risks of property expropriation are negligible. Tariffs and quotas are practically nonexistent. All freely permit income repatriation.

Nauru

The island of Nauru has a population of between 5000 and 8000, depending on whether foreign workers are included in the count. Inhabitants live entirely off the proceeds of the country's rich phosphate mines. Average per capita income runs around US$20,000, approximating that of the United States. Imported laborers do all the work and the native population lives lavishly—by island standards. Education and health care are free. The Nauruans have developed a propensity for junk food and consumer luxuries.

Recognizing that the phosphate deposits are running out and that the days of plenty are numbered, the Nauruan government has asked the World Court to force Australia to compensate it to the tune of US$60 million for phosphate mined prior to the island's independence in 1968. Australia's reply was not only "no," but "hell, no!"

Liberal company and trust laws plus zero taxes could make Nauru an enviable tax haven for foreign companies and individuals. To date, the government has done little to promote this advantage, but with the nation's future prosperity in doubt, look for active promotion efforts in the next few years. Substantial tourism promotions are also likely.

U.S.-Dominated States

In the three states comprising the former U.S. Trust Territory of the Pacific Islands—the Federated States of Micronesia (FSM), the Republic of the Marshall Islands, and the Republic of Palau—there is no tax on foreign source income. Local source personal income is taxed at rates of only 6 to 12 percent, local businesses at 4 percent of gross revenue. Several "shell" banking corporations have been set up in the Marshalls, but as of this writing, their worth to traders remains dubious.

The Marshalls and the FSM have entered into Compacts of Free Association with the United States; Palau remains a Trust territory. All three are treated as U.S. possessions for U.S. tax purposes.

Palau is the most developed of the three states. Tourism flourishes there, world-class diving attracts a plethora of visitors, and, with substantial aid coming from the United States, islanders have little interest in industrializing their paradise.

To date, Japanese firms have dominated tourism investment. Palau is strategically located a stone's throw from the Philippines and just north of the Indonesian outer islands. Positioning a facility here to tap Southeast Asian markets could be an excellent strategy, considering all the advantages that accrue from locating in a U.S. territory.

The FSM states of Yap, Chuuk, Pohnpei, and Kosrae are far less developed than Palau. Chuuk and Pohnpei (which seats the FSM government) are the furthest along. Yap remains the least developed. Kosrae fits in the middle. English is the official language on all the islands, along with Palau, although local dialects are widespread.

Yap probably offers the best opportunities for foreign investment. It is trying to become a world-class diving center but has just two small resort hotels. Many more are needed, as is a deep-water port and retail boutiques to attract cruise ships. The island state also desperately needs new medical facilities and personnel. American companies are missing the boat by not looking at Yap.

Cook Islands

The Cook Islands, located in southern Polynesia, use the New Zealand dollar and extend New Zealand citizenship to all Cook Islanders. The state is pushing hard to secure a small place among the world's tax havens and offshore financial centers. Offshore banking and insurance activities, international corporations and partnerships, and exempt trusts are not subject to any income tax or exchange controls (except on transactions involving the New Zealand dollar). Strict secrecy laws apply to all offshore business.

At last count, the Cook Islands boasted registration of the following foreign entities: 885 international corporations; 10 international insurance companies; 2 class *A* banks, 6 class *B* banks, 16 class *C* banks; 266 international trusts; and 5 international partnerships. Excellent communications facilities tie the capital, Rarotonga, to worldwide financial centers.

Vanuatu

Vanuatu, located about 300 miles west of Fiji and just north of New Caledonia, is the premier tax haven and offshore financial center of the South Pacific. The country has no taxes of any kind, either corporate or personal, other than very modest annual registration fees. Any foreign company may register as an exempt company provided that all its business is conducted offshore. Strict secrecy regarding company affairs is demanded by local law. Breach of this secrecy carries a large fine, imprisonment for up to twelve months, or both.

In addition to representation from virtually every major international corporation, bank, and insurance company, Vanuatu claims a large number of financial and professional service firms (accounting, legal, and trust management). The state maintains excellent air and shipping links with Australia and Fiji and has state-of-the-art communications facilities, including satellite stations.

The only negative, other than the state's remote location, is the continued animosity between the old English and French cultural and legal systems. Although these old antagonisms have little affect on foreign companies, the two political parties continue to harbor disagreements reminiscent of their English and French heritage.

Fiji

The most populous of the small island states, Fiji is wracked by political bickering that originates from racial unrest. The opposing forces—Fijians of Melanesian or Polynesian descent, and Fijians of Indian descent—seem to be doing everything in their power to dissuade foreign companies from investing in the island state. Coups and ethnic repression have become common. Yet, other than New Guinea, Fiji has the only economy of the Pacific islands capable of relatively significant export trade. For that reason alone, foreign companies continue to be interested. In 1989, Fiji's exports totaled US$388 million, broken down as follows (data from IMF and EIU):

Sugar	36%
Reexports	17%
Gold	13%
Clothing	9%
Fish	7%
Timber	5%
Other	13%

In addition, more than 250,000 tourists visit Fiji each year—provided there isn't a coup in progress. Japanese and French companies have been the predominant investors. To date, American companies do not have a significant presence.

Index